DISTINGUISHED ASIAN AMERICANS

A Biographical Dictionary

EDITED BY HYUNG-CHAN KIM

Contributing Editors:
Dorothy Cordova
Stephen S. Fugita
Franklin Ng
Jane Singh

Greenwood Press
Westport, Connecticut • London

Library of Congress Cataloging-in-Publication Data

Distinguished Asian Americans : a biographical dictionary / edited by
  Hyung-chan Kim ; contributing editors, Dorothy Cordova . . . [et al.].
      p.   cm.
    Includes bibliographical references and index.
    ISBN 0–313–28902–6 (alk. paper)
    1. Asian Americans—Biography—Dictionaries.   I. Kim, Hyung-chan.
  E184.O6D57   1999
  920'.009295073—dc21   98–41423

British Library Cataloguing in Publication Data is available.

Library of Congress Catalog Card Number: 98–41423
ISBN: 0–313–28902–6

First published in 1999

Greenwood Press, 88 Post Road West, Westport, CT 06881
An imprint of Greenwood Publishing Group, Inc.
www.greenwood.com

Printed in the United States of America

The paper used in this book complies with the
Permanent Paper Standard issued by the National
Information Standards Organization (Z39.48–1984).

10 9 8 7 6 5 4 3 2 1

Copyright Acknowledgments

The editors and publisher gratefully acknowledge permission for use of the following
material:

Excerpts from "Yellapragada Subba Row, 1896–1948." *Lederle Laboratories Newsletter,* Pearl
River, NY, pp. 6–9. Reprinted with the permission of the Manager of Library Services,
Wyeth-Ayerst Research Library, Pearl River, NY.

Every reasonable effort has been made to trace the owners of copyright materials in this
book, but in some instances this has proven impossible. The editor and publisher will be
glad to receive information leading to more complete acknowledgments in subsequent
printings of the book and in the meantime extend their apologies for any omissions.

Contents

Contents

Contents

Contents

Introduction

This reference book features biographical profiles of 166 distinguished Asian Americans who have made significant contributions to American society. For the purpose of this work, an Asian American may be native or foreign-born. If foreign-born, the person has immigrated to the United States, most likely since the end of World War II. If native-born, the person may be a second-, third-, or fourth-generation descendant of an Asian immigrant.

For the purpose of this biographical work, the term *Asian American* denotes those immigrants and their descendants who came from China, India, Japan, Korea, Pakistan, the Philippines, Cambodia, Laos, or Vietnam. For the sake of convenience, four separate groups—namely Chinese, Japanese, Koreans, and Filipinos—are identified in terms of their ancestry, whereas people from India and Pakistan are grouped as South Asians and those from Cambodia, Laos, and Vietnam are grouped as Southeast Asians. The latter two groupings are owing mainly to the fact that (1) the number of entries on prominent people from these countries is rather small, or (2) the boundaries of their native lands make it almost impossible to categorize them as separate groups.

Immigrants from Asian countries arrived on these shores with an American dream. The first group who came to America in large numbers were from the Chinese province of Guangdong, located in southeastern China. They began to arrive in the late 1840s after gold was discovered in California in 1848. Many came with the hopes of striking it rich and going home to live out the rest of their lives in comfort. This dream was very American. After the U.S. Congress excluded Chinese laborers from coming to America as immigrants in 1882, Japanese laborers were brought in large numbers between 1895 and 1905 to work on sugar plantations in Hawaii and vegetable and fruit farms in California. Japanese workers often went on strike for higher wages and better living conditions. This too was very American. In 1903 Koreans were brought in large numbers as strike breakers against Japanese workers in Hawaii. About the same time, the Hawaiian Sugar Planters Association brought in Filipinos, some of whom also were used as strike breakers. They were also brought in to work on asparagus and other vegetable farms in central California. People from India, at the time a British colony, began to arrive in the Pacific Northwest at the turn of the century, but their numbers in America remained rather small until 1965, when Congress liberalized America's immigration policy toward Asians. The most recent group of Asian ancestry to arrive in America is from Cambodia, Laos, and Vietnam. Many came as refugees in the spring of 1975, at the end of U.S. involvement in the War in Vietnam, leaving behind their war-torn countries in search of new places for resettlement. Whether they came from Korea or Vietnam, they came with the dream of sharing America's wealth and the new opportunity it promised.

The dream of freedom, equality, and wealth was shattered for Japanese Americans during World War II by U.S. government policies to evacuate and intern them because they were considered likely to be enemy aliens. Approximately 110,000 persons of Japanese ancestry who lived on the West Coast were sent to concentration camps (also called internment camps) for no other reason than the fact that they looked Japanese. Persons of Korean ancestry in Hawaii were under military order to observe blackout and curfew laws during World War II. Even after the end of the war, Japanese and Korean resident aliens could not become American citizens until 1952, when Congress passed the McCarran-Walter Immigration Act.

The Asian American population remained small through the 1960s because of numerous laws passed by the U.S. Congress against Asian immigration between 1882 and 1952. Some of the most important anti-Asian immigration laws were the Chinese Exclusion Act of 1882, the Immigration Act of 1907, the Asiatic Barred Zone Act of 1917, the National Origins Act of 1924, and McCarran-Walter Immigration Act of 1952 which restricted Asian immigration to the national quota whereas European immigrants faced no quota restriction. The number of Asians immigrating to America grew steadily after 1965, when legal restrictions against their immigration were lifted. The American demographic landscape has changed considerably since then owing to increasing numbers of immigrants from Latin America as well as from Asian countries. According to a 1990 report released by the Bureau of the Census, there were 7,554,000 Asian and Pacific Americans in the United States on July 1, 1990, and it was estimated that this population, as shown in the table, would grow by leaps and bounds, surpassing the ten million mark on September 1, 1997.

Asian American Population

	July 1, 1992	July 1, 1994	July 1, 1996	July 1, 1997	September 1, 1997
Population (Million)	8,300	9,025	9,743	10,086	10,146
(Percentage of Total Population)	3.3	3.5	3.7	3.8	3.8
Median Age	29.9	30.3	30.8	31.0	31.1
Male	4,051	4,388	4,719	4,876	4,903
Female	4,250	4,637	5,024	5,210	5,242

According to another census report by the U.S. Department of Commerce (1993), the Asian American population was the fastest-growing minority during the 1980–1990 decade. Although the Latino American population increased by more than 50 percent during the decade, the Asian American population grew by almost 100 percent. There were 3,726,440 persons of Asian ancestry in the United States in 1980; but this population grew rapidly to reach 7,554,000 in 1990. The magnitude of deep changes taking place in American demographics and culture is evident in the fact that this population grew by 600 percent since 1970, when it numbered 1,356,638. More astonishing to some observers is the fact that certain ethnic groups within this population increased by more than 1,000 percent. For instance, the Korean American population in 1970 was 69,510, but it grew to reach 798,848 in 1990.

Asian Americans are highly concentrated in the West. In 1991, 58.5 percent lived in California, Oregon, Washington, and Arizona. Almost four out of every ten Asian Americans (39 percent) resided in California during that year. Only 17.3 percent of Asian Americans live in the Northeast. In 1980 only seven states had more than 100,000 Asian Americans, but a decade later California, Florida, Hawaii, Illinois, Massachusetts, Michigan, New Jersey, New York, Pennsylvania, Texas, Virginia, and Washington each claimed more than 100,000 Asian Americans as residents. More than nine out of ten Asian Americans (94.4 percent) live in a metropolitan area today. Among those who are residents of metropolitan areas, about half live in central cities and half in suburbs. In contrast, one out of every two white Americans lives in a suburban area, and almost one out of every four (23.6 percent) whites resides in a nonmetropolitan area, where only 5.6 percent of Asian Americans are found.

Asian Americans share many values with other Americans. They strongly believe in the importance of family. Indeed, the family is the primary institution for preserving cultural tradition and generational continuity. Family members of different generations come together frequently to interact and support each other. The Asian American family emphasizes success through hard work and self-discipline. Children are encouraged to work hard in and out of school to be worthy of the many sacrifices their parents make for them. Self-control is another important value children are taught in the family. They learn that a mature person does not show feelings too readily. In many Asian American families, especially among immigrant families, one's duty to the family is considered more important than one's rights. One is to fulfill one's duties before one claims one's rights.

Although Asian Americans share many ideas, values, and religious beliefs, they are as culturally diverse among themselves as they are different from other Americans. The cultural diversity among Asian Americans originates from a variety of physical, environmental, and historical factors. Language and religion are just two such factors. Major languages spoken by Asian Americans include Mandarin Chinese, Cantonese, Hindi, Japanese, Korean, Tagalog, and Vietnamese. Asian Americans practice the world's major religions such as Buddhism, Christianity, Confucianism, Hinduism, Islam, and Shintoism. Because of these pronounced differences, it is important for readers of this book to hold in respect the uniqueness of each individual experience profiled in these biographies and the cultural heterogeneity that the experiences reflect.

The 166 Asian Americans profiled in this work have made notable contributions not only to American society but also to the world. America has been more energized socially, and the world more enriched culturally, because of what they have done for others. These people have been chosen for their outstanding accomplishments in professions that range from labor leaders to political leaders, tennis players to football players, scientists to distinguished inventors, Hollywood actors to Wall Street investors, schoolteachers to scholars, and comedians to community activists. Many of these people, however, had to overcome physical and/or cultural obstacles. Some had to learn English as a second language before they were able to compete in their profession; others had to learn skills through training and education in America because they did not have the opportunity for education in their native countries, and still others had to transcend psychological barriers resulting from violence perpetrated against them in their native lands (particularly Vietnam, Cambodia, and Laos). Despite overwhelming odds they have succeeded in their chosen fields because they were determined to make the most out of their lives, being strongly motivated to achieve something of value, willing to search for new knowledge and skills, and self-disciplined to concentrate on their goals.

The task of selecting the people included in this volume was difficult in view of the fact that so many deserve to be mentioned. Five major criteria were consistently applied in choosing them. First, it was considered very important to choose those whose life stories would inspire Americans, particularly Asian Americans, to examine their own lives for some future action. Second, they were chosen because their life stories were pedagogical in that they could teach Americans of Asian ancestry, particularly Asian American youth, about the individual efforts and struggles to become more giving and less self-serving on their way to maturity. Third, they were selected because they have made significant contributions that helped to improve both the quantity and the quality of Asian Americans' collective memory. Fourth, they were chosen because of their contributions to their respective professional fields and to American society. Last but not least, an overwhelming majority of them were chosen in the hope that they would be regarded by Asian American youth as role models.

This biographical dictionary will serve the reader in a variety of ways. First, it will provide readers with essential biographical information on 166 noted Asian Americans, many of whom have not been profiled elsewhere. It will also help familiarize readers with the names of individuals, organizations, events, and places in Asian American communities that would go otherwise unrecognized.

For ease of use by American readers, each entry is written with the biographee's surname last. Because of a wide variety of practices used by the biographees to write their names, no particular systems of transliteration (e.g., the Reischauer-McCune system) have been applied to the present work. Each individual's unique way of spelling his or her name was honored, and no attempt was made to change it. For instance, *Syngman Rhee*, which should be written as *Yi, Seung-man* in accordance with the Reischauer-McCune system, is retained in the present work. The information in each entry is based on a variety of published resources whenever possible. Many of the profiles benefitted from personal interviews with biographees, who were also asked to present their life stories in writing for this work. The facts in those profiles were supplied by the subjects. The entries are organized in alphabetical order. Each entry concludes with a short list of further readings about the person. Appendix A groups the biographees by profession. Appendix B groups them by ethnicity.

ACKNOWLEDGMENTS

Many professional colleagues worked together to make this volume possible. I would like to acknowledge my indebtedness to each of the contributing editors, whose knowledge of their ethnic community and its history were sine qua non for completing this work. Each group of entries was written by specialists who have been engaged in teaching and doing research about the specific ethnic group for many years: Franklin Ng for the Chinese Americans, Steve Fugita for the Japanese Americans, Jane Singh for the South Asian Americans, and Dorothy Cordova for the Filipino Americans. I prepared the entries on the Korean Americans. Four other individuals should be acknowledged for their contributions to this volume: Visi R. Tilak, Tapan Mukherjee, Dildar Gill Pisani, Anu M. Mitra, and Zillur Khan for working with Jane Singh to complete the South Asian American entries, and Le Hong Phan for preparing entries on the Southeast Asian Americans. In addition, Lisa Lollock and Minh Hoang should be recognized for their able assistance to Steve Fugita in his research and writing of the Japanese American entries. My special thanks go to Jennifer Kang, whose able assistance helped me through the ups and downs in the process of writing and research. Chae Reed deserves special recognition for her library research and clerical and editorial assistance. She gave her time and energy to this book beyond the call of duty. My very special thanks go to Barbara Rader, Greenwood Press executive editor, whose words of encouragement and support sustained me while I was struggling against Bell's Palsy during the various stages of working on the book.

Hyung-chan Kim
Bellingham, Washington

KYUTARO ABIKO

(1865–1936)

Newspaper Publisher, Community Leader

Kyutaro Abiko, leader of the Japanese Community of San Francisco, was a newspaper publisher, farm colony pioneer, and head of the Japanese American Business Promotion Company (Nichibei Kangyosha). Abiko was born in 1865 in the town of Suibara, in Niigata prefecture, Japan. Since his mother died soon after he was born, his maternal grandparents raised him. As a youngster he contributed to the family business by selling candles and paper in nearby villages. At the age of seventeen Abiko and several friends ran away from home, intending to move to the city and then stow away on a ship to America, where he hoped to make his fortune. He lived for several years in Tokyo, where he took English classes and converted to Christianity in 1883.

Inspired by the American ships that sailed into Tokyo's harbors, Abiko decided to sail abroad. He immigrated to America in 1885 under the patronage of the Fukuinkai (Gospel Society), the first Japanese immigrant organization in San Francisco, founded by Methodists and Congregationalists. Abiko settled in San Francisco, where he worked as a schoolboy in an English-speaking home and attended the Lincoln Grammar School. Following graduation from the Boys' High School he enrolled in the University of California at Berkeley. While attending Berkeley, Abiko became an influential leader and instructor of the Methodist Branch Fukuinkai.

After graduation from U. C. Berkeley, Abiko began a laundry business and a restaurant, both of which earned only small profits. In 1897 he purchased a Japanese newspaper, and in 1899 he combined his paper with a second to form one newspaper, the *Nichibei Shimbun* (Japanese American News). The newspaper, written in Japanese, was especially helpful to those who had recently immigrated to the West Coast from Japan; it eventually became the most widely circulated of the Japanese immigrant newspapers. During the 1920s it came out in two editions, one in Los Angeles and the other in San Francisco, with a combined press run of 25,000 and subscribers throughout California, the Pacific Northwest, and the Rocky Mountain region. The newspaper's long-term aims included protection of the rights of Japanese in America, exploration of new fields of enterprise for urban and rural Japanese, and encouragement of further Japanese immigration to the United States. While publishing the newspaper, Abiko provided part-time jobs for Japanese students who needed sponsorship to study in the United States.

The *Nichibei Shimbun* reported news from Japan and America in addition to giving advice to readers on American customs. Through the newspaper Abiko encouraged readers to settle in America and begin families via the *shashin kekkon*, or "picture bride" system, whereby Japanese immigrant men had their relatives in Japan arrange marriages by writing letters and sending photographs. He criticized the Japanese Foreign Ministry and the Japanese Association of America for the decision to stop issuing passports to the picture brides in 1920, believing that discontinuing the practice would impede the progress of community formation. Abiko advocated that Issei (first-generation Japanese immigrants) permanently settle, believing that many of their problems resulted from their status and orientation as migrant laborers. He strongly encouraged education for the Issei, stating that ignorance contributed significantly to their problems. He also encouraged education for non-Japanese, believing that ignorance about the Japanese influenced the racial discrimination, economic fear, and political maneuvering that led to the exclusion movement against the Japanese. He disparaged the *dekasegi* (traveling for temporary employment) mindset of the Japanese, which he perceived as a cause of gambling and immoral behavior as well as an obstacle to establishing stable Japanese immigrant communities.

In October 1906, Abiko organized a protest against the San Francisco School Board's decision to enforce its 1905 resolution that segregated Japanese students. After October 15, 1906, the Board ordered all Japanese children to attend a segregated "Oriental School" in Chinatown, which had been established for the Chinese students in 1885. Abiko and others sent a letter of complaint to the Japanese ambassador in Washington, D.C. Abiko's efforts, and additional pressures from the Japanese government via the Japanese consul general in San Francisco, influenced President Roosevelt to challenge the San Francisco Board of Education. In 1907 the Board rescinded its order as it applied to Japanese children.

After the school segregation issue was settled, Abiko led a protest against the Gentlemen's Agreement, signed by Japan and the United States, whereby Japan agreed to stop allowing laborers to immigrate to America.

In addition to political activities, Abiko worked to fulfill his dream of establishing a permanent Japanese Christian utopian community. In 1902 he established the Nichibei Kangyosha (Japanese American Industrial Company) to handle contract labor and the acquisition of farmland in central California. As a major labor contractor Abiko supplied laborers to the railroad, agricultural, sugar-refining, and mining industries in several states. His company also attracted Hawaiian workers to the mainland. Abiko opened a savings and loan company, the Nichibei Kinyusha, which loaned money to Japanese immigrants for purchasing land to start farms.

With the profit from his companies Abiko founded the Bikoku Shikusan Kaisha (American Land and Produce Company) in 1906. The company purchased land in Merced County to be subdivided and resold to establish his first settlement, the Yamato Colony in Livingston, California. Issei families began to settle on the company's land in 1907. By 1920 this colony grew to 2,450 acres. Abiko began two other colonies, Cressey in 1918 and Cortez in 1919, located near Livingston and Turlock, California. Abiko's investments were successful in helping the Japanese farm laborers to become farm owners. Although the colonies eventually flourished and remain in operation today, the Bikoku Shikusan Kaisha soon encountered financial difficulties. Overextended by purchases, the company folded in 1913. The colony settlers also encountered hardships as they transformed the sand wasteland into suitable land on which to establish farms.

In 1924 Abiko added an English section to the *Nichibei Shimbun* for the English-speaking Nisei children (children born of Issei, that is, second-generation Japanese immigrants). Besides covering the news, this section had many lessons in American etiquette. Abiko shifted the newspaper's emphasis to include the Nisei because he viewed them as the future of America once the Oriental Exclusion Act was passed in 1924. Through the *Nichibei Shimbun*, Abiko encouraged the Issei to recognize their moral obligation and duty to support the Nisei. Following the enactment of the 1924 Immigration Act, Abiko envisioned the Nisei playing a pivotal role in future United States–Japan relations. In 1925 he began to sponsor Nisei excursions to Japan.

Abiko died in 1936. His wife, Yona Tsuda Suto, served as the publisher of the *Nichibei Shimbun* until 1942, when it ceased publication as a result of the forced removal of all West Coast Japanese Americans to internment camps.

Selected Bibliography

Fukuda, M. *Legal Problems of Japanese-Americans: Their History and Development in the United States.* Tokyo: Moritoshi Fukuda, 1980.
Ichioka, Y. "A Study in Dualism: James Yoshinari Sakamoto and the *Japanese American Courier,* 1928–1942." *Amerasia Journal,* vol. 13 (1986–1987): 48–82.
Kim, H. ed. *Dictionary of Asian American History.* Westport, CT: Greenwood Press, 1986.

Steve Fugita

ELEANOR ACADEMIA

(1958–)

Musician

A consummate musician who plays the classics, pop, jazz, funk, and most recently the ancient music of the Philippines on the kulintang (gong), Eleanor Academia started as a child prodigy at age three playing the piano. Born in Honolulu in the late 1950s to Filipino immigrants, she moved with her family several times before settling in San Diego when she was eight.

Recognizing her musical gifts, Academia's teachers encouraged her to study music. Eleanor received private tutoring and training in violin, piano, voice, flute, clarinet, cello, bass, and percussion. She won solo competitions in violin and also arranged and conducted her school ensembles. A "straight A" student in high school, the multitalented Eleanor was also captain of her top-ranked tennis team, was editor of the school newspaper, and was voted "Most Likely to Succeed" in ninth and twelfth grades.

At age sixteen, after hearing the great jazz pianists Oscar Peterson and Art Tatum, Academia realized there were new music vistas to explore and began frequenting San Diego's jazz clubs. A copy of a song she wrote when she was sixteen caught the attention of Quincy Jones, who asked to meet her. He was impressed with her musical background and the fact that she was attending the University of Southern California on a full scholarship. She became the conductor and musical director for the Quincy Jones Workshop, a practical music school for underprivileged blacks who want to learn how to break into the music business. Wanting

Eleanor Academia

to experience all kinds of music, Eleanor played in Los Angeles clubs near Watts while attending USC during the day.

In 1980, Academia met Fulbright scholar Bayani DeLeon, who introduced her to the ancient music of the Philippines, and Eleanor's musical horizons expanded some more. She settled in Los Angeles, playing key boards, writing, recording, arranging, and singing at clubs with various artists including Stevie Wonder, Thelma Houston, Diana Ross, and Earth Wind and Fire.

Producer Maurice White was impressed with Academia's musical gifts and offered to produce her first album. However, on her own Eleanor signed a contract with Epic/Sony Records to write and produce an album herself. The album *Adventure* was produced in Japan in 1987. In the United States it came out as *Jungle Wave* on Columbia Records. Supporting her decision to produce the album herself, White contributed his vocals on two of her cuts. The debut album received critical acclaim for its innovative, pioneering musical textures—using "rhythmic Indian tablas, Philippine gongs, tasty sizzling keyboard work, pop melodies, in-the-pocket grooves and sultry vocals."

On May 7, 1988, Academia's 12" dance mix of the single moved into the highly sought-after No. 1 spot on the Billboard Dance Charts across the United States and more doors began to open. Pop artist Cyndi Lauper immediately hired Academia to be her percussionist and background singer for the 1988 MTV awards. That same year she also performed in Vancouver, British Columbia, at the CBS International Convention with a giant CBS All-Star lineup playing percussion and keyboard. When she opened as a solo act for Nancy Wilson she shocked the audience by playing the Philippine kulintang—an instrument most never had seen or heard of before.

Eleanor Academia is not only a jazz, rock, rhythm and blues, funk, and pop musician, she is also a respected musicologist. Her research on ancient Philippine music, which began with Bayani Mendozas DeLeon, continues with frequent trips to Philippine villages and provinces to study with the masters.

In 1988, Academia received a $21,000 grant from the National Endowment for the Humanities to found a center—the World Kulintang Institute and Research Studies Center, Inc.—for the preservation, education, and presentation of kulintang music. Academia is the executive and artistic director, as well as principal performer, of the Center. Her work with the Institute is strictly traditional and adheres to ritual in performance; it is a dramatic contrast to her contemporary recording work.

Eleanor Academia is a hardworking, creative musician who has blended her remarkable skill as a percussionist in the ancient rhythms of the Philippines with her knowledge and experience in western music. She epitomizes the concept of world music. No one sounds like her.

Selected Bibliography

Asian Music in America Program, April 13, 1991.
RICE magazine, November 1987, pp. 22–23, 43.
World Kulintang Institute Newsletter, Winter 1994, pp. 6–9, 11.

Dorothy Cordova

CHUN AFONG

(1825–1906)

Entrepreneur, Politician

Many Chinese who came to Hawaii did well in business. Chun Afong became well known as the first Chinese millionaire in the Hawaiian Islands. Born in 1825 in the village of Yeong Mui Cha, he came from the

Heungshan (later renamed Chungshan) district of Guangdong province, as did the majority of Chinese who migrated to Hawaii. In 1849 his uncle took the nephew to Honolulu to work in his retail store. Hawaiian officials assumed "Ah Fong" to be his last name and the surname "Chun" to be his given name, so *Chun Fong* was mistakenly changed to *Chun Afong*.

After gaining experience at his uncle's store, Afong set up his own store known as Ah Fong and Ah Fat to sell goods. But the store eventually burned in a fire, and he reopened it with the new name of Afong and Ahchuck. As Afong and other Chinese merchants prospered, they became more visible in Hawaiian society. Along with other members of the foreign community, they mixed with the Hawaiian royalty. In fact, to cultivate good relations between themselves and the Hawaiians, the Chinese organized a ball on November 13, 1856, in honor of King Kamehameha IV and Queen Emma. Afong took charge of the arrangements, and the Chinese even practiced quadrilles so that they could join in the social dancing. The gala affair elicited much praise in the local press and society, and it heightened the prestige and prominence of the Chinese in the Hawaiian and foreign communities.

Since most of the Chinese who initially migrated to Hawaii were men, they found few Chinese women whom they could marry. Many of them chose instead to marry Hawaiians and to raise families in the islands. They loved their wives and the children of Hawaiian-Chinese ancestry, in some cases even sending them back to China to live with their natal families or to receive a Chinese education. Afong followed this practice by marrying Julia Fayerweather on June 18, 1857. Of mixed Hawaiian, American, and English ancestry, she was the ward of Gerrit P. Judd, a well-known missionary. In order to marry her Afong decided to become a naturalized citizen, as was required by Hawaiian law for any foreigner who wished to wed a Hawaiian girl.

In the 1870s, Afong was a partner in a sugar plantation along the Hamakua coast on the island of Hawaii known as Pepeekeo Plantation. In 1884 he incorporated the Huelo Sugar Company on Hamakua. It already had a sugar mill and employed Chinese laborers. Being a very enterprising man, he soon acquired interests in other sugar and coffee plantations. Then, to carry cargo back and forth efficiently and conveniently, he even operated a ship, the 'China Packet,' which sailed back and forth between Hong Kong and Honolulu.

Because of his prominence, Afong was appointed a noble of the Hawaiian Kingdom in 1879. He resigned, however, before he served in the legislature, so that he could act as a commercial agent for China (a position similar to that of a consul). His appointment to the post showed an awareness on the part of China that the Chinese population in Hawaii by now constituted a sizable community. Afong was personally involved in Hawaiian politics, too, supporting King David Kalakaua against Queen Emma, the widow of Kamehameha IV. In part this was owing to his wife, Julia, being a foster sister of Kalakaua. Many sugar planters also sided with Kalakaua, who had agreed to support a reciprocity treaty with the United States. In 1889, Chun Afong aligned himself with Kalakaua against a revolt by Robert Wilcox, organizer of the Liberal Patriotic Association who attempted to overthrow the native government in Hawaii.

After his oldest son, Chun Lung, died, Chun Afong decided to return to China in 1890 with his son Toney. He disposed of all but one-third interest in Pepeekeo Plantation, selling it to Alexander Young for $600,000. He settled in his home village of Yeong Mui Cha in the Heungshan district of Kwangtung province. He bought a large home there and also purchased property in Macao, and Hong Kong. His son Toney (Chun Chik Yee) was appointed governor of Kwangtung province in 1922 by Sun Yat-sen, founder of the Republic of China, and remained in that office until 1930.

Living in Yeong Mui Cha, Afong became a benefactor and contributor to the welfare of the people in the area. His role was highly regarded, and the memorial gates to the village were erected in his memory. When he died in 1906, he had fathered four sons and twelve daughters.

As a "merchant prince" in Hawaii, Afong was the subject of much attention and curiosity. The writer Jack London wrote a fictional account of Chun Afong in *The House of Pride* (1909), in the story "Chun Ah Chun." Many years later Eaton Magoon Jr., a great-grandson of Chun Afong, produced the musical comedy *13 Daughters*, which drew on the Chinese merchant's life. For artistic reasons, however, Magoon's 1956 musical story portrayed Chun Afong's family as consisting of thirteen daughters instead of the four sons and twelve daughters he had in real life.

Selected Bibliography

Dye, Bob. "The Great Chinese Merchants' Ball of 1856." *Hawaiian Journal of History*, vol. 28 1994: 69–78.

Taylor, Clarice B. "The Story of the Afong Family." *Honolulu Star-Bulletin*, October 7–December 25, 1953.

Franklin Ng

Tosan Ahn Ch'ang Ho

CH'ANG HO AHN

(1878–1938)

Political Activist

Ch'ang Ho Ahn, better known among Koreans by his nom de plume, Tosan, was born on November 9, 1878, in Koil village, Tongjin township, Kangso county, South P'yeongan province, which is now located in North Korea. His father died when Tosan was young, and he was taken by his older brother to live with his grandfather. He was taught Chinese classics by his grandfather until he was about nine years of age, when he was taken to a private school known as Sodang, or Hall of Learning. Tosan stayed in the village of his birth until he and his family members were forced to flee from the village during the Sino-Japanese War in

1895. It was during this period that Tosan was exposed to the injustice
and indignity the two giant neighboring nations imposed on their weak
neighbor, Choson Dynasty. Tosan came to the full realization that his
country and people were being victimized by two imperialistic nations
because of its own lack of national power.

Immediately after the war Tosan moved to Seoul, where he entered a
modern school, Kuse Haktang (Save the World School), which was established and run by American missionaries. Here Tosan was exposed
to Western civilization by means of Western science and Christianity. He
was baptized soon after he entered the school. He attended the school
until he was eighteen years old, at which time he returned home to
establish an elementary school. During this period Tosan joined an organization known as Tongnip Hyeop-hoe, or the Independent Club,
founded by Seo Jae-p'il, or **Philip Jaisohn**. He toured the countryside in
order to encourage people to work toward maintaining Korea's independence by refusing to sell land to foreign land speculators. He told
his people that selling land would be like selling their own flesh and
blood.

After the club was ordered disbanded by Korea's emperor Kojong,
Tosan decided to come to the United States for his education. He planned
to prepare himself for a career in education. He left for the United States
in 1902, reaching his first port of call, Honolulu, Hawaii. While his ship
was nearing Honolulu he saw the towering peaks of the Hawaiian Islands; they made such unforgettable impressions on him that he gave
himself a nom de plume, Tosan, or "island mountain." Continuing his
journey he reached Seattle, Washington, where he and his wife, Heryeon
(Helen Lee Ahn), spent five days before arriving in San Francisco on
October 14, 1902.

Upon arrival in California he worked as a houseboy while studying
at local elementary schools. Changing his plan for study, he decided to
work toward the goal of improving the living conditions among Korean
immigrants in California. He moved to Riverside, where he worked as
a fruit-picker at local orchards and organized Korean workers for better
work efficiency and political activities toward Korean independence. In
December 1906 he helped found a political organization, Sin Koryeohoe
(the New Korea Association), made up of people willing to dedicate their
lives to Korea's independence. Korea became a Japanese protectorate in
1905, and Tosan was compelled to return to Korea in 1907 in order to
help his people restore their political independence. In one of his letters
to his wife he wrote that he was returning to Korea because "today our
nation is about to disintegrate and our twenty million people are about
to perish. I have decided to go because I have to do what I can in order
to help our country and our people. Let us not bemoan either our separation or hardship, since we have resolved even to give up our lives."

Tosan worked in Korea between 1907 and 1911 in order to strengthen Korean educational, economic, and political institutions. He believed that Korea would regain its true independence only after its people were educated to have knowledge and skills, and when their traditional institutions were changed to effectively solve problems. Therefore he helped to found a number of key schools, including Taesong School in P'yeongyang. He worked hard to establish key industries such as the P'yeongyang Ceramics Company. More important, he helped found a secret political organization, Sinminhoe (the New People's Society), dedicated to creating a new people born of new civic values. Because of his leadership in this organization, he was imprisoned and then released later. Tosan and his colleagues decided to go into exile because of Japanese political oppression. He came back to San Francisco by way of Beijing, Vladivostok, Chita, St. Petersburg, Berlin, London, and New York, where he arrived on September 3, 1911.

Tosan's second sojourn in America lasted for almost eight years. During this period he worked hard to strengthen the Korean community in North America, Mexico, and Hawaii. He traveled to Hawaii in August 1915 to smooth out a serious community conflict among local leaders and made a trip to Yucatan, Mexico, where he helped organize a branch office of the Korean National Association. One of the most important accomplishments in Tosan's life was the founding of Heungsadan, or the Young Korean Academy, established in San Francisco in 1913. The philosophy of the organization was grounded on the three key concepts: (1) *musil yeokhaeng*, or seeking the truth and practicing it; (2) *cheongeui donsu*, or promoting mutual love; and (3) *tongmaeng yeonsu*, or cultivating unity of virtue, body, and knowledge. The purpose of the Young Korean Academy was to promote among Korean youth at home and abroad the renewing of moral character through self-cultivation. This organization, with large numbers of Koreans both young and old, is very active to this day with social, educational, and cultural programs.

On March 1, 1919, Koreans launched a nationwide protest movement against Japanese colonial rule, and later the leaders of the independence movement established a provisional government-in-exile in Shanghai, China. Tosan was named minister of home affairs and was asked to rush to Shanghai. Upon arrival in Shanghai he was made acting premier of the government in the absence of **Syngman Rhee**. Tosan resigned from the government and worked toward establishing an ideal community in either Manchuria or China. He even made a trip to Manila in 1929 in order to investigate the availability of suitable land for his project.

With the Japanese invasion of China in 1937, Korean independence movement leaders were compelled to change their strategy of fighting against Japanese imperialism; Kim Ku, a close associate of Tosan, chose to use terrorism against the Japanese military. He recruited a number of

Korean patriots, including Yun Pong-gil who hurled two bombs at a gathering of Japanese dignitaries at Hungk'ou Park in Shanghai as they held a military parade to celebrate the emperor's birthday. Although Tosan had nothing to do with this incident, he was arrested because of his association with Kim Ku and the provisional government-in-exile. He was extradited to Korea, prosecuted on charges of violation of security laws, put on trial in Seoul, and found guilty as charged. He was imprisoned for a period of three years before he was released from Taejon Prison. He was later imprisoned for his involvement in other independence activities. He died on March 10, 1938, in a hospital room in Seoul while on bail owing to his poor health. He left his wife with five children; **Philip Ahn**, Philson, Susan, Soorah, and Ralph. His wife and his oldest son, Philip, have passed away, and the rest of his family members are living in the Los Angeles area.

Tosan did not leave any books in his name, although he wrote a few journal articles. Many of his ideas are found in numerous speeches he delivered in Korea, China, and the United States. Letters he wrote to his wife and children are available for those who are interested in doing research on him. Tosan is today considered one of the greatest national leaders by Koreans, not only for his involvement in the independence movement but also for the political, educational, and social leadership he provided for the moral and ethical regeneration of his people.

Selected Bibliography

Choy, Bong-youn. *Koreans in America*, Chicago: Nelson-Hall, 1979.
Gardner, Arthur. "The Korean Nationalist Movement and An Ch'ang-ho, Advocate of Gradualism." Doctoral dissertation, University of Hawaii, 1979.
Kim, Hyung-chan. *Tosan Ahn Ch'ang-ho: A Profile of a Prophetic Patriot*. Seoul: Tosan Memorial Foundation, 1996.

Hyung-chan Kim

PHILIP AHN
(1905–1978)
Actor

Actor Philip Ahn, known for his performances in more than three hundred Hollywood films, was born on March 29, 1905, the first son of **Ch'ang Ho Ahn**, who was married to Helen Lee Ahn (Heryeon). He

Philip Ahn

attended public schools in the Los Angeles area. While still a high school student in Los Angeles, he visited Douglas Fairbanks's *Thief of Bagdad* set and was introduced to Fairbanks and R. Walsh through **Anna May Wong**. Fairbanks thought Philip would be a good character in his picture. Ahn took the news to his mother, who did not think it was a wonderful thing because acting was not done by the upper class in Korea.

Philip Ahn later went to California Polytechnic, where he became interested in dramatics although he prepared to become an electrical engineer. As his interest in dramatics grew, he took as many courses in dramatics and speech as possible. He participated in school plays, which often cast him as an Oriental character. In one of the plays, "Turtle Dove," he was cast as a lover. In another play, Booth Tarkington's "Trusting Place," he was given the part of Ingolsby, for which he wore horn-rimmed glasses and powdered his hair to look like an Occidental. Although the effort was not successful, it was a good experience, according to Philip.

He entered the University of Southern California, where he became a member of many honorary societies and was also assistant to the dean of men. At the university he prepared himself for two separate professions. On the one hand, he wanted to become an actor but felt that it was a profession with a very uncertain future. In order to have something to fall back on in case acting proved not to be lucrative, he chose foreign commerce as his academic major and speech as his minor. He prepared to go into the business of importing and exporting between the United States and Asia. He learned acting by taking courses at the university, by appearing on the stage in "Merrily We Roll Along," and by working in motion pictures such as *Anything Goes* (directed by Lewis Milestone) and *Klondike Annie*.

Philip Ahn was so often cast as a bad guy in motion pictures and television programs that he was listed as No. 1 in the picture index of "The Bad Guys" in a book by William K. Everson. In real life, however, he was a kind man who worked hard to support his mother, two brothers, and two sisters because his father, Tosan Ch'ang Ho Ahn, was often away from home to work for Korea's independence. The family was poor and lived above the laundry located at First and Figueroa in Los Angeles. While going to a local high school, Philip used to drive his sweetheart, Anna May Wong, who later became a renowned actress, to the movies in her car because she did not know how to drive.

During World War II Philip Ahn served in the U.S. Army Infantry, and during the Vietnam War he visited Vietnam to entertain American and Korean soldiers. In spite of his failing health he even volunteered to go abroad to entertain the U.S. armed service personnel in Korea and Vietnam in 1968. He appeared in more than three hundred motion pictures, including *Stowaway, Back to Bataan, Halls of Montezuma, Battle Hymn*, and *Love Is a Many-Splendored Thing*, in both major and minor supporting roles. Hollywood recognized his contributions by inscribing his name on the "Walk of Fame." Before his death in February 1978 he played a major role in the television series *Kung Fu* as Master Kan.

Selected Bibliography

Halliwell, Leslie. *The Filmgoer's Companion*. New York: Hill and Wang, 1974, p. 8.
International Motion Picture Almanac. New York: Quigley, 1977, p. 23.
Kim, Hyung-chan. *Tosan Ahn Ch'ang-ho: A Profile of a Prophetic Patriot*. Seoul: Tosan Memorial Foundation, 1996.

Hyung-chan Kim

JOHN FUGUE AISO

(1909–1987)

Judge

Judge John Fugue Aiso was born in Burbank, California, on December 14, 1909. He attended LeConte Junior High School in Hollywood, where he ran for—and won by a margin of 600 votes—the office of student body president. However, pressure from angry parents, local newspapers, and an anti-Asian student petition resulted in the school administration's suspension of student government until after Aiso graduated.

Aiso attended Hollywood High School, where he applied for but was rejected from the Junior ROTC program. When he tried out for cheerleader, the principal "advised" him to drop out. He did join the debate team and eventually became its captain. Aiso led the Hollywood High School debate team to a Southern California High Schools championship in 1926. He was the first Japanese American to be elected to the honorary Ephebian Society. Aiso was also selected by faculty members to be the valedictorian of his class.

At a preliminary oratorical contest on the U.S. Constitution sponsored by the American Legion, Aiso took first place. This made him eligible to become the representative of his high school at the next level of competition. At this point, the principal called him to his office and told him to choose between the valedictory position or continuing in the oratorical contest. Aiso chose the valedictory position. The second-place winner, Herbert Wenig, represented the school amid much controversy about the ultimatum that forced Aiso to make the choice. Wenig went on to win $500, a paid trip to Europe, and the right to represent the Pacific Coast in the final contest held in Washington, D.C. Aiso served as Wenig's coach.

While on the East Coast, Aiso called on Ambassador Matsudaira of Japan, who encouraged him to apply to colleges on the East Coast. Matsudaira gave him an introductory letter to Brown University's president, Dr. W. H. P. Faunce. On meeting Aiso, Faunce promised him a scholarship if he attended Brown.

Immediately after Aiso graduated from high school at age sixteen he studied the Japanese language for ten months at Seijo Gakuen in Tokyo. In the fall of 1927, when he was almost seventeen years old, Aiso returned to the United States to enter Brown University. In college Aiso participated in many activities. He won a varsity award on the cross-country team and captained Brown's debate team to an Eastern Intercollegiate Championship in 1928–1929. Aiso also joined the Brown Chapter of Delta Upsilon, a national social fraternity, serving on its interfraternity governing board for one semester. In addition Aiso was selected valedictorian of his class, graduating cum laude with final honors in economics in 1931.

Aiso then entered Harvard Law School, the first Nisei (children of Japanese immigrants) from the mainland United States to do so. He graduated from Harvard Law School in 1934. He was admitted to the Bar in New York and was hired as a clerk for Patterson, Eagle, Greenough, & Day on Wall Street. From 1936 to 1937, Aiso studied Japanese law at Chuo University. He next went to Shanghai to work for the Shanghai Branch of Domei News Service. He was promoted from head of the Legal Department to director of the corporation, staying in Manshoukuo (Manchuria) for almost three years.

In 1940, Aiso returned to the United States after contracting hepatitis. In December 1940 he was notified that he would be drafted under the Selective Service Training Act. He reported for active military service in April 1941. Stationed at Ft. MacArthur in San Pedro, California, Aiso became a 31-year-old private second class. He was then transferred to Company D, 69th Quartermaster Battalion, at Camp Haan, near the Riverside air force base. Aiso was given the job of repairing trucks, even though he had no such skills.

After several months of service Aiso was released on furlough. He resumed his law practice in Los Angeles and became engaged. When he returned to pick up his discharge papers at Camp Haan, he was ordered to attend the Japanese language school at Crissy Field in the Presidio of San Francisco. He was not allowed to discuss the situation with his fiancée, Sumi Akiyama of Westminster, Orange County. In a matter of hours he was on his way to the Presidio.

Lieutenant Colonel John Weckerling assigned Aiso to an assistant instructor position. A few days later he was appointed head instructor. The school formally opened on November 1, 1941, with forty-five Nisei and Kibei (Nisei sent to Japan for education) and fifteen men of other ethnicities. Aiso was promoted to master sergeant, the highest grade to which he could be promoted. Subsequently the school was moved to Camp Savage near Minneapolis. The school grew and was renamed the Military Intelligence Service Language School (MISLS). It also expanded its curriculum to include Japanese history, geography, military, language, general conversation, translation, and the reading of *sosho*, or grass writing. As it grew, the school was relocated again, this time to Fort Snelling, which was four to five miles away. Aiso was subsequently commissioned as a major.

On October 1, 1945, Aiso turned over the directorship of the MISLS to Tsutomu Tekawa and left for a new assignment in occupied Japan under General MacArthur in Tokyo. Soon thereafter the MISLS was moved to the Presidio in Monterey and was renamed the Defense Language Institute.

In Tokyo, Aiso became a legal assistant in the Civil Information Section of MacArthur's Allied Headquarters, led by Major General Charles A. Willoughby. Aiso took a leave of absence to return to Los Angeles in February 1947. By then he was a lieutenant colonel. Aiso was not called back to Tokyo.

Aiso passed the California State Bar examination in 1941. Upon leaving active duty in 1947, he returned to general practice until he was appointed commissioner of the Los Angeles Superior Court in September 1952. A year later he was appointed a judge of the Municipal Court of the Los Angeles Judicial District. In November 1953 he was promoted to Superior Court of Los Angeles County, where he served in civil and criminal cases. Chief Justice Taynor appointed him chief judge of the Appellate Department in December 1967, and a year later Governor Reagan appointed Aiso associate justice of Division Five of the California Court of Appeal for the Second Appellate District (Los Angeles, Ventura, Santa Barbara, and San Luis Obispo counties). He was also justice pro tem of the California Supreme Court for three months, appointed by Earl Warren, until his retirement from public office. Thereafter he worked as special counsel to the law firm of O'Melveny & Meyer for ten years.

Before Aiso retired in 1983, the Japanese-American Bar Association set up a scholarship fund named in his honor. Aiso suffered a slight stroke in February 1984. On Japan's Bunka-no-Hi (Literary Holiday), November 1984, the Japanese government conferred on Aiso its Third Class Order of the Rising Sun medal.

Aiso was killed by a mugger in December 1987.

Selected Bibliography

Daniels, Roger. *Asian America: Chinese and Japanese in the United States since 1850.* Seattle and London: University of Washington, 1988.

Hosokawa, Bill. *Nisei: The Quiet Americans.* New York: William Morrow, 1969.

Inchinokuchi, Tad. *John Aiso and the MIS.* Los Angeles: MIS Club of Southern California, 1988.

Niiya, Brian, ed. *Japanese American History: An A-to-Z Reference from 1868 to the Present.* New York: Facts on File, 1993.

Uyeda, Clifford, and Barry Saiki, eds. *The Pacific War and Peace: Americans of Japanese Ancestry in Military Intelligence Service, 1941 to 1952.* San Francisco: Military Intelligence Service Association of Northern California, 1991, pp. 15–20.

Steve Fugita

Chang Apana

(1864–1933)

Law Enforcement Officer

Chang Apana, a Honolulu detective, was the person who became the basis for Earl Derr Biggers's famous fictional character Charlie Chan. He was born in Waipio on the island of Oahu in Hawaii on December 26, 1864. His father, Chang Jong Ton, and his mother, Chun Shee, were both farmers who came from Oo Syak village in the Gook Do area of Chung-shan district in Guangdong province. They named their son Chang Ah Ping. When the son was three years old, his parents took him back to China. At age ten he returned to live with his uncle, C. Y. Aiona, in Waipio.

Although his given name was Ah Ping with the surname Chang, he eventually became known as Chang Apana. Because of his ability to handle horses, he was hired to tend horses for the Wilder family on their Esbank estate in 1891. Three years later he was enlisted by Helen K. Wilder to work for the Hawaii Humane Society, which she had founded.

In 1898, Chang Apana joined the Honolulu Police Department. Over the years he rose through the ranks. In 1916 he was promoted to detective. In 1925 he attained the rank of detective 2nd grade, and in 1928 he became a detective 1st grade. A shrewd and meticulous investigator, he solved cases dealing with crime such as gambling and opium smuggling. Fluent in Hawaiian, Chinese, and Pidgin English, he communicated with a wide network of informants who provided him with the information to crack cases and arrest felons.

While vacationing in Hawaii in 1919, writer Earl Derr Biggers (1884–1933) read in the local papers about the exploits of Chang Apana. This became the basis for his popular series of mysteries centered on a Chinese detective in Honolulu named Charlie Chan. *House without a Key*, published in 1925, was the first book to introduce Charlie Chan. It was a success, and in rapid succession other novels appeared. Other mysteries featuring Charlie Chan included *The Chinese Parrot* (1926), *Behind That Curtain* (1928), *The Black Camel* (1929), *Charlie Chan Carries On* (1930), and *Keeper of the Keys* (1932).

In a letter dated June 28, 1932, and sent to the *Honolulu Advertiser*, Earl Derr Biggers acknowledged that Chang Apana was the inspiration for Charlie Chan. Although the public grew to know Charlie Chan as a portly detective, Chang Apana was actually a short, slender person. But researchers have nevertheless noted a number of coincidences. For example, Apana had a daughter named Rose, and in *The Black Camel* Charlie Chan also had a daughter named Rose. In the same novel Chan is said to have served for twenty-seven years. Apana at that time would have been a detective for about a similar amount of time. Apana once lived in the Punchbowl area of Honolulu, and Chan lived on Punchbowl, too.

Hollywood wanted to capitalize on the success of the detective, and many films were made. Different actors portrayed Charlie Chan for the various studios. They included English actor E. L. Park, and Japanese actors George Kuwa and Kamiyama Sojin. In 1931, Fox acquired rights to *Behind That Curtain* and cast the Swedish-born actor Werner Oland in the title role. Oland had wide audience appeal and starred in sixteen films. His death in 1938 led to Sidney Toler as his replacement, and later Roland Winters.

The detective Charlie Chan was based on Chang Apana, but the role has never been portrayed by a Chinese on the screen. In recent years some Chinese American activists have felt that such renditions of Charlie Chan have perpetuated negative images and stereotypes of Asian Americans. Thus the filming of a new Charlie Chan movie in 1980, *Charlie Chan and the Curse of the Dragon Queen*, starring Peter Ustinov in the main role, triggered angry protests and demonstrations. More recently the writer Jessica Hagedorn edited an anthology of contemporary Asian American fiction, giving it the title *Charlie Chan Is Dead* (1993).

Chang Apana retired from the police force in 1932 and died on December 8, 1933. He was buried in the Lin Yee Chung cemetery in the Manoa valley of Honolulu. His reputation was so great that newspapers such as the *San Francisco Chronicle, Chicago Tribune*, and *New York Times* mentioned his passing. Apana had been married three times. He married Annie Lee Kwai, the sister of his second wife, on April 12, 1914, in Honolulu. He had ten children from the different marriages.

Selected Bibliography

"Black Camel Kneels at Home of Chang Apana." *Honolulu Star-Bulletin*, December 9, 1933.
Chin, Frank. "Interview: Roland Winters." *Amerasia Journal*, vol. 2 (Fall 1973): 1–19.
Connor, Edward. "Charlie Chan in Hawaii." *Honolulu Star-Bulletin*, March 19, 1955.
Martines, Gilbert. "Chang Apana the Man." *Hawaii Herald*, February 4, 1983.
———. "In Search of Charlie Chan." *Hawaii Herald*, January 21, 1983.
Yim, Susan. "In Search of Chan." *Honolulu Star-Bulletin*, August 22, 1982.

———. "The Real Charlie Chan?" *Honolulu Star-Bulletin*, October 21, 1976.
                                                                                Franklin Ng

---

GEORGE RYOICHI ARIYOSHI

(1926–   )

Governor, Politician, Attorney

George Ryoichi Ariyoshi, the former governor of Hawaii, has had a distinguished career in law and politics and is the first American of Japanese ancestry to be elected a governor in the nation. On November 2, 1982, he was reelected to a third consecutive term as governor of Hawaii. On December 6, 1982, he was officially sworn into office, culminating a successive series of elections to territorial and state offices.

Born on March 12, 1926, in Honolulu, he grew up in the downtown and Kalihi sections of Hawaii's capital. His late father, Ryozo Ariyoshi, was a sumo wrestler from Fukuoka prefecture in Japan. After coming to Hawaii, his father was a stevedore and owner of a dry-cleaning shop. Ariyoshi's mother, Mitsue (Yoshikawa) Ariyoshi, came from Kumamoto, Japan. He attended McKinley High School in Honolulu and graduated in 1944; he was president of his senior class. He subsequently served as an interpreter with the U.S. Army's Military Intelligence Service in Japan at the end of World War II.

Returning to Hawaii, Ariyoshi attended the University of Hawaii, then transferred to Michigan State University, where he received a Bachelor of Arts degree in history and political science in 1949. He earned a law degree (Juris Doctor) from the University of Michigan Law School in 1952.

In 1953, Ariyoshi entered law practice in Hawaii. In 1962 he became a director of the First Hawaiian Bank, and in 1964 he became a director of the Honolulu Gas Company (later Pacific Resources). In 1966 Ariyoshi became a director of the Hawaiian Insurance and Guaranty Company. While gaining this recognition in the business community, he advanced in the legal profession as well. Ariyoshi was elected vice-president of the Hawaii Bar Association in 1968 and president in 1969. He was also a charter member and president of the Hawaii Bar Foundation in 1969–1970 and a member of the American Bar Association House of Delegates in 1969. After being elected lieutenant governor in 1970, Ariyoshi with-

George Ryoichi Ariyoshi

drew from private law practice and also resigned his various director-ships.

Ariyoshi's political career began in 1954. Urged by former governor John A. Burns, then Hawaii Democratic Party chairman, to enter politics, he ran for the territorial House of Representatives and was elected to the 28th Legislature, Territory of Hawaii. He served for four years before moving up to the territorial Senate in 1958. Following the achievement of statehood in 1959, Ariyoshi remained in the state Senate. In 1964 he became chairman of the Ways and Means Committee; then majority leader of the Senate in 1965–1966. He also served as majority floor leader of the Senate in 1969–1970.

In 1970, Ariyoshi was elected lieutenant governor. When Governor Burns fell ill in October 1973 he became acting governor, serving in that capacity through the balance of the term. In 1974, Ariyoshi was elected governor and reelected in 1978 and 1982. When he was reelected to a third term, he became one of the nation's senior governors in terms of service. He also has the distinction of never having lost an election.

Ariyoshi served as chairman of the Western Governors' Conference in 1977–1978 and was president of the Pacific Basin Development Council in 1980–1981. The council includes the governors of American Samoa, Guam, Hawaii, and the Northern Mariana Islands. When two separate

Western Governors' organizations were merged into one new Western Governors' Association comprised of sixteen western states and three Pacific territories, he was elected its first chairman in February 1984.

The Japanese government presented Ariyoshi with one of its highest decorations, the Order of the Sacred Treasure, First Class, in 1985, and the Emperor's Silver Cup in 1987. The Japanese-American Citizens' League presented him with its Japanese-American of the Biennium award in 1984.

George Ryoichi Ariyoshi married Jean Miya Hayashi in February 1955 in Honolulu. They have three children: Lynn Miye, born in 1957; Todd Ryozo, born in 1959; and Donn Ryoji, born in 1961. For recreation, Ariyoshi enjoys golf. He is active in a number of business and cultural organizations.

Selected Bibliography

Current Biography Yearbook. New York: H. W. Wilson, 1985.
Niiya, Brian, ed., *Japanese American History.* New York: Facts on File, 1993.
Who's Who in American Politics, 1997–1998. 2 vols. 16th ed. New Providence, NJ: Marquis Who's Who, 1997.

Steve Fugita

JOSE ARUEGO

(1932–)

Cartoonist, Artist

As a young boy in the Philippines, Jose Espiritu Aruego spent hours doodling and drawing, especially at school where he decorated the bulletin board, chalkboards, and classroom. He was born on August 9, 1932, in Manila into a family of lawyers, and it was expected that he would join his father and sister in that profession. The elder Mr. Aruego also taught law at the University of Manila and wrote legal books. When the Republic of the Philippines was granted independence from the United States on July 4, 1946, he participated in the important discussions and conventions that shaped the constitution of the new nation.

Aruego wanted to please his father, so he enrolled in the University of the Philippines in preparation for a career in law. He earned a Bachelor of Arts degree in 1953 and went on to law school, getting his law degree in 1955. He was not really interested in law and did not study much for the bar exam, and he barely passed. His career as a lawyer lasted only three months. When he lost his first case, Aruego decided he would pursue his first dream and become an artist.

Aruego's parents supported his decision, and his father encouraged him to go to Paris to study. However, he wanted to go to New York City, the comic book capital of the world. As a child he had collected comic books, and he was intrigued by their artwork. He wanted to draw cartoons and comic books. He enrolled in the Parsons School of Design, and at first he was lonely and wanted to return to the Philippines. After the first year Aruego adjusted to life in New York. After the second year at Parsons he went to Europe for the summer to study art. There he learned a technique of line drawings that he now uses in his own illustrations. Aruego graduated from Parsons in 1959 with a certificate in graphic arts and advertising. During the next six years he worked for advertising agencies and magazines doing a variety of jobs.

Aruego joined the International House in New York City, which gave him the opportunity to meet other people—including another artist, Ariane Dewey, whom he married in 1961. As part of a group interested in international friendship, Jose traveled throughout the United States and other countries.

Aruego constantly drew cartoons and submitted them to various magazines. Eventually his cartoons were accepted by the *Saturday Evening Post, Look*, and *New Yorker*. As his confidence and income increased with each new sale, he left his job and became a fulltime cartoonist. However, he later described how discouraging it was that only one in every twenty cartoons submitted would be accepted. Despite this, Aruego remained a freelance cartoonist for two years.

While he was cartooning, Aruego also wrote and illustrated a children's book, *The King and His Friends*, which he dedicated to his newborn son, Juan. One publisher rejected the book, but it was later accepted by another publisher, Charles Scribner's Sons, because an editor was impressed with his illustrations. The book was published in 1970. He also illustrated *Whose Mouse Are You?* written by Robert Kraus. It was selected as an American Library Association Notable Book.

During his second year as an illustrator and writer of children's books, Aruego had five books published—including three he illustrated and two that were entirely his own. One of his own creations, *Juan and the Asuangs*, won an award as an Outstanding Picture Book of the Year from the *New York Times*. This was just the first of many awards he was to receive. In his early years of writing and illustrating children's books, Aruego sometimes collaborated with his wife, Ariane Aruego. They illustrated several books for other writers and together wrote and illustrated *A Crocodile's Tale*. The couple was divorced in 1973 but continue to collaborate. Ariane has resumed her maiden name, Ariane Dewey.

Aruego has written and illustrated mostly animal stories, which could be a reflection of a happy childhood spent among the menagerie of animals his family kept in Manila and on a farm where he spent some summers. He has combined his lifelong fascination with animals and his love of humor with brilliant, colorful drawings that reflect his roots in the tropical climate of the Philippines. His pictures depict memorable characters and humorous situations.

Over the past twenty years Aruego has illustrated over sixty books and has written at least ten of those. He enjoys traveling around the country meeting people, talking with schoolchildren, and exchanging ideas with other artists and writers. Although America is now his home, Jose still visits the Philippines. In 1976 he made a special trip there to receive an award as the Outstanding Filipino Abroad in Arts. Jose Aruego, lawyer turned illustrator, plans to continue for many more years in his chosen career.

Selected Bibliography

Fil-American Courier, June 1990, p. 27.
International Examiner, August 5, 1994, p. 27.
Kent Valley Daily News, November 5, 1994, p. 13.

Dorothy Cordova

TAI BABILONIA
(1960–   )
Figure Skater

Tai Babilonia is a talented figure skater whose lifelong involvement in skating has brought her fame, financial success, and personal heartbreak. The daughter of a retired Los Angeles police detective of Filipino descent and an African American mother, Tai was introduced to the sport at age nine by her Japanese godfather when he took her to an outing at a skating rink. He was also responsible for her first name, which means "beautiful, tranquil, lovely."

Babilonia's parents were both sports-oriented and were eager for her to excel. They supported the hectic and rigorous schedule their daughter underwent to develop and hone her skills. She first skated with her future partner, Randy Gardner, as the characters Dr. and Mrs. Doolittle at a local club show when she was nine and he was eleven. Coach Mable Fairbanks saw their potential and urged them to try competitive pair skating. After a few months of training, the young couple made their debut in the 1971 Southwest-Pacific Regional and placed sixth among ten novice pairs. The next year she took second in the Regionals and third in Pacific Coast Novice Pairs. At the end of the season, Gardner's parents felt it was time for the young couple to receive expert training and approached John A. W. Nicks, who coached U.S. Pair Champions and World Bronze medalists Jo Jo Starbuck and Ken Shelley.

Babilonia and Gardner blossomed under Nicks, who put them on a grueling schedule and had them practice and perform their routines for many hours each day but Sunday. They went on to win four straight National Pairs titles; fifth place in the 1976 Olympic Winter Games at Innsbruck (when Babilonia was only fifteen years old); third place in the 1978 World Championships; and the Gold Medal at the United States Olympic Committee's National Sports Festival in 1978 and 1979. In 1979, when Babilonia was nineteen years old, the duo broke an unchallenged Soviet monopoly by winning the World Championships in Vienna, scoring a perfect 6.0.

By the 1980 Olympic Winter Games in Lake Placid, New York, Babilonia and Gardner were considered to be the major competition of the Soviet husband/wife team, Irina Rodnina and Aleksndr Zaitsev, who were returning to competition after taking a year off to have a child. The American pair thrilled rink-side observers with their elegant line, athletic prowess, and musical interpretation. Pressure began to build. They were expected to win Olympic gold. However, a groin injury incurred by Gardner during practice forced the pair to drop out during the Olympic competition, and years of unresolved frustration for Babilonia began.

The press called Babilonia and Gardner the "heartbreak kids." In an interview with *People* magazine, Babilonia recalls never discussing their great disappointment or mutual sorrow with Gardner. Shortly after the Olympics, they signed a three-year contract with the Ice Capades and began the grueling, fast-paced, "sometimes glamorous, mostly lonely" life of professional ice skaters. At the same time, Tai began the dating she had missed during her teenage years. The loneliness of being away from her family, and weight gain because of junk food, began to take its toll. She started to take drugs and drink alcohol to cope. Despite this, her career was on a roll. However, she was on the verge of a nervous breakdown and wanted to quit but hesitated to do so because she did not want to let Gardner down. Her drinking continued, and in 1988, after a final performance at Harrah's at Lake Tahoe, she announced her retirement from skating.

She dropped out of sight, shut out friends, slept until noon, and demonstrated other evidence of depression. A suicide attempt was aborted, and Babilonia began to see a therapist to finally deal with the rage and bitterness she had held in at the time of the Olympics. She realized she had to find out who she was and how she could have a life of her own—without Randy Gardner. Babilonia now began to heal herself and talk more openly about her feelings. After years of pleasing others, she learned to do things just for herself.

In 1989 after a year away from performing, Babilonia rejoined Gardner for an engagement in Atlantic City. The "heartbreak kids" began a successful comeback. They now perform professionally in the United States and abroad.

Selected Bibliography

Journal American Family Weekly, February 3, 1980, p. 4.
People, April 17, 1989, pp. 88–93.
People, December 9, 1996, pp. 176–178.
Philippine News, March 19, 1980, p. 1.

Dorothy Cordova

BOBBY BALCENA
(1926–1990)
Baseball Player

Robert Rudolph Balcena was born on August 1, 1926, in San Pedro, California. Both his parents were immigrants from the Philippines. His father, Fred, came from Iloilo, and his mother, Lazara, was from Cavite. He had one sister, Florence.

Balcena began playing baseball when he was six years old and went on to excel in football and track and field as a student at San Pedro High School. While still a teenager he joined the U.S. Navy during World War II and served for three years. After the war Balcena returned to civilian life and played briefly with a Yugoslav-American baseball team. He played semi-pro baseball with the San Pedro Independents from 1946 to 1947.

From 1948 to 1949 Balcena was with the Mexicali Aguilas (Eagles) of the Sunset League, and he led the league in batting with a .369 average in 1948. The next year he led the league once again with 132 runs batted in and 295 total bases. An injury incurred while playing with the Eagles prevented him from continuing as a pitcher—his preferred position. However, Balcena continued his baseball career as an outfielder with Toronto (1950–1951), San Antonio (1952–1953), and Kansas City (1954). He was with the Baltimore Orioles for spring training in 1955, and that same year he went to play for the Seattle Rainiers.

In Balcena's first year with the Rainiers the team won a championship. He was a valuable member of the team, third in runs batted in with an average of .290. In 1956, playing center field for Seattle, he led the Coast League in doubles and batted .295. Later he was drafted by the Cincinnati Red Lights (now known as the Cincinnati Reds) and played as a utility outfielder. His career in the major leagues was short-lived, and he returned to Seattle the following year. He was one of the most popular players for the Rainiers and was often referred to as the Filipino Flyer.

Balcena played with or against many baseball greats; among them were Maury Wills, Darrell Johnson, Hank Aaron, Roberto Clemente, and Tom Lasorda. He was a professional baseball player for more than fifteen years.

When Balcena retired in 1962 he pursued his other hobbies, collecting jazz and big band records and tinkering with and maintaining old cars. Maintaining an attachment to both Seattle and San Pedro, where he was born, Balcena had homes in both places. He was also engaged in a construction business in Seattle.

Balcena died on January 5, 1990. At his funeral there were many tributes, including one by a sports reporter who described Bobby Balcena as "one of a kind with no other ball player like him before or since."

Selected Bibliography

Fil-American Moderator, December 1957, p. 2.
Heritage magazine, March 1990, pp. 8–9.
San Pedro News Pilot, October 24, 1995, pp. A1, A8.

Dorothy Cordova

THANG NGUYEN BARRETT
(1960–   )
Judge

The third child of the late Nguyen Thong Tri, a high-ranking Vietnamese diplomat and former general consul to Laos, and Bui Thi Dung, Thang Nguyen was born in 1960 in Saigon. His father had sent the family to Belgium in anticipation of an assignment, but he passed away before he could join them. Nguyen was then fourteen years old. He remained in Europe and eventually was adopted by Lieutenant Colonel (Ret.) Robert Barrett, who brought the family to Virginia in 1977.

Thang Nguyen Barrett did not speak English then but completed his last year in high school, struggling to overcome the language barrier. Following high school he supported himself as a waiter for three years before entering college. He attended the American University and graduated with honors in philosophy in 1985, then came to California where he received his Juris Doctor degree from the University of California, Hastings College of Law, in 1988. Barrett was the first Vietnamese American research attorney for the San Francisco Superior Court, and he became the first Vietnamese American deputy district attorney in Santa Clara County in 1989. His trial work included a three-year assignment with the elite Sexual Assault Team.

He was the first prosecutor in Santa Clara County to obtain a jury conviction under California's hate crime laws, to demonstrate the reliability of DNA (RFLP, or restriction fragment length polymorphism) evidence in court, and to obtain a jury conviction under the one-strike sex crime law. His work in a death penalty case resulted in California's first reinstatement of a death sentence following an appeal by the prosecution. Barrett has been regarded as a highly skilled trial lawyer and an accomplished appellate attorney.

When appointed by Governor Pete Wilson to the Santa Clara Municipal Court on February 22, 1997, Judge Thang Nguyen Barrett became the first Vietnamese American judge in California.

In addition to his responsibilities on the bench, Judge Barrett has taught legal writing and research at the University of California, Hastings College of Law, and Moot Court at Peninsula Law School. In 1992 he received the Hastings Legal Opportunity Education Program's Out-

standing Services Award. Later Judge Barrett was awarded a commendation in recognition of outstanding contributions to the delivery of pro
bono legal services in Santa Clara County, in which he taught trial advocacy at Santa Clara University School of Law.

Judge Barrett believes that as a public servant an important part of his
responsibility is toward the community. His community services include
serving on the Board of Directors of the Southeast Asian Refugee Resettlement; the Asian Law Alliance; the Girl Scouts of Santa Clara County;
the blue ribbon committees to select county officials; and the San Jose
mayor's steering committee on the Vietnamese language television program "The Law and You." In 1997 he received the Asian Americans for
Community Involvement's Freedom Award.

Judge Barrett says he will continue to take time to encourage others,
especially fellow Vietnamese Americans, to pursue work in the public
sector.

Selected Bibliography

Recorder March 25, 1997.
San Jose Mercury News, February 26, 1997.

Le Hong Phan

LYNDA BARRY
(1956–)
Author, Cartoonist

Irreverent Lynda Barry has been called the funniest redhead in America.
A philosopher and an artist with a keen insight into human dynamics,
she is considered one of the three top female cartoonists in the United
States. Her whimsical work, which chronicles in satirical form the mating
game (love, romance, and breakup), can be found monthly in *Esquire*
magazine, is nationally syndicated in newspapers, and has appeared in
Playboy, Vogue, and other national publications.

An *Elle* magazine article described Lynda Barry "as the reigning queen
of adolescent pop psychology" and said she "has a monopoly on growing pains."

Barry was born in Minnesota to an Irish-Norwegian father and an immigrant Filipino mother. When she was very young her parents separated. Her mother moved the family to a multiracial working-class neighborhood in Seattle, where Barry lived within a five-block radius of fifty Filipino relatives who often dropped in to visit. She looked like a "regular white kid" but had a Filipino mother and was raised in a family run in "pretty traditional Filipino ways." Many of her early cartoons reflect the influence of her Filipino heritage.

Barry has said that as a youngster she was obsessed with drawing. She remembers fondly one of her first teachers who "punished" out-of hand students by sending them to the back of the room with a pencil and pad to draw. She said drawing calmed her.

She did not begin drawing cartoons until she was studying fine arts at Evergreen State College in Washington. The editor of the school paper was Matt Groening, who also became a syndicated cartoonist and the creator of "The Simpsons." Another friend from her high school days who was working at the University of Washington *Daily* in 1976 published her first cartoons, which she had mailed to him. That strip led to another in the *Seattle Sun* that was eventually picked up by the publisher of the *Chicago Reader*. It was just a matter of time before other papers—including the *Village Voice*—picked up her strip and her work went into syndication. From 1984 to 1989, Barry had a regular strip in *Esquire* magazine.

During her adolescent years Barry often hung out with her male friends, and she has been acclaimed as a female cartoonist who understands men. She is also known not to hesitate to poke fun at women's magazines. When she was in college, an art professor encouraged his students to tell the story of their lives. Her cartoons aptly portray the sometimes funny, sometimes sad experiences of childhood and the anxieties of adolescence, but they are not completely autobiographical because they do not feature Filipinos. Barry has said that one day she may write about passing as white, and she has acknowledged that she receives "breaks" that would not have been extended to her cousins who look Filipino.

Barry's one-woman exhibits have received positive reviews. A series of her comics have been turned into a National Public Radio miniseries. She lectures to packed halls. Several of her books have gone into multiple printings. She has adapted her first novel, *The Good Times Are Killing Me* (1988) into a successful off-Broadway play that tells the bittersweet story of an interracial friendship in a working-class neighborhood. With this play Lynda Barry has managed to share her life story with her legions of admirers. She has also written a second novel, *Cruddy* (1998).

Selected Bibliography

Coburn, Maria Froelke. "Her So-Called Life." *Chicago*, March 1997.
McCalls, November 1991, p. 130.
Mifflin, Margot. "A Not So Perfect Life: The Anxious Humor of Lynda Barry."
  Elle, April 1992.
Oppenheimer, Judy. "Lynda Barry Outstrips Them All." *Mirabella*, April 1991.
Pacific Northwest Magazine, December 1986, pp. 36–39.
Seattle Weekly, July 12, 1995, pp. 16–17.

Dorothy Cordova

AMAR GOPAL BOSE

(1931–)

Entrepreneur, Inventor, Educator

The Massachusetts-based Bose Corporation, founded by Amar Gopal Bose, is one of the world's foremost manufacturers of loudspeakers and audio equipment. With over three thousand employees worldwide, the company has subsidiaries in fifteen countries and manufacturing units in the United States, Mexico, Canada, and Ireland. The company boasts an estimated annual sales of over $600 million and has been growing at an average of 20 percent per annum over the last decade. Apart from being a successful entrepreneur and inventor, Bose is a professor of electrical engineering at the Massachusetts Institute of Technology (MIT).

Bose grew up in a Philadelphia suburb. His mother, Charlotte, a schoolteacher, was an American of French-German descent, and his father, Noni, emigrated to the United States from Calcutta, India, to escape British rule. Bose describes how his family experienced racial discrimination during his childhood: "there wasn't a restaurant where we could be served as a family because they thought my father was black" (quoted in Mayer 1990). Although he was often harassed by neighborhood kids, his father told him to "never, never fight." After one occasion when Bose was physically attacked, his father changed his approach. His father "lectured him on racism, taught him how to box and told him to never start a fight—or lose another one. He didn't" (Walker 1992).

Bose's interest in electronics began when his violin teacher allowed him to play with an electric train set that he owned. When he was still in high school Amar Bose opened a radio repair shop, which he ran for four years. This entrepreneurial experience developed into a quest for knowledge about electronics design.

After spending nine years as an engineering student at the Massachusetts Institute of Technology, where he got his B.S., M.S., and Ph.D. in electrical engineering, he decided to buy a stereo system to help him relax while he prepared to write his thesis. With his knowledge of electrical theory he bought the system with the best specs. When he brought it home, put it together, and played a violin recording that sounded terrible, it was the beginning of his research for the ultimate stereo.

Bose took his new acquisition to the school's acoustics lab and started tinkering with it. He was trying to find out why speakers that seemed impressive from an engineering standpoint sounded so awful. Bose's research showed that the textbook information on loudspeaker design was incorrect. As his knowledge about speaker design and psychoacoustics grew, his MIT professor, Y. W. Lee, suggested that Bose start a company. Lee invested his life savings of $10,000 toward the formation of Bose Corporation in 1964. That investment yielded $250,000 when the company bought back Lee's stock in 1972.

Bose holds numerous patents in the fields of acoustics, electronics, nonlinear systems, and communication theory. His electronic patents formed the basis of the research and development contracts that Bose secured with the armed forces, NASA, DOT, and AEC. Along with his acoustical and electronic patents, Bose Corporation has a strong research team to ensure the future of its technological leadership in the field of sound.

Bose Corporation is privately held, and 100 percent of the profits are re-invested in the company's growth and development. The company's objective is to create products that combine high technology with simplicity and thereby provide the best possible sound system that is easy to use and accessible to all consumers. Bose, a fierce and thoroughgoing critic of the mystique of high fidelity, is described as a music lover's best friend. He is considered a level-headed, plain-spoken ally who will defend the consumer's right not to care about arcane electronics but just to "plug in" to some great sounds.

The Bose Corporation's first products were high-power amplifiers produced under contract to the U.S. military. Patented technology created for those highly sophisticated units has since been used by Bose in a variety of consumer products. Today the Bose Corporation produces home professional audio systems, home theater systems, automotive music systems, and Bose Acoustic Noise Canceling headsets for general aviation pilots and passengers.

Bose strongly believes that a product cannot be better than its competitor's unless it is different. The 901 Direct/Reflecting loudspeaker, the company's first product, bewildered technical professionals in the industry but continues to be one of Bose's best-selling products. The company followed the 901s with several other innovations, including its Acoustimass system, the Acoustic Wave music system, and the Wave Radio (for which the Intellectual Property Owners Association named Amar Bose inventor of the year). His Auditioner system, released in fall 1994, helps architects design buildings with good acoustics.

Bose speakers are the best-selling models in Japan, home to many of the world's largest stereo manufacturers. Bose, who attributes his success to having quality products and personnel, says that there is nothing magical about dominating the Japanese market.

In 1979 Bose Corporation started designing speakers for the auto market, and today its car audio components account for 25 percent of revenue of the company. Bose is supplying audio systems to some eleven car makers, representing some thirty-one different vehicles. Bose believes that car stereo systems can surpass home systems. He says that engineers who design sound systems for cars benefit from knowing the precise furnishings of the listening space and from being able to anticipate the listener's location within that space.

Bose does not let his business interests affect his teaching career. A dedicated professor, he considers his students his first priority. Many of Bose's students work with him. According to Bose, hiring the right people is critical to success. He has an advantage—he has some of the brightest people around as graduate students, and he already knows their abilities and character. He first hired a few of them after they graduated; his company continues to attract students.

Both at MIT and Bose Corporation, Bose sees his role as that of motivator. His philosophy of teaching and managing reflects his belief that people are capable of great things, if given the chance. In the 1960s Bose participated in a Ford Foundation experiment at MIT to see if students who face extraordinary challenge in the classroom learn at more rapid rates. According to him, the students proved that people tend to meet higher standards.

Bose believes in educating the consumer in the same way that a professor educates a student to appreciate finer things. His view is that once a person recognizes and becomes accustomed to quality, the person never goes back to mediocrity.

Selected Bibliography

Balagopal, Sudha. "Sound Success." *India Today*, February 15, 1994.
"Concert Hall on Wheels." *Motor Trend*, March 1990, p. 12.
Griffith, Victoria. "Mr. Motivator." *Financial Times*, March 17, 1995, p. 12.
Mayer, Barbara. "Tête à Tête: Who's Got the Button?" *Elle Decor*, 1990.
Teague, Paul E. "Engineering's 'Mr. Speaker.' " *Design News*, March 6, 1995, p. 98.

Walker, Blair S. "Revenue Growth Music to Bose's Ears." *USA Today*, September
    22, 1992.

Visi R. Tilak

CARLOS BULOSAN

(1911–1956)

Author, Poet

Carlos Bulosan has been called the most important Filipino American writer. He spent a lifetime speaking out in a very eloquent manner against the inequities he found in America. He spoke on behalf of the tens of thousands of immigrants from the Philippines who came to the United States during the 1920s and 1930s with great hopes for a better life, only to find intolerance and personal loneliness.

Bulosan was born in Binalonan, Pangasinan, Philippines, on November 2, 1913. Although his family was middle class, through his writings in America he chose to identify with and champion the poor, working-class Filipino immigrant. He was a teenager when he came to America in 1930 to join Aurelio, his older brother, who had been a teacher in the Philippines and who was determined that Carlos finish his education. The two brothers began a long-lasting arrangement. Aurelio would work—usually in menial kitchen jobs—so that Carlos could concentrate on his studies and, later, his writings.

A brilliant student, Bulosan enrolled in high school in Los Angeles. However, after only two weeks he stopped attending class. He told his brother he was not learning anything and wondered why he should spend time in this school. The two brothers resolved the problem by having Bulosan spend most of each day reading books on different subjects in the local public library. He was a voracious reader who literally educated himself.

In 1932 Bulosan sent several of his poems to a poetry publication in California and was selected by the editors to be the poet laureate of the state. This honor gave him the incentive to become a writer. During the next few years, essays he submitted to different university publications around the country were published—for free.

Although he was breaking into the literary world, Bulosan mingled with ordinary farmworkers who liked and trusted him because they re-

Carlos Bulosan (*center*; courtesy of the Filipino
American National Historical Society Collection)

alized he was a brilliant Filipino who could express their plight in words. Believing that the main problem in this country was racial discrimination, he began his lifelong work to articulate in his writings the struggles of racial minorities in America.

Bulosan became ill with tuberculosis in 1937. Fearing his brother would die, Aruelio gave the doctor permission to remove several ribs and the diseased portion of Carlos's lung. While recuperating in the hospital and preparing for a second operation, Carlos was often visited by different Hollywood writers—all Caucasian—who had befriended him. Some brought him books, and all encouraged him to continue writing and submitting his poetry to publishers.

After the second operation Aurelio rented a house far from the city so his brother could recuperate among the trees. The brothers' Hollywood friends, including James Wong Howe, a famous Chinese cameraman, often invited them into their homes. According to Aurelio, this was the real beginning of Carlos's friendship with true intellectuals.

When World War II began Aurelio was drafted, but because of his illness Carlos remained a civilian. He was recruited by the Philippine Commonwealth government-in-exile to publish a journal.

During the early part of the war, President Franklin Delano Roosevelt asked the editors of the *Saturday Evening Post* to find four writers to develop essays on the Four Freedoms. On the recommendation of several writers around the country, Carlos Bulosan was selected to write *Freedom from Want*. The four essays were printed in the *Saturday Evening Post* along with illustrations by Norman Rockwell. *The Laughter of My Father*— a collection of modernized folktales—was published by Harcourt, Brace, and Company in 1944. It was the first of Bulosan's works to be translated into several European languages.

America Is in the Heart, a poignant record of the life of Filipino workers in the United States during the Great Depression, was published in 1946. Although the experiences Bulosan wrote about were not his own, he faithfully chronicled what actually happened to countless Filipino immigrants.

In 1950 Bulosan was summoned to Seattle by the Filipino-run Alaska Cannery Workers Union, Local 37, to write their yearbook. Despite his failing health he continued his work on behalf of Filipino workers. On September 13, 1956, Carlos Bulosan died at the age of forty-three. He left a legacy of inspiring works that addressed the struggle to fulfill the "prophecy of a new society of men: of a system that knows no sorrow or strife or suffering."

Selected Bibliography

Bayanihan Tribune, May 1981, p. 6.

Bulosan, Carlos. *America Is in the Heart: A Personal History*. New York: Harcourt Brace, 1946.

Philippine News, February 5, 1985, p. 13.

Seattle Post Intelligencer, September 16, 1956, obituary.

Seattle Post Intelligencer, October 3, 1974, p. A9.

Susan Sinott. *Extraordinary Asian Pacific Americans*. Chicago: University of Chicago Press, 1993, pp. 64–67.

Dorothy Cordova

BENJAMIN J. CAYETANO

(1939–)

Lieutenant Governor, Politician

Benjamin J. Cayetano, Hawaii's eighth lieutenant governor and the first of Filipino ancestry, considers his being in public office a miracle. He was born on November 14, 1939, in Honolulu, Hawaii, to Filipino immigrants. His father, who had only a third grade education and worked as a waiter, raised his young son alone after his marriage broke up. Cayetano was bright and did well in his early days in school. However, by the time he attended Farrington High School he ran with a tough crowd and his grades suffered because he skipped school. He began hanging out in pool halls, got involved in fights, and barely finished high school. The young Cayetano had little direction until he married his high school sweetheart, Lorraine Gucco, at age eighteen. He soon had others to think of, and his life changed when the couple had two children.

These were the last days of territorial Hawaii before statehood was achieved in 1959. He said Filipinos never assumed there were many opportunities because the Haoles (Caucasians) dominated everything. He worked in the junkyard and became an electrician's apprentice before getting a state job with the Transportation Department. When Cayetano was turned down for a promotion, he realized it was because of discrimination. He followed the advice of a Filipino American friend who had moved to Los Angeles, and after saving money for one year he moved his young family to the mainland. He swore that he would not return to Hawaii until he became successful.

He recalled experiencing cultural shock on the mainland when he saw Haoles working in menial jobs, whereas in Hawaii they managed things. After working a while for the California Highway Department, Cayetano decided to return to school and become a lawyer. His ambition to be a lawyer arose because he wanted to be in control and liked the idea of helping people.

At age twenty-four Cayetano enrolled at Harbor Junior College in Los Angeles. He later attended the University of California at Los Angeles and Loyola University Law School. For the next seven years Cayetano attended school in the morning, worked in the afternoon, and returned home to bring his wife to the Los Angeles airport where she worked as a waitress. After feeding the children, he would study. At midnight he would pick up his wife. This hectic schedule ended in 1971 when he received his law degree. It was now time to return to Hawaii.

Cayetano had lived through the civil rights movement, the assassinations of John and Robert Kennedy and Dr. Martin Luther King, the race riots in Watts, and the anti-war protests. Cayetano said he began to realize the importance of politics. He was content to work in the background because he never believed he could get elected. In 1972 the late governor John A. Burns appointed him to the Hawaii Housing Authority. The post gave him the opportunity to watch state legislators in action. He began to think he could do as well or even better than many of them.

In 1972 Cayetano ran for a seat in the state House of Representatives from his district of Pearl City, a Honolulu suburb dominated by Japanese American voters. He surpassed the Japanese American incumbent by 250 votes. He said he had no chance to win, but he found that when he spoke to the people he found they had many shared values. Cayetano served two two-year terms in the House and two four-year terms in the state Senate. He was called one of the four best legislators in the 1975 session and was described as "accessible and honest." In 1986 the *Honolulu Star-Bulletin* recognized him as a "standout" in its listings of Ten Most Effective Legislators. Cayetano introduced a number of significant bills, including one to create the Pacific International Center for High Technology Research at the University of Hawaii, and another to establish the first program in Hawaii to test Vietnam veterans suffering from the effects of Agent Orange. He also practiced law for fifteen years.

In 1986 Cayetano announced his candidacy for the position of lieutenant governor. Along with the state's first elected Hawaiian governor, John Waihee, Ben Cayetano was inaugurated into office on December 1, 1986. He has a reputation of being outspoken and intense and has aligned himself with the liberal dissidents of the dominant Democratic Party.

Governor John Waihee will not be able to seek another term because Hawaiian state laws limit governors to two four-year terms. Lieutenant Governor Ben Cayetano is the leading contender for the Democratic nomination for governor. If he wins his bid, he will become the first Filipino American governor in the United States.

Selected Bibliography

Balitaan, Fall/Winter 1995, pp. 1, 8.
Filipino Reporter, May 24–30, 1996, p. 3.
Hawaii Filipino News, December 1982, p. 6.

RICE magazine, December/January 1989, pp. 76–79.
Star Bulletin & Advertising, October 8, 1989, p. A1.

Dorothy Cordova

SUCHENG CHAN

(1941–   )

Educator, Author

Sucheng Chan, professor, was born on April 16, 1941, in Shanghai, China. Her father, Kock K. Chan, studied engineering in Germany. His family, originally from Guangdong province, had moved to Malaysia soon after British colonization. Her mother, Dora K. W. Chan, moved all around China with her family when she was young but later settled in Shanghai and was one of the first women to earn a sociology degree from the University of Shanghai.

At age four Chan contracted both polio and pneumonia. Though the doctors told her parents she would not live, she survived. During the next four years she taught herself to walk again, and when she was nine years old her family moved to Malaysia. There, her health improving, Chan attended the Anglo-Chinese Girls' School in Penang and the Methodist Girl's School in Singapore. In 1957 the family immigrated to the United States to pursue medical treatment for Chan and higher education for the children.

In New York, Chan attended William Cullen Bryant High School in Long Island City. After struggling with the racial bias and low expectations of her teachers, Chan graduated as salutatorian in a class of over 1,000. She was the first student in her high school ever to receive a perfect score of 800 in the Verbal Section of the Scholastic Achievement Test, a remarkable achievement that gives her great satisfaction.

Chan then attended Swarthmore College in Pennsylvania, originally as a premedical student and later as a student of economics and political science. While at Swarthmore, Chan became active in the emerging civil rights movement. She received a Bachelor of Arts degree in economics in 1963. In 1965 she received a Master of Arts degree in Asian studies from the University of Hawaii, and she spent the next two years doing anthropological fieldwork in the Philippines and traveling in Asia.

Next, Chan began doctoral studies in city and regional planning, but

Sucheng Chan

soon she changed to political science. She received her Ph.D. from the University of California at Berkeley in 1973. Chan's political activities included work in the anti–Vietnam War movement and the movement to develop ethnic studies as a legitimate field of university study.

Chan began her teaching career as assistant professor of ethnic studies at California State University in Sonoma, California, from 1971 to 1973. In 1974 she returned to the University of California at Berkeley as assistant professor (and later associate professor) of Asian American studies. During this time she struggled with the university and her colleagues to establish Asian American studies as a legitimate academic field of inquiry. In 1984, after ten years at Berkeley, Chan accepted the position of provost of Oakes College at the University of California at Santa Cruz. There, in addition to serving as professor of history and American studies, Chan revitalized Oakes College as the multicultural center of the university.

In 1988, seeking more time for her research and writing, Chan accepted a position as professor of history and Asian American studies at the University of California at Santa Barbara and chair of its Asian American studies program. Since 1992 Chan has been professor of Asian American studies and affiliate professor of history at Santa Barbara.

Chan has been recognized for her outstanding teaching throughout her career. She received the Distinguished Teaching Award from the University of California at Berkeley in 1978. In 1994 Chan received the Margaret T. Getman Service to Students Award from the University of California at Santa Barbara.

Chan has written and edited many books and articles during her career and is at work on more. *This Bittersweet Soil: The Chinese in California*

Agriculture, 1860–1910 (1986) won the Theodore Saloutos Memorial Book Award for best book in American agricultural history (1986), the American Historical Association Pacific Coast Branch Award for best first monograph (1987), and the Association for Asian American Studies Outstanding Book Award (1988). *Quiet Odyssey: A Pioneer Korean Woman in America* (1990), which Chan edited, won the Association for Asian American Studies Outstanding Book Award in 1991. *Asian Americans: An Interpretive History* (1991) received the Gustavus Myers Center for the Study of Civil Rights Outstanding Book Award in 1992.

Since 1988 Chan has been suffering from post-polio syndrome, a degenerative neuromuscular condition. This condition has led her to focus more on her writing and to decline most invitations to give public lectures, participate in conferences, and consult on projects. Chan is married to Mark Juergensmeyer, who is dean of the School of Hawaiian, Asian, and Pacific Studies in Honolulu, Hawaii.

Selected Bibliography

Chan, S. *Asian Americans: An Interpretive History*. Boston: Twayne Publishers, 1991.

————, ed. *Quiet Odyssey: A Pioneer Korean Woman in America*. Seattle: University of Washington Press, 1990.

————. *This Bittersweet Soil: The Chinese in California Agriculture, 1860–1910*. Berkeley: University of California Press, 1986.

Lomotey, K. "Sucheng Chan." In M. Seller, ed., *Women Educators in the United States, 1820–1993*. Westport, CT: Greenwood Press, 1994.

Franklin Ng

SUBRAHMANYAN CHANDRASEKHAR
(1910–1995)
Astrophysicist

Astrophysicist Chandrasekhar was giving a colloquium. Three walls of the lecture room had blackboards on them, all spotlessly clean when he began his lecture. During the course of his lecture he filled all the blackboards with equations, neatly written in his fine hand, the important ones boxed and numbered as though they had been written on paper for publication. As his lecture came to an end, Chandra leaned against a table, facing the audience. When the chairman invited questions, some-one in the audience said, "Professor Chandrasekhar, on blackboard . . . let's see . . . 8, line 11, I believe you've made an error in sign." Chandra was absolutely impassive, without comment, and did not even turn around to look at the equation in question. After a few moments of embarrassing silence, the chairman said, "Professor Chandrasekhar, do you have an answer to this question?" He responded, "It was not a question; it was a statement, and it is mistaken," without turning around.

Born on October 19, 1910, in Lahore (then a part of India, now in Pakistan), Subrahmanyan Chandrasekhar was the first son and the third of ten children of Chandrasekhara Subrahmanya Ayyar, an Indian government official and musicologist, and Sita Balakrishnan Chandrasekhar, a literary scholar and linguist. His maternal uncle was the Nobel Prize–winning physicist Dr. C. V. Raman.

Chandra, as he was always known, was educated at home by his parents and tutors until 1922, when he joined the Hindu High School in Madras, India, when his family moved there in 1918. Chandrasekhar studied arithmetic on his own, working ahead of the lessons and exercises that his father assigned. It did not take Chandrasekhar's father and family very long to realize that he was an exceptionally bright child.

After graduating from high school in 1925 he joined the famous Presidency College of the University of Madras, where he majored in theoretical physics and followed with interest the latest developments in astrophysics. As an undergraduate student in 1928 he published a paper analyzing the thermodynamics of the Compton Effect, with reference to the interior of the stars. This was an extraordinary time for Chandrasekhar, when he had the benefit of watching his uncle make a fundamental discovery in the molecular scattering of light. He had the opportunity to work in the lab where the discovery was made in Calcutta, India. He earned a B.S. with honors in 1930.

Chandrasekhar's father wanted him to take the Indian Civil Service (ICS) exams and enter government service. However, Chandrasekhar had no interest in government service. He wanted to do basic research in either mathematics or physics. In 1930 Chandrasekhar found out that he was going to be the recipient of a government scholarship to go to England for graduate study at Cambridge University. This scholarship was special; it was more or less created for him. It was not to be advertised in the usual way, by inviting applications from all qualified candidates. An exception was even going to be made regarding the strict rule that any scholarship for a specific year be included in the budget of the previous year.

In 1930 Chandrasekhar set sail for England. There were a dozen or so other students from various parts of India on board. The Indians were all seated together in the dining hall, ostensibly for the convenience of serving their special dietary needs, though in reality it was an arrangement to ensure that the whites on board would not be "contaminated" through proximity to the browns.

Just before his departure from Madras, Chandrasekhar had made notes, further developing the famous physicist Ralph Howard Fowler's theory of white dwarfs. According to this theory, once all stars exhaust the fuel sustaining their nuclear reactions they collapse under their own weight, radiating excess energy into space. A star such as the sun would shrink to an earth-size, white-hot ball, called a white dwarf, with a density of 10 tons per cubic centimeter, after which it would simply cool but remain otherwise unchanged forever.

During the voyage Chandrasekhar read a book he had received as a prize in a physics competition, Arthur Eddington's *The Internal Constitution of the Stars*. With the help of two other books that he read during the voyage, Compton's *X-Rays and Electron* and Sommerfield's *Atomic Structure and Spectral Lines*, he had all the theoretical tools he needed to incorporate the changes in Fowler's theory due to relativity.

At Trinity College, Cambridge, Chandrasekhar investigated the behavior of dying stars, under the physicist Fowler, and within a year at age twenty-one he published three papers—"The Highly Collapsed Configurations of a Stellar Mass," "The Maximum Mass of Ideal White Dwarfs," and "The Density of White Dwarf Stars." These papers contradicted Eddington's views and that of Fowler as well, since Fowler supported Eddington's views to a large extent. Their view was that the stars would collapse to form objects of planetary size, becoming whiter dwarfs that were hot and relatively bright brown dwarfs that were cool and relatively dim.

Chandrasekhar spent his last year of doctoral studies at Copenhagen with the famous scientist Niels Bohr at the Institute for Theoretical Physics. He completed his Ph.D. in 1933 and continued in Cambridge as a fellow of Trinity College for four years. Chandrasekhar continued his research on stars, and his calculations predicted what are now known as black holes. By 1934 these calculations led to the discovery of another stellar event—supernovas.

In 1936 Chandrasekhar returned to India to marry Lalitha Doraiswamy, whom he had met when they were students in the physics honors course at Presidency College in Madras. Lalitha, like Chandrasekhar, was an avowed vegetarian; other than that, she was prepared to be "modern" to live in the West.

Chandrasekhar and Lalitha spent October to December 1941 at the Institute for Advanced Studies in Princeton. In 1942 he became an associate professor at the University of Chicago, and in the following year, he was promoted to full professor and Hull Distinguished Service Professor of Astrophysics in 1947. Chandrasekhar was elected to the Royal

Society in 1944 and won the Gold Medal of the Royal Astronomical Society in 1953. No other astronomer had received both these honors by the age of forty-two, with the exception of Eddington.

In 1953 Chandrasekhar and Lalitha became American citizens, much to the displeasure of Chandrasekhar's father. Lalitha wrote a letter to her father-in-law explaining the important step they had taken and their reasons for doing so. Over the years they had developed strong ties and had become less and less the outsiders. "I have one advantage here in the United States," Chandrasekhar said in an interview to John Horgan, "I have enormous freedom. I can do what I want. Nobody bothers me."

Chandrasekhar has authored many books that have been praised for their breadth and clarity. He always sought to present his findings in as elegant, even literary a form as possible. He read novels by Henry James and Virginia Woolf to study the fluidity of their writing. Chandrasekhar's books are now physics classics.

As the sole editor of the *Astrophysical Journal* from 1951 to 1972, he sought to encourage good writing in the premier publication of his field. According to Chandrasekhar, too few scientists write well or even carefully. He used to tell authors that their papers were scientifically correct but that they should have colleagues in the English department read them as well.

Between 1974 and 1983 he explored black holes, coming back full circle to the work that had launched his career. The "Chandrasekhar Limit" has become one of the foundations of modern astrophysics, leading to the recognition of neutron stars and black holes. The quasi-stellar object, or quasar, may be a black hole in the center of a galaxy. Black holes are detected by radiation emitted by matter accelerated to very high energy as it is drawn into the black hole.

Chandrasekhar was awarded the 1983 Nobel Prize for Physics "for his theoretical studies of the physical processes of importance to the structure and evolution of the stars." He shared the prize with William A. Fowler. Chandrasekhar also won numerous other awards, including the Bruce Gold Medal of the Astronomical Society of the Pacific (1952), the Rumford Medal of the American Academy of the Arts and Sciences (1957), the Royal Medal of the Royal Society of London (1962), the National Medal of Science of the National Science Foundation (1966), the Dannie Heineman Prize of the American Physical Society (1974), the Padma Vibhushan from the Government of India and the Coplye Medal from the Royal Society (1984).

Chandrasekhar was both a theorist and a teacher. He was an avid reader of literary classics and appreciated classical music and art. He once said that he felt the same thrill from a Michaelangelo sculpture as from a beautiful mathematical relationship.

A striking photograph that hung in his office showed a man climbing a ladder that leans against a vast, abstract structure. Like the ascending man, Kameshwar Wali says, Chandrasekhar was constantly aware of how much more there is to know and of his own inadequacies. In an interview with John Horgan, Chandrasekhar—who was working on Newton's *Principia* at the time—said, "No, that's the end. I don't expect to do science after I finish work on the *Principia*. Obviously I can go on doing work of a quality that is below my standards, but why do that? So the time must come when I say, Stop."

Chandrasekhar's last book, *Newton's Principle for the Common Reader*, is a look in depth at Newton's formation of the science of gravitation and mechanics. His penetrating analysis of Newton's overly concise geometrical way of looking at things fully illustrates the genius of Newton. This parting gift to the scientific community from a great physicist was published two months before Chandrasekhar's death.

Subrahmanyan Chandrasekhar contributed immensely to the world of science. An article published in a German newspaper claimed that if all the formulas, equations, and text that have appeared in Chandrasekhar's publications were put end to end, they would cover the distance between the earth and moon. In his Nobel Prize acceptance speech Chandrasekhar quoted some lines of poetry written by Rabindranath Tagore: "Where the mind is without fear and the head held high; where knowledge is free; into the heaven of freedom let me awake."

Select Bibliography

Current Biography, 1986, pp. 85–88.

Horgan, John. "Confronting the Final Limit." *Scientific American*, March 1994.

Nobel Prize Winners: An H. W. Wilson Biographical Dictionary, 1987.

Parker, Eugene N. "Genius Unlimited." *India Today*, September 15, 1995.

The Who's Who of Nobel Prize Winners, 2nd ed., 1991.

Wali, Kameshwar C. *Chandra*. Chicago: University of Chicago Press, 1991.

Visi R. Tilak

MICHAEL CHANG
(1972–   )
Sports Figure (Tennis Player)

Many Asian Americans become scientists, educators, and businessmen. Very few aspire to become world-class athletes, but tennis player Michael Chang may be changing that image. Michael Chang was born on February 22, 1972, in Hoboken, New Jersey. His father and mother, Joe and Betty Chang, are research chemists who left mainland China for Taiwan. After immigrating to the United States in the 1960s, they met in New York and eventually married. They have two sons, Michael and his older brother, Carl.

At an early age Michael Chang began to play tennis. His parents introduced the game to their sons when they were very young. When the family moved to San Diego, the children were able to practice tennis without regard to the seasons. In the new setting Chang began to win junior tournaments, including the Junior Hard Court singles title of the United States Tennis Association (1984). In 1987 he won the United States Tennis Association junior championship.

In 1988 Chang decided to turn professional at age sixteen. In 1989 he entered the French Open in Paris and surprised the tennis world. In the fourth round he achieved an amazing victory over top-seeded Ivan Lendl, a three-time French Open winner. After losing two sets to Lendl he won the next three sets in a grueling match that stunned the spectators. The final result was an unbelievable come-from-behind victory at 4–6, 4–6, 6–3, 6–3, 6–3. Chang also defeated top-ranked Stefan Edberg in a 1–6, 6–3, 6–4, 4–6, 2–6 final match. At age seventeen Chang had become the youngest person to win the men's singles title at the French Open.

In the following year he broke his hip and was unable to play on the professional tennis circuit for a while. But in the years since he has maintained high rankings among world-champion tennis players. In 1997 he was ranked second in the ATP (Association of Tennis Professionals) world tennis rankings. He continues to win major tournaments, and his earnings have made him a millionaire many times over.

In Asia, Michael Chang is popular with young people for whom tennis is a flourishing sport. To the delight of fans in Asia and the Pacific region, Chang is willing to play in new ATP tournaments in Jakarta, Kuala Lumpur, Osaka, Hong Kong, and Beijing. His youthful look, calm demeanor, modesty, and world-champion status enhance his appeal. In a sport populated by temperamental personalities, Chang's civility, politeness, and religious piety are a refreshing contrast. Many see him as an important ambassador for tennis, helping to promote the sport in the Asian region. He founded a Tennis Stars of the Future Program, funded through the Michael T. P. Chang Foundation, that since 1992 has provided free equipment and tennis instruction to children in Hong Kong. He has also funded a tennis scholarship at the University of California, which his brother, Carl Chang, attended.

Chang sees himself as an Asian American and a Chinese American. He is interested in Asia and its culture, and he enjoys eating Chinese food. In fact, his mother prepares noodles for him to eat on his tours with the professional tennis circuit. For Asian Americans, Michael Chang is an inspirational model that they can follow in sports. Despite his small build he is a formidable player because of his quickness, mental attitude, and deceptive play. He also knows how to mix his play and has solid baseline play. Along with champion figure skaters such as **Kristi Yamaguchi** and **Michelle Kwan**, and other Olympic athletes profiled in this work, Michael Chang is showing that Asian Americans can indeed excel in sports.

Selected Bibliography

"Asia's Tennis Ambassador." *Asiaweek*, November 2, 1994, pp. 56–57.
Bonk, Thomas. "Boy Wonder." *Los Angeles Times Magazine*, August 27, 1989, pp. 8–16.
Callahan, Tom. "Youth Will Be Served." *Time*, June 26, 1989, p. 90.
Cohen, Paul. "Strokes of Genius." *World Tennis*, April 1989, pp. 62ff.
Kirkpatrick, Curry. "Giant Killers." *Sports Illustrated*, June 19, 1989, pp. 34–43.
"Purring over Michael the Cat." *Asiaweek*, November 23, 1990, p. 77.
"Tennis: Michael Chang." *U.S.A. Weekend*, January 27–29, 1995, p. 10.
Walker, Jeremy. "A Slice of the Action." *Asia Magazine*, April 9–11, 1993, pp. 14–17.

Franklin Ng

ELAINE L. CHAO

(1953–   )

Business Leader

Elaine L. Chao, business, government, and nonprofit executive, was born in Taiwan. Her parents, James and Ruth Chao, had each emigrated from mainland China to Taiwan in 1949. Chao's father became a sea captain, and when Chao was five years old he immigrated to America. Three years later Chao and her mother and sister joined him. The family settled first in Queens, New York, and later moved to Long Island and then to Westchester County. James Chao established a successful shipping business, and the family's six daughters attended Ivy League and Seven Sisters colleges. After beginning to learn English at age eight, Chao graduated from high school near the top of her class and went on to attend Mount Holyoke College. She received a degree in economics in 1975. She received a Master of Business Administration from Harvard Business School in 1979.

Elaine L. Chao

From 1979 to 1983 Chao specialized in transportation finance at Citibank in New York City; from 1983 to 1994 she served as a White House fellow. In 1984 Chao became vice president of syndications at Bank-America Capital Markets Group in San Francisco, California.

Chao became deputy administrator of the United States Maritime Administration in 1986, and in 1988 she became chairman of the Federal Maritime Commission. Chao was appointed deputy secretary of the Department of Transportation in 1989 and served in that capacity until she was appointed director of the Peace Corps in 1991. At the Peace Corps, Chao was instrumental in establishing programs in the Baltic nations and in the newly independent states of the former Soviet Union. Chao rose be the highest-ranking Asian Pacific American ever appointed in the executive branch in U.S. history.

In 1992 Chao accepted the challenge of becoming president and chief executive of United Way of America. Under her leadership the United Way began an aggressive program to rebuild public trust and confidence in the organization. This included implementing new governance structures and new financial and management controls, undertaking comprehensive reviews of programs and services, visiting scores of key local United Way communities, and meeting with local volunteers and professionals. In 1996, with confidence and sound fiscal practices instituted in the organization, Chao announced her resignation. Not long thereafter she accepted a position as a distinguished fellow with the Heritage Foundation, a think tank in Washington, D.C. In 1998 she was named chairman of its Asian Studies Center Advisory Council.

Chao has received several honorary doctorate degrees and won the Outstanding Young Achiever Award from the National Council of Women in 1986. She also received the Harvard University Graduate School of Business Alumni Achievement Award in 1993.

Chao is married to Senator Mitch McConnell of Kentucky.

Selected Bibliography

Baum, Geraldine. "An Insider Moves Up." *Los Angeles Times*, January 19, 1993.
Canna, Elizabeth. "Free Market Peace Corps." *American Shipper*, March 1992.
MacLachlan, Suzanne L. "United Way Hit by Weak Economy, Old Scandal and Competition." *Christian Science Monitor*, May 18, 1992.
Melillo, Wendy. "United Way Names New President." *Washington Post*, August 27, 1992.

Franklin Ng

TIN-YUKE CHAR

(1905–1990)

Historian, Business Leader

Tin-Yuke Char, a historical researcher and businessman, was born in Honolulu, Hawaii, on July 4, 1905. His father, Char See Yick, had emigrated from the Chungshan district of South China to Hawaii in the 1890s after working for a period in the tin mines of Singapore. In Honolulu he worked as a handyman for Peacock & Co., a wholesale liquor dealer. He married Chong Fo, who migrated at age twenty-one to Hawaii in 1893 to be his bride.

Tin-Yuke Char was the fourth son in a family of five sons and four daughters. He went to McKinley High School and graduated in its first class of 1924. Other members of that class included businessmen **Chinn**

Ho and **Hung Wai Ching**, U.S. senator **Hiram Fong**, Yale professor Chi-toshi Yanaga, and Hawaii Supreme Court justice Masaji Marumoto.

After briefly attending the University of Hawaii, Char enrolled at Yenching University in Beijing, China. After getting his bachelor's degree in 1928, he became an instructor of history at the Nankai Middle School in Tientsin from 1928 to 1930. He then returned to the University of Hawaii, receiving an M.A. in 1932. From 1930 to 1936 Char was also an instructor in Chinese language and history at the university, after taking some time off in 1934–1935 for further graduate study at Columbia University. From 1936 to 1938 he served as registrar and director of admissions at Lingnan University in Canton, China.

Because of the expanding Sino-Japanese conflict, Tin-Yuke Char journeyed home to Honolulu and worked as a special agent for the Home Insurance Company of Hawaii from 1939 to 1952. During this time he was the first person in the territory to receive national professional designation as a certified property and casualty underwriter. In 1952 he became co-founder and president of the Continental Insurance Agency of Hawaii. The successful company expanded quickly, developing a large staff and acquiring its own headquarters building. Retiring in 1969, Char served for a year until 1970 as a volunteer student counselor at Chung Chi College at the Chinese University of Hong Kong.

Like many of his generation, Tin-Yuke Char was interested in Chinese history and culture. While at Yenching University, he had been encouraged by Professor William Hung to study the Hakka Chinese and their migrations. At the University of Hawaii, his M.A. thesis of 1932 focused on the legal restrictions against the Chinese in the English-speaking countries of the Pacific. Char shared his knowledge about China by writing articles for the *Honolulu Star-Bulletin* and the *Honolulu Advertiser*. Even while working as a businessman, he continued to research and lecture on his Hakka and overseas Chinese heritage.

His retirement from the insurance business gave him more time to research and to write. Among his publications after 1969 was a book about the Hakka Chinese that he co-authored with Chan-Hoon Kwock. He also wrote a book on Chinese proverbs in 1970 and edited a volume entitled *The Sandalwood Mountains: Readings and Stories of the Early Chinese in Hawaii* (1975).

His wife, Wai Jane Chun, was an important collaborator in his research and writing. They married on January 30, 1934, and had four children—David, Judith (Mrs. John Flagg), Peter, and Janice (Mrs. Arthur A. Chung). Together they published articles about the early Chinese in the *Hawaiian Journal of History* and edited several volumes about Chinese historic sites and pioneer families on the islands of Oahu, Hawaii, and Kauai.

In 1970, while in Hong Kong, Char arranged for **Him Mark Lai** of the

Chinese Historical Society of America in San Francisco to talk about Chinese American history in Honolulu. The meeting led to the formation of the Hawaii Chinese History Center in 1971. Tin-Yuke Char and Wai Jane Char steadfastly supported the activities of the center. Working with Irma Tam Soong, they assembled others interested in the history of the Chinese of Hawaii, such as Diane Mark, Douglas Chong, Ted Gong, C. Fred Blake, and Puanani Kini. The Chars helped initiate a program of field trips, workshops on genealogy and oral history, lectures, publications, archival collection, and fundraising. These efforts helped spark much local interest in the experiences and contributions of the Chinese in Hawaii. In 1991, Kapiolani Community College in Hawaii dedicated its Tin-Yuke Char and Wai Jane Char Asian Pacific Reading Room in recognition of their work on behalf of the community and Chinese American history.

An active community leader, Tin-Yuke Char held many posts and offices. He was vice-president of the Chinese Chamber of Commerce in 1954 and president of the Hawaii chapter of the Chartered Property and Casualty Underwriters (CPCU) in 1961. He served as an officer or director of the Hawaii Congress of the PTA, the Palolo Chinese Home, the Nuuanu YMCA, and the Community Church of Honolulu. He also was a trustee of the Hawaii Foundation for History and the Humanities and was a member of the Chinese Historical Society of America and the Hawaiian Historical Society. He passed away on June 17, 1990. His wife died on June 12, 1991.

Selected Bibliography

Char, Tin-Yuke. *The Bamboo Path: Life and Writings of a Chinese in Hawaii* (1977).

———. "The Chinese in Hawaii." *Chinese Sociology and Political Science Review*, vol. 14 (1930):13–40.

———. "Chinese Merchants, Adventurers, and Sugar Masters in Hawaii: 1802–1852." *Hawaiian Journal of History*, vol. 8 (1974): 3–9.

———. *Chinese Proverbs* (1970).

———, ed. *The Sandalwood Mountains: Readings and Stories of the Early Chinese in Hawaii* (1975).

Char, Tin-Yuke, and C. H. Kwock. *The Hakka Chinese: Their Origin and Folk Songs* (1969).

Char, Tin-Yuke, and Wai Jane Char. "The First Chinese Contract Laborers in Hawaii." *Hawaiian Journal of History*, vol. 9 (1975): 128–134.

———. "S. P. Aheong, Hawaii's First Chinese Christian Evangelist." *Hawaiian Journal of History*, vol. 1 (1977): 69–76.

———, comps. and eds. *Chinese Historic Sites and Pioneer Families in Rural Oahu* 1987.

———. *Chinese Historic Sites and Pioneer Families of Kauai* (1979).

———. *Chinese Historic Sites and Pioneer Families of the Island of Hawaii* (1983).

Franklin Ng

BOONA CHEEMA

(1945–)

Community Leader

For over twenty years Boona Cheema has dedicated her life to her community. As executive director of Building Opportunities for Self-Sufficiency, the largest provider of comprehensive services to the homeless and people of low income in Alameda County, California, Cheema has fought homelessness, hunger, and poverty; created housing, job support services, and opportunities; and built collaborations between service providers, businesses, churches, schools, and voluntary organizations.

Born in Peshawar, now Pakistan (then India), on August 6, 1945, the day Hiroshima was bombed, into a family of Sikhs, she was a victim of the partisan riots that occurred in India during the struggle to end British colonial rule. Her father, Dr. Amrik Singh Cheema, was a civil servant, agricultural commissioner in India, agricultural expert, Green Revolutionist (the Green Revolution refers to a method for planting higher yielding rice seedlings), and holder of the Padma Sri Medal, one of the highest honors in the country. Her mother, Raminder Kaur Gill, was a village organizer and farmer. Boona Cheema was one of three children. One brother, Jatinder Cheema, works for USAID/Africa; the other, Jagdeep Cheema, is a farm consultant and organizer of young farmers in India.

Boona Cheema and her family were separated from their father when they moved to India as refugees when she was two years old. India and Pakistan had just gained independence from Britain, but the partition of two nations led to massive movement of people across the border. Subsequently the conflict that arose over partition took countless lives on both sides of the India-Pakistan border. Cheema recounts that the violence that took place during partition remains vivid in her memories: "I'll try to do anything to change the way people see, the way people think, the way people act, so that violence is not the result" (Camp 1989). The experience made her sensitive at a young age to the suffering and special needs of the disenfranchised and the displaced. Her train ride from Pakistan to India during the summer of 1947 left a strong impact on Boona Cheema's life. The family was reunited in Faridkot, Punjab, where Cheema lived with thirty-five relatives in a three-bedroom house.

Cheema graduated from Punjab University with a B.A. in sociology and an M.A. in journalism, following which she worked for a year as a salesperson for Brooke Bond Tea Company, New Delhi, and then as a reporter for the *Times of India*, New Delhi. In 1968 she had the opportunity to visit the United States as a member of India's International Farm Youth Exchange program.

In the United States she met an International Voluntary Services worker who persuaded her to join a very worthwhile project that was being conducted in Laos. Instead, the service organization directed her to Vietnam. "I got a telegram saying 'Report to Saigon,'" she recalls. "I was in Vietnam one year and three months too long" (Camp 1989). She worked in Saigon as a teacher and volunteer with the Committee for Responsibility, an organization that air-lifted injured children for care to San Francisco General Hospital. She came away from Vietnam with a great deal of respect for Vietnamese people and their courage.

The stint in Vietnam resulted in her marriage to an American from Kentucky in 1970. The couple was married in India and traveled for six months before arriving in Berkeley, California. Cheema was pregnant, and the couple had neither money, nor family, nor friends to help them. They turned to the Hillel Street Project for assistance. The project began operating in Berkeley in 1971, the year Cheema's son Azad was born. The organization's object was to provide advocacy and support to the de-institutionalized mentally disabled and the homeless. Once Cheema's own life was back in order, she became a volunteer for this small, caring, community-based organization.

The Hillel Street Project went on to become Building Opportunities for Self-Sufficiency (BOSS), and Cheema rose from the rank of worker to that of executive director in nine years. Since 1979 Cheema has been executive director of Berkeley Oakland Support Services, which serves about 5,500 clients per year.

Cheema has been the driving force behind BOSS and its growth to eleven sites countywide with a $3.6 million budget. Aid ranges from overnight shelter, shower, laundry facilities, and meals to money management, legal and crisis counseling, and use of phones and facilities such as a bank and post office. It also provides help with transitional housing and employment placement. Her mission is to make things better—individual lives, programs, services, communication between cultures and organizations, planning structures, inclusive grassroots organizing.

Through Cheema's leadership and hands-on program development work, the Transitions Project, a federally funded effort to provide housing subsidies and support services (the first program of its kind), has become very successful with over fifty individuals in permanent housing. The most significant part of the program is the strong involvement of program participants in the planning and problem-solving process concerning community, personal, and political issues. Program participants take part at all levels of the Transitions Project. At each site participants may become staff members, serve on advisory committees, or sit on the board of directors. Additionally, Cheema continues to advocate for the involvement of program participants in fund development activities, mandating their inclusion in site-based and agency-wide fundraising committees and events.

Apart from working for BOSS, Cheema is a volunteer with many other community organizations. She is committed to working with larger-scale policy and advocacy organizations to try to impact the root economic and social problems that exacerbate the crises in neighborhoods.

Cheema has also worked with Berkeley youth by volunteering and helping establish the Children's Learning Center, a project to provide family literacy services and after-school tutoring to homeless children; SAY-YAY (Save American Youth—Youth Advocates for Youth); and Encampment for Citizenship, a nonprofit organization that sponsors activities for teenagers from diverse backgrounds to help them learn about and address challenging social or political issues.

Cheema has worked on issues of education, poverty, and social justice all her adult life. She has been recognized for her activities in numerous ways. In 1987 the city of Berkeley declared a Boona Cheema Day and the county of Alameda, a Boona Cheema Week. She has won several awards for her dedication and hard work toward the cause of the homeless, such as the Bruce Springsteen Award for Outstanding Community Service; the National Women's Political Caucus Award for Service to the Homeless; Woman of the Year, City of Berkeley Commission on the Status of Women; and the Anti-Defamation League's Woman on the Move Award.

Selected Bibliography

Camp, Roya. "Making a Difference." *India Currents*, January 1989, pp. 11–13, 26.
Cook, Geoffrey. "Personal Crusade." *India Today*, June 15, 1994.

Visi R. Tilak

ANNA CHEN CHENNAULT

(1925–)

Aviation Executive, Author, Journalist

Anna Chen Chennault, an aviation executive, author, and lecturer, was born in Peking, China, on June 23, 1925. She received a Bachelor of Arts degree in Journalism from Lingnam University in Hong Kong in 1944, and an honorary Doctor of Literature degree from Chungang in Seoul, Korea, in 1967.

Chennault began her career as a journalist, serving as a war correspondent for the Central News Agency from 1944 to 1948. She was a feature writer for the *Hsin Ming Daily News* in Shanghai, China, from 1944 to 1949. She served as a special Washington correspondent for the Central News Agency from 1965 to the present and as a U.S. correspondent for the *Hsin Shen Daily News* from 1958 to the present. In addition, she was a broadcaster for the Voice of America from 1963 to 1966.

In 1946 Chennault began her work with Civil Air Transportation in Taipei, Taiwan, serving as an editor and public relations officer until 1957. From 1968 to 1976 she was vice-president of international affairs for the Flying Tiger Line, Incorporated, of Washington, D.C. She has served as president of TAC International from 1976 to the present.

Chennault is the author of *Chennault and the Flying Tigers: Way of a Fighter* (1963); the best-seller *A Thousand Springs* (1963); and *The Education of Anna* (1980). She is also the author of a number of works in Chinese, including *Song of Yesterday* (1961); *M.E.E.* (1963); *My Two Worlds* (1965); *The Other Half* (1966); *Letters from the U.S.A.* (1967); and *Journey among Friends and Strangers* (Chinese edition, 1978).

Active in public affairs, Chennault has been a member of the President's Advisory Committee for the John F. Kennedy Center for the Performing Arts since 1970. She also served as a member of the United States National Committee for UNESCO from 1970 to the present. Chennault was president of Chinese Refugee Relief from 1962 to 1970 and has served as president of the General Claire Chennault Foundation from 1960 to the present.

Chennault has long been active in Republican Party activities and has served as a committeewoman of the Washington, D.C., Republican Party since 1960. She was the founder and chairperson of the National Republican Asian Assembly. In recent years she has advocated greater political participation by Chinese Americans and Asian Americans in both major parties and has given frequent addresses on the subject. She has also talked about the development of relations between the United States and China.

Chennault has been honored with many awards. In 1966 she received the Freedom Award of the Order of Lafayette and the Freedom Award from the Free China Association. She received the Award of Honor from the Chinese-American Alliance in 1971. She has been a member of the National Aeronautics Association Board of Directors, the National League of America, PEN Women, Writers Association, Free China Writers Association, 14th Air Force Association, USAF Wives Club, Flying Tiger Association, American Newspaper Women's Club of Washington, and Theta Sigma Phi. She is the founder and chairperson of the Military Families Association.

Chennault was married in 1947 to Claire Lee Chennault, who died in 1958. She has two children, Claire Anna and Cynthia Louise.

Selected Bibliography

Byrd, M. *Chennault: Giving Wings to the Tiger*. Tuscaloosa: University of Alabama Press, 1987.
Chennault, A. *Chennault and the Flying Tigers*. New York: P. S. Eriksson, 1963.
————. *The Education of Anna*. New York: Times Books, 1980.
————. *A Thousand Springs: The Biography of a Marriage*. New York: P. S. Eriksson, 1962.
————. *Way of a Fighter: The Memoirs of Claire Lee Chennault*. New York: G. P. Putnam's Sons, 1949.

Franklin Ng

NG POON CHEW

(1866–1931)

Journalist, Activist, Newspaper Publisher

Ng Poon Chew was a well-known Chinese American journalist and activist. Some authorities consider him to be the father of Chinese journalism on the West Coast.

Ng Poon Chew was born in the Toisan area of Guangdong province to Ng Yip and Wong (Shee) Hok. Although his surname was Ng, in the United States many people assumed that his last name was Chew. In

China he underwent training to be a Taoist priest. But when an uncle returned from California in 1879 with money and stories about his experiences, the young boy decided to go to the United States. He arrived at San Francisco in 1881, going shortly thereafter to San Jose where he worked and attended local schools. Having converted to Christianity when he was at the Presbyterian mission, he later graduated from the San Francisco Theological Seminary in 1892.

Ng Poon Chew was ordained as a pastor in the same year and appointed an assistant pastor to the Chinese Presbyterian Church in San Francisco's Chinatown. He married Tso Chun Fah of San Francisco in 1892. From 1894 to 1899 the Presbyterian Board of Foreign Missions assigned him to serve as a pastor in the Chinese Presbyterian Church in Los Angeles. A decision by the Board in 1898 had important consequences for Ng's career as a journalist. They decided to withdraw support from much of their work with the Chinese in the United States to fund missions abroad. Ng protested the decision, saying that Chinese in America often contributed to the success of the Christian outreach in China. This meant, however, that Ng had to find other means of financial support, and in 1899 he started the *Hua Mei Sun Po*, a Chinese weekly newspaper in Los Angeles.

Learning of his activities, Chinese merchants in San Francisco's Chinatown asked Ng Poon Chew to move his paper north. On February 16, 1900, he started publishing the *Chung Sai Yat Po* in San Francisco, with himself as its managing editor and English-language translator. Teng I-yun served as its first editor, and John Fryer, a professor of Chinese literature at the University of California at Berkeley, worked on its editorial staff. The paper was published for fifty years as a Chinese daily newspaper, missing publication only during the famous San Francisco earthquake of 1906.

As a Christian, Ng Poon Chew used his paper to espouse reform and progressive ideas. He claimed that *Chung Sai Yat Po* should be a beneficial influence on the Chinese community, contributing to its enlightenment, morals, and welfare. As a result the paper attacked what it perceived to be antiquated customs such as the use of opium, footbinding, polygamy, the wearing of the queue (a traditional hair style for men), and idolatry. It promoted education and adaptation to American society. Ng himself adopted Western dress. He also was involved with the *Radiator (Kuang Pao)*, a multi-denominational Chinese language monthly journal started in 1905 for Chinese Christians. He served on its board of managers, helping it to promote information and fellowship among Chinese Christians. The *Radiator* did not last long, however, and Ng devoted most of his attention to the *Chung Sai Yat Po*, arguably the Chinese paper with the largest circulation in the United States for much of its existence.

Ng Poon Chew wanted *Chung Sai Yat Po* to be nonpartisan in Chinese politics, but that was not always possible. He was willing to support reformer K'ang Yu-wei's Pao-huang hui (Protect-the-Emperor Society) in 1900. Later his disaffection with the Pao-huang hui led him to side with the revolutionary figure Sun Yat-sen. In fact, when Sun was detained by U.S. immigration officials in San Francisco in 1904, Ng and others hired lawyers and helped obtain his release. As Ng became closer to Sun, he agreed to print 11,000 copies of Tsou Jung's *Ko-min Chun* (Revolutionary Army) for distribution in the United States. This was a revolutionary tract that aroused enthusiasm for Sun Yat-sen and increased anti-Manchu sentiment among Chinese in the Americas (Manchu people overthrew the Ming dynasty).

Ng Poon Chew's changing attitudes toward Sun Yat-sen may have been influenced by the anti-Chinese sentiment in the United States. In 1901, Chinese Christians in San Francisco sent him on a national tour to educate the public about the Chinese and the need for changes in immigration laws. But gradually he was convinced that China's military weakness had led to injustices against Chinese in this country in violation of treaty agreements. Reaction to the abuses and indignities by U.S. immigration authorities against Chinese led to the anti-American boycott in 1905 by Chinese in China, Southeast Asia, Hawaii, and the Americas. *Chung Sai Yat Po* endorsed the boycott and carried news about its progress.

As a noted Chinese leader, Ng Poon Chew was asked in 1905 to speak to American audiences at forums and schools. He explained to them that the widespread boycott was not aimed at the American people but at the U.S. exclusion policy against the Chinese. Thus, he spoke at the National Civic Federation Conference on Immigration held in New York City. The Chinese Six Companies sent him on a tour, during which he met with President Theodore Roosevelt. Though not much came of it, Ng felt that one result was the categorization of Chinese ministers and newspaper editors as "educators" instead of "laborers," thereby exempting them from exclusion. He wrote with Patrick J. Healy *A Statement for Non-Exclusion* (1905) about the immigration issue. Three years later he delved again into the topic with another publication, *The Treatment of the Exempt Classes of Chinese in the United States* (1908).

As Ng Poon Chew's reputation grew, he was in constant demand as a speaker. He lectured on the Chautauqua and Lyceum circuits, educating Americans about China and the Chinese. He tried to foster good relations between the United States and China and was recognized for his expertise and skill in addressing a wide variety of topics. His sense of humor, keen wit, and fluency in English made him exceptionally popular with audiences. He participated in activities with the Commonwealth Club of San Francisco, the American Academy of Political and Social Science, and the American Economic Association. He was a Mason and the first Chinese in California to become a Shriner. In 1913 the University of Pittsburgh conferred on him the honorary degree of Litt. D.

He also served as an adviser to the Chinese consulate general in San Francisco from 1906 to 1913 and served as a vice-consul for China from 1913 until his death on March 13, 1931. His survivors included his wife and five children—Mansie, Effie, Rose, Edward, and Caroline. Mansie managed the *Chung Sai Yat Po*, which continued to be influential in the Chinese community during the 1930s and 1940s.

Selected Bibliography

Chinn, Thomas W. *Bridging the Pacific: San Francisco Chinatown and Its People*. San Francisco: Chinese Historical Society of America, 1989.
"Dr. N. P. Chew Dead; Chinese Editor." *New York Times*, March 15, 1931.
Hoexter, Corinne K. *From Canton to California: The Epic of Chinese Immigration*. New York: Four Winds Press, 1976.
Hummel, Arthur W. "Ng Poon Chew." In Dumas Malone, ed., *Dictionary of American Biography*. New York: Charles Scribner's Sons, 1962, pp. 479–480.
Ma, L. Eve Armentrout. *Revolutionaries, Monarchists, and Chinatowns: Chinese Politics in the Americas and the 1911 Revolution*. Honolulu: University of Hawaii Press, 1990.
McKee, Delber L. *Chinese Exclusion versus the Open Door Policy, 1900–1906: Clashes over China Policy in the Roosevelt Era*. Detroit: Wayne State University Press, 1977.
Ng, Poon Chew. *The Treatment of the Exempt Classes of Chinese in the United States*. San Francisco: Author, 1908.
Ng, Poon Chew, and Patrick J. Healy. *A Statement for Non-Exclusion*. San Francisco: n.p., 1905.
Tsai, Shih-shan Henry. *The Chinese Experience in America*. Bloomington and Indianapolis: Indiana University Press, 1986.
Woo, Wesley. "Protestant Work among the Chinese in the San Francisco Bay Area, 1850–1920." Ph.D. dissertation, Graduate Theological Union, Berkeley, California, September 10, 1983.

Franklin Ng

FRANK (CHEW JR.) CHIN
(1940–   )
Author, Playwright

Frank (Chew Jr.) Chin, an author and playwright, was born on February 25, 1940, in Berkeley, California. For his undergraduate studies he attended the University of California at Berkeley, the State University of

Iowa, and the University of California at Santa Barbara, from which he received his Bachelor of Arts degree in 1965.

Upon graduation Chin worked on several jobs with various railroads before turning to the King Broadcasting Company in Seattle, Washington. He was employed there as a writer and editor from 1966 to 1969. He then moved to California and lectured in Asian American Studies at the University of California at Davis and at San Francisco State College in 1969 and 1970. He also taught creative writing at the University of California at Berkeley in 1972. Starting in 1976 he was for a while the artistic director of the Asian American Theater Workshop in San Francisco, which he had founded in 1972.

Living in the San Francisco Bay Area, Chin joined with other Asian American writers to form a Combined Asian American Resources Project (CARP) to collect materials such as literature and oral histories about Asian Americans. Among the members of the group were the poet **Lawson Fusao Inada** and the writers Shawn Wong and Jeffrey Paul Chan. During the period 1974–1976 they collected oral interviews that were then rendered in transcript form and deposited in the Bancroft Library at the University of California at Berkeley.

Much of Frank Chin's reputation as a writer stems from his plays. Chin's play *The Chickencoop Chinaman* was first staged in 1972 at the American Place Theatre in New York City. *The Year of the Dragon*, staged in 1974 at the same theater, was televised on PBS in 1975 on its *Theatre in America* series. Both plays provided powerful insights into Chinatown life and the tensions between generations, and both received critical acclaim. For many Asian Americans and members of the larger public, the two plays unveiled the drama of conflict in everyday life in a Chinatown enclave that they might have visited but never really known.

In 1974 Chin co-edited *Aiiieeeee! An Anthology of Asian-American Writers* (1974). His co-editors were Lawson Inada, Shawn Wong, and Jeffrey Paul Chan. With its iconoclastic title and angry introduction, the anthology proved to be an immediate sensation. From the start, it sought to define an "Asian-American sensibility" in authentic Asian American writing. It demarcated the differences between Asian and Asian American writers and their contrasting voices. It also provided a brief but informed history of Asian and Asian American writing in the United States and the failure of many people to discern the differences between the two. Many recognize Chin as the pioneer in focusing attention on an Asian American literature distinct from Asian literature.

In his talks and writing, Chin has tried to separate the "fake" from the "authentic" in Chinese American literature. He sees the former as the product of assimilation, Christian conversion, and the denigration of the folk culture of the Chinese. He tries to encourage the recovery of the culture and voices of the common folk and Asian American history.

Toward this end, he has investigated *muyu*, or "wooden fish songs," and the cult of Guan Gong in Guangdong and the Chinese American community. He also researched and wrote about the internment of members of the Japanese American community during World War II and frequently criticized what he felt was an accommodating and complicitous stance on the part of the Japanese American Citizens League. Often writing in a flamboyant and angry vein, he won a large following in the 1970s.

Chin's literary battles are legendary. In 1972 and 1973, journalist Frank Ching and he engaged in an exchange over the place of foreign-born Chinese in Chinese American culture. Ching claimed that the foreign-born had a role to play, whereas Chin argued that they were too different from the American-born Chinese. Printed in the pages of *Bridge* magazine, one issue drew attention to the debate by headlining it as "Who's Afraid of Frank Chin, or Is It Ching?"

Chin has also engaged in criticism of the work by authors such as **Maxine Hong Kingston, Amy Tan**, and **David Henry Hwang**. He feels that their work is assimilationist, presenting what non-Asians want to see, and that it perpetuates stereotypes about Chinese Americans. In rebuttal, there are frequent charges that he is threatened by their greater fame and visibility. Moreover, it is argued that he has tried to champion Asian American manhood at the expense of Asian American women.

In recent years Chin has revealed an interest in presenting Chinese mythology through children's literature and Chinese-style comics. In addition, he wrote *The Chinaman Pacific and Frisco R.R. Co.: Stories* (1988). He and his co-editors followed his earlier *Aiiieeeee!* anthology with a sequel named *The Big Aiiieeeee! An Anthology of Chinese American and Japanese American Literature* (1991). The same year he also wrote *Donald Duk: A Novel* (1991). Three years later he came forth with *Gunga Din Highway* (1994).

Chin received the Joseph Henry Jackson Award in 1965 for his unpublished novel *A Chinese Lady Dies*. Chin received a James T. Phelan Award for short fiction in 1966, and an East-West Players Playwriting Award in 1971 for *The Chickencoop Chinaman*. In 1974 Chin received a Rockefeller Playwrights Grant and a National Endowment for the Arts Creative Writing Grant. In 1992 he received a Fiction Fellowship from the Lannan Foundation.

Selected Bibliography

Chin, F. *The Chickencoop Chinaman and The Year of the Dragon: Two Plays*. Seattle: University of Washington Press, 1981.
———. *The Chinaman Pacific and Frisco R.R. Co.: Stories*. Minneapolis: Coffee House Press, 1988.

———. *Donald Duk: A Novel*. Minneapolis: Coffee House Press, 1991.

———. *Gunga Din Highway*, 1994.

Chin, F.; Ching, Frank. "Who's Afraid of Frank Chin, or Is It Frank Ching?" *Bridge*, vol. 2, no. 2 (December 1972): 29–34.

Chin, F., et al., eds. *Aiiieeeee! An Anthology of Asian-American Writers*. Washington, DC: Howard University Press, 1974. (Includes F. Chin, Act 1 of *The Chickencoop Chinaman*)

Chin, F., et al., eds. *The Big Aiiieeeee! An Anthology of Chinese American and Japanese American Literature*. New York: Meridian, 1991.

Franklin Ng

HUNG WAI CHING

(1905–)

Community Leader, Business Leader

Hung Wai Ching, real estate broker, was born on August 1, 1905, in Hawaii. His parents, Yei and Lin Fong Ching, came to Hawaii in 1898 from the Chung Shan district of Guangdong province, China. Ching attended McKinley High School in Honolulu, graduating in 1924, and received a Bachelor of Arts degree in engineering from the University of Hawaii in 1928. He attended Yale University from 1931 to 1932.

After completing his studies, Ching served as secretary of the Nuuanu YMCA in Honolulu from 1928 to 1939, and as executive secretary of the University YMCA from 1939 to 1941. During World War II he advocated for Japanese Americans in Hawaii; he was later made an honorary member of the 442nd Veteran Club. After the war Ching became a real estate broker and land developer, as well as continuing to be a leader in the community. He has served on the Board of Directors of Liberty Bank, Aloha Airlines, Pacific Insurance Company, Pacific Management Company, and the Honolulu Stadium, and as a partner in Pacific Land Hui and Oahu Homes.

Ching has served the Honolulu community in a number of ways; he was a regent of the University of Hawaii (1953–1960) and a trustee for the University of Hawaii Foundation. He served as director of the Honolulu Community Chest, president of the Advisory Board of St. Francis Hospital, and president of the Rotary Club of West Honolulu. Chin was one of the founders of the Community Church of Honolulu in 1934. He has been an active leader in the Honolulu Chamber of Commerce, the Council of Social Agencies, the Honolulu Academy of Arts, Leahi Hospital, and Hawaii 4H Foundation.

Chin married Elsie Tong in 1934. They have three children.

Franklin Ng

THOMAS W. CHINN
(1909–   )
Business Leader, Journalist, Historian

Thomas W. Chinn, typographic company executive, journalist, and historian, was born in Marshfield, Oregon, on July 28, 1909. He moved with his family to San Francisco in 1919. Chinn attended public schools in Oregon and California, but after his father's death in 1926 he was unable to continue his formal education. He later attended Healds College and the University of California at San Francisco, taking classes in business administration, advertising, and journalism. In his youth Chinn was an all-around athlete and won trophies in track, handball, basketball, and football. In 1936 he was the Chinese national tennis singles champion, and he was also a doubles champion for many years. (Many overseas Chinese participated in their homeland events, be they music or sports.)

From 1935 to 1937 Chinn founded and edited the *Chinese Digest*, the first English-language weekly newspaper for Chinese Americans. From 1937 to 1942 he was the proprietor of Chinn Linotype Company in San Francisco. Chinn founded, published, and edited the *Chinese News* during this time, from 1940 to 1942. Chinn's publishing and typography profession was interrupted in 1942 when he served as a civilian executive for the U.S. Army Quartermaster General's Office, Quartermaster Market Center Program, stationed in San Francisco. Chinn returned to his profession in 1949 as owner of California Typesetting Company, and in 1971 he became president of Gollan Typography, Inc., a position he held until his retirement in 1980.

Chinn has been active in a number of historical associations. In 1963 he was the primary founder of the Chinese Historical Society of America, he served as its president in 1963, 1964, 1965, 1966, and 1975. From 1963 to 1980 he edited the Society's research papers and its monthly *Bulletin*. In 1966 Chinn planned and established the Society's museum, which has

Thomas W. Chinn

been open ever since. In 1971 Chinn worked with the San Francisco Public Library to take, on long-term loan, the Society's research material so that it could be available for public use. The collection was transferred in 1983 to the Asian American Studies Library at the University of California at Berkeley.

Chinn's articles on history have appeared in the California Historical Society's *California History*, the Book Club of California's *Vignettes in California History*, and the San Francisco Corral of Westerners publications. Chinn edited *A History of the Chinese in California—A Syllabus* in 1969. His first book, *Bridging the Pacific—San Francisco Chinatown and Its People*, was published in 1989. In 1993 a book of his reminiscences, *A Historian's Reflections of Chinese-American Life in San Francisco*, was published by the University of California at Berkeley.

In 1969 Chinn spearheaded the drive to place bronze memorial plaques to commemorate the centennial of the first transcontinental railroad in the United States—at both Sacramento, California, and Promontory Point, Utah. He was chairman of the First National Conference on Chinese American Studies, held at the University of San Francisco in 1975, and edited and published the *Conference Proceedings* in the following year. In 1980 Chinn received the Scroll of Honor from the Chinese Historical Society of America and the Chinese Culture Foundations, cosponsors of the 1980 Second National Conference on Chinese American

Studies. In 1975 Chinn received a presidential appointment to the American Revolution Bicentennial Administration National Advisory Committee on Racial, Ethnic, and Native American Participation. He also served as a member of the History Committee of the San Francisco Twin Bicentennial.

In 1970 Chinn received an Award of Merit from the California Historical Society, and in 1976 and again in 1982 he received an Award of Merit from the Conference of California Historical Societies. The American Association for State and Local History awarded him its Award of Merit in 1976 as well. In 1987 Chinn received the City of San Francisco's Laura Bride Powers Award for "enhancing the historic renown of San Francisco."

Chinn married Daisy Lorraine Wong Chinn in 1930. She is one of the seven founders of the Square and Circle Club, the largest and oldest active Chinese women's service organization in the United States; a past president of the Chinese Historical Society of America; and a former Chinese women's tennis doubles champion (1929). They have one son, three grandchildren, and seven great-grandchildren.

Selected Bibliography

Chinn, T. *Bridging the Pacific: San Francisco Chinatown and Its People*. San Francisco: Chinese Historical Society of America, 1989.

————. *Genealogical Methods and Sources for the Chinese Immigrants to the U.S.* Presented at the World Conference on Records. Salt Lake City, Utah, August 6, 1969.

————. *A Historian's Reflections of Chinese-American Life in San Francisco, 1919–1991*. Berkeley: Regional Oral History Office, Bancroft Library, University of California, 1993.

————, ed. *A History of the Chinese in California—A Syllabus*. San Francisco: Chinese Historical Society of America, 1969.

                                                                                        Franklin Ng

MARGARET CHO

(1968–)

Comedienne, Actress

Comedienne Margaret Cho was the first Asian American to star in her own television show. *All American Girl*, the first prime-time network series with a primarily Asian American cast, was aired on ABC in 1994.

Through her comedy act she has taken the opportunity to break the color barrier and shed light on a still-foreign culture, that of Korean Americans.

Margaret Cho was born on December 5, 1968, to Seung-Hoon Cho and his wife, Young-Hie, who had immigrated to the United States in 1964 to continue their college education. They later owned a bookstore in the Haight-Ashbury district of San Francisco's Bay Area, where she and her younger brother, Hahn Earl, were raised.

After graduating from the High School of Performing Arts in San Francisco she attended San Francisco State University to study theater. Never finishing college, she turned to stand-up comedy after becoming frustrated with the limited acting roles available to Asian women. She developed her comedy act while working in her parents' bookstore. Cho's routines address many aspects of her own life as a second-generation Asian American woman growing up with Korean culture in Western society. She often pushes the envelope on controversial topics such as the gender war and ethnicity.

In 1991 Cho moved to Los Angeles and won the West Coast division championship of the U.S. College Comedy competition that led to a billing with Jerry Seinfeld. Afterwards she performed in comedy clubs and appeared on "Evening at the Improv," the "Arsenio Hall Show," "Star Search," MTV's "Half-Hour Comedy Hour," Lifetime's "Six Comics in Search of a Generation," and Fox's "Comic Strip Live." Cho starred in the film *The Doomed Generation* with Dustin Nguyen. She also portrayed a Brooklyn nurse in *Angie*, which starred Geena Davis.

In 1994 Cho was the first Asian American of Korean descent to produce and star in her own television sitcom, called *All-American Girl*. In 1993 Cho caught the attention of Disney and ABC, which designed the show around her stand-up persona. As the first prime-time, high-profile show to star and feature an Asian American cast, the sitcom (in which Cho portrayed a college student torn between the allure of Western society and tradition-bound parents) faced high expectations and intense scrutiny by the Asian American community. After just one season, the sitcom was canceled in 1995 due to poor ratings and much criticism of its unrealistic depiction of a Korean immigrant family.

Cho opened the door to exploration of Asian Americans in Western society and of their subsequent portrayal in a media forum. Her ambitions are to continue working to break cultural barriers and be part of the rise of Asian Americans in this country. She is currently performing her stand-up act in comedy clubs across the United States.

Selected Bibliography

Kang, K. Connie. " 'Girl' Undergoes Major Changes Amid Criticism." *Los Angeles Times*, Saturday, March 11, 1995, F1.

Lee, Elisa. "Margaret Cho Brings APA Twenty-Somethings to Television." *Asian Week*, November 19, 1993, p. 19.

McNamara, Mary. "The New Feminist Comics." *Ms*, January/February 1992, p. 23.

Polkinghorne, Rex. "Comic Cho Proves Laughter Can Sever Racial Stereotypes." *Daily Bruin* (Los Angeles) February 22, 1994, p. 21.

Chae Reed

MARTHA C. CH'OE

(1954–   )

Business Leader, Government Administrator, Community Leader

Through a variety of community services aimed at improving the quality of life for those who live in the Puget Sound area, Martha Ch'oe has shown her ability to work with people of diverse backgrounds and lead them to reach their goals. She has been involved in many social, cultural, and educational programs to help Asian American youth develop strong identity with their cultural and historical roots. Through her work with many people and organizations in the greater Seattle area, she is a role model for young people.

Martha Ch'oe was born on November 16, 1954, in New York City to Korean immigrant parents, Edward Kesoon and Yang Ja Ch'oe. In 1966 the family moved to Seattle, where she attended Roosevelt High School. Upon graduation she went to the University of Washington and graduated with a Bachelor of Arts degree in 1976. She continued her education at Seattle University, from which she graduated with an M.B.A. degree in 1986. While studying for her business degree, she was busy developing her career as a banker. The Bank of California hired her as a trainee in 1982 for a cash management marketing position. She was soon promoted to various positions with increasing responsibilities: corporate banking officer, 1984; vice-president for private banking, 1986; vice-president of credit administration, 1989; and vice-president for

Martha C. Ch'oe

commercial lending, 1990. In 1991 she was elected to the Seattle City
Council with 70 percent of the vote.

In 1996 she was reelected with over 81 percent of the vote. She is
currently chair of the Finance and Budget Committee, the Seattle Employees' Retirement System and the Police Pension Board. She has previously chaired the Transportation and Economic Development
Committee and the Regional Transit Authority (RTA) Task Force on
Women and Minority Business Enterprise. Other committees she has
served in the past include the Parks and Recreation Committee, Business
and Labor Committee, and Metro Transit Committee.

Today, as chair of the Finance and Budget Committee, Martha Ch'oe
is responsible for oversight of the city's $1.8 billion Capital Improvement
Program and the $450 million General Fund budget. Concerning her abil-
ity to work on successful legislation, she initiated a transportation plan
for Seattle and led the city's efforts on the Regional Transit Authority
(RTA) ballot measures for 1995 and 1996. The latter was approved by
the voters. She is credited with legislative accomplishments that include
drafting and sponsoring new election policies for the City of Seattle, and
spearheading the City's apprenticeship program to train disadvantaged
populations for long-term, livable-wage jobs.

Since 1984 Martha Ch'oe has been involved in many community organizations for a variety of purposes and goals: Asian Youth At-Risk, organized to help Asian youth struggling with their identity; King County Advisory Committee on Open Space and Trail Bond Issues, to improve the quality of life in the region; Western Washington University's Board of Trustees, to oversee education; and the Seattle Housing Authority. She has been active in many Asian American organizations, including the Asian Pacific American Municipal Officials, the Asian Pacific American Women's Leadership Institute, and the Wing Luke Museum.

For her active involvement in community services and leadership she was given the Japanese American Citizens League Leadership Advisory Board Community Leadership Award as well as the Korean American Professionals Society Pioneer Award. She was named one of *Newsweek* magazine's thirty "movers and shakers" in Seattle (1996) and one of the Seattle *Chinese Post*'s 1990 Women of the Year.

Selected Bibliography

Who's Who among Asian Americans, 1994–95 ed. Detroit: Gale Research, 1994, p. 107.

Hyung-chan Kim

BONG YOUN CHOY
(1914–   )
Author, Activist, Educator

Choy is author of four major books that have contributed to understanding of issues and problems related to Korea, Korean American relations, and Korean Americans. His earlier work included *Korea: A History* (1971), which provides a comprehensive overview of Korean history, people, and culture. In the book Choy suggests that Korean unification could be achieved only if *minjung*, or the masses of people, rise to oppose the unification policies of both Koreas and march toward the Demilitarized Zone to tear down the wall that separates North and South Korea. In his later work, *Koreans in America* (1979), Choy presents a collection of biographical and autobiographical stories of Korean immigrants since their coming to America in 1903.

Bong Youn Choy

Bong Youn Choy (Bong-yun Ch'oe) was born on May 25, 1914, in a small farming village called Jadong, P'yeongan pukto now located in North Korea. Although his family was poor, his father sent him to a village school where he learned to read and write Chinese characters. Despite his father's plan to make him a farmer, Choy persuaded his father to send him to an elementary school with the promise that he would pay his own way. Before he completed elementary school, he took an entrance exam for a middle school and was accepted by Sung'in Commercial School in P'yeongyang, now the capital of North Korea.

During this period he converted to Christianity and began attending church every Sunday. He was active in church work, teaching Sunday school and working for the Young Men's Christian Association. While attending school, Choy was given opportunities to become acquainted with Cho Man-sik, Han Kyeong-jik, Kim Chae-sun, and **Ch'ang Ho Ahn**, who were all Korean national leaders just released from a Japanese prison. His exposure to such patriotic leaders of the Korean national movement inspired him to follow in their footsteps and work for the cause of Korean national independence.

Upon graduating from the Sung'in Commercial School, Choy decided to go to Japan to study at Aoyama Gakuin in Tokyo, where he concentrated on reading about Japanese history, nationalism, and militarism in addition to his regular studies. While studying in Tokyo, he felt he was not free from Japanese police surveillance on all Korean students, and he decided to come to the United States. He received financial assistance from Cho Man-sik and Han Kyoeng-jik. Arriving in the United States in 1938, he enrolled first in Pasadena College, then transferred to Los Angeles City College, and finally attended Los Angeles Junior College, from which he graduated. After graduation Choy enrolled in Chapman College, where he began to study political science and later graduated in 1942.

The Japanese surprise attack on Pearl Harbor in 1941 helped open a new chapter in Choy's life. He was asked by the U.S. government to work as an interpreter of Japanese. With acceptance, he was appointed as an instructor in Oriental languages at the University of California at Berkeley. While teaching at the university, he also worked with the Office of War Information in San Francisco on Saturdays and Sundays as a broadcaster in Korean. He was also asked to teach Japanese to the Special Army Training Program classes. In addition, he was frequently called on by the federal court to translate Japanese documents in connection with Japanese property. Indeed, the six years he spent immediately after Pearl Harbor were the busiest in his entire life.

After the end of World War II, Choy returned to Korea in June 1946 and worked for the reconstruction of his native land as a political education specialist in the American military government in South Korea. He focused on teaching democracy to his people by arranging programs that invited people to learn about democratic ideals as well as writing articles about democracy for newspapers, academic journals, and monthly magazines. He was later given the responsibility of creating a Department of Political Science at Seoul National University. After successful establishment of the department, he was promoted to deputy director of the Department of Public Information.

When **Syngman Rhee** and his associates successfully established a government in South Korea, Choy was disappointed in the political development that kept his native land divided between North and South. He decided to return to the United States, arriving in San Francisco on August 17, 1948. When asked by the Seattle Pacific College to teach political science and Far Eastern history, he accepted the position and moved to Seattle, Washington, where he also ran a hotel business. During this period he encountered trouble with the Immigration and Naturalization Service, primarily because he was against the dictatorship of Syngman Rhee in South Korea. Rhee wanted to have Choy expelled from the United States so that he could punish him. He returned to Berkeley, where he concentrated on studying and writing his book, *Korea: A History*.

Choy has contributed to the Korean American community in the Bay Area by teaching Korean language classes, writing Korean language textbooks when there were none available for language instruction, and running summer classes for children who otherwise would have not known the language of their parents. For his outstanding contributions Choy was awarded two medals of honor by the Republic of Korea. The first one, given in 1988, was for his contributions to the social development of Korea; the other, given in 1995, was for his contributions to Korean national independence.

Selected Bibliography

Choy, Bong-youn. *Koreans in America*. Chicago: Nelson-Hall, 1979, pp. 324–334.
Contemporary Authors, vol. 69. Edited by Jane A. Bowden. Detroit: Gale Research, 1978, p. 128.

Hyung-chan Kim

HERBERT C. CHOY
(1916–   )
Judge

Herbert C. Choy, the former ninth circuit judge on the U.S. Court of Appeals, was the first person of Asian American descent to rise to that position when President Richard Nixon appointed him in 1971. Choy was named Senior Judge of the Court of Appeals in 1984, and during his tenure he has taken special interest in Native American treaty disputes over land.

The second of five children, Herbert Choy was born on the Island of Kauai, Hawaii, in 1916 and was raised by his parents, who were Korean immigrants. The Choy family later relocated to Honolulu when his father, Poo Wok Choy, opened a business supplying military uniforms.

Choy attended grammar school at the Royal School, which specialized in training children of royalty to become future leaders of Hawaii. After graduating from high school in 1934, Choy went to the University Hawaii. It was there that he found a passion for law. His other interests included the college debate team, singing, and the theater guild—all of which helped enhance the communication skills he needed to become a lawyer. After earning a law degree from Harvard, Choy entered the military service and was sent to the School of Military Government in Charlottesville, Virginia. While stationed there he met his future wife, Helen Schilar, and married her in 1974.

After he was discharged from the service in 1946, he began practicing law at the firm of Fong and Miho. After six months of grueling work, he was made a partner. In 1957 Choy left law to pursue a stint as attorney general of the Territory of Hawaii, but after only one year he returned to practice law.

Choy has no children of his own, but rather has "adopted" dozens of law clerks who still keep in touch.

Selected Bibliography

Chase, Harold, Samuel Krislov, et al. *Biographical Dictionary of the Federal Judiciary.* Detroit: Gale Research, 1976, pp. 325–26.
Judicial Conference of the United States. *Judges of the U.S.* Washington, D.C.: U.S. Government Printing Office, 1978, p. 69.
Kobayashi, Ken. "Herbert Choy, Hawaii's Most Retiring Judge, Retires." *Sunday Star-Bulletin & Advertiser*, December 16, 1984.
Reincke, Mary, ed. *The American Bench.* Minneapolis, MN: Reginald Bishop Foster and Associates, 1977, p. 3.

Jennifer Kang

LOUIS CHU

(1915–1970)

Author, Broadcaster

Louis Chu was a pioneering Chinese American writer and a community-minded leader. His novel, *Eat a Bowl of Tea* (1961), provided rich insights into the bachelor society of New York's Chinatown of the 1940s. In the 1970s, as Asian Americans expressed interest in their literary traditions, Louis Chu was rediscovered and proclaimed a vital resource for the understanding of a Chinese America not often described in other published novels.

Louis Chu was born on October 1, 1915, in the Toishan district of China. This was one of the four districts of the Sze Yup area, in Guangdong province, that had sent many Cantonese immigrants to the United

States in the nineteenth century. His name was Louie Hing Chu, with *Louie* as his surname. Later he converted his last name to *Louis* and give himself the name Louis Chu.

At the age of seven he left his mother and his village to join his father and grandfather in the United States. His father owned a successful Chinese restaurant called Sui Wu in Newark's Chinatown. Louis Chu went to the Blairstown Academy and graduated from Upsala College in East Orange, New Jersey, in 1937 with a major in English. From New Jersey, it was easy to participate in many of the activities in the larger New York Chinatown. Chu traveled there often and worked with the Edserbro organization—a boys' group in New York's Chinatown that performed community service and held social functions with other youth. In 1937 Chu attended New York University for graduate study in sociology. His thesis for his M.A. degree, which he received in 1940, focused on the topic "The Chinese Restaurants in New York City."

After being away from China for seventeen years, Louis Chu returned to Toishan to visit his mother in 1940. While in China, he married Gim Kang. Because of restrictions in the immigration laws, he could not bring back his wife to the United States. During World War II, Chu served in the U.S. Army Signal Corps from 1943 to 1945 in the China-Burma-India theater. At the end of the war he returned to his village to bring his wife and first-born child, a daughter, back to the United States under the provisions of the War Brides Act of 1945. The couple eventually had four children, one son and three daughters—son Pong Fey and daughters May Jean, May Jane, and May Joan.

The family settled in New York, and Louis Chu opened a record store known as the Acme Company in 1950. He also pursued additional graduate work at the New School for Social Research from 1950 to 1952 and got an M.A. in social work. In 1961 he founded and directed the first senior citizens' program in Chinatown, the Golden Age Club at the Hamilton-Madison Settlement House.

Being bilingual in Chinese and English and raised in a Chinatown, Louis Chu understood intimately the experiences and struggles of the first-generation Chinese immigrants. In 1951 he and his wife became broadcasters, hosting an hour-long "Chinese Festival" radio program on station WHOM-FM in New York. Because of the popularity of the program, its length was extended to ninety minutes. The format of the successful program had Chu speaking in English and his wife conversing in Chinese. During its ten-year run until 1961, the couple supplied the Chinese community with news, interviews, commercials, and Chinese recorded music, especially traditional Cantonese opera. Active in the Chinatown community, Louis Chu also was a member of the Soo Yuen Benevolent Association and served as its executive secretary.

Louis Chu had wanted to write a book about the life of New York's

Chinatown, and his friend, Lyle Stuart, encouraged him in the project. In 1961 Lyle Stuart published Chu's *Eat a Bowl of Tea*, which captured the inner life of Chinatown's bachelor society of the 1940s. Accurately capturing the language and concerns of a predominantly male environment, Chu made reference to an era that was ultimately eclipsed by the immigration acts of 1952 and 1965. The book did not enjoy the attention that was won by **Jade Snow Wong**'s *Fifth Chinese Daughter* (1950) and Chin Yang Lee's *Flower Drum Song* (1957). He was writing another novel, *Double Trouble*, and had an unfinished autobiography when he died of a heart attack on February 27, 1970.

After his death, a younger generation of Asian American writers wanting to learn more about their predecessors discovered anew the sensitivity and realism of Louis Chu's work. The ground-breaking *Aiiieeeee! An Anthology of Asian-American Writers* (1974) edited by **Frank Chin**, Jeffery Paul Chan, **Lawson Fusao Inada**, and Shawn Wong, revived interest in *Eat a Bowl of Tea*. The novel was reissued in 1979 by the University of Washington Press as part of its series on Asian American studies. It was performed on stage by groups such as the Pan Asian Repertory Theater in New York. In 1989 **Wayne Wang** directed a film production of *Eat a Bowl of Tea* that was released for distribution to movie theaters across the country.

Selected Bibliography

Chin, Frank, Jeffery Chan, Lawson Fusao Inada, and Shawn Wong, eds. *Aiiieeeee! An Anthology of Asian American Writers*, 1974.

Chua, Cheng Lok. "Review of *Eat a Bowl of Tea* by Louis Chu." *Explorations in Ethnic Studies*, vol. 3 (January 1980): 67–69.

Kim, Elaine H. *Asian American Literature: An Introduction to the Writings and Their Social Context*, 1982.

New York Chinatown History Project. "Tribute to a Pioneer Chinese American Writer: Louis Chu (1915–1970)." *East Wind*, vol. 5, no. 1 (Spring/Summer 1986): 39–41.

Wong, Shawn. "Introduction to the 1979 Edition." In Louis Chu, *Eat a Bowl of Tea* 1979 (1961).

Franklin Ng

CONNIE CHUNG

(1946–)

Television Journalist

Connie Chung, broadcast journalist, was born in Washington, D.C., on August 20, 1946. Her full name is Constance Yu Hwa Chung. Her father, William Ling Chung, was a diplomat in Chiang Kai-shek's government in China, and during the 1944 Japanese bombing of China he moved his family to Washington, D.C. Five of William Ling and Margaret (Ma) Chung's first nine children had died while in China, and Connie Chung was the only child born in the United States. She grew up in the Maryland suburbs of Washington, D.C., and had a childhood dream of becoming a ballerina. She attended the University of Maryland from 1965 to 1969, switching from biology to journalism after spending a summer internship in the office of Congressman Seymour Halpern of New York.

Even before her graduation, Chung began a job as copyperson at WTTG-TV, a Washington television station, and soon moved up to newswriter, assignment editor, and reporter. In 1973 Chung was hired by CBS News' Washington Bureau as a news correspondent. She covered George McGovern's presidential campaign, Richard Nixon's trips to the Middle East and the Soviet Union in 1972, the Watergate hearings in 1973 and 1974, and Nelson Rockefeller's vice-presidency. From 1976 to 1983 Chung was news anchor at KNXT (now KCBS) in Los Angeles. While there, she won an award for best television reporting from the Los Angeles Press Club in 1977, local Emmy awards in 1978 and 1980, and a George Foster Peabody Award from the Maryland Center for Public Broadcasting for her documentary *Terra, Our World* in 1980.

In 1983 Chung accepted a position anchoring *NBC News at Sunrise* in New York City. During the next six years she contributed to the network's news lineup as political correspondent for *NBC Nightly News*, anchor of the Saturday evening news, chief correspondent of *American Almanac*, co-anchor of *1986*, and developer of a series of prime-time documentaries. These included *Life in the Fat Lane* (1987), *Scared Sexless* (1987), *Stressed to Kill* (1988), and *Guns, Guns, Guns* (1988). During a moving series of five news broadcasts from China in 1987, Chung interviewed her own relatives and visited her grandparents' graves. In 1989 Chung moved back to CBS, anchoring *West 57th* (later *Saturday Night with Connie Chung*) and *CBS Sunday Night News* (later *CBS Evening News with Connie Chung*), and substituting for Dan Rather on *CBS Evening*

News. In 1993 Chung became co-anchor with Rather on *CBS Evening News,* the second woman and the first Asian American ever to co-anchor one of the major network news evening broadcasts. She also hosted her own weekly newsmagazine, *Eye to Eye with Connie Chung.* In 1997 Chung joined *ABC News* as an anchor and correspondent. She also joined its *20/20* program with Barbara Walters.

In addition to those she received in 1978 and 1980, Chung received another Emmy award in 1987. She received the Metro Area Mass Media Award from the American Association of University Women in 1971. Chung was recognized for enhancing public awareness of the cruelties of seal harvesting by the United States Humane Society in 1969. She received an award for Outstanding Excellence in News Reporting and Public Service from the Chinese-American Citizens Alliance in 1973. California State University in Los Angeles honored Chung with its Women in Communications Award in 1979. The Anti-Defamation League of B'nai B'rith presented her with its First Amendment Award in 1981.

Chung is married to Maury Povich, host of Fox Television's *Current Affair.*

Selected Bibliography

Anderson, Kurt. "Does Connie Chung Matter?" *Time,* May 31, 1993.
Romano, Lois. "Stories That Changed Their Lives: Connie Chung Witness to Truth." *Redbook,* October 1991.
Yang, Jeff, and Betty Wong. "Power Brokers." *A. Magazine,* December 15, 1993, pp. 25–34.

Franklin Ng

EUGENE Y. CHUNG

(1969–   )

Football Player

Eugene Y. Chung, a current National Football League star, plays right guard for the New England Patriots. Chung was the third Asian American to play professional football in the United States.

Born on June 14, 1969, in Prince George's County, Maryland, Eugene moved to northern Virginia and was brought up by his father, Choon Chung. Choon had come to the United States in 1956 from Korea and attended City College of New York, then enrolled at Columbia University, where he studied political science. Afterwards he went to Yale and received a degree in law. Choon guided Eugene through school by telling his son not to believe in stereotypes and that he could do whatever he wanted because America is a free country.

Eugene took his father's advice to heart and continued his pursuit of athletics. His career started at Oakton High School in Virginia, where he earned three letters in football and track; he was elected All-District and All-Region with a stellar performance recording eighty-six tackles, eight sacks, and six fumble recoveries. He also competed in judo, which enhanced his speed and agility in football, and won the Virginia State Judo Championship in 1990.

Attending Virginia Tech University, Eugene started as a freshman and was voted best offensive lineman in 1990. At the end of his college career he was selected first team All-American and All–Big East.

Eugene Chung was drafted in the third round by the New England Patriots in 1992 and had a dismal start, battling with contract disputes as well as his father's death in the same year. However, after conquering all these obstacles in 1993, Eugene played like a first-round choice with all the promise in the world. He still plays today.

Selected Bibliography

Conroy, Steve. "Chung Strong on Rebound." *Boston Herald*, September 25, 1993.
Freeman, Mike. "For Chung, NFL Dream Has Special Glow." *Washington Post*, April 15, 1992, pp. D1, D3.
May, Peter. "Chung Is Starting to Feel Comfortable." *Boston Globe*, October 22, 1992.
Price, Terry. "Chung Now Ready to Give Pats His All." *Attleboro Sun Chronicle*, August 18, 1993, pp. 29, 32.

Jennifer Kang

ANANDA COOMARASWAMY

(1877–1947)

Author, Art Critic, Historian

Ananda Coomaraswamy is hailed as "one of the most important writers and thinkers of this century" because of his ground-breaking work in such differing fields as science, art theory, and religion and metaphysics

(Singam 1979). A man of diverse abilities, he began his work as a young scientist—a botanist, geologist, petrologist, and mineralogist—who was appointed director of the Mineralogical Survey of Ceylon at the age of twenty-six. He went on to a second career as an art historian and critic. He wrote prolifically in several South Asian and European languages on subjects including the geology of Ceylon, Kandyan art and architecture, and the ancient cultures and spiritual traditions of South Asia.

Coomaraswamy was born on August 22, 1877, in Colombo, Ceylon (now Sri Lanka). An only child, his father was Sir Mutu Coomaraswamy and his mother was Lady Elizabeth Clay Beeby Coomaraswamy of Kent, England. His middle name, Kentish, was derived from the name of his mother's birthplace. His father became the first South Asian barrister in England in 1863 and the first Asian to be knighted by the British monarchy in 1874. The couple made their home in Colombo, but due to ill health Lady Coomaraswamy returned to England in 1878 with her one-year-old son. His father was to follow them, but he fell ill and died in Ceylon on the day he was scheduled to leave for England. Ananda remained in England with his mother.

Little is known about his days as a student. It is presumed he was tutored at home as a child. At the age of twelve he attended Wycliffe College at Stonehouse in Gloucestershire, where he stayed for six years. Later he attended the University of London, from which he received the degree of Bachelor of Science with first-class honors in geology and botany in 1900. He returned to Ceylon after graduation. He contributed his first paper on "Ceylon Rocks and Graphite" to the *Quarterly Journal of the Geological Society* in 1900 when he was twenty-three years old. Two years later in 1902, he was appointed director of the Mineralogical Survey of Ceylon, where he published the two-volume *Mineralogical Survey of Ceylon*.

He traveled all over Ceylon during his tenure as director. During these travels he became interested in the fine traditional arts and crafts of Ceylon. He found that the local arts were languishing as a result of the invasion and impact of European industrialism, as well as the lack of official patronage and support. At this time he also discovered a new mineral of high specific gravity that he named "thoranite."

He returned to London in 1906 to receive the degree of Doctor of Science in geology from the University of London on the basis of his work in Ceylon. During the next few years Coomaraswamy continued his scholarly work and helped found a publishing house in Gloucestershire. He advised and directed the printing of some of his own as well as others' books. Besides becoming an art critic and historian, Coomaraswamy developed his skills as an adept photographer, draftsman, and fine artist. Some of his earlier books in limited editions were illustrated with his own precise drawings.

Between 1906 and 1917 Coomaraswamy continued writing. This time his focus was on subjects ranging from arts and crafts to nationalism and political conditions in India and Ceylon. He discovered Rajput painting in 1915. The two volumes he published on Rajput painting in 1916 proved to be a landmark in the appreciation of Kangra painting in the West. He contributed numerous articles to journals in India, Ceylon, and England. In addition he compiled the songs of Kashmir and Punjab, and in cooperation with Sister Nivedita he completed the *Myths of the Hindus and Buddhists* in 1914.

In 1917 Coomaraswamy left for the United States to join the staff of the Boston Museum of Fine Arts. The museum had acquired an exceptional collection of Indian art and invited Coomaraswamy to arrange, study, and catalog its contents. Although he took the position as a temporary assignment, Coomaraswamy remained a member of the museum staff for the rest of his life, some thirty years. In 1933 he became the research fellow in Indian, Persian, and Muslim art at the museum.

Coomaraswamy married Dona Louisa Zlata Llama, an Argentinian national of Basque origin. She also was a Sanskrit scholar who shared her husband's enthusiasm for South Asian literary and cultural traditions.

Between 1917 and 1947 Coomaraswamy published more than 120 books and monographs, 300 learned articles, and some 50 scholarly book reviews, and numerous technical notes and letters. In 1947 he announced plans to retire from the Boston museum and to settle down in the foothills of the Himalayas. Before his plans could materialize, on September 9, 1947, the seventy-year-old Coomaraswamy passed away at his home in Needham, Massachusetts.

Ananda Coomaraswamy was remarkable not only for his command over so many fields but for his ability to synthesize his myriad ideas and thoughts. He was a linguist in the true sense of the word. His knowledge of and great familiarity with languages both in a literary and philosophical sense were exemplary. He was fluent in Greek, Latin, Sanskrit, Pali, English, French, German, Spanish, Tamil, Persian, Hindi, and Sinhalese. Besides displaying his wide-ranging scholarship, the countless quotations in his footnotes reinforced his persistent thesis that "there is nothing new." His belief was that in every age, writers "rediscovered" what had already been written and revered (quoted in Chandrasekhar 1977).

Selected Bibliography

Chandrasekhar, S. *Ananda K. Coomaraswamy: A Critical Appreciation*. Bombay: Blackie & Son Publishers Pvt. Ltd, 1977.
Narasimhaiah, C. D., ed. *Indian Writers Series*, vol. 8, 1974.
Singham, Durai Raja. *Ananda Coomaraswamy: A Biographical Record Arranged Chronologically*. Kuala Lumpur, Malaysia: n.p., 1984.

————. *Ananda Kentish Coomaraswamy: A Handbook.* Kuala Lumpur, Malaysia: privately published, 1979.

Visi R. Tilak

TARAKNATH DAS
(1884–1958)
Political Activist, Educator

A revolutionary, exiled patriot, author, lecturer on international politics, and educator, Taraknath Das championed the cause of India's freedom in the United States for over fifty years. He was born on June 15, 1884, in Majhipara near Calcutta. From early boyhood he was obsessed with nationalist ideals. While in high school, he joined an underground revolutionary cell in Calcutta where he attended study-circles, carried out secret propaganda against the British government, and learned rudimentary military tactics. Although he was a brilliant student, he left college after two years to organize secret societies in different towns in the Bengal province.

In 1905 Taraknath left India for Japan to study at the University of Tokyo, and his foreign study was extended to other countries including the United States, Canada, Germany, and China. In the United States he attended the University of California at Berkeley, where he organized Indian students and laborers. He started a night school in Oakland and established the first nationalistic newspaper in America, *Free Hindustan*. He moved to Seattle, Washington, where he attended the University of Washington. He established United India House in Seattle and Vancouver as meeting places for Indian students and immigrants. When the Gadar Party, an Indian nationalist organization based in San Francisco, California, began to publish its news weekly, the *Gadar*, he contributed articles. He also organized the Hindustan Association of America and published its magazine, the *Hindustani Student*.

Das studied political science at the University of Washington, graduating in 1910 with a B.A. degree. In the following year he earned a M.A. degree and a teaching certificate. A resident of the United States since 1906, Das made several attempts to become an American citizen. In 1914 his application was finally approved and he became a naturalized citizen.

With the outbreak of World War I, Das moved to Berlin, Germany, in

December 1914 and became involved in revolutionary activities against the British government in India. As part of his revolutionary work he became a member of the Suez Canal Mission that was charged with the task of destroying the British-controlled railway tracks along the canal. However, the mission failed due to inadequate German and Turkish support. Das came back to Hebron in Palestine to recuperate from desert sickness.

Das then traveled to China and Japan on behalf of the Berlin-based Indian Independence Committee to organize the Pan-Asiatic League and to spread the doctrine of "Asia for the Asiatics." While in China he published books and articles on Asian unity and sovereignty. He asserted that Japan had the power to challenge European, particularly British, aggression in Asia. He also demanded that India be free and that European domination of Asia be terminated through joint opposition by India, China, and Japan.

The United States declared war against the Central Powers on April 6, 1917, and ordered that Indians suspected of plotting with Germany against the British government be arrested for conspiring to violate the Neutrality Act. A warrant was issued for the arrest of Das, who was given the choice of asylum or safe passage to Russia by the Japanese foreign minister. He chose to return to the United States to stand trial. He was convicted along with other Indian revolutionaries in the famous Hindu-German conspiracy case of San Francisco, and he served 18 months of a 22-month sentence in the U.S. penitentiary in Leavenworth, Kansas.

Upon release from prison he settled in New York City and became a prominent spokesperson in the Indian community's struggle against the discriminatory immigration policy of the U.S. government. After the passage of the 1917 Immigration Law, he advised American and Indian activists Agnes Smedley and Sailendranath Ghose to form a society called Friends for Freedom of India. The organization launched a full-scale campaign to educate the American public about the U.S. government's discriminatory policies toward Indians.

In 1923 he received his Ph.D. from Georgetown University, and in the following year he married Mary Keatinge, who came from a Quaker family of revolutionary war heritage. Soon after their marriage, both Das and his wife lost their U.S. citizenship rights. Das was denaturalized because of a 1923 U.S. Supreme Court decision declaring that people from the Indian subcontinent were not eligible for citizenship. Mary Das lost her citizenship because of the 1922 Cable Act, which stipulated that American women who married men ineligible for naturalization would lose their citizenship. The Dases launched a campaign to have their citizenship rights reinstated. Their efforts were successful, but only after years of filing court petitions.

Das and his wife also traveled in Europe for extended periods. He wrote and lectured in Geneva, Rome, Paris, Munich, and other European cities. He formed a Cultural Committee in Germany for the exchange of students between the United States and Germany, and he made arrangements for Indian students to study in Germany.

In 1930 the Dases co-founded the Taraknath Das Foundation for the promotion of cultural and educational cooperation between India and the United States. The foundation is based at Columbia University, and it still provides annual grants to American university scholars for programs and research on India studies.

Das became a traveling lecturer in the United States and a radio commentator on contemporary politics. In 1943 he testified before the House Committee on Immigration and Naturalization supporting the repeal of the Chinese Exclusion Act and the measure to permit Chinese immigrants to become naturalized citizens. In 1948 he became an adjunct professor of public affairs at New York University, and in 1949 he was a lecturer in Columbia University's History Department. He later taught international studies at the University of Virginia.

Das traveled on a lecture tour to Japan, India, Israel, and Germany in 1952 on a grant from the Watumull Foundation. It was his first visit to India after a 46-year absence. Wherever he went, large crowds greeted the aged patriot. Major newspapers in Calcutta and New Delhi covered his visit on front pages and in editorials.

Upon his return to the United States, Das continued to teach and deliver public lectures. He died in New York City on December 22, 1958.

Selected Bibliography

Banerjee, Kalyan Kumar. *Indian Freedom Movement: Revolutionaries in America.* Calcutta: Jijnasa, 1969, pp. 5–7.

Jensen, Joan M. *Passage from India: Asian Indian Immigrants in North America.* New Haven: Yale University Press, 1988, p. 273, *passim.*

Who Was Who in America, vol. 3 (1951–1960). Chicago: A. N. Marquis Co., 1963, p. 208.

Tapan Mukherjee

Hisaye Yamamoto DeSoto

HISAYE YAMAMOTO DESOTO

(1921–)

Author, Newspaper Publisher

Hisaye Yamamoto DeSoto, newspaper and short story writer, was born in Redondo Beach, California, on August 23, 1921. As a child she was an avid reader. She began writing for Japanese American newspapers at the age of fourteen, beginning with the *Kashu Mainichi* (Japan California Daily News). DeSoto attended Compton Junior College between 1938 and 1940 and was the class salutatorian. During the 1942–1945 World War II years, DeSoto was interned at the Colorado River Relocation Center (Poston I). In the late 1940s, Desoto participated in numerous anti-war and anti–Jim Crow demonstrations and sit-ins sponsored by the Committee of Racial Equality in Los Angeles. From 1945 to 1948 DeSoto wrote for the *Los Angeles Tribune*. In 1950 she received the John Hay Whitney Opportunity Fellowship. DeSoto lived at Peter Maurin Farm on Staten Island, New York, from 1953 to 1955, working with the Catholic Worker Movement and writing for the *Catholic Worker* monthly newspaper. In 1986 DeSoto won the Lifetime Achievement Award from the Before Columbus Foundation.

DeSoto's writings focus on Japanese American protaganists, and her work draws heavily from her own personal experiences. For example, her widely reprinted "Seventeen Syllables" tells her mother's story. Other works focus on the internment camps, her postwar resettlement experiences, and the dilemmas faced by Japanese American women. Having experienced both the Japanese American and white worlds, DeSoto not only portrays a multitude of forms of interethnic and intraethnic racism but also positive relationships that develop among diverse peoples.

DeSoto has published two books of short stories: *Seventeen Syllables / Five Stories of Japanese American Life* (1985) and *Seventeen Syllables and Other Stories* (1988). In addition, her work has been widely anthologized in such works as *The Big Aiiieeeee!, Charlie Chan Is Dead, Before Columbus Foundation Fiction Anthology, The Heath Anthology of American Literature,* and *The Harper Anthology of Fiction*. She has given readings at numerous universities across the country. Emiko Omori's film *Hot Summer Winds* was loosely based on several of DeSoto's short stories.

Hisaye Yamamoto DeSoto is married to Anthony DeSoto. They have five children and several grandchildren.

Selected Bibliography

A Directory of American Poets and Fiction Writers, 1993–1994 ed. New York: Poets & Writers, 1992.
Seventeen Syllables and Other Stories: Hisaye Yamamoto. Introduction by King-Kok Cheung. Kitchen Table; Women of Color Press, 1988.

Steve Fugita

KARTAR DHILLON

(1915–)

Author, Political Activist

Kartar Dhillon, writer and political activist, was born in Simi Valley, California, on April 30, 1915, the fourth of eight children. Her father, Bakhshish Singh, had been a farmer in Punjab, India, a soldier in Singapore, and a merchant marine. He first traveled to San Francisco in the 1890s as a merchant marine and, after his final trip, settled there in 1899. Her mother, Rattan Kaur, immigrated in 1910. After Dhillon's birth the

Kartar Dhillon

family moved to Astoria, Oregon, where her father worked in a lumber mill and was a major force in organizing Indian workers to support a strike called by the International Workers of the World (IWW) to improve working conditions.

Both her father and her mother were among the founding members of the Gadar Party (Party of Revolution), whose purpose was to bring an end to British rule in India. The organization was established in 1913 and had its headquarters in San Francisco.

In 1922 Dhillon's family returned to California and purchased a farm. They were unable to keep the farm, however, due to increasingly rigid Alien Land laws that forbade Asians to own property. The family moved from place to place in search of work. This resulted in frequent disruptions in Dhillon's schooling as she changed schools often; however, her level of academic achievement remained high. By the time Dhillon graduated from high school in 1932, she had attended thirteen different schools. During high school she edited and wrote for the school paper and was an art editor for the yearbook. A graduation gift of a diary started her on a lifetime of journal-keeping.

Dhillon's father died in 1926, and her mother in 1932. This ended her dreams of higher education, because she and her brother Budh assumed care of the younger children. At the age of seventeen Dhillon married

Surat Singh Gill, a University of California student and activist in the Gadar Party. Her husband and brother worked together, leasing land and sharecropping and, at times, hiring out as day laborers on other farms. Within the decade Dhillon was caring for three children of her own as well as her four siblings.

In the 1930s Dhillon and her family lived in Los Angeles, where she planned to attend the university. These plans were again frustrated. Instead she worked as a domestic, a waitress, and an "extra" in Hollywood films. Dhillon and her husband applied for passports to migrate to India in 1940, but they were denied because of wartime conditions. They moved to San Francisco instead, where her husband worked in the naval shipyards.

Dhillon divorced in 1942. She and her children remained in San Francisco, where she worked as a waitress, a machinist, a secretary, and a driver for the Marine Corps, while frequently taking classes in night school. She managed a community music school, where her three children studied piano and violin. Between convoys, while working for the Marine Corps, Dhillon sketched portraits of her fellow workers.

In 1952, with her two oldest children working their way through the University of California at Berkeley, Dhillon took her youngest child and hitchhiked to New York to study art. After living and studying there briefly, she moved back to San Francisco and worked in a trade union office and for the *People's World*, a West Coast workers' paper. In addition to working fulltime, Dhillon was politically active (e.g., supporting the United Farm Workers, striking Pakistani merchant marines, and political prisoners). A popular source of fundraising for these causes was Indian dinners cooked by Dhillon.

In 1972 Dhillon was denied a visa to visit the now-independent India. She risked flying to India without a visa and appealed to the head of immigration to allow her this, her first opportunity to visit the land of her parents. She was granted a four-month visa. She later learned that the reason for the initial denial was that her name appeared on a list generated by the former British colonial government. This list consisted of the names of approximately 200 people who were to be denied entry into India because they were active in the independence movement.

While in India, Dhillon met many people who held her parents and brother in high esteem for their work toward India's freedom. In New Delhi she was asked by Dr. G. Adhikari, a founder of the Communist Party of India, to sponsor a research trip to the United States and Canada by Sohan Singh Josh, a historian of the Gadar movement. Dhillon not only helped the author go to these countries but also spent months gathering materials and researching documents in the U.S. and Canadian archives. The history was published in 1978 in New Delhi.

After retiring in 1983, Dhillon began auditing classes at the University of California at Berkeley, studying rhetoric and Hindi. Once again a new child in the family claimed her attention, and she cared for him for the next ten years. During that time she was asked to submit a piece of writing to an anthology being prepared by Asian Women United of California. Her autobiographical essay "The Parrot's Beak" was published in their book *Making Waves* in 1989 and again, in another anthology, *Growing Up Asian American: An Anthology*, in 1993.

Dhillon continues to write and remains politically active. She is a member of the Gadar Memorial Committee. She participates in writing groups and a literary group in the San Francisco Bay Area, but invitations to speak take her to forums in Canada and the United States to engage in dialogue on politics, culture, and the status of women. She has given presentations at the Desh Pardesh festival and conference in Toronto, at the University of British Columbia in Vancouver, at the University of California at Berkeley, and at Stanford University. Her work also will appear on film. Her film-maker granddaughter, Erika Stuart Andersen, is producing a narrative film based on Dhillon's memoir of her childhood in Oregon. Dhillon gave the plenary keynote address at the 1998 South Asian Students Association national meeting in Atlanta, Georgia.

"The Parrot's Beak" has been translated into the Punjabi language by Professor Sadhu Binning of the University of British Columbia and published in the literary journal *Sirjana* in Chandigarh, India. It is currently being translated into Urdu and Hindi, thus bringing Dhillon's voice once again to the homeland of her parents.

Selected Bibliography

Asian Women United of California. *Making Waves: An Anthology of Writings By and About Asian American Women*. Boston: Beacon Press, 1989.

Dhillon, Kartar. "Astoria Revisited: A Search for the East Indian Presence in Astoria." *Cumtux, Clatsop County Historical Society Quarterly* (Astoria, Oregon), Spring 1995, pp. 2–9.

———. "Sikhs in Oregon: A Journey into the Past." *Samar* (New York), 1996, pp. 45–48.

Hong, Maria, ed. *Growing Up Asian American: An Anthology*. New York: William Morrow, 1993.

Dildar Gill Pisani

VICTORIA MANALO DRAVES

(1924–   )

Olympic Medalist (Diver)

Vicki Manalo Draves was a sports pioneer who broke barriers both as a Filipino and as a woman. In 1948, as a member of the U.S. Olympic team in London, she became the first woman to win two gold medals in diving competition. She was also the first Filipino woman to represent the United States.

Draves—a fraternal twin—was born in San Francisco's South-of-Market district in 1924. Her father was a musician who came from the Philippines, and her mother was an Englishwoman. Draves was often told by her father that her two names meant "double victory," because *Manalo* in Tagalog meant "to win."

Like most Filipino American families in those days, the Manalos did not have much money. Draves worked while going to junior college. Then she fell in love with diving. Without money it was difficult to access swimming clubs. However, she had enough natural talent and the drive to excel to elicit the guidance and free training of swimming coaches Charlie Sava, Jimmy Hughes, and Lyle Draves (whom she eventually married).

Draves first gained national attention in 1942 when she won the Junior National 3-Foot Springboards. In 1944 she met Lyle, who was coaching Zoe Ann Olsen—the girl Vicki would beat in the Olympics High Diving finals. Draves's big titles came when Lyle began coaching her. In 1946 she swept the Junior and Senior National High Platform titles. That same year Vicki and Lyle were married. **Sammy Lee**—another champion diver who was Korean American—was their best man. In 1947 and 1948 she successfully defended her senior title.

Draves trained hard for the 1948 Olympics. Lyle believed she could win both the platform and the springboard events at the Games. Her biggest competition was Zoe Ann Olson. Her friend, Sammy Lee, had finished medical school and returned to compete as a member of the U.S. team. When it was time to go to London, Lyle almost did not make the trip because the Olympic Committee felt it was better for the athletes not to have family at the games. Draves was upset because Lyle was not only her husband but also her coach, and he had made it possible for her to make the team.

Victoria Manalo Draves (courtesy of the Filipino American National Historical Society Collection)

The couple raised money for Lyle's passage to London. Once there, he eventually was able to assist his former mentor, Fred Cady, the head coach of the U.S. Women's Team. His presence meant a lot to Draves. During the opening day ceremonies of the Olympic Games, as she entered the stadium with the rest of the American delegation, Draves suddenly realized that she would be competing against representatives of all the other nations of the world for her country—the United States. She felt a bond with those athletes from around the world.

Draves began to focus on the six dives she had to execute in both Women's High Diving and Springboard finals. She would not be allowed to perform two dives with a higher degree of difficulty—the "two and a half tuck" and "forward two and a half pike." The competition was spread over two days with the springboard scheduled first. When it was official that Draves had won, she was ecstatic because she had not been the favorite.

However, she was the favorite on the platform. She became apprehensive, though, when she learned that if she won the platform she would become the first woman in the history of the Olympics to win both gold medals in the diving competition. Although she did not dive her best on the platform, Draves did well enough to win her second gold medal. She was not only the first woman in the history of the Olympics to win both gold medals in the diving competition, but she was also the only U.S. athlete in 1948 to win two gold medals at the Olympic Games. Victoria Manalo Draves fulfilled the name her father had given her—Double Victory.

After her Olympic successes, Draves and her husband continued diving and raised a family. Their four sons also became world-class professional divers. Although her Olympic gold medals were won over forty years ago, Victoria Manalo Draves has remained one of the best role models for Filipino American youths.

Selected Bibliography

Bamboo magazine, October–November 1953, pp. 3–5.
Philippine News, March 9–15, 1984, p. 14.

Dorothy Cordova

EDITH MAUD EATON
(1865–1914)
Author

The eldest of fourteen children, Edith Maud Eaton was born in 1865 in Macclesfield, England, to an English father, Edward Eaton, and a Chinese mother, Grace Eaton. The couple had met in China, returned to England, lived in the United States, and finally moved to Canada.

As a young girl Edith Eaton helped to sell her artist father's paintings by going door to door. As a woman she worked as a stenographer, a journalist, and a writer, occasionally combining several jobs. Her many travels took her to the West Indies, San Francisco, and Seattle. While in Seattle she also worked for a while with several law firms. Charles Lummis, the editor for *Land of Sunshine*—a California magazine—encouraged her writing endeavors in short stories and essays.

Although her health was delicate, Edith Eaton was a sensitive and thoughtful observer of the world around her. Assuming the pen name of Siu Sin Far, which means "Narcissus," she started writing stories about the Chinese, how they were perceived and treated by European Americans, and the place of Eurasians in both communities. Her stories were published in a variety of different magazines, including the *Chautauquan, Century, Good Housekeeping*, The *Independent, Land of Sunshine*, and the *New England Magazine*. In 1912 she published many of her pieces in a book entitled *Mrs. Spring Fragrance*, published by the Chicago firm of A. C. McClurg and Company.

To take such a stance as a writer required strong convictions and a rare degree of courage. The United States had passed a Chinese Exclusion Act in 1882, barring most Chinese from coming to this country, and anti-Chinese attitudes were still strong at the turn of the century. Moreover, across the Pacific a weak China in dynastic decline and threatened by Western imperialism was being derided as the "sick man of Asia."

Her autobiographical piece "Leaves from the Mental Portfolio of an Eurasian," published in 1909 in the *Independent*, offers insight into her thinking. It records the pain and indignation that she felt when people slighted her Chinese ancestry or teased her with epithets such as "Chinky, Chinky, Chinaman, yellow-face, pig-tail, rat-eater." Seeking solace, she learned about her Chinese heritage and took pride in the grandeur and richness of Chinese civilization.

When other Chinese were beset by problems or troubles, she often tried to help them. This included writing to newspapers, and she was heartened when a Chinese immigrant from New York publicly thanked her for coming to their defense. At the same time, she knew that there are good and bad people everywhere, and that both Chinese and white may hold prejudice against Eurasians, those of mixed ancestry. Daring to look into the future in her autobiographical essay, she ventured to think that "only when the whole world becomes as one family will human beings be able to see clearly and hear distinctly." She cheered herself by musing that "one day a great part of the world will be Eurasian." In that sense, she was a pioneer who foresaw the blending of different peoples as being commonplace in the future.

In other writings Edith Eaton dealt with the pain caused by the clash between old and new ways among the Chinese in America. She also showed empathy for the women's point of view as well as that of ordinary people. Throughout her work Eaton conveyed a sense of authenticity that arose from the insider's perspective, the views of one who lived in Chinatowns and among the Chinese. For example, in one story published in 1909 in the *Independent*, she recreated for her readers the heartbreak and pain experienced by the Chinese who had to deal with the barriers thrown in their path by the U.S. immigration authorities. The irony of the situation was not to be missed by her audience, for she titled the piece "In the Land of the Free."

As Edith Eaton submitted her articles to different publications, there were some who suggested that she write about the exotic East to cater to the public's curiosity about the mystery of the Orient. Indeed, her younger sister Winnifred Eaton adopted the pen name Watanna Onoto. Presenting herself as Japanese, she wrote popular novels such as *Miss Nume of Japan* (1899) and *A Japanese Nightingale* (1901). But Edith Eaton refused to follow a similar path, even for the sake of greater notoriety and commercial success. As a result, her sister—under the persona Watanna Onoto and the author of seventeen books—was much better known to the reading public of the early twentieth century. Edith Eaton never married. She died in Montreal on April 7, 1914.

In recent decades, researchers and scholars have rediscovered Edith Eaton's work. Literary scholar S. E. Solberg, in particular, has found many of her essays and stories that were published in various journals and periodicals. He has called her the "first Chinese-American fictionist," and many other authorities agree with this assessment. They see in her a distinct Asian American sensibility, a consciousness of one who endeavored to negotiate her Chinese identity in the United States.

Selected Bibliography

Dong, Lorraine, and Marlon K. Hom. "Defiance or Perpetuation: An Analysis of Characters in *Mrs. Spring Fragrance.*" In Him Mark Lai, Ruthanne Lum McCunn, and Judy Yung, eds., *Chinese America: History and Perspectives.* San Francisco: Chinese Historical Society of America, 1987.

Eaton, Edith. (1897). "The Chinese Woman in America." *Land of Sunshine*, vol. 6, no. 2: 59–64.

———. (1913). "Chinese Workman in America." *Independent*, vol. 75, no. 3370: 56–58.

———. (1909). "In the Land of the Free," *Independent*, vol. 67, no. 3170: 504–508.

———. (1909). "Leaves from the Mental Portfolio of an Eurasian." *Independent*, vol. 66, no. 3138: 125–31.

———. *Mrs. Spring Fragrance.* Chicago: A. C. McClurg and Co., 1912.

Ling, Amy. "Edith Eaton: Pioneer Chinamerican Writer and Feminist." *American Literary Realism*, vol. 16, no. 2 (1983): 285–298.

Solberg, S. E. "Sui Sin Far/Edith Eaton: First Chinese-American Fictionist." *MELUS*, vol. 8, no. 1 (1981): 27–39.

White-Parks, Annette. "Naming as Identity, Sui Sin Far." In Annette White-Parks et al., eds., *A Gathering of Voices on the Asian American Experience.* Fort Atkinson, WI: Highsmith Press, 1994, pp. 73–79.

———. *Sui Sin Far/Edith Maude Eaton: A Literary Biography.* Champaign-Urbana: University of Illinois Press, 1995.

Franklin Ng

BOBBY ENRIQUEZ

(1932–   )

Jazz Pianist, Musician

Nicknamed the "Wild-man of Mindanao" by saxophonist Richie Cole, jazz artist Bobby Enriquez has been critically acclaimed for his unique, exciting, rhythmic piano-playing style. Born in 1932, Roberto Delprado Yulo Enriquez was raised in Bocolod City, the sugar capital of the Philippines. Enriquez began playing piano at the age of two by imitating his two older sisters. By the time he was twelve he was performing professionally as a member of a group called the Coca Cola Tops—which did promos for Coca Cola while playing for audiences in the barrios. At fifteen years of age Enriquez had been expelled from five different schools, and his parents enrolled him in a special school directed by nuns. He could not take the discipline and ran away to Manila. A friend got him a job playing music in Hong Kong. For the next nine years Enriquez played different entertainment venues throughout Southeast Asia. He also played jazz festivals throughout Asia with great artists like Lionel Hampton, Tito Puentes, Chico Hamilton, and Mel Torme.

In 1967 the actor William Conrad invited Enriquez to the United States. While living in Los Angeles he joined a band called the Sunspots. He went with the group to Hawaii, where he eventually performed in most of the major jazz clubs there and developed a large following of fans. Enriquez also became the popular Hawaiian singer Don Ho's musical director. Richie Cole later discovered him in Hawaii and invited him to join his band. Cole introduced Enriquez to mainland music buffs at the Russian River Jazz Festivals in California, where he received a standing ovation from the crowd of 6,000. Enriquez has continued to perform in international jazz festivals and has six internationally released albums.

New York Times critic John S. Wilson wrote, "Mr. Enriquez has such a lively and attractive mixture of melodic appeal, rhythmic excitement and imaginative ability that he could be for the 80's what (Errol) Garner was to the 50's." A resident of the United States for twenty-five years, Enriquez still returns to the Philippines for concerts and benefit shows.

Selected Bibliography

Bobby Enriquez CD jacket. 1988.
Filipinas magazine, March 1993, p. 19.
Hawaii Philippine News, July 1–15, 1981, p. 10.

Dorothy Cordova

MARINA ESTRELLA ESPINA

(1934–   )

Educator

Marina Estrella Espina, known for her research on "Manilamen," eighteenth-century Filipino pioneers in Louisiana, was born in Bocolod City, Negros Occidental, Philippines, on September 8, 1934. Her father was the senior stenographer for the American Trading Company. Within two years he was promoted to supervising manager for the province of Negros. When World War II broke out the family returned to Cebu, their island home. Marina's father spoke fluent English and Spanish and became regional district manager for several insurance companies.

Marina attended public elementary and secondary schools and studied at the University of San Carlos in Cebu City. She was a consistent scholar in college, majoring in zoology, and she planned to study medicine in Manila. However, because of the distance, her father opposed the idea. Mr. Estrella was promoted to district manager of the Insular Life Assurance Company in Manila and in 1957 the entire family moved to Manila—leaving Marina to finish her senior year at the University of San Carlos. She graduated with honors on October 12, 1957, with a B.S. in zoology. Three weeks later she joined her family in Manila.

On December 12, 1960, Marina married Cipriano L. Espina, who was from San Isidro, Leyte. He was then a senior at the Philippine Law School in Manila. There he underwent rigid training in international trade and was assigned to be commercial analyst at the Philippine Consulate in New Orleans, Louisiana. This brought Espina and her family to America on March 17, 1967.

Life in America with four small children ranging from two to five years of age was difficult for Espina, who had had maids to help take care of her children and do housework in the Philippines. Despite homesickness and culture shock she realized her adjustment was easier than what had faced earlier Filipino immigrants. At least her husband had a job with the Philippine Consulate, and Marina's sister had come with them to help tend the children.

The larger consular community in New Orleans—established in 1948— helped the Espinas find an apartment and get adjusted. In time Espina became a librarian at the University of New Orleans. Because of her husband's position in the Philippine Consulate they were invited to various functions, and before long they were absorbed as bona fide members of the Filipino community. Through these contacts Espina came across descendants of the eighteenth-century Filipino pioneers in Louisiana.

Thus began a new phase in Espina's life as she embarked on her all-consuming, intensive research on the history of the "Manilamen" who had fled Spanish galleons and built several remote villages in the bayous of Louisiana as early as 1763. She recalled that the existence of these Filipino seamen had been chronicled in Philippine history books—but to actually meet their descendants was exciting. They became her friends, and she began to write about their family history. To gather new material, Espina spent countless hours and her own money interviewing families, traveling to archives, and following clues that brought her to Mexico. Soon she was sharing the story of the "Manilamen" with Filipinos in other cities.

Her work caught the attention of the Demonstration Project for Asian Americans, and from 1980 through 1982 she became part of a national team of Filipino and Korean scholars sharing their research through public programs. Espina's valuable research now had a nationwide audience and made many people—especially those teaching Asian American studies—reexamine their perceptions about the immigration of Asians to America.

Espina was a Fulbright Scholar to the Philippines in 1983, and over the years she has been involved in a variety of community work in New Orleans and Louisiana. She was a founding member (1977) and has served on the board of directors of the National Association for Asian and Pacific American Education (NAAPAE). She served as president and trustee for both the Filipino American National Historical Society (FANHS) and the Filipino American Women's Network (FAWN). She has received many honors at both the local and national level.

Espina retired in 1986 as head of the Education/Psychology Department, Earl K. Long Library, University of New Orleans. She is continuing her research and is writing a book on the history of Filipinos in Louisiana.

Selected Bibliography

Clippings (NAAPAE Newsletter), June 1983, p. 1.
Filipino American National Historical Society. *Filipino Women in America.* (expected for publication in 1999)
Philippine News, August 14–20, 1976, p. 1.

Dorothy Cordova

MARCH FONG EU

(1922-   )

Politician, Ambassador

March Fong Eu, U.S. ambassador to Micronesia, was born in Oakdale, California, on March 29, 1922. The daughter of Chinese immigrants, Yuen Kong and Shiu Shee Kong, she received a B.S. degree from the University of California at Berkeley. In 1951 she received a M.Ed. degree from Mills College, and in 1954 she was awarded an Ed.D. from Stanford University.

She has done postdoctoral work at Columbia University and at California State College at Hayward. During World War II, Eu was a dental hygienist at the Presidio in San Francisco. Before beginning her career in public service, Eu was chairman of the Division of Dental Hygiene and professor of health education at the University of California Medical Center in San Francisco; dental hygienist with the Oakland Public Schools; supervisor of dental health education at Alameda County Schools; and lecturer in health education at Mills College.

From 1956 to 1966 Eu was a member of the Alameda County Board of Education, serving as its president from 1961 to 1962 and as its legislative advocate in 1963. In 1967 she was elected to the California State Assembly from the 15th District and served there until 1974. She served as chairman of the Select Committee on Agriculture, Food, and Nutrition (1973–1974) and as a member of the Committee on Natural Resources and Conservation, the Commerce and Public Utilities Committee, and the Select Committee on Medical Malpractice. She may be best known for authoring a bill to outlaw pay toilets in public bathrooms in California. She was the first Asian American woman to be elected to statewide office in California, and from 1975 to 1994 she served as secretary of state, overseeing elections and initiating statewide get-out-the-vote efforts. In 1986, after surviving an attack during a robbery at her Los Angeles home, Eu launched an anti-crime initiative and ran briefly for U.S. Senate. She withdrew from that race when her husband, businessman Henry Eu, refused to disclose his financial holdings. In 1994 Eu was appointed U.S. ambassador to Micronesia.

Eu received the Phoebe Apperson Hearst Distinguished Bay Area Woman of the Year Award (1967), the Merit Citation from the California Adult Education Administrators (1970), the Outstanding Woman Award from the National Women's Political Caucus (1980), the Woman of Achievement Award from the Los Angeles Hadassah (1983), and the Woman of Achievement Awards from several chapters of the National Federation of Business and Professional Women. In 1988 *Ladies Home Journal* named her "One of America's 100 Most Important Women." Eu was awarded honorary Doctor of Law degrees from Western State University (1975), the University of San Diego (1977), and Lincoln University (1984). Eu is a member the American Dental Hygienists Association, the Business and Professional Women's Club, the League of Women Voters, the Navy League, the Chinese American Citizens Alliance, Hadassah, and the American Association of University Women.

Eu has two children, Matthew Kipling Fong and Marchesa Suyin Fong, and five stepchildren—Henry, Adelina, Yvonne, Conroy, and Alaric.

Selected Bibliography

California Secretary of State. *Biography, Secretary of State March Fong Eu*. Sacramento: California Secretary of State, 1976.
Eu, M. *A History of the California Initiative Process*. Sacramento: California Secretary of State, 1979, 1985, 1988, 1989.
————. *Legislative Research Materials in the California State Archives*. Sacramento: California Secretary of State, 1985.
Locke, L. "March Fong Eu, Profile." *C.J. Weekly*, October 18, 1993.

Franklin Ng

HIRAM FONG

(1907–)

Politician, Attorney, U.S. Senator

Hiram Leong Fong, former U.S. senator from Hawaii, was born in the Kalihi district of Honolulu, Hawaii, on October 1, 1907. His parents, Lum Fong and Lum Fong Shee, had immigrated from Guangdong province in China in 1872 to work on a sugar plantation. Fong was the seventh of eleven children and attended Kalihi-Waena Grammar School. He graduated from McKinley High School in Honolulu and then worked as a clerk in the Supply Department of the Pearl Harbor Naval Shipyard from 1924 to 1927 to earn money for college.

Hiram L. Fong

Fong attended the University of Hawaii and received a Bachelor of Arts degree in 1930, after only three years. During this time he was editor of the student newspaper, *Ka Leo;* associate editor of the yearbook, *Ka Palapala;* adjutant of the Reserve Officers Training Corps; member of the Hawaii Civilian Rifle Team at the National Matches at Camp Perry, Ohio (1929); and member of the school debating, volleyball, and rifle teams. He also worked as a bill collector, tour guide, and college correspondent for the *Honolulu Advertiser* newspaper.

After graduation Fong once again worked to save money to continue his education. From 1930 to 1932 he was chief clerk of the Suburban Water System of the City and County of Honolulu. He entered Harvard Law School and received his Doctor of Jurisprudence degree in 1935. Returning to Honolulu, Fong worked as a municipal clerk and deputy city attorney before founding the first deliberately multiethnic law firm in Honolulu: Fong, Miho, Choy & Robinson.

Fong served in the U.S. Army Air Corps from 1942 to 1944, entering with a rank of first lieutenant and later promoted to major. He was judge advocate of the 7th Fighter Command of the 7th Air Force. Fong also served as a reserve officer of the U.S. Army for over twenty years, and he retired as a colonel in the U.S. Air Force Reserve. He is a member of The Kau-Tom Post of the American Legion and Post 1540 of The Veterans of Foreign Wars.

In 1938 Fong, a Republican, was elected to the legislature of the Territory of Hawaii. He served there for fourteen years, including four years as vice-speaker of the House of Representatives (1944–1948) and six years as speaker (1948–1954). A strong proponent of statehood for Hawaii, Fong was elected as one of the state's first U.S. senators on July 28, 1959. He was sworn into office on August 24, 1959, the first American of Asian ancestry to be elected to the U.S. Senate.

During Fong's three terms as U.S. senator (1959–1977) he served on the Post Office and Civil Service Committee, the Appropriations Committee (including subcommittees on Agriculture and Related Agencies; Defense; HUD-Independent Agencies; Labor, Health, Education, Welfare and Related Agencies; State, Justice, Commerce, the Judiciary and Related Agencies; and Treasury, Postal Service, and General Government), the Judiciary Committee (including subcommittees on Antitrust and Monopoly; Constitutional Amendments; Constitutional Rights; Immigration and Naturalization; Juvenile Delinquency; Patents, Trademarks, and Copyrights; and Refugees and Escapees), and the Special Committee on Aging. Fong was appointed in January 1975 to serve on the Commission on Revision of the Federal Court Appellate System. Fong was also a member of the U.S. delegation to the Canada–United States Interparliamentary Conferences in 1961, 1965, 1967, and 1968. He was a U.S. delegate to the 55th Inter-parliamentary Union World Conference in Teheran, Iran (1962), and to the 61st Inter-parliamentary Union World Conference in Tokyo (1974). He was a U.S. delegate to the Mexico–U.S. Inter-parliamentary Conference in Honolulu (1968), and a presidentially appointed member of the U.S. congressional delegation to the People's Republic of China in 1974. In 1974 Fong made a fact-finding and inspection tour of U.S. State and Defense Department installations in Japan, Okinawa, Korea, the Republic of China, the Island of Guam, and the Trust Territory of the Pacific. In 1975 Fong was a member of the official U.S. delegation to attend funeral ceremonies in Taiwan for the late president Chiang Kai-shek.

Fong has been active in many service and civic organizations throughout his career, and he has received numerous awards and honors. In 1970 he was the first citizen of Hawaii to receive the Horatio Alger Award for outstanding success in law, business, and public service despite humble beginnings. In the same year Fong was honored for outstanding public service by the Japanese American Citizens League. He was honored by the Pacific Asian Studies Association for his outstanding contribution to the promotion of understanding and unity among the peoples of the Pacific Asian world in 1974. Ambassador James Shen presented Fong with the Order of Brilliant Star with Grand Cordon on behalf of the Republic of China in 1976. Fong received the Order of Diplomatic Service Merit, Gwanghwan Medal, presented by Consul General Lee Yoon Hee on behalf of the Republic of Korea in 1977. The University of Hawaii Alumni Association honored Fong with its Distinguished Alumnus Award (1991), and the Public Schools of Hawaii Foundation honored him with the Kulia I Ka Nu'u Award in the same year.

Fong was married to the former Ellyn Lo in 1938; she is a graduate of the University of Hawaii and a former schoolteacher. The couple have four children: Hiram Jr., Rodney, Merie-Ellen, and Marvin Allan. They also have nine grandchildren.

Selected Bibliography

Chou, M. *The Education of a Senator*. Doctoral thesis, University of Hawaii at Manoa, 1980.
Chou, M., and M. Dahlquist. *Hiram L. Fong: The American Dream Comes True*. Honolulu: Boys & Girls Club of Honolulu, 1991. [Video-recording]

Franklin Ng

PHILIP KAN GOTANDA
(1953–   )
Playwright

Playwright Philip Kan Gotanda was born in the diverse Sacramento Delta city of Stockton, California, in 1953. Gotanda spent a lot of time fishing and hunting with his family in his youth. He was raised as a Buddhist. His writing has been greatly influenced by the extended Japanese American community in the area. Moreover, his works are almost always influenced by autobiographical elements drawn from his relationship with family members.

Gotanda attended the University of California at Santa Cruz, the University of California at Berkeley, and International Christian University in Tokyo. He received a B.A. degree in Japanese art from the University of California at Santa Barbara and a degree from Hastings College of Law.

Gotanda's plays have been produced extensively throughout the country. His works have played at Berkeley Repertory Theater, East West Players, Manhattan Theater Club, Asian American Theater, A Contemporary Theater, Group Theater, Northwest Asian American Theater, Playwrights Horizons, Wisdom Bridge, Los Angeles Theater, Asian

Philip Kan Gotanda (photo by Hideo Yoshida)

American Theater Center, Studio Theater, Mark Taper Forum, Eureka Theater, Asian American Repertory Theater, Toronto Free Theater, ESIPA, Pan Asian Repertory Theater, and Theater of the Open Eye. He was recently a recipient of the prestigious National Theater Artist Residency Program. Among his other honors are the Guggenheim Fellowship, the Lila Wallace–Reader's Digest Writer's Award, as well as the National Arts Club's Kesselring Prize and the Ruby Schaar–Yoshino Playwright Award.

Gotanda's play *Day Standing on Its Head* premiered in 1994 at New York's Manhattan Theater Club. It explores the midlife crisis of a cerebral Japanese American law professor whose memories of a 1970s campus strike create surreal fantasies. He has collaborated with composer Dan Kuramoto, head of the fusion band Hiroshima, on a full-length spoken word piece entitled "In the Dominion of Night," a synthesis of narrative poetry and jazz. Gotanda and Kuramoto have also toured with the beat-retro performance jazz combo the New Orientals. His newest play, *Ballad of Yachiyo*, is loosely based on an aunt who died in Hawaii when she was seventeen years old. She killed herself after having an affair with a married man to avoid shaming her family. It was performed at the Berkeley Repertory Theater in California and at the Joseph Rapp Public Theater in New York City in 1997.

Other critically acclaimed plays and productions that Gotanda has written include *Fish Head Soup* (1991), *Yankee Dawg You Die* (1988), *Jan Ken Po* (1986), *The Wash* (1984), *The Dream of Kitamura* (1982), *Bullet Headed Birds* (1981), *A Song for a Nisei Fisherman* (1980), and *The Avocado Kid* (1980). The screenplays he has produced include *The Wash, Aiko Yoshinaga Story,* and *Play of Light and Shadows.*

Gotanda resides in San Francisco and is married to actress Diane Takei.

Selected Bibliography

Ballad of Yachiyo. New York: Theatre Communications Group, 1977.

Berney, K.A., ed. *Contemporary American Dramatists.* London: St. James Press, 1994.

———. *Contemporary Dramatists,* 5th ed. London: St. James Press, 1993.

Kamp, Jim, ed. *Reference Guide to American Literature.* Detroit: St. James Press, 1994.

Omi, Michael. "Introduction." In *Fish Head Soup and Other Plays by Philip Kan Gotanda.* Seattle and London: University of Washington Press, 1991.

Steve Fugita

CARL SADAKICHI HARTMANN
(1867–1944)
Author, Art Critic, Journalist

Carl Sadakichi Hartmann, writer and art critic, was born in 1867 on the island of Deshima in Japan. His father was Oskar Hartmann, a German trader, and his mother was a Japanese woman named Osada. Osada died in 1868 during his birth, and Hartmann and his older brother, Taru, were sent to Hamburg, Germany. There the brothers were raised by their grandmother in the home of their uncle, Ernst Hartmann. Carl's uncle was wealthy and had an extensive art collection, and it was here that Carl was first exposed to fine art.

Hartmann's father remarried a widow who had two daughters, but Hartmann was sent to a naval academy in Kiel. However, he rebelled at the naval academy and ran away to Paris. His father subsequently disowned him and sent him to live with his uncle in Philadelphia in 1882. Soon thereafter he left his relatives to live on his own.

In 1883 Hartmann began working for Wells & Hope, a lithographic firm, copying designs onto stone. He later worked as a stippler for another lithographic house and as a negative retoucher for a photographer in Philadelphia.

For a while Hartmann studied to be an artist and attended Spring Garden Institute, where he took evening drawing classes. He often consulted landscape painter Carl Weber to critique his sketches. However, he decided he lacked the necessary talent to become an artist. Nonetheless some of his pastels were exhibited in 1894. In an effort to educate himself, Hartmann read books in a Philadelphia bookstore, studying hundreds of photographic reproductions of world art by the Soule Photographic Company before he was asked to leave the store.

Hartmann paid many visits to Walt Whitman at his Camden Cottage, befriending him and translating his German correspondences for him. During this time Hartmann started his literary and journalistic career and began selling freelance articles on art, literature, and theater to newspapers in Boston, Philadelphia, and New York.

Hartmann visited Europe four times between 1885 and 1893 to study theater and visit art galleries in London, Copenhagen, Antwerp, Paris, Munich, and Berlin. During these trips to Europe, Hartmann learned of the symbolist movement. In 1893 he wrote the symbolist play *Christ*. The New England Watch and Ward Society burned most of the copies of the controversial play. Hartmann was arrested and jailed. *Christ* included scenes in which a young Jesus fought against sexual temptations of harlot queen Zenobia. Even though the play was extremely moralistic, he was charged with obscenity.

Hartmann also wrote the symbolist plays *Buddha* (1897), *Confucius, Mohammed*, and *Moses*, and a collection of short stories entitled *Schopenhauer in the Air* (1899). During the same year he wrote *Christ*, Hartmann also began his own art and literary magazine in Boston called the *Art Critic*. This magazine emphasized the French symbolist movement as well as American and European art. It ceased publication after four issues because of Hartmann's arrest. The resultant attorney's fees and a $100 fine left him without the necessary funds to continue publication.

After that episode Hartmann moved to New York and continued freelancing for several magazines for ten years. In 1896 he worked as Richard Hovey's art critic for The *Daily Tattler*, a daily literary magazine. Unfortunately, daily publication turned out to be overly ambitious and the magazine folded.

Hartmann's interest in photography as art began to be expressed at about the same time that the Society of Amateur Photographers and the New York Camera Club merged on May 7, 1896. These two groups formed the Camera Club of New York. Hartmann's first known essay on photography was published in German for the newspaper *New York Staats-Zeitung* on January 30, 1898. It was entitled "Art Photography and Its Relationship to Painting." Hartmann's first major English essay on photography and the first in a long series of interviews with photographers was called "An Art Critic's Estimate of Alfred Steiglitz," which first appeared in the *Photographic Times* in June 1898. Hartmann first met Alfred Steiglitz at the New York Camera Club. Steiglitz founded the magazine *Camera Notes*.

Between 1898 and 1902 Hartmann wrote some 250 sketches on New York life for *New York Staats-Zeitung*. He wrote under a number of pseudonyms, such as Chrysanthemum, Hogarth, Juvenal, Caliban, A. Chameleon, and Sidney Allan. He used the name Sidney Allen for his essays and writings on photography. Hartmann also lectured under this name. In 1903 he published a two-volume work entitled *History of American Art*, the first standard textbook on the modern history of American art.

Steiglitz resigned from *Camera Notes* in February 1902 and began *Camera Works* in January 1903. Hartmann contributed many writings to this magazine sporadically over the years, depending on his relationship with Steiglitz. Hartmann was the magazine's most prolific writer, contributing forty-two essays and poems.

In 1906 Hartmann published his Japanese tanka and haiku poems. He also dabbled as an art, dance, and most especially a photography critic. Moreover, though he never achieved excellence in photography himself, he was a favorite subject of well-known photographers who relished capturing his rapidly changing moods and expressions.

After 1912 Hartmann's critical essays decreased, and he began concentrating on journalistic articles with popular appeal. He ceased writing articles in 1919. In 1923 Hartmann moved to southern California and tried his hand at motion pictures. He wrote a motion picture script called *Don Quixote* but could not produce it. Hartmann was also known as the King of Bohemia after he walked out on Douglas Fairbanks while filming some scenes as the court magician in *The Thief of Bagdad*. Fairbanks had to reshoot the film, which cost him $250,000. Between 1925 and 1931 Hartmann was a correspondent for an English theatrical magazine called the *Curtain*.

Hartmann's first marriage was to Elizabeth Blanche Walsh, and he had five children with her. He had several more children with his second wife, Lilian Bonham. Hartmann was always in difficult financial straits. This poverty, combined with his bad health, led him to unethically obtain money by selling his previously published essays. Hartmann was even known to telegram his friends, saying he was stranded in a hotel unable to pay the bill and in need of funds. In his last years he existed largely on the patronage of others, including Ezra Pound and George Santayana.

In his last years Hartmann lived in a one-room shack he built on the

Morongo Indian Reservation near Banning, California. Here he was near his daughter Wisteria Hartmann Linton, who was married to a Cahuilla Indian cattle rancher. His health declined and his alcoholism worsened during these years; he became John Barrymore's drinking partner. Hartmann managed to avoid the Japanese American incarceration during World War II.

Hartmann took a bus to St. Petersburg, Florida, in November 1944, when he was seventy-seven years old. He went to visit his daughter Alma Dorothea Gilliland, intending to collect some of his writings to compile an unfinished book. Hartmann died suddenly hours after arriving in St. Petersburg.

Selected Bibliography

Hartmann, S. *Buddha, Confucius, Christ: Three Prophetic Plays*. New York: Herder & Herder, 1971.
———. *Conversations with Walt Whitman*. New York: E. P. Coby & Co., 1895.
Hosokawa, Bill. *Nisei: The Quiet Americans*. New York: William Morrow, 1969.
Knox, G., and H. Lawton, eds. *The Whitman-Hartmann Controversy: Including Conversations with Walt Whitman and Other Essays*. Bern: Herbert Lang, 1976.
Niiya, Brian. *Japanese American History: An A-to-Z Reference from 1868 to the Present*. New York: Facts on File, 1993.
Weaver, J. *Sadakichi Hartmann: Critical Modernist. Collected Art Writings*. Berkeley: University of California Press, 1991.

Steve Fugita

S. I. HAYAKAWA

(1906–1992)

U.S. Senator, Educator, Politician

Samuel Ichiye Hayakawa, U.S. senator, semanticist, and college president, was born on July 18, 1906, in Vancouver, British Columbia. Hayakawa was a Nisei (second-generation Japanese immigrant), raised and educated in the United States, whose Japanese immigrant Issei (first-generation Japanese immigrant) father worked in the import/export business. Hayakawa's father initially came to the United States in 1901, then returned to Japan before moving to Canada. From Canada, he returned to Japan in 1929.

Hayakawa graduated from the University of Manitoba in 1927 and received a master's degree from McGill University in Montreal in 1928. In 1935 Hayakawa received a doctorate from the University of Wisconsin, where he taught English and wrote the book *Language in Action: A Guide to Accurate Thinking, Reading, and Writing* (1941). The book was widely read and cited, establishing Hayakawa's reputation as a semanticist.

Hayakawa taught at the Armour Institute of Technology, the Illinois Institute of Technology, and the University of Chicago. He also wrote a column for the *Chicago Daily Defender*, an African American newspaper. Hayakawa was a spokesperson for and a proponent of the civil rights movement. He also lectured on psychology, sociology, and language. Additionally he hosted a radio program on the history of jazz and was even highly regarded as a jazz historian.

In 1955 Hayakawa moved to San Francisco and became the first Japanese American faculty member at San Francisco State University. Here he gained much of his notoriety and visibility. In 1968 leftist students at the university demanded a more multicultural curriculum. Hayakawa became the spokesperson for the Faculty Renaissance Committee, a conservative group that strongly opposed this student movement. When Robert R. Smith resigned as president of what was then called San Francisco State College on November 26, 1968, Hayakawa became president.

Hayakawa retired as president in 1972, and in 1976 he ran for a seat in the U.S. Senate. He was seventy-two years old. He won the seat running against Democratic incumbent John Tunney. Hayakawa had changed his party affiliation from Democrat to Republican in 1973.

As a U.S. senator, Hayakawa opposed demands for reparations for the Japanese Americans interned during World War II. He even suggested that the incarceration had befitted them, claiming that the "camps allowed us to escape from our ethnic enclaves" and that "the relocation forced them [Japanese Americans] out of their segregated existence to discover the rest of America." Hayakawa himself was never interned because he was, at the time, a Canadian citizen living in Chicago, which was outside the designated evacuation area. However, he co-sponsored Senate Bill 1647, which established a commission to investigate the "facts and circumstances surrounding the internment and recommended appropriate remedies." It was called the Commission on Wartime Relocation and Internment of Civilians (CWRIC).

Another indicator of Hayakawa'a assimilationist orientation was his feelings about the persistence of Japanese American social organizations. "I believe Nisei social organizations should cease to exist . . . these are social crutches that are not needed anymore—but so long as we use them, we shall imagine they are needed." Such sentiments led to an outcry from parts of the Japanese American community. For example, when the Japanese American Citizens League (JACL) asked Hayakawa to be a speaker at a dinner, pressure from the younger members forced the JACL to withdraw its invitation.

In response to the tension associated with the Iranian revolution and the taking of American hostages on March 11, 1980, Hayakawa stated that all Iranians in the United States should be put in camps similar to the Japanese American internment camps of World War II. He even announced plans to introduce a bill, called the Sovereignty Protection Act, to make such actions possible.

In 1975 Dr. Clifford Uyeda, the JACL, **William K. Hosokawa**, Wayne Merritt Collins, and others began a sustained campaign for a presidential pardon for Iva Toguri d'Aquino, who was accused of treason during World War II for being "Tokyo Rose." Decades earlier, Toguri d'Aquino had left the United States for Japan on July 5, 1941, to take care of her ill aunt. Instead of a passport, she left the United States with only a "Certificate of Identification to Facilitate Return to the United States of America." This allowed her to stay six months in Japan. When the war began, d'Aquino tried unsuccessfully to obtain a passport and was denied passage home because her U.S. citizenship could not be proven. Due to financial constraints and illness for which she was hospitalized, d'Aquino could not go home on the repatriation ship that sailed in September 1942. In the following year she was ordered by the Japanese government to be a radio broadcaster on Radio Tokyo. She was one of several female broadcasters known as "Tokyo Rose" to American troops.

D'Aquino was arrested for allegedly trying to "demoralize American troops in the Pacific during the war." At the trial, she faced a prejudicial judge and witnesses who had been pressured by the government, and a generally hostile media and public. She was found guilty of a minor charge, served more than eight years in prison, was fined $10,000, and lost her U.S. citizenship.

During the movement to gain a presidential pardon for d'Aquino, then senator-elect Hayakawa wrote a newspaper article in her defense entitled "The Woman Who Was Not Tokyo Rose." He also discussed the petition for a pardon with President Ford. On January 19, 1977, Ford pardoned Iva Toguri d'Aquino.

After leaving public office in 1982, Hayakawa became active as an honorary chairman of U.S. English, the movement to make English the official language of California.

In 1937, Hayakawa married Margedant Peters. He died in 1992.

Selected Bibliography

Daniels, Roger. *Asian America: Chinese and Japanese in the United States since 1850.* Seattle: University of Washington, 1988.

Daniels, Roger, Sandra C. Taylor, and Harry H. L. Kitano, eds. *Japanese Americans: From Relocation to Redress.* Seattle: University of Washington, 1991.

Hayakawa, S. I. *Language in Action: A Guide to Accurate Thinking, Reading, and Writing.* New York: Harcourt, Brace, 1941.

Hosokawa, Bill. *JACL in Quest of Justice.* New York: William Morrow, 1982.

Howe, Russell Warren. *The Hunt for "Tokyo Rose."* Lanham, MD: Madison, 1990.

Niiya, Brian, ed. *Japanese American History: An A-to-Z Reference from 1868 to the Present.* New York: Facts on File, 1993.

Wilson, Robert A., and Bill Hosokawa. *East to America.* New York: William Morrow, 1980.

Steve Fugita

SESSUE HAYAKAWA

(1889–1973)

Actor

Screen actor Sessue Hayakawa was born in Honshu, Japan, on June 10, 1889. He was the youngest of five children born to Hayakawa Yoichiro, the governor of Chiba prefecture. Kinturo (Sessue's birth name) enrolled in the Naval Preparatory Academy of Tokyo at age fifteen and was accepted by the Naval Academy in Etajima at age nineteen. His dream of establishing a naval career ended in 1908 when he ruptured an eardrum while abalone diving. The injury prevented him from passing physical examinations before his scheduled cadet training at the Naval Academy. His expulsion from the Academy led to severe depression and an attempted suicide. In 1909, after he recovered from the depression, Hayakawa's family sent him to the University of Chicago. He graduated in 1913 with a Bachelor of Arts degree in political science, and he planned to return to Japan and become involved in government and politics.

On his way back to Japan, Hayakawa passed through the Little Tokyo area of Los Angeles and attended a play in the Japanese theater. His disappointment in the play provoked him to challenge the theater owner that he could do a better job of producing the play *Hotogisu,* which received very good reviews from the Japanese newspaper. Motivated to become known outside of Little Tokyo, Hayakawa directed and performed in his first major theater production, *Typhoon*. Good reviews of the play prompted Thomas Ince to produce *Typhoon* as a motion picture, featuring Hayakawa as the lead. During this early phase of his career, Hayakawa decided to assume the name *Sessue* in place of *Kinturo*. While making *Typhoon*, he began working for the Jesse Lasky Feature Play Company.

In 1915 Hayakawa completed the film *The Cheat*, directed by Cecil B. deMille. DeMille became a major artistic influence in Hayakawa's life. Hayakawa began to star in more films, including *Alien Souls, The Victorian Cross*, and *The Clue* in 1916; *The Bottle Imp, The Jaguar's Claw, Each to His Kind, Forbidden Paths, Hashima Togo, His Honorable Friend, The City of Some Faces*, and *The Soul of Kura San* in 1917; and *The Secret Game, Hidden Pearl, The Call of the East, The Honor of His House*, and *The Bravest Way* in 1918. Also during 1918 Hayakawa began his production company, Haworth Pictures Corporation, with money lent by the family of a good college friend, William Connery. The company produced twenty-three pictures in three years, including *His Birthright* and *The Temple* in 1918 and *Heart in Pawn, Gray Horizon, Courageous Coward, Bonds of Honor, The Dragon Painter*, and *House of Intrigue* in 1919. The production company netted over $2 million within these first two years of operation. This success allowed Hayakawa to live a lavish lifestyle and socialize with stars such as Rudolph Valentino and Mary Pickford.

In 1922 Hayakawa's company worked with the Robertson-Cole company to produce *The Vermilion Pencil*, starring Hayakawa. He completed the production; however, he immediately left Hollywood after discovering that the members of Robertson-Cole had participated in the anti-Japanese movement that had begun in California during the early 1920s.

In the spring of 1922 Hayakawa sailed with his wife to Yokohama to visit his family. He moved to New York during the fall of that year and starred in the play *Tiger Lily*. In January 1923 he accepted an offer by Vandal-Delac Studios in France to star in *La Bataille* (which was later shown as *The Danger Line* in America). The international success of this film earned Hayakawa an invitation to act in *The Samurai*, which was performed for Britain's royalty. During this time he also performed vaudeville acts at the Casino de Paris night club and wrote a novel, *The Bandit Prince*. After the royal performance, Hayakawa remained in England for a year to make two films. He returned to France to film *J'ai Tue* and work for the Casino.

In 1926 Hayakawa moved back to New York and performed in the play *The Love City*. He then produced a dramatization of his novel *The Bandit Prince* in vaudeville. In 1928 he performed in the theater production of *The Man Who Laughed*. In 1931 he moved back to Japan to produce the play *The Honorable Mr. Wong*, in which he performed the title role. He remained in Japan to make several films until 1933, when he was called back to Hollywood to make his first sound film, *Daughter of the Dragon*. In 1934 he returned to Japan to star in *Hamlet* and remained in Tokyo until 1937. During that year he moved to Paris with the intention of staying a short time to make films; however, the onset of World War II forced him into an eleven-year exile in France and a prolonged separation from his family. While in Paris he made the films *Yoshiwara, The Cheat,* and *Macao.* He also painted to supplement his income during the war. In 1947 Hayakawa participated as a judge in the International Film Festival in Venice, Italy.

Hayakawa returned to Hollywood in 1949 after being asked by Humphrey Bogart to star in *Tokyo Joe.* He then starred in *Three Came Home.* In the same year Hayakawa was reunited with his family in Japan and continued to make films in Tokyo, one of which was the production of his novel *The Life of Buddha.* While in Japan he was ordained a Zen Buddhist priest. In 1956 Hayakawa returned to Hollywood to star in *The Bridge on the River Kwai,* which earned him an Academy Award and the 1957 Golden Globe Award. Throughout Hayakawa's acting career he often portrayed characters in the military, thus utilizing his early military education.

Sessue Hayakawa was married to Tsuru Aoki, who died in 1966. They had a son and two daughters: Yukio (1929), Yoshiko (1936), and Fugiko (1938).

Selected Bibliography

Hayakawa, S. *Zen Showed Me the Way . . . to Peace, Happiness, and Tranquility.* London: George Allen and Unwin Ltd., 1961.
Kim, H., ed. *Dictionary of Asian American History.* New York: Greenwood, 1986.
Niiya, B., ed. *Japanese American History: An A-to-Z Reference from 1868 to the Present.* New York: Facts on File, 1993.

Steve Fugita

LE LY HAYSLIP

(1949–)

Author, Community Leader, Philanthropist

Le Ly Hayslip, known for autobiographical books about her experience in Vietnam and America, was born Phung Thi Le Ly in 1949 in Ky La, Quang Nam, Vietnam, to a devout Buddhist family. The youngest of six children, she was born at a time when her country was under French colonialism, and Ho Chi Minh and his guerrilla soldiers were fighting against the French colonial administration in an attempt to gain national independence. At an early age Hayslip was drawn into the war, sometimes as a tunnel digger in support of the cause of Viet Cong—soldiers of national liberation led by Ho Chi Minh, who was sometimes called Uncle Ho.

When she was fifteen years old she worked as a lookout for the Viet Cong and was arrested by the South Vietnamese police, who tortured her. She was released but was later sentenced to death by the Viet Cong, who suspected that she had been a collaborator of the South Vietnamese government. Two Viet Cong soldiers who were responsible for executing her raped her instead and set her free.

Le Ly fled from her village with her mother to Saigon, where they found work as domestic help for a wealthy Vietnamese businessman, who seduced Le Ly and made her pregnant with his child. When she was delivered by the mistress of the house, she and her mother were expelled from the house. Le Ly then worked as black-market vendor, waitress, and drug courier. She also worked as a nurse's assistant in a Saigon hospital before she married an American, Ed Munro, who worked as a civilian contractor. Her husband died in 1973, leaving her with a son. She then married Dennis Hayslip, who brought her and her relatives to America after Vietnam fell into the hands of the Viet Cong in 1975. Le Ly's marriage to Dennis was never a happy one, and Dennis was later found dead in a parked van outside a school building. However, he left her with a trust fund and an insurance policy that paid the mortgage of the house in which Le Ly and the family lived. She began to invest her money wisely and was able to make money.

In her memoir, *When Heaven and Earth Changed Places: A Vietnamese Woman's Journey from War to Peace* (1989), she tells her side of the story of a young girl whose life was ravaged by individual and organized violence committed by soldiers of both sides in the name of national liberation and democracy. She also tells her private perspective of the war, a perspective that has been lacking in books and articles written about the armed conflict chronicled extensively by foreign correspondents and writers.

In another book, *Child of War, Woman of Peace* (1993), she focuses on her life with her husband in America in 1970. She describes her struggle to become financially independent after his death, her determination to change "from a self-conscious immigrant to a self-confident American," as Frances McCue characterized her in the *New York Times Book Review*. Both of her books formed the basis for a screenplay written by Oliver Stone, a film director.

Selected Bibliography

Booklist, January 1, 1993, p. 787.

Contemporary Authors. Detroit: Gale Research, 1995, pp. 187–189.

Hayslip, Le Ly. *Child of War, Woman of Peace.* New York: Anchor Books, 1993.

———. *When Heaven and Earth Changed Places: A Vietnamese Woman's Journey from War to Peace.* New York: Doubleday, 1989.

Los Angeles Times Book Review, June 25, 1989, p. 4.

New York Times Book Review, June 25, 1989, pp. 1, 37; April 11, 1993, p. 15.

Hyung-chan Kim

GORDON KIYOSHI HIRABAYASHI

(1918–)

Educator, Community Leader

Gordon Kiyoshi Hirabayashi, known for his courage to challenge the U.S. government policy to evacuate, relocate, and intern all persons of Japanese ancestry during the Pacific War, was born in Seattle on April 23, 1918. He was a student at the University of Washington when, during World War II, he disobeyed a curfew law imposed on persons of Japanese ancestry living within Military Area No. 1. The law was instituted by General John Lesesne DeWitt on March 24, 1942, requiring all persons of Japanese ancestry residing or within limits of the zone to be in their residence between the hours of 8:00 P.M. and 6:00 A.M. Hirabayashi deliberately violated this curfew law to test its constitutionality because he believed that a curfew law should be imposed on everyone, not on a select group of people on the basis of their race.

Hirabayashi was arrested, tried, and convicted on misdemeanor charges. He was ordered to serve six months in jail. In addition, as punishment for his failure to register for the armed services under the Selective Service Training Act, he had to serve ninety days of work on a government road crew. Hirabayashi appealed to the Ninth Circuit Court, which referred the case to the Supreme Court of the United States. The Court handed down its decision on June 21, 1942, unanimously upholding the decision of the lower court. Hirabayashi was released after five months of incarceration.

After the end of the Pacific War he moved to Canada, where he continued his study in sociology and worked for a research organization in

Vancouver, British Columbia, before joining the faculty of sociology at the University of Alberta.

In 1981 Hirabayashi, along with **Fred Korematsu** and **Minoru Yasui**, was informed by Peter Irons, a Massachusetts legal scholar, that government lawyers involved in their cases against the U.S. internment of Japanese Americans from 1942 to 1944 had lied to the justices of the Supreme Court and suppressed evidence. Hirabayashi, with the help of a special team of attorneys including **Dale Minami**, petitioned for the government to have his original conviction in *Hirabayashi v. United States* overturned. On February 10, 1986, Judge Voorhees handed down a ruling charging the government with concealment of information from the Supreme Court as well as from the lawyers who represented Hirabayashi in 1943. In his decision, Judge Voorhees stated that the internment of Japanese Americans was a tragic mistake for which American society as a whole must accept responsibility.

Selected Bibliography

Bondi, Victor, ed. *American Decade: 1940–1949*. Detroit: Gale Research, 1995, pp. 305–306.
Kim, Hyung-chan, ed. *Dictionary of Asian American History*. Westport, CT: Greenwood Press, 1986, pp. 292–294.
Ng, Franklin, ed. *The Asian American Encyclopedia*. New York: Marshall Cavendish, 1995, p. 509.
Spickard, Paul R. *Japanese Americans: The Formation and Transformations of an Ethnic Group*. New York: Twayne Publishers, 1996, pp. 102–103, 156–157.

Steve Fugita

CHINN HO

(1904–1987)

Entrepreneur, Business Leader

He was called the Chinese Horatio Alger or the Chinese Rockefeller. The character Hong Kong Kee, who bested the white oligarchy in James Michener's novel *Hawaii* (1959), was supposedly based on him. Rising from humble roots, Chinn Ho became a legendary businessman as a self-made millionaire in contemporary Hawaii.

Chinn Ho's family established roots in Hawaii when his grandfather,

Ho Tin Hee, came to work as a caretaker for a coconut grove and then as a rice farmer on the island of Oahu. His son Ho Ti Yuen married Ho Kam Lan and operated a small store. One of nine children, Ho Chin was born on February 26, 1904. He later became known as Chinn Ho by adopting the Western practice of placing the surname last and adding an additional "n" to his name to distinguish himself from someone else.

Chinn Ho graduated from McKinley High School in Honolulu in 1924. He soon showed a flair for entrepreneurship by organizing Commercial Associates with his classmates; the group was a combination of a savings club, mutual insurance plan, and investment group. He also got his first job in 1924 at the Bishop Bank, now the First Hawaiian Bank. A year later his interest turned to securities and he joined Duisenberg, Wichman and Co., the predecessors to Dean Witter & Co. in Hawaii. He remained with the firm until 1943.

In 1944 Chinn Ho organized the Capital Investment Company with about $200,000. Though his firm prospered, he attracted little notice until his purchase of land in Makaha Valley in 1947. Informed that Waianae Sugar Company with 9,000 acres of land on Leeward Oahu was available for sale, he bought its stock for $1.2 million. The transaction sent tremors through Hawaii's business community, for this was the first time that an Asian had organized such a large stock purchase. A few years later Capital Investment Company reportedly made over $4 million from the deal by subdividing and selling off 4,000 acres of land.

An astute and daring businessman, Chinn Ho realized that profits could be gained by investment in the land. He foresaw very early that future business profits could come from population growth, development of the tourist industry, and the influx of foreign capital. In 1959 he built the largest condominium apartment-hotel complex in Hawaii, the Ilikai, with 1,000 units and convention facilities. In 1974 he sold the hotel to United Airlines, Inc. for $35 million, realizing reportedly an after-tax profit of $11.4 million.

Chinn Ho engaged in many land, financial, and commercial transactions and diversified his operations. He extended his interests to buying and developing in 1958 in California the 2,200 acres on San Pablo Bay in Marin County. His dealings spanned across the Pacific, where he built and operated the Empress Hotel in Hong Kong in the 1960s and had a minority interest in the Great Wall Hotel in Beijing, China. It was not surprising that he should have invested in China. As early as 1969 he had been asking for normalization of relations with the People's Republic of China. He believed that trade between the United States and China would be advantageous to both countries and to Hawaii.

Not one to remain still, Chinn Ho acquired the *Honolulu Star-Bulletin* for $11 million in 1961. Ten years later he sold it to the Gannett chain for $35 million while remaining a chairman of the Gannett Pacific Corporation. At the same time he advocated an arrangement with the Hawaii Newspaper Agency that allowed Honolulu to keep two major daily papers. While president of the Honolulu Stadium, he brought Triple-A Pacific Coast League baseball to Hawaii. And he helped to develop successfully the Hawaiian Independent Refinery for Pacific Resources, Inc.

Not all of Chinn Ho's efforts were endowed with the Midas touch, although it certainly appeared so to many of his peers. Some of his resort and hotel investments in Makaha and elsewhere did not fare as well as he hoped. Moreover, in the 1960s his wish to develop a portion of Diamond Head on Oahu aroused controversy from opponents touting the cry "Save Head." In the end, Governor John Burns asked the U.S. Department of the Interior to designate it as a National Natural Landmark, and it gained protected status from further development around the crater.

Ultimately, however, Chinn Ho's reputation as a visionary and pioneering businessman seems likely. At a time when Asians were denied access to Hawaii's old-time elite, he was able to breach their barriers by his bold moves. In the companies that he worked with, he tried to ensure that their boards would be multiethnic instead of exclusively *Haole*, or Caucasian. He became the first Asian to be appointed a trustee to manage a landed estate in Hawaii, the Robinson estate. He also became the first Asian director for one of Hawaii's "Big Five" business firms, Theo. H. Davis & Co. Winning the respect of the financial community, he became the first Asian president of the Honolulu Stock Exchange. And he was appointed the first Asian board chairman of a major Honolulu paper, the *Honolulu Star-Bulletin*.

Always busy with his many businesses and investments, Chinn Ho still found time to be generous with his time and money. He served as a volunteer and director on many boards and civic organizations. He headed the Hawaii Visitors Bureau and the Bishop Museum Associates. He paid for the restoration of the Kaneaki Heiau, a Hawaiian temple, and contributed to local projects and charities. His Chinn Ho Foundation funded a reading room—named in his honor—at Harvard University's Harvard-Yenching Library. It also funded a California Parks Foundation study for a Chinese cultural center in Marin County, California. Ho himself gave a grant to the Capital Hospital in Beijing, where he had once been hospitalized during a trip to China.

Chinn Ho married Betty Ching in October 13, 1934. They had six children—Stuart Tse Kong, Dean Tse Wah, Karen Seu Han (Mrs. Stanley Hong), John Tse Nien, Robin Seu Moy (Mrs. John Lee), and Heather Seu Chinn (Mrs. Malcolm Lee). The oldest son, Stuart, is well known in Hawaii business circles. Chinn Ho died of heart failure on May 12, 1987.

Selected Bibliography

"Chinn Ho, 1904–1987." *Honolulu Star-Bulletin*, May 13, 1987.
"Chinn Ho: Office Boy to Multi-Millionaire." In Robert M. Lee, ed., *The Chinese in Hawaii: A Historical Sketch*. Honolulu: Advertiser Publishing Co. for Chinese Chamber of Commerce, 1961, p. 116.
"Chinn Ho: Pioneer in Hawaii Business." *Honolulu Star-Bulletin*, May 13, 1987.
"Chinn Ho Talks about—My Image." *Honolulu*, vol. 2, no. 10 (1968): 22–23.
Daws, Gavan, and George Cooper. *Land and Power in Hawaii: The Democratic Years*. Honolulu: Benchmark Books, 1985.
Folkart, Burt A. "Hawaii Multimillionaire Chinn Ho Dies: Known as 'Chinese Rockefeller' of the Islands." *Los Angeles Times*, May 14, 1987.
Hartwell, Jay. "Chinn Ho Dies at Age 83." *Honolulu Advertiser*, May 13, 1987.
Ho, Chinn. *The Story of Capital Investment Company*. Honolulu: n.p., 1962.
Smyser, A. A. "He Led the Way for Isle Asians." *Honolulu Star-Bulletin*, May 13, 1987.
Spellman, Julius. "Hawaii's Horatio Alger: Chinn Ho." *Finance*, vol. 88, no. 6 (1970): 8–13.
Turner, Wallace. "Chinn Ho, 83, a Major Figure in Success of Hawaii's Asians." *New York Times*, May 14, 1987.

Franklin Ng

PING TI HO

(1917–)

Author, Educator

Ping Ti Ho, educator and writer, was born in the city of Tientsin in Hopei, China, on September 1, 1917. His father, Shou-ch'uan Ho, was a judge; his mother was Yun-lan Chang. Ho received his Bachelor of Arts degree from National Tsing-hua University in Peking, China, in 1938 and his Ph.D. in 1952 from Columbia University.

Ho began his teaching career at National Tsinghua University in K'unming, China, as a history professor from 1939 to 1945. He then taught at the University of British Columbia in Vancouver, serving as instructor (1948–1952), assistant professor (1952–1956), associate professor (1956–1960), and professor of history and Asian studies (1960–1963). Ho was professor of Chinese history and institutions at the University of Chicago from 1963 to 1965, and the James Westfall Thompson professor of history since 1965. From 1987 to 1990 he was a visiting distinguished professor of history at the University of California at Irvine.

Ho has written and edited a number of important books on different periods in Chinese history. His *Studies on the Population of China, 1368–1953* (1959) was a pioneering work on the demography of China from the Ming period into the modern era. A second study, *The Ladder of Success in Imperial China: Aspects of Social Mobility, 1368–1911* (1962), was a wide-ranging examination of social mobility over a long period. His *Chung-kuo hui-kuan shih-lun* (History of Landsmannschaften in China) (1966) was another significant study. It examined the role of locality (regional) associations in providing support for and promoting commerce in China. But beyond China itself, the study afforded new insight into the study of the social organization of overseas Chinese in North America, Southeast Asia, and elsewhere.

China in Crisis: China's Heritage and the Communist Political System (edited with Tang Tsou, 1968) was an attempt to understand both the historical and contemporary China. Scholars of China met at the University of Chicago to exchange insights and perspectives that might shed light on a China going through the turmoil of a cultural revolution. The anthology included an influential essay by Ho on the significance of the Ch'ing period in Chinese history that reshaped conventional thinking about Manchu rule. A year later Ho published *Huang-t'u yu Chung-kuo nung-yeh ti ch'i-yuan* (The Loess and the Origins of Chinese Agriculture) (1969). A remarkable study, it discussed the significance of the loess, a friable but immensely fertile soil in North China, for the history of Chinese people and their agriculture. The study has continued to influence studies of Chinese history and geography.

Rethinking the formation of early Chinese civilization, Ho published *The Cradle of the East: An Inquiry into the Indigenous Origins of Techniques and Ideas of Neolithic and Early Historic China, 5000–1000 B.C.* (1975). Although the study has not been without controversy, it was a bold attempt to reexamine the roots of early China from many different angles. In his many studies, Ho has shown himself to be a master of interdisciplinary approaches in analyzing the Chinese past. For his numerous contributions in illuminating Chinese history and civilization, he was president of the Association of Asian Studies from 1975 to 1976. But the election was important in other way, for he was the first Chinese American and Asian American to be selected to preside over this organization.

Ho married Ching-lo Shao in 1940. They have two children.

Selected Bibliography

Contemporary Authors, New Revisions Series, vol. 11. Detroit: Gale Research, 1984.
Directory of American Scholars, 8th ed., vol. 1: History. New York: R. R. Bowker, 1982.

Who's Who in America (1990–1991). Wilmette, IL: Marquis Who's Who, 1990.
Franklin Ng

WILLIAM K. HOSOKAWA

(1915–   )

Journalist

William K. Hosokawa, an award-winning journalist, was born in Seattle, Washington, on January 30, 1915. He grew up in a Japanese-speaking home and spoke no English when he entered first grade. At the age of fourteen he spent the summer as a laborer in an Alaska salmon cannery, as did many other Japanese American youths. He was sports editor of his high school newspaper. Hosokawa attended the University of Washington in Seattle from 1933 to 1937 and received a B.A. in liberal arts with a minor in journalism. During his university years he was news editor of the *University of Washington Daily*. He was also elected to Sigma Delta Chi.

Hosokawa began his journalism career at the weekly *Japanese American Courier* in Seattle in 1933–1936 while attending the University of Washington. He next became managing editor of the *Singapore Herald* from 1939 to 1940, and then writer for the *Shanghai Times* and the *Far Eastern Review* in Shanghai, China, from 1940 to 1941. After his return to the United States in 1941, Hosokawa was interned with other Japanese Americans and edited the *Heart Mountain Sentinel* during his internment.

Hosokawa's professional career continued at the *Des Moines Register*, where he was copy editor from 1943 to 1946. In 1946 Hosokawa began a long association with the *Denver Post*, serving as war correspondent in 1950 (in Korea), editor of *Empire* magazine (1950–1957), executive news editor (1957–1958), assistant managing editor (1958–1960), Sunday editor (1960–1962), associate editor (1963–1977), editorial page editor (1977–1983), and columnist (1983–1992). In addition, Hosokawa served as war correspondent in Vietnam in 1964. He was a columnist for the *Rocky Mountain News* from 1985 to 1992 and a lecturer in journalism at the University of Northern Colorado (1973–1975), the University of Colorado (1974, 1976), and the University of Wyoming (1985).

During Hosokawa's distinguished career with the *Denver Post*, he was

William K. Hosokawa

responsible for the news-gathering and editing operations of a major regional newspaper and for establishing and implementing the editorial policy of the newspaper. These responsibilities enabled him to make a significant contribution to the life of the Rocky Mountain West and led to his recognition by the Denver Press Club as "Outstanding Colorado Communicator" in 1985.

Hosokawa has made an outstanding contribution to an understanding of the Japanese American experience through his many books. His works include *Nisei: The Quiet Americans* (1969), *The Two Worlds of Jim Yoshida* (1972), *Thunder in the Rockies* (1976), *35 Years in the Frying Pan* (1978), *East to America* (1980, with Robert W. Wilson), *JACL in Quest of Justice* (1982), and *They Call Me Moses Masaoka* (1987, with Mike Masaoka).

William Hosokawa married Alice Tokuko Miyake on August 28, 1938. They have four children: Michael, Susan Hosokawa Boatright, Peter, and Christie Hosokawa Harveson.

Selected Bibliography

Hosokawa, Bill. *Nisei: The Quiet Americans*. New York: William Morrow, 1969.
Niiya, Brian, ed. *Japanese American History: An A-to-Z Reference from 1868 to the Present*. New York: Facts on File, 1993.

Wilson, Robert A., and Bill Hosokawa. *East to America: A History of the Japanese in the United States*. New York: William Morrow, 1980.

Steve Fugita

JEANNE WAKATSUKI HOUSTON
(1934–   )
Author

Author Jeanne Wakatsuki Houston was born on September 26, 1934, in Inglewood, California, and was the youngest of ten children. She was seven years old when Pearl Harbor was bombed, and her family spent three and a half years in Manzanar internment camp for Americans of Japanese ancestry. Houston considers this experience the most definitive in her life. After the war, Houston's family was "relocated" to a defense housing project in Long Beach, a ghetto of sorts where defense workers from all parts of the United States lived during and after the war. This was Houston's first contact with individuals from many different ethnic groups. She learned to speak Spanish during this time, and her interest in international relations was born because of this crosscultural living experience.

Houston attended San Jose State University from 1952 to 1956, studying journalism, psychology, sociology, and Spanish; she received her B.A. in social welfare. She also attended San Francisco State University from 1956 to 1957 and studied at the Sorbonne in France from January 1960 to August 1960.

Houston is co-author (with James D. Houston) of *Farewell to Manzanar* (1973), a book, screenplay, and movie based on her family's experience during and after World War II and the internment of Japanese Americans. This book, now in its seventeenth printing, has become a standard work in schools and on campuses throughout the United States. For the script of the movie, Houston received a Humanitas Prize and a 1976 Emmy Award nomination. Houston has also written *Don't Cry, It's Only Thunder* with Paul Hensler, and *Beyond Manzanar, Views of Asian American Womanhood*. Houston's essays, articles, and reviews have appeared in *Mother Jones, California, West*, the *San Francisco Review of Books*, the *San Francisco Chronicle, San Jose Mercury News, Reader's Digest* (Japan edition), *New England Review*, and *Pen*. Her works have also appeared in numerous collections such as *Ethnic American Woman, Asian Americans: Social*

Jeanne Wakatsuki Houston

and Psychological Perspectives, Ethnic Lifestyles and Mental Health, Common Ground, Crossing Cultures, and the *Borzoi College Reader*.

In addition to *Farewell to Manzanar* (1976), Houston's film projects (with James D. Houston) include *Barrio* (1978), a treatment and pilot script for an original four-part television drama dealing with three generations of a Mexican American family in California and the Southwest; and *The Melting Pot* (1980). *The Melting Pot* is a treatment and two-hour pilot script for an original television drama dealing with two young Cubans who cross to America during the Freedom Flotilla of May 1980.

Houston has received a number of awards and honors throughout her career. In addition to the Humanitas Prize in 1976 for the film *Farewell to Manzanar*, Houston received the Christopher Award in the same year for the book. In 1979 Houston received a Woman of Achievement Award from the National Women's Political Caucus. In 1984 she received a travel grant to Asia from the United States Information Service (USIA) and lectured in Japan, Korea, Hong Kong, the Philippines, Okinawa, and Indonesia. Houston was one of fourteen American women honored in 1984 with the Wonder Woman Award for making outstanding achievements in the pursuit of truth and positive social change. Houston received a Special Award from the Hawaii International Film Festival in 1989, and the U.S./Japan Artist Exchange Fellowship for 1991.

Selected Bibliography

Houston, Jeanne Wakatsuki. Autobiographical profile in *Contemporary Authors Autobiography Series*, ed. Joyce Nakamura, vol. 16. Detroit: Gale Research, 1992.

Houston, Jeanne Wakatsuki, and James D. Houston. *Farewell to Manzanar*. New York: Bantam Books, 1973.

Steve Fugita

FRANCIS LANG KWANG HSU

(1909–   )

Anthropologist, Educator, Author

Francis Lang Kwang Hsu, an anthropologist, professor, and author, was born on October 28, 1909, in Chuang-ho, China. He received his Bachelor of Science degree from the University of Shanghai in 1933 and his Doctor of Philosophy degree from the University of London in 1940. Hsu taught at National Yunnan University in Kungming, China, from 1941 to 1944. He lectured at Columbia University in New York from 1944 to 1945 and became an assistant professor at Cornell University in Ithaca, New York, from 1945 to 1947. He then joined Northwestern University in Evanston, Illinois. From 1947 to 1978 he successively served as assistant professor, professor, and later chairman of its Department of Anthropology. After his retirement from Northwestern University in 1978, he was professor of anthropology and director of the Center for Cultural Studies in Education at the University of San Francisco from 1978 to 1982. During his career he has lectured frequently to academic, parent-teacher, business, and religious groups.

Hsu is a member of the American Anthropological Association and was its president from 1978 to 1979. For his graduate studies, he was the recipient of a Sino-British Boxer Indemnity Fund Scholarship from 1937 to 1941. He received numerous grants and fellowships from many organizations, such as the Viking Fund (1944–1945), the Wenner-Gren Foundation (1949–1950, 1955–1957, 1975–1976, 1985–1987), the Social Science Research Council (1949–1950), the Rockefeller Foundation (1955–1957), Carnegie Corporation (1964–1965), and the East-West Center in Honolulu (1969–1970, 1978–1979).

In the early part of his career as a social anthropologist, Hsu wrote about his fieldwork and ethnographic studies in north central and southwestern China. An example of this is his monograph *Under the Ancestors' Shadow: Chinese Culture and Personality* (1948, 1967). Some of his other early works on China include *Magic and Science in Western Yunnan: The Problem of Introducing Scientific Medicine in a Rustic Community* (1943) and *Religion, Science, and Human Crisis: A Study of China in Transition and Its Implications for the West* (1952).

After he came to the United States, he increasingly became interested in the differences between Americans and Chinese. His book *Americans and Chinese: Two Ways of Life* (1953) became a popular classic as he elaborated on the contrasts between the societies, drawing even from literature to underscore his points. Later the book was reissued as *Americans and Chinese: Purpose and Fulfillment in Great Civilizations* (1970).

Hsu has long been interested in psychological anthropology and has written widely in that particular field. Among his important publications on this topic are several edited works: *Aspects of Culture and Personality* (1954), *Psychological Anthropology: Approaches to Culture and Personality* (1961), *Psychological Anthropology* (1972), *Iemoto: The Heart of Japan* (1975), *Rugged Individualism Reconsidered: Essays in Psychological Anthropology* (1983), and *Culture and the Self: Asian and Western Perspectives* (1985).

Diverse in his research interests, Hsu has studied the Chinese of Hawaii. Some of this work was incorporated in his book *The Challenge of the American Dream: The Chinese in the United States* (1971). He has also believed that complex and large civilizations merit attention, as is shown in his book *The Study of Literate Civilizations* (1969). Aware of ethnocentrism, prejudice, discrimination, and the need for crosscultural understanding, he has addressed these issues in "Prejudice and Its Intellectual Effect on American Anthropology: An Ethnographic Report," *American Anthropologist* (1973); "Intellectual Understanding: Genuine and Spurious," *Anthropology and Education Quarterly* (1977); and "The Cultural Problem of the Cultural Anthropologist," *American Anthropologist* (1979).

Even before President Jimmy Carter restored full diplomatic relations with China in 1979, Hsu had visited China and co-authored his impressions on a visit in *China Day by Day* (1974) with Eileen Hsu-Balzer and Richard Balzer. He has also written *Clan, Caste and Club: A Comparative Study of Chinese, Hindu and American Ways of Life* (1963), edited *Kinship and Culture* (1971), and co-edited *Moving a Mountain: Culture Change in China* (1979) and *China's New Social Fabric* (1983).

Selected Bibliography

Chu, G., and F. Hsu, eds. *China's New Social Fabric.* Boston: Kegan Paul International, 1983.
———. *Moving a Mountain: Cultural Change in China.* Honolulu: University Press of Hawaii, 1979.

Hsu, F. *Americans and Chinese: Two Ways of Life*. New York: H. Schuman, 1953.
———. *The Challenge of the American Dream: The Chinese in the United States*. Belmont, CA: Wadsworth Publishing, 1971.
———. *Clan, Caste, and Club*. Princeton, NJ: Van Nostrand, 1963.
———. *Exorcising the Troublemakers: Music, Science, and Culture*. Westport, CT: Greenwood Press, 1983.
———, ed. *Kinship and Culture*. Chicago: Aldine Publishing, 1971.
———. *Rugged Individualism Reconsidered: Essays in Psychological Anthropology*. Knoxville: University of Tennessee Press, 1983.
———. *Under the Ancestors' Shadow: Chinese Culture and Personality*. New York: Columbia University Press, 1948.
Hsu-Balzer, E., R. Balzer, and F. Hsu. *China Day by Day*. New Haven: Yale University Press, 1974.
Marsella, A., G. DeVos, and F. Hsu, eds. *Culture and the Self: Asian and Western Perspectives*. New York: Tavistock Publications, 1985.

Franklin Ng

DAVID HENRY HWANG

(1957–   )

Playwright, Screenwriter

David Henry Hwang, playwright and screenwriter, is perhaps best known for his play *M. Butterfly*. He was born on August 11, 1957, in Los Angeles, California. Hwang's father, Henry Yuan Hwang, immigrated from Shanghai, China, and was president of a Los Angeles bank. His mother, Dorothy Yu Hwang, a pianist and music teacher, was born in China and grew up in the Philippines. Hwang attended Calvin Coolidge Elementary School, Jefferson Intermediate School, and San Gabriel High School, all in San Gabriel, California. He was recruited by Harvard School of North Hollywood, California, for its debate team. He graduated in 1975.

Hwang attended Stanford University and received his Bachelor of Arts degree in English with an emphasis on creative writing in 1979, cum laude and Phi Beta Kappa. While at Stanford, Hwang was theme associate for Junipero House, an Asian American theme house. Hwang's first play, *FOB*, was produced at Junipero House in 1979. He also founded the Asian American Theatre Project. Hwang attended the Yale School of Drama Playwriting Program in 1980 and 1981.

Hwang's plays have been widely produced and have won numerous awards. His first play, *FOB*, was produced at the New York Shakespeare

Festival in 1980 and won a 1980 Drama-Logue Award and the 1981 OBIE for the Best New Play. *FOB* stands for "Fresh Off the Boat," or a recent arrival. The play itself focuses on the question of identity and authenticity among different generations of Chinese Americans. *The Dance and the Railroad* premiered at the New York Shakespeare Festival in 1981 and won a CINE Golden Eagle Award and a 1982 Drama Desk Nomination. This play centers on the struggles of Chinese railroad workers working on the transcontinental railroad in the 1860s. Also in 1981, Hwang's play *Family Devotions* premiered at the New York Shakespeare Festival; this play also won a 1982 Drama Desk Nomination. This play, the third in his Chinese American trilogy, examines stereotypes, assimilation, and identity. In 1983 the same festival presented *The House of Sleeping Beauties & the Sound of a Voice*, which won a 1985 Drama-Logue Award.

M. Butterfly, a play about gender and conflicting notions of East and West, premiered in 1988 on Broadway and ran there for two years; it also had a one-year run on London's West End. It has been produced in over three dozen countries and has enjoyed numerous U.S., British, and international tours. *M. Butterfly* won the 1988 Tony Award, Drama Desk Award, John Gassner Award, and Outer Critics Circle Award. Warner Brothers produced *M. Butterfly* as a film based on Hwang's screenplay in 1993, directed by David Cronenberg and starring Jeremy Irons and **John Lone**.

Hwang co-created with Philip Glass and Jerome Sirlin a musical theater piece, *1000 Airplanes on the Roof*, in 1988; it premiered in Vienna and Berlin and toured in North America and Europe. Hwang worked with Philip Glass again in 1992, writing the libretto for the opera *The Voyage*, which premiered at the Metropolitan Opera House in New York City. Another play, *Bondage*, was produced at the ATL Humana Festival of New American Plays in 1992. Other recent works are *Face Value* (1993), *The Alienist* (Screenplay, 1995), *The Monkey Kings* (1995), *The Importance of Reading Ernest* (a stage adaptation of Oscar Wilde's play, 1995), and *The Golden Child* (1996). Hwang wrote the screenplay for the film *Golden Gate*, released in 1994 by Samuel Goldwyn Company and directed by John Madden.

Hwang has won grants and fellowships from the Guggenheim and Rockefeller Foundations, the New York State Council on the Arts, and the National Endowment for the Arts. He is a member of the Board of Directors of the Dramatists Guild, Young Playwrights, Inc., and the China Institute. He is also on the advisory boards of Broadway-Asia, the ACLU Anti-Censorship Project, and the Theatre Development Fund. He is a former member of the Board of Directors of the Theatre Communications Group and PEN America, and in 1992 he served as honorary co-chair of the Asian-Pacific Americans for Clinton/Gore.

Hwang is married to actress Kathryn Layng and lives in New York City and Los Angeles.

Selected Bibliography

Asian American Theater Company. *The Dance and the Railroad*. Berkeley: University of California, Educational Television Office, 1984. [Videotape]

Delgado, R., ed. *The Best Short Plays, 1985*. Radner, PA: Chilton Book Co., 1985.

Du, Wenmei. "The Chinese America Drama: In Search of Gender and Identity—Focusing on David Henry Hwang." In Annette White-Parks, ed., *A Gathering of Voices on the Asian American Experience*. Fort Atkinson, WI: Highsmith Press, 1994, pp. 165–173.

Glass, P., D. Hwang, and J. Sirlin. *1000 Airplanes on the Roof*. Salt Lake City: Gibbs-Smith, 1989.

Hwang, D. *Broken Promises: Four Plays*. New York: Avon Books, 1983.

———. *The Dance and the Railroad; and Family Devotions: Two Plays*. New York: Dramatists Play Service, 1983.

———. *FOB and Other Plays*. New York: New American Library, 1990.

———. *M. Butterfly*. New York: New American Library, 1989.

Hwang, D., J. Takagi, and C. Choy. *Homes Apart: Korea*. New York: Third World Newsreel, 1991. [Videotape]

Isaacson, R., and E. Wilson. *David Henry Hwang, Playwright*. Santa Cruz, CA: Audio Visual Services, University Library, University of California, Santa Cruz, 1991. [Videotape]

Street, D. *David Henry Hwang*. Boise, ID: Boise State University, 1989.

Franklin Ng

BONG HAK HYUN

(1922–)

Physician, Educator, Political Activist

Bong Hak Hyun is still active in spite of his official retirement in 1988 from research, teaching, and community service. As his most recent autobiographical book, *No Retirement for Me* (1996), strongly suggests, he continues to be involved in many community projects in order to provide mature leadership for fledging organizations and institutions in Korean American communities across this country. In 1996 he accepted the responsibility for co-chairing the SAT II (Scholastic Achievement Test) Korea Committee that was organized to raise money for use in Korean-language instruction in the United States. He was appointed during the same year to represent the Committee for Restoration of Korean American Historical Monuments. He also serves as president of the U.S.

Bong Hak Hyun

China Korean Fellowship Association, which was founded by him to assist Chinese people of Korean ancestry living in China.

Born on June 23, 1922 in Seongjin, Hamkyeong namdo, which is now located in North Korea, into a Christian family of six sons and one daughter, he was brought up to respect learning and Christian faith because his father was a schoolteacher and chaplain. When he was three years old he was suddenly struck by polio, from which he has never recovered completely. He still suffers now and then from post-polio syndrome. After completing his elementary education in his hometown he moved to Hamheung, the capital of Hamkyeong namdo, where he attended Hamheung Public High School established by the Japanese colonial government primarily for Japanese children.

Upon graduation from high school, he sent in an application to Severance Medical School in Seoul in March 1941 and was accepted. His medical college education was financed by two Canadian missionaries, who were later asked to leave Korea in 1942 by the Japanese colonial government after the outbreak of the Pacific War. When he graduated from the medical school in 1944, he was recommended by his benefactor, Dr. Myeong-seon Kim, to do his internship at the P'yeongyang Christian

Hospital, where he chose to work until the end of the Pacific War in 1945. He returned to Hamheung with the hope of working at a local hospital but later decided to come to Seoul toward the end of 1945.

In 1947 he was offered an opportunity to come to the United States to study clinical pathology at Medical College, Richmond University, in Virginia. After a two-year stay in America he returned to his native country on February 28, 1950, less than four months before the Korean War broke out. During the first few days of the war he volunteered to take care of those who were wounded in air raids conducted by American airplanes that mistook civilians for enemy soldiers. He continued to follow South Korean soldiers in their retreat to the Taegu defense perimeter before he was asked to work as interpreter for the U.S. 25th Army Division. He was later asked to work for the commanding general of the U.S. 10th Army Corps, whose headquarters was located in Hamheung. When the U.S. Army decided to retreat from the city, Hyun helped to evacuate more than 100,000 civilians aboard American naval ships from Heungnam to Pusan. This was one of the greatest accomplishments of his life.

He came to America for further study in 1953 and received a Doctor of Science degree in pathology from the University of Pennsylvania in 1959. His first teaching position in America was with the Medical College, University of Pennsylvania, in 1955. Before his retirement from teaching he reached the rank of full professorship in pathology at the Rutgers Medical School, New Jersey, which he held until 1988. While teaching and conducting research as a college professor, he engaged in a variety of community projects, one of which was to promote the humanitarian ideals of **Philip Jaisohn**. A group of Korean American physicians established the Philip Jaisohn Memorial Foundation in 1976 and invited Hyun to direct it. He served as chair of the foundation from 1976 to 1985.

Selected Bibliography

American Men and Women of Science, Physical and Biological Sciences, 13th edition. New York: R.R. Bowker, 1979, p. 2076.

Hyun, Bong-hak. *Na ege eunt'oe neun eopta* (No Retirement for Me). Seoul: Yeoksa pip'yeong-sa, 1996.

Hyun-chan Kim

SOON HYUN

(1879–1968)

Political Activist

Soon Hyun (Hyeon Sun) was a remarkable man of many great achievements. He was a national hero who sought the fusion of Korean culture with American Christianity and democracy as the way to Korea's freedom from Japan. His accomplishments were fourfold. First, in Korea and Hawaii, he advocated the preaching and practice of American Christianity and democracy as part of Korean life (1903–1919). Second, during 1919 Hyun planned and organized the first March First Declaration and Demonstrations of Korean Independence in Korea, China, and the United States. Third, he was responsible for organizing the provisional government of the Republic of Korea in China, Hawaii, and the United States (1919–1923). Fourth, from 1923 to 1968 Hyun led the Korean Christian Methodist churches and the Korean independence movements.

Born on March 21, 1879, as son of Hyun Chae-ch'ang, a magistrate of Jiksan whose ancestors served as *Yeokgwan* or translator-diplomat, in the Yi dynasty, he grew up studying the Chinese classics according to the family tradition. When he was twenty years old, however, he was sent to Hansong Public English School where he learned the English language, among others. In 1899, before his graduation from the school, he and two of his friends, Chang Eung-chin and Kim Kyeong-min, went to Japan, where he continued his study in mathematics and science at Junten Jugako located at Kanda-ku, Tokyo.

Upon graduation from the school in April 1902, Hyun came back to Korea and was employed as an English interpreter by the East-West Development Company established by David Deshler, an agent for the Hawaiian Sugar Planters Association who recruited Korean workers to come to Hawaii. In early February 1903 he and his wife sailed for Hawaii aboard the SS *Coptic*. The ship anchored at Honolulu on February 20. He and his wife stayed there until 1905, when he was sent to Lihue, Kauai, as a roving preacher by John W. Wadman, superintendent of the Hawaiian Missions of the Methodist Episcopal Church. During their sojourn in Hawaii, three children were born to them: Alice on May 8, 1903, and Elizabeth on March 19, 1905, in Honolulu; Peter on August 15, 1907, in Lihue.

In May 1907 the Hyuns returned to Korea to see their country falling

Soon Hyun

increasingly under Japanese pressure to accommodate their terms for modernizing its old institutions. Hyun began to work at Paejae Haktang, or Paejae Hall of Learning, which was under the leadership of D. A. Bunker serving as the school's principal. Hyun taught English, mathematics, geography, general science, and world history while also preaching at the Young Men's Christian Association every Sunday afternoon. He also conducted revival meetings at Cheongdong Methodist Church. He subsequently resigned from Paejae Haktang and worked with the pastor of Cheongdong Methodist Church as an assistant.

While working as assistant minister, Hyun enrolled in the Union Methodist Theological Seminary of Seoul to study theology and graduated from the college in 1911. He spent a few months in P'yeongyang preaching and establishing churches before he was brought back to Seoul to work as interpreter for Bishop M. C. Harris, who had come from Japan to Korea to assume leadership of the Methodist Church. Hyun served as pastor of Cheongdong Church from 1913 to 1915 before being succeeded by Reverend Son Cheong-to, a famous patriot who served as chairperson of the Provisional Assembly of the Korean provisional government-in-exile in Shanghai in the 1920s.

In January 1919, Hyun was invited to conduct two weeks of revival meetings at a Korean Presbyterian church in Euiju, located at the bank of the River Yalu. After the end of the revival meetings he led a big parade with a group of Sunday school children, calling for Korea's independence. In February he returned to Seoul, where he was asked to join a group of seven Korean Methodist Christian patriots to plan for a nationwide independence movement to be staged with a mass demonstration. Hyun was chosen to carry the message of this movement to Shanghai, China, where a group of patriotic Korean leaders gathered to launch Korea's independence movement and diplomacy. Hyun left Korea on February 24, 1919, and reached Shanghai on the eve of March 1, when Koreans declared their independence from Japan by staging the nationwide mass demonstration.

Hyun was chosen as general secretary by a group of Korean leaders in Shanghai who opened the Temporary Office for Independence to coordinate independence movements launched by Koreans in Japan, China, and Korea. He was a key member of the group that organized and elected the members of the Provisional Assembly and those of the Korean provisional government-in-exile. The Declaration of Independence written by Ch'oe Nam-seon in Korean was translated into English by Hyun and Yi Kwang-su, and a copy was sent to local newspapers. Cables were sent to the British, American, French, Italian, Dutch, and Chinese delegations at the Peace Conference held after the end of World War I in Paris, and telegrams were dispatched to the Korean National Association in San Francisco and Honolulu to inform them of the March First Independence Movement. Hyun's telegram reached **Ch'ang Ho Ahn** on March 9, when Ahn was in San Francisco to preside over the regular annual meeting of the Central Congress of the Korean National Association. Hyun served as vice-minister of foreign affairs in the Korean provisional government in Shanghai under Kim Kyu-sik, foreign affairs minister, a graduate of Roanoke College. He was appointed by **Syngman Rhee**, president of the provisional government, as Korean Minister to the United States on October 6, 1920.

As Minister, Hyun founded the legation, conducted strategic diplomatic relations, and submitted to the secretary of state, Charles E. Hughes, a request for recognition of the Republic of Korea by the United States on May 11, 1921. Friendly acknowledgment of receipt of Hyun's request was made by the office of the vice-president, which guaranteed that his request would receive his attention. However, Hyun was physically forced out of the office, and his request for recognition was withdrawn with allegations that he used false credentials.

After Hyun was relieved of his office, he returned to Shanghai by way of Honolulu and Manila to continue his involvement in the Korean independence movement. Upon arrival in Shanghai he was joined with his family, who had succeeded in escaping from Korea. He made a trip to Moscow, where he met Lenin and Trotsky for consultation on Korea's independence movement, and he returned to Shanghai before being asked to come back to Hawaii by William Fry, Wadman's successor. He came back to Honolulu with his first daughter, Alice, and was later joined by Elizabeth, Peter, David, and Mary in Honolulu on May 25, 1924, and by his wife, Maria, Paul, and Joshua one year later.

He continued to struggle for Korea's independence while working as pastor of many Korean Methodist churches located at such places as Hanamaulu, Kapaa, Kealia, Kilauea, Huleia, Puhi, Koloa, Lawai, Eleele, Makaweli, Kekaha, and Man on the Island of Kauai. He was responsible for establishing a number of political organizations among Koreans in Hawaii. They were the Hawaiian Branch of the Korean National Revolutionary Party, of which he was chairperson; and the Korean National Information Bureau located in Honolulu, Hawaii. He worked closely with Kim Kyu-sik and Kim Ku, president of the Korean provisional government in Chungking, China, in 1940.

In February 1946, after Korea was liberated from Japan and was placed under the American military government, Hyun wrote a letter to the commanding general of the United States Army Forces, Middle Pacific, asking permission to visit his native country. His purpose was to make immediate contact with Kim Kyu-sik and Kim Won-bong, who later had to flee to North Korea. He made this request as chairperson of the Hawaiian Branch of the Korean National Revolutionary Party without being aware of the fact that the party and its members had been placed under surveillance by the FBI and the Immigration and Naturalization Service. His request was denied, probably because of his affiliation and leadership position within the Korean National Revolutionary Party and his close ties with Kim Won-bong. He was not allowed to come back to his native country even for a short visit while **Syngman Rhee** was serving as president of Korea between 1948 and 1959.

Hyun retired from active life in 1940 and moved to Los Angeles in 1947, where he died on August 11, 1968. He was buried in Los Angeles, but the Republic of Korea, in recognition of his contributions to Korea's independence, requested in 1975 that his body be exhumed for reburial in Korea's national cemetery. His family complied with the request, and he is now resting in peace in his native land.

Selected Bibliography

Hyun, Peter. *Man Sei! The Making of a Korean American*. Honolulu: University of Hawaii Press, 1986.
———. *In the New World: The Making of a Korean American*. Honolulu: University of Hawaii Press, 1991.
Hyun, Soon. *P'owa yuram-gi* (Records of the Trip to Hawaii). Seoul: Hyun Kong-yeom, 1909.

Hyung-chan Kim

LAWSON FUSAO INADA

(1938–)

Poet, Educator

Lawson Fusao Inada, poet and educator, was born on May 26, 1938, in Fresno, California. His grandparents founded the first store in the Fresno region in 1912, the Fresno Fish Market on "F" Street. Inada grew up in the heart of the multicultural business district known as Chinatown, a vibrant, culturally vital community. His earliest significant event was being removed from this community when he and his family were locked up in the county fairgrounds, shipped to an internment camp in Arkansas, then to a camp in Colorado during the World War II "relocation" of Japanese Americans. When he and his family returned to Fresno, he went about the business of growing up and going to school, but he says his main teacher was jazz. Artists such as Charlie Parker and Lester Young were "household names" in his Asian, black, and Chicano neighborhood.

Inada has published his poetry in several collections, including *Legends from Camp* (1993), *In This Great Land of Freedom: The Japanese Pioneers of Oregon* (1993), and *Before the War: Poems as They Happened* (1971). He has co-edited several anthologies: *The Big Aiiieeeee! An Anthology of Chinese American and Japanese American Literature* (1991), and *Aiiieeeee! An Anthology of Asian American Writers* (1975, 1991). His essays, fiction, and poetry have been published in numerous periodicals and collections, including *Dreamers and Desperadoes: Contemporary Short Fiction of the American West* (Craig Lesley, editor, 1993), and *Moment's Notice: Jazz in Poetry and Prose* (Art Lange and Nathaniel Mackey, editors, 1993).

Inada has performed his work in concert with numerous musicians, including Russel Baba, Marion Brown, Andrew Hill, Jon Jang, Johnny Hammond Smith, Mal Waldron, and Francis Wong. His multimedia performances include "Concentrated Images," with photographer Joan Myers and composer Greg Steinke; and "Always Reaching for Something: Tribute to Jacob Lawrence," with composer Todd Barton.

Inada has received many honors and awards for his work. In 1991 he was named Oregon State Poet of the Year. In 1988 Inada received the American Book Award. He was the subject of a documentary film called "I Told You So: Lawson Fusao Inada" in 1975.

Inada is professor of English at Southern Oregon State University in Ashland, Oregon. He is married and has two children.

Selected Bibliography

Inada, Lawson Fusao. *Before the War: Poems as They Happened.* New York: Morrow, 1971.

—————. *Legends from Camp: Poems.* Minneapolis: Coffee House Press, 1992.

Kikumura, Akemi, Lawson Fusao Inada, and Mary Worthington, eds. *In This Great Land of Freedom: The Japanese Pioneers of Oregon.* Los Angeles: Japanese American Museum, 1993.

Steve Fugita

Daniel Ken Inouye

(1924–   )

Senator, Politician

Daniel Ken Inouye, U.S. Senator, was born in Honolulu, Hawaii, on September 7, 1924. He was the eldest son of Hyotaro and Kame Inouye. Inouye's father, Hyotaro, came to Hawaii from Japan with his parents at the age of four. His mother, Kame, was the orphaned daughter of a family from Hiroshima that had come to Hawaii as contract laborers for the sugar plantations. Inouye was named after a Methodist minister who had adopted his mother and lived with his family in a small Japanese ghetto in Honolulu. His father worked as a clerk in the jewelry department of one of Hawaii's largest stores.

Inouye attended the Honolulu public schools, earning pocket money by parking cars at the Honolulu Stadium and giving haircuts to fellow students. He graduated from McKinley High School, then nicknamed "Tokyo High" because of its predominantly Japanese American enrollment.

During the Japanese attack on Pearl Harbor of December 7, 1941, Inouye was one of the first Americans to care for civilian casualties. He had taken medical aid training and was pressed into service as head of a first-aid litter team. At the beginning of the war, Americans of Japanese ancestry were discharged from National Guard units in Hawaii and rejected by the Selective Service System. But after the U.S. Army announced plans to accept a limited number of Americans of Japanese descent to form a combat team, eighteen-year-old Inouye, a freshman in premedical studies at the University of Hawaii, enlisted in March 1943. He was accepted into the 442nd Regimental Combat Team and trained

Daniel Ken Inouye

at Camp Shelby, Mississippi. The all-Nisei 442nd Combat Team (all second-generation Japanese) sailed to Naples, Italy, and joined another Nisei unit from Hawaii, the 100th Infantry Battalion.

Sergeant Inouye slogged through nearly three bloody months of the Rome-Arno campaign with the U.S. Fifth Army. Early in the action he established himself as an outstanding patrol leader with the "Go for Broke" regiment, the phrase used as a rallying cry in infantry attacks. Inouye's unit was relocated to the French Vosges Mountains and spent two of the bloodiest weeks of the war rescuing a Texas battalion surrounded by German forces. The rescue of the "lost battalion" is listed in U.S. Army annals as one of the most significant military battles of the century. Inouye became a platoon leader, won the Bronze Star, and received a battlefield commission as a second lieutenant.

Back in Italy, the 442nd was assaulting a heavily defended hill in the closing months of the war when Inouye was shot through the abdomen; the bullet narrowly missed his spine before coming out his back. He continued to lead the platoon and advanced alone against a machine gun nest that had his men pinned down. He tossed two grenades with devastating effect before his right arm was shattered by a German rifle grenade at close range. Inouye threw his last grenade with his left hand, attacked with a submachine gun, and was finally knocked down the hill by a bullet in the leg. He spent twenty months recovering in Army hospitals after losing his right arm. Inouye came home as a captain with a Distinguished Service Cross (the second-highest award for military valor), Bronze Star, Purple Heart with cluster, and twelve other medals and citations. Ironically, on his way back to Hawaii to be reunited with his family, while in full uniform, Captain Inouye was refused a haircut by a San Francisco barber.

The loss of Inouye's right arm shattered his hopes for a career as a surgeon. Instead, he entered a prelaw course at the University of Hawaii, graduating in 1950. There he met his future wife, Margaret (Maggie) Awamura, the daughter of a Honolulu jeweler. She had returned to Hawaii to teach after receiving her Masters degree in counseling at Columbia University. Maggie Inouye helped support her husband as he worked his way through George Washington University Law School in Washington, D.C. Inouye received his law degree in 1952. They have one child.

In 1953 Inouye returned to Honolulu and was appointed deputy public prosecutor for the City and County of Honolulu. He was elected to the Territorial House of Representatives in 1954 and was immediately elected House Majority leader, a position he held through 1958 when he was elected to the Territorial Senate. In 1959 Inouye won election as the first U.S. representative from the new state of Hawaii. Based on his awareness of discrimination against fellow Japanese Americans, Inouye strongly supported efforts to pass civil rights legislation. He backed Lyndon Johnson's candidacy for the Democratic presidential nomination and, at Johnson's request, gave the seconding speech at the 1960 Democratic National Convention.

Inouye was elected to the U.S. Senate in 1962. His career in the Senate has been long and illustrious. He has been a strong supporter of civil rights and social welfare legislation. Among his many accomplishments, Inouye delivered the Keynote Address at the 1968 Democratic Convention in which he appealed for racial understanding and progressive change through democratic institutions. He gained national exposure and respect as a member of the Senate Watergate Committee in 1973 and 1974. In 1976 he became the first chairman of the Senate Select Committee on Intelligence, a post he voluntarily relinquished after a two-year term. Inouye served as the third-ranking leader among Senate Democrats as secretary of the Democratic Conference from January 1979 through 1988. In 1984 Inouye chaired the Senate Democratic Central America Study Group to assess U.S. policy and served as senior counselor to the National Bipartisan Commission on Central America (also known as the Kissinger Commission). In January 1987 he became the chairman of the Senate Select Committee on Secret Military Assistance to Iran and the Nicaraguan Opposition, which held public hearings on the Iran-Contra affair from May through August 1987.

Inouye's present leadership positions in the Senate include chairman of the Committee on Indian Affairs, chairman of the Senate Appropriations Subcommittee on Defense, and chairman of the Senate Commerce, Science, and Transportation Subcommittee on Communications.

Selected Bibliography

Inouye, Daniel K. (with Lawrence Elliott). *Journey to Washington*. Englewood Cliffs, NJ: Prentice-Hall, 1967.
Notable Asian Americans. Detroit: Gale Research, 1995.
Who's Who in American Politics. New York: R. R. Bowker, 1993.
Yang, Jeff. "Power Brokers." *A. Magazine*, vol. 2, no. 3 (December 15, 1993): 25–34.

Steve Fugita

LARRY ITLIONG

(1913–1977)

Union Organizer, Community Leader

During the 1970s, Larry Itliong constantly challenged young Filipino American activists to understand that in order to successfully organize themselves in the difficult struggle for equality, they needed to identify specific objectives. For forty years he did just that: he fought to give the average laborer better working conditions.

A native of the Philippines, Itliong was born on October 25, 1913, in San Nicolas, Pangasinan. He was one of six children of Artemio and Francesca Itliong. He had only a sixth grade education when at age fifteen he decided to come to the United States in 1929. Filipinos were American nationals and only needed the price of a boat ticket to go to America—considered the land of milk and honey. He hoped to continue his studies, but because of the Great Depression there was a scarcity of jobs and Itliong found it difficult to sustain himself.

Itliong worked on the railroads, in the sugar beet fields of Montana, in South Dakota, and in the agricultural camps of California. He also worked in canneries in the San Pedro–Wilmington area while continuing the life of a migrant farm worker in Washington state and California. Life was hard for Filipino laborers, and Itliong was disturbed by their plight.

In the 1930s, Itliong became involved in the lettuce strike at Monroe,

Washington. He later helped organize the salmon cannery workers union (ILWU Local 37). He first served as a shop steward, and later in 1953 he was elected vice-president of Local 37. At the same time he was involved in the asparagus strikes in Stockton, California.

By the 1960s Itliong was raising a family in the Delano area. In 1965 he organized Filipino farm workers working in the grape fields to strike for higher wages and better working conditions. The grape strike began. When Mexican farm workers led by Cesar Chavez later joined the strike, the United Farm Workers union (UFW) was born. At first the growers did not take the strike seriously, thinking that the strikers would starve during a prolonged strike. However, the strikers were supported by fellow Filipino Americans as well as other community members who kept them alive with donations of food, clothing, and money. According to Itliong, the most difficult issue in the Delano strike was that the growers did not want Filipino workers to have a union and a way to bargain collectively. Eventually Larry Itliong acted as vice-president of the UFW and gradually withdrew from active participation in the grape boycott.

Always active in Filipino American community concerns, Itliong became president of FAPA, a national political action group, and was instrumental in the formation of Agbayani Village—a retirement center for elderly Filipino American farm workers in the Delano area.

On February 10, 1977, Larry Itliong died at the age of sixty-four.

Selected Bibliography

Filipino American Herald, April 16, 1973, p. 2.
Filipino Forum, March 1969, p. 2.
Freedom Socialist, September–November 1986, pp. 3, 4.
Sacramento Bee, December 28, 1996, pp. A1, A20.
Stockton Record, March 28, 1971, p. 12.

Dorothy Cordova

LANCE A. ITO
(1950–   )
Judge

Lance A. Ito, Los Angeles superior court judge, was born in Los Angeles on August 2, 1950, and grew up in the city. He attended John Marshall High School and the University of California, Los Angeles, where he was a political science major and graduated cum laude. In 1975 he was awarded a law degree from Boalt Hall School of Law at the University of California at Berkeley. He was admitted to the bar in 1976.

A veteran jurist, Judge Ito has presided over two very high-profile trials. In 1991–1992 he was the judge in the securities fraud case of Charles H. Keating Jr. Keating was tried for his role in the collapse of Lincoln Savings & Loan and its parent company. The thrift's failure was the largest in U.S. history, costing taxpayers some $2.6 billion. After initially dismissing many of the charges against Keating, when he was found guilty, Ito handed down the maximum sentence of ten years in prison. Ito was also the presiding judge over the 1994–1995 O. J. Simpson case. The televised trial of this popular football player for the murder of his wife, Nicole Brown Simpson, and her friend, Ron Goldman, was the subject of intense media scrutiny. Through this trial Ito became a widely recognized celebrity.

After being admitted to the bar, Ito worked in private practice for two years before joining the Los Angeles County district attorney's office. Here he worked prosecuting cases of gang violence. In 1987, then Republican governor George Deukmejian appointed Ito, a Democrat, a municipal court judge. Two years later Deukmejian appointed him to the Superior Court bench. In 1992 the Los Angeles Bar Association named Ito Trial Judge of the Year. In 1996 the alumni association at Ito's high school, John Marshall, presented him with its Distinguished Alumni Award.

Ito has been characterized as well prepared, hardworking, no-nonsense, low key, and fair. Further, he is known to be affable as well as somewhat of a prankster. It is said that he gets to work at 6 A.M. and has a pillow and blanket in his chamber. Judge Ito frequently points out that his parents, schoolteachers, were imprisoned during World War II in internment camps, as were other West Coast Japanese Americans. He says that this strongly influenced his choosing the law as a career.

Ito's personal interests include long-distance marathon running. He is also an amateur photographer and collects fountain pens. Ito first met his wife-to-be, Margaret York, when he was working as a young prosecutor. She was then a Los Angeles police detective. York is now a captain who heads up the bunco-forgery unit, the highest-ranking woman in the Los Angeles Police Department. The couple do not have children, live in Pasadena, and often spend weekends at their second home in Baja California, Mexico.

Selected Bibliography

Gleick, Elizabeth, Danelle Morton, and Lois Armstrong. "Order in the Court: The
O.J. Files." *People* magazine, O.J. Central on the World Wide Web.
Granelli, James S. "Judge Gives No Hints about Keating Sentencing." *Los Angeles
Times*, April 10, 1992, p. D2.

Steve Fugita

PHILIP JAISOHN (SEO, JAE-P'IL)
(1864–1951)
Political Activist, Physician

Born on November 28, 1864, in Tongbok district in South Cheolla province of Korea, into an elite class called the *yangban* during the Yi dynasty
(1392–1910), Jae-p'il Seo was sent as an adoptive son to another magistrate who had no male heir. He had many disagreements with his new
family but was still expected to bring fame, fortune, and honor to them
by passing the civil service examination, called *kwageo*. Because of the
poor condition of education in his district he was sent to an uncle who
lived in Seoul, and there he attended a private school that prepared him
for this important state-administered examination.

After passing the test with top scores and atop his class at age thirteen,
Seo became the youngest graduate of the school. Upon graduation, he
and his classmates went to Japan to study military science at the Toyama
Junior Military School in Tokyo, where he learned military tactics, modern sciences, geography, and history. In 1884 Seo and his nine friends
graduated from the school with honors and immediately came back to
their native country in hopes of using their skills to strengthen their
nation's military power.

Disappointed deeply in the government's inability or unwillingness to
call on them to serve the nation, Seo and his friends decided to stage a
coup d'etat on December 4, 1884. It was successful, and they took over
the reigns of government. But due to the Chinese intervention in the
Korean government's affairs, he and his associates had to give up their
power three days later and flee to Japan, where Jaisohn taught Korean
language to American missionaries. Dissatisfied with the lack of Japanese
support for them, Seo and two of his friends, Pak Yeong-hyo and Seo

Kwang-peom, decided to come to the United States, where they arrived in April 1885. Upon arrival in San Francisco, Seo attended English classes while working at odd jobs.

Seo left San Francisco in 1887 for Harry Hillman Academy in Wilkes-Barre, Pennsylvania, to continue his study with the support of an American, J. W. Hollenback, who wanted to train him as an evangelical missionary to be sent back to Korea. Upon graduating from the academy in three years, Seo entered Lafayette College but could not complete his study due to lack of money. Leaving Easton, Pennsylvania, in search of opportunity to work and study, he found a job at the Army Medical Library in Washington, D.C., as a Japanese language translator. He entered George Washington University Medical School, graduating with his medical degree in 1895. That same year he married Muriel Armstrong, daughter of George Armstrong, a major in the United States Army. By this time Seo had become a naturalized citizen of the United States with an American name, Philip Jaisohn.

When Seo was invited by his friend, Pak Yeong-hyo, to join him in his effort to modernize Korea, he gladly accepted the invitation and came back to Korea in January 1896 with his wife. He was later appointed advisor to the Privy Council to advise King Kojong on national and international affairs. While serving in that capacity he established Korea's first modern newspaper, *Tongnip Sinmun* (the Independent), and founded a political organization, Tongnip Hyeop-hoe, or the Independent Club. Many prominent Koreans joined the Club and worked toward the goal of maintaining and strengthening Korea's independence.

Because the club he helped to found became very successful in bringing about political changes, Seo became a persona non grata in the eyes of conservative politicians in the Korean court, including King Kojong. The king asked the American minister to have Seo removed from Korea, and when he was refused, he used other means to expel him. Seo came back to the United States in 1898 and resumed his medical practice.

In 1947 Seo was invited again to come to Korea as chief advisor on Korean affairs to the commanding general of the U.S. Army forces in Korea. The commanding General was L. General John R. Hodge. Seo disagreed with **Syngman Rhee** on the method of bringing into existence one government that would include both southern and northern parts of Korea, occupied by American and Soviet Russian forces, respectively. Seo also disagreed with Kim Ku and Kim Kyu-sik for their plan to go to North Korea. When Seo realized that he could no longer work with General Hodge and Korean political leaders, he left Korea to come back to America in September 1948. Seo died on January 5, 1951.

Selected Bibliography

Liem, Channing. *America's Finest Gift to Korea: The Life of Philip Jaisohn*. New York: William Frederick Press, 1952.

———. *Philip Jaisohn*. Elkins Park, PA: Philip Jaisohn Memorial Foundation, 1984.

Hyung-chan Kim

INDIRA FREITAS JOHNSON
(1943–   )
Artist, Cultural Worker

Indira Freitas Johnson, known for her art and social work around the world, was born on August 17, 1943, as the second of six girls and three boys. Her family lived in Bombay, India, where her father was an art director for the newspaper *Times of India* and her mother was the founder of a social work organization that focused on leprosy control and community development. As a student, Johnson received poor grades throughout her school career, including zero marks in her high school art classes. Her teachers advised her not to continue her art studies, but her father encouraged her to pursue her interest in art. Her parents, in fact, were convinced that she would become an artist.

Johnson did well on her yearly examinations and graduated from high school at the age of fourteen. She entered Sofia College and later transferred to Sir J. J. Institute of Applied Art in Bombay. She also attended the University of Bombay and in 1964 graduated from both institutions, receiving a B.A. in English from the University as well as an arts diploma from the Institute of Applied Art. She came to the United States to further her studies on a full scholarship to St. Xaviers College on the south side of Chicago. She soon transferred to the School of the Art Institute of Chicago, from which she graduated in 1967 with a Master's degree in fine art.

During her studies at the Chicago Art Institute, Johnson met and later married Karl Johnson. Together they traveled to Sweden, where her husband studied at the University of Lund. She first starting working with clay and sculpting during this period, attending a small art center called a Folk Universitet. Before going to Sweden, all of Johnson's formal training had been in advertising design, a field in which she worked after returning to Chicago. She gave up the advertising business when she was expecting her second child in order to become a fulltime artist and mother.

Johnson has exhibited her ceramic sculptures widely in the United States, as well as in Europe and India. She incorporates both Indian and American symbols, images, and experiences in her work. "Two vastly different . . . worlds come together in her life. She uses her sculpture to express and balance these dichotomies" (Price 1996). Her work also reflects her efforts to combine her interest in Buddhist philosophy with her Indian Christian upbringing. Many of her sculptures represent life as a "spiritual journey" in which "life's daily occurences exert their own push and pull, challenging us at different levels. How we deal with these challenges helps us accumulate various strengths and energies" (quoted in Price 1996).

Many of her works address these life challenges. In one piece, "Suspended Balance," Johnson places a woman's torso on top of a wheel. The precariously balanced figure represents the many roles that women must juggle in their lives. She also has sculpted an on-going series of baggage carts, inspired by a cart commonly used in India by the working poor and homeless to move their goods from place to place. To Johnson the cart represents the psychological as well as physical baggage that each individual carries. "What is often not immediately apparent in her baggage carts is that each is created in the form of the human body with shoulders, hips or feet ready to be grasped" (Price 1996).

Johnson has consistently integrated her art with pressing social concerns. She has collaborated on a series of projects with community groups such as SHARE (Support the Handicapped's Rehabilitation Effort), a Bombay-based group of women and persons with disabilities. In 1993 she founded the Shanti: Foundation for Peace, an organization that uses art to bring people together to address issues of mutual concern. The Chicago-based foundation focuses on programs that foster positive relations and peace between cultures and communities through education, the arts, and grassroots community development.

In 1994, under the directorship of Johnson, the Shanti Foundation initiated the "Getting Along/Peace Bus" project with the Chicago Children's Museum and the Chicago Transit Authority. The children's visions and expressions of a peaceful community were transformed into public art work that appears on the sides of a public bus. As director of the project, Johnson had the opportunity to work directly with many inner-city children. She notes, "They have such a simple ways of expressing themselves, of coming right to the point. . . . You see how violence affects children most of all. Some of them told me that if there was peace they would be able to go out and play in their yard. That seems like such a basic wish" (quoted in Lindegard 1995).

In connection with the Shanti project, Johnson has launched a pilot program in four Chicago public schools called Nonviolence in Action. It uses art to teach and explore nonviolent practices. She also has collaborated on an art installation project with women from the domestic violence shelter, Apna Ghar, in Chicago.

Johnson is widely recognized for her work and has received many awards given by institutions such as the Illinois Arts Council, Arts Midwest, Arts International Travel Grant, and the Kohler Company. Her work appears in many public and private collections, including the State of Illinois Building, College of DePage, Arkansas Arts Center, University of Illinois Law School, Air India Corporation, Kohler Company, and High Museum of Art.

In 1997 Johnson received the Governor's Award for the Arts, which is given biannually to an Illinois artist in recognition of artistic distinction and achievement.

Selected Bibliography

Bonesteel, Michael. "Sculptors Face Off in 'Contrast.' " *Pioneer Press*, March 12, 1992, p. D5.

Coburn, Marcia Froelke. "Throwing Curves." *Chicago Magazine*, October 1993, pp. 29–31.

Lindegard, Janice. "Small Steps toward Peace Go Long Way." *Today's Chicago Woman*, April 1995.

Padgett, Deborah McWatters. "Valuable Offerings: The Ceramic Sculpture of Indira Freitas-Johnson." *Ceramics Monthly*, April 1996, pp. 58–60.

Price, Sandra. "Indira Freitas Johnson: Journey of an Artist." *Ceramics: Art and Perception*, no. 26 (1996): 1–3.

Jane Singh

K. CONNIE KANG

(1942–)

Journalist, Author

K. Connie Kang, an award-winning reporter for the *Los Angeles Times*, was the first Korean woman journalist in the United States and the first Korean to work for a major American daily newspaper. K. Connie Kang (Kang, Kyonshill), whose name means "steady," was born on November

K. Connie Kang

11, 1942, in Hamheung, South Hamgyeong province, now in North Korea, not far from her ancestral home of Tanch'eon. She is the first child of Kang, Joo Han, a teacher of English and German. His family was among the first to embrace Christianity in Korea at the turn of the century. His religion and love of the English language were two things that have influenced Kang's life profoundly.

It was for Christianity that her family left everything behind in Tanch'eon, where the Kang clan had lived for six hundred years. It also was his father's love of the English language, which Connie Kang inherited from him, that inspired her career in journalism that began in the summer of 1964.

Kang's introduction to English came at age three, when her father sat her on his lap and taught her to memorize John 14:6 in English. So, when her father, who taught English at Seoul National University, left for the United States in the spring of 1950 as a Fulbright scholar, young Connie felt as if America was part of her life.

Her journey from Tanch'eon on the northern tip of the Korean peninsula in 1946 to Los Angeles in 1950 was a tumultuous and circuitous one that spanned three countries—Korea, Japan, and the United States—and three languages and cultures.

In her critically acclaimed book *Home Was the Land of Morning Calm: A Saga of a Korean American Family*, Kang has interwoven her family's story with 100 years of modern Korean and Korean American history. She pulls the reader into her mind, heart, and soul on a journey of the extraordinary family—from the privileged life of landed gentry to the hard life of operating a grocery store in urban California. Hers is a story of the Korean diaspora and 75 million ethnic Koreans everywhere.

Growing up in Japan, Connie was introduced to two new cultures almost simultaneously. She lived among Japanese, speaking their language in public but using Korean in the privacy of home, while attending an international school where her education was conducted in English. She made friends with people of many ethnic backgrounds.

Her dream was to write in English. Finding no role models among Korean women, she looked for role models in non-Koreans like Pearl S. Buck and journalists Marguerite Higgins and Inez Robb. By the time she was a high school sophomore and began to edit her school paper, she was determined to become a newspaper woman.

She chose the world's oldest school of journalism at the University of Missouri to pursue her dream. While a student at the School of Journalism, she worked at a local newspaper. She received her B.A. degree in journalism in 1963, the first Korean woman to do so. From there she went on to the Medill School of Journalism at Northwestern University, where she earned a Master of Science degree in journalism—again the first Korean to do so. A week later she moved clear across the country to Rochester, New York, to work as a reporter at the *Democrat and Chronicle*.

In the ensuing three decades she has worked for seven American news organizations, including the *Los Angeles Times, San Francisco Examiner*, and *San Francisco Chronicle*, United Press International, and for newspapers and magazines in Asia as a reporter, editor, foreign correspondent, editorial writer, and columnist. Her coverage of the California Supreme Court, both its law and politics, has won her more than thirty professional awards. In 1997 Kang was awarded the Lifetime Achievement Award by the Asian American Journalists Association.

In her book *Home Was the Land of Morning Calm*, Kang writes that her encounter with America has changed her life: "It opened my eyes to a world where people made choices based on their individual preferences. In America, individualism reigned, not family consensus. America provided me with a new set of eyes to judge my own culture and value systems, and my contact with America sparked an internal revolution that continues to this day" (p. xiv).

Kang was among a handful of Korean American journalists who founded the Korean American Journalists Association. She has spent many years in service to the Korean American community, conducting seminars and workshops and mentoring many aspiring journalists.

However assimilated she might feel at times, and however much her profession and her acculturation pull her into mainstream America, she says she identifies with immigrants because she is one of them. In mind and body, she travels back and forth between several worlds—a lifelong struggle to reconcile her many worlds of vast differences. "Within me, the duality of being a Korean and an American requires me to continue the mental gymnastics of moving back and forth between these often-conflicting two worlds. The tensions of being both remain, but have eased somewhat. I am more American than Korean in my mind, but I am more Korean than American in my soul," states Kang in *Home Was the Land of Morning Calm* (p. xiv).

Selected Bibliography

Kang, K. Connie. *Home Was the Land of Morning Calm: A Saga of a Korean American Family*. Reading, MA: Addison-Wesley, 1995.

Kyo, Nobuko (trans.), and K. Connie Kang. *Harukanaru Shizukeki Asano Kuni* (A Faraway Land in Serene Morning. Tokyo: Aoyama Shupan, 1995.

Lee, Young-A. *Hankookin imni-da, Jarang seureowun Hanin kyop'odeul* (I am Korean: Overseas Koreans who give us pride). Seoul: Doseo ch'ulp'ansa, 1997.

Stolz, Preble. *Judging Judges: The Investigation of Rose Bird and the California Supreme Court*. New York: Free Press, 1981.

Hyung-chan Kim

SEN KATAYAMA

(1860–1933)

Union Organizer

Sen Katayama, socialist and union organizer, was born Sugataro Yabuki on January 8, 1860, close to Hadeki in central Okayama, Japan. His father and mother were Kunizo and Kichi Yabuki. They had two sons, firstborn Mokutaro and Sugataro (Sen Katayama). The family wanted a daughter, and consequently Sugataro's birth was somewhat of a disappointment. Kunizo, caught up in a family quarrel, was forced to dissolve his marriage with Kichi and left the household for a monastery in 1864. This left Sugataro a fatherless child with no legal share of the family property, which all passed to the eldest son, Mokutaro.

Katayama's education in the pre-Meiji period consisted of private tutors and the *terakoya*, or Buddhist temple schools. However, during the Meiji era a new school opened in Hadeki, and Katayama enrolled in it at age fourteen, graduating in November 1874. The school had an innovative teaching method and a new curriculum, focusing less on Chinese classics. Katayama blossomed under this new teaching style and curriculum.

Subsequently the family experienced financial difficulties, and Katayama quit school to help his mother with field work. He began self-schooling and received a teaching position in Yuge, near Hadeki. In the following year he taught at the Uetsuki primary school.

Kichi, fearing conscription for Suataro, arranged for his adoption by Ikutaro Katayama, a peasant in nearby Shimo-Kamine. Sugataro Yabuki thus became Sen Katayama. With this adoption, he escaped the draft and cut all ties with his family.

Katayama began to prepare for the competitive entrance examinations into the Normal School in Okayama City. He made the top of the list of eligible candidates. At the end of the summer of 1881, after completing his studies at the Normal School, Katayama planned to continue his studies in Tokyo. Unfortunately, travel expenses to Tokyo depleted his savings, leaving nothing for education. Katayama was forced to concentrate on making money. His first job was with Sekibun-Sha, a printing operation in downtown Tokyo, working with the press machine. His second assignment was as a typesetter.

In order to reduce the cost of living and save money, in the winter of 1882 Katayama moved to Oka Juku, a small preparatory school and lodging house. Here he could resume his studies. Soon thereafter he quit Sekibun-Sha and worked as the school servant at Oka Juku. He was also the student assistant for Oka Shikamon, accompanying him on lecture tours about Confucius.

In the spring of 1883 Katayama entered the Kodama-Sha, a private preparatory school for those who wanted a career in the navy. Again, he worked as a school servant. As Kodama-Sha was not to his liking, he soon left and returned to Oka Juku. Soon thereafter he left to teach Chinese studies in Fujioka, a provincial town northwest of Tokyo.

In 1884 a close friend who was living in San Francisco informed him of the good prospects for students in the United States. Prompted by this, Katayama borrowed money for passage to the United States. He arrived with one Mexican peso to his name, which amounted to 60 cents in U.S. currency.

Poor English skills forced Katayama to continue working in menial jobs, with little time to study. When he obtained a position as a domestic in Alameda, he was able to take English night classes at a Chinese mission. At this time he converted to Christianity. He then attended Hopkins Academy of Oakland, which was one of two private boarding schools in the area that allowed students to matriculate into universities without having to take examinations.

Katayama left California in December 1887 and headed east to attend

Maryville College in Tennessee. Finances again forced him to change schools and transfer to Grinnell College in Iowa. He obtained his B.A. degree from Grinnell in 1892. Katayama next attended Andover Theological Seminary in Massachusetts while working as a cook to support himself. In September 1894 he moved to New Haven to attend the Yale Divinity School, where he earned his B.D. degree in 1895.

Katayama returned to Japan in 1895 as an English instructor at Waseda Preparatory School. At this time he began his long writing career. His first book was *Tetsudo Shinron* (Essay on the Railroad Problem). After suffering from smallpox, he was dismissed from Waseda Preparatory in 1896.

At this time Reverend Daniel C. Greene offered Katayama a position as the director of a settlement house in Japan. Katayama formed Kingsley Hall, a college settlement named after the famous English Christian Socialist and located in Kanda, a poor section of Tokyo. It opened on March 1, 1897. He gave orientation sessions for the students who wanted to go to the United States. In 1901, drawing on his experiences in the United States, Katayama wrote *Gakusei Tobei Annai* (Student Guide to America), which sold 2,000 copies the first week after its release. He also gave lectures on socialism, sociology, economics, German, and English.

Through arrangements made by a friend, Katayama married Fude Yokodzuka in 1897. At the time he was thirty-eight years old. The couple had two children: daughter Yasuko, born in 1899, and son Kan'ichi, born in 1907. Kan'ichi died of double pneumonia in 1922.

Katayama became a union organizer in 1897, establishing the Rodo Kumiai Kiseikai (Society for the Promotion of Trade Unions). This was Japan's first trade union. He edited the *Rodo Sekai* (Labor World), the first labor journal, produced by the Rodo Kumiai Kiseikai. As secretary general of the Iron Workers Union and as editor of its publication, *Rodo Sekai*, Katayama fought for improved working conditions and workers' rights.

Katayama became a member of the Shakaishugi Kenkyukai (Socialist Study Society), which was the start of the Japanese socialist movement. In 1901 Katayama and three others, Abe Isoo, Kaneko Kiichi, and Kotoku Shusui, formed the Shakai Minshuto (Social Democratic Party), the first socialist party in Japan. However, Minister for Home Affairs Baron Suematsu suppressed the Shakai Minshuto and prevented its printed materials from being circulated. In order to continue its existence, the party became an educational organization and was led by Abe Isoo. It sponsored public lectures on socialism and labor problems.

In 1902 Katayama founded the Association for the America-Bound in Tokyo, printing pamphlets and travel guides to encourage immigration to the United States. The organization also began a rice farming colony in Texas in 1906. Katayama purchased 160 acres of land in Colorado

County, but the venture was unsuccessful. The organization did, however, become financially successful through the popularity of the guidebooks and magazines. In July 1903 Katayama published his book *Waga Shakai Shugi* (Socialism to Me), which examined the evolution of industrial capitalism.

Katayama's second visit to the United States in 1904 consisted mostly of lectures and tours. He attended the National Convention of the American Socialist Party in Chicago. He lectured on socialism to Japanese immigrants in San Francisco and organized the Soko Nihonjin Shakaito (San Francisco Japanese Socialist Party). This party was short-lived, but the thirty-eight members did convene for an antiwar meeting at the San Francisco Methodist-Episcopal Church. Katayama left for Amsterdam to attend the 6th Congress of the Second International as a delegate from the Japanese Socialist Association. In Amsterdam he was the only Asian in attendance, but he was elected vice-president of the convocation. After Europe, Katayama returned to Texas to study agricultural settlements. His wife, Fude, passed away soon after he left for the United States.

Katayama returned to Japan in January 1906. In May 1907 he remarried 31-year-old Hara Tama of Aomori, Honshua, and in 1908 their daughter Chiyoko was born. Years later, during Katayama's fourth trip to the United States, Hara Tama left him.

When the government disbanded the socialist newspaper *Nikkan Heimin* (Commoner's Daily), Katayama sought to continue to keep the Japanese workers informed about socialism by founding the *Shakai Shimbun* (Socialist News) in June 1907. This newspaper survived for more than four years.

In June 1908 Morkchika, the editor of the *Osaka Heimin*, was released from prison. Gathered at his release were the parliamentarian socialists and "direct action" anarchists/socialists. The police were also there, as they anticipated demonstrations. At the end of the program, two flags were unfurled by two direct action proponents. Inscribed on the flags were "Anarchism" and "Common Property under Anarchism." Police rushed in and made many arrests. After this skirmish, known as the Red Flag Affair, the police and government increased their pressure on the socialists, crippling the movement.

Another incident that led to increased government pressure was a strike against the Tokyo trolley owners. The owners "capitulated" on January 15, 1912. Katayama and sixty others were arrested, and he was charged with incitement to strike. After spending three and one half months in jail, he was sentenced to five more months in Chiba Prison. Due to constant police harassment after his release, Katayama returned to the United States in 1914. During this time he attended several labor league meetings, where it was suggested that he become manager of the adjunct labor club. However, because he was listed as a subversive by the Japanese government, his involvement as a leader in the league was likely to discredit it. As a result, he was asked to sever his ties with the league. Many Japanese immigrants regarded Katayama as "a dangerous man."

In 1915 Katayama founded the Japanese Labor Federation of America, and in 1916 he began publishing the *Heimin* (Commoner), a Japanese/English monthly magazine. In the same year Katayama brought his older daughter, Yasuko, and her cousin, Nobuko, to San Francisco. His wife in Japan, harassed by the police because of her relationship to Katayama, moved back home and stopped using her married name.

With a ticket to New York from S. J. Rutgers, leader of the left-wing faction of the Dutch Socialist Party, Katayama and his daughter left San Francisco for New York in November 1916. Because he was the only internationally known Japanese socialist, Rutgers wanted Katayama to be an ally in his political party, which was sympathetic to Lenin and the Bolsheviks. In New York, Katayama met with Russian socialists such as Leon Trotsky, as well as American socialists. He made many political connections and was given a leadership position in what later became the American Communist Party.

In 1917 Katayama began to write a series of articles entitled "The Labor Movement in Japan" for the *International Socialist Review*. This series was later consolidated into a book of the same title. The articles focused on the socialist and labor movements in Japan between 1897 and 1912. During speeches, he often supported the Bolshevik Revolution. As a result, Katayama was subjected to the "Palmer raids" of Attorney General Alexander Mitchell Palmer, in which 3,000 suspected "subversive aliens" were rounded up. After this, Katayama moved to Mexico to start agitating for Communism.

On December 14, 1921, at the age of sixty-two, Katayama moved to Moscow. Though attempts to create a proletarian revolutionary movement in Japan failed, Katayama obtained a permanent position in the Comintern (Communist International organization). At the 3rd Congress he was the Japanese Communist Party's representative, and at the 4th Congress he was elected to the Executive Committee of the Comintern (ECCI) and to a seat in the Presidium, a twelve-man committee. He retained these positions at the 1924 5th Congress and the 1928 6th Congress. On December 7, 1929, on Katayama's seventieth birthday, he was honored in Russia by being nominated for membership in the exclusive Bolshevik Club.

Katayama's health declined sharply in 1932. He suffered from a heart condition, the grippe, and fatigue. On November 5, 1933, at seventy-four, he died. Katayama was buried in the Kremlin, with 150,000 people in attendance at his funeral.

Selected Bibliography

Ichioka, Yuji. *The Issei: The World of the First Generation Japanese Immigrants, 1885–1924*. New York and London: Free Press, 1899.

Katayama, S. *The Labor Movement in Japan*. Chicago: C. H. Kerr, 1918.

Kublin, Hyman. *Asian Revolutionary: The Life of Sen Katayama*. Princeton, NJ: Princeton University Press, 1964.

Niiya, Brian, ed. *Japanese American History: An A-to-Z Reference from 1868 to the Present*. New York: Facts on File, 1993.

Steve Fugita

JAMES K. KEALOHA
(1908–1983)
Politician

James K. Kealoha was the first elected lieutenant governor when Hawaii became a state in 1959. With his victory, he also became the first Hawaiian Chinese to be elected to a statewide office in the United States.

James Kealoha was born on April 29, 1908, in Pahoa on the island of Hawaii to Lee Chau and Alice Makinui Kealoha. His father was a Cantonese immigrant who had come to Hawaii as a plantation laborer. While growing up James was raised by his grandparents, whose name he assumed. Later he decided to add *Kimo* as his middle name. In the Chinese community in Hawaii, he was commonly known as Lee Yat Wo. He graduated from Hilo High School in 1926 and started working as a clerk for Kwong See Wo, a grocery store in Hilo. In 1929 he married Muilan Young, with whom he had two daughters, Leihulu Emma and Leiohu Lillie. In the next year he opened his own grocery, which he operated until 1948 when he devoted full time to his candidacy for the chairmanship of Hawaii County.

In 1934, when James Kealoha was twenty-six years old, he won election to the Territorial House of Representatives and reelection two years later. In 1938, at age thirty, he successfully ran for a seat in the Territorial Senate. Held in high esteem by his colleagues, he was a speaker pro-tem while in the House and a president pro-tem while in the Senate. His large margins and the surprising ease with which he won elections led him to be regarded by observers as the "Wonder

Boy" of Hawaiian politics. In that same year he switched to the Republican Party, saying that he was unhappy with internal fighting within the Democratic Party.

In 1940 Kealoha was elected to the Hawaii County Board of Supervisors. Reelected to three successive terms, he suffered one defeat in 1946 in his bid for county chairman. The setback was only temporary, however, and he subsequently won six successive terms as Hawaii County chairman, starting in 1948. His popularity and leadership bolstered the Republican cause in Hawaii County, for it was the only area to withstand the Democratic landslide in the territorial elections of 1954, an event that some historians have dubbed the "bloodless revolution" against the traditional power structure of Hawaii.

Such a distinction could not escape notice. In 1959 the Republican Party selected Kealoha to be its candidate for lieutenant governor in the state of Hawaii's first gubernatorial election. Local born and well liked, he balanced the ticket by running alongside William F. Quinn, the party's candidate for governor. The formula worked as the pair successfully defeated their Democratic opponents—the gubernatorial candidate, John Burns, and the candidate for lieutenant governor, Mitsuyuki Kido.

While Republicans were delighted by the victory, the next few years were unpleasant for Kealoha. The pairing of Quinn and Kealoha was not as successful as it was presumed to be. Accustomed to being a powerful Hawaii County chairman, Kealoha chafed at being a lieutenant governor with little to do except presiding at ceremonial functions. He also disagreed with Quinn over the awarding of political patronage. In 1962 he challenged Quinn in the Republican gubernatorial primary. He presented himself as a "native son" and a "local boy" in a bitter contest but lost the primary. Seeking reconciliation with Kealoha, Quinn appointed him to a three-year post as the executive officer for the Hawaii exhibit at the New York World's Fair. Later in the general election of that year, Quinn was in turn defeated by his Democratic opponent, John Burns.

James Kealoha still harbored political ambitions but failed to make a comeback. In 1966 he ran unsuccessfully for a seat in the U.S. House of Representatives against incumbent Democrat **Masayuki "Spark" Matsunaga**. In the course of the campaign Kealoha shocked the Republican Party by taking a strong stand against the war in Vietnam. He opposed further expansion of the war and proposed an end to the bombing of North Vietnam without any conditions demanded from Hanoi. His statements stunned fellow Republicans and cheered Democrats in their election efforts. In 1968 he ran for mayor on the island of Hawaii but was again unsuccessful.

Along with his political defeats, James Kealoha experienced business difficulties. Representing a group of investors from Hawaii operating a restaurant and show concession at the Montreal World Expo in Canada, he was forced to file bankruptcy in 1967. In 1977 he and his wife became the victims of a hotel and condominium scam that also resulted in bankruptcy. In his later years Kealoha grew papayas in Hawaii and owned a farm in Salem, Oregon. He died on August 24, 1983, in Honolulu.

Selected Bibliography

Black, Forrest. "Kealoha Campaigns for Governor as 'Native Son.'" *Honolulu Star-Bulletin*, August 31, 1962.
Borg, Jim. "James Kealoha Dead at 75." *Honolulu Advertiser*, July 25, 1983.
Casey, Brian. "Mr. Kealoha's 'Sunny Jim.'" *Honolulu Advertiser*, December 13, 1959.
Cavaliero, Eric, and Eddie Sherman. "Kealoha Files Bankruptcy for Exhibition." *Honolulu Advertiser*, September 11, 1967.
Goodfader, Al. "Quinn for Governor; Suggests Kealoha for 'No. 2' Post." *Honolulu Advertiser*, April 5, 1959.
Harada, Wayne. "Kealoha Stand Surprises Spark." *Honolulu Advertiser*, October 8, 1966.
McManus, Larry. "Kealoha's Speech Cheers Democrats." *Honolulu Advertiser*, October 8, 1966.

Franklin Ng

FAZLUR RAHMAN KHAN
(1929–1982)
Engineer, Educator

Eulogized by the *New York Times*, the *Chicago Tribune* and *Time* magazine, among other publications, as one of the greatest structural engineers of modern times, Fazlur Rahman Khan, a Bangladesh-born structural engineer, is credited with designing some of tallest concrete and steel buildings in the world. In 1968 Khan became known as the designer of the world's tallest concrete skyscraper. He used pioneering techniques of combining concrete with steel to design the skyscraper in Houston, Texas. Khan then led the design teams that produced the tallest and fourth tallest office buildings in the world, the Sears Tower and the John Hancock Center in Chicago.

Khan was born on April 3, 1929, in Dhaka, Bengal, in what was then British India, to Abdur Rahman and Khadija Khatun. His father had been granted the title Khan Bahadur by the government for his contributions to public education, and his mother, though not formally educated herself, shared her husband's commitment to education. When young Fazlur refused to begin formal schooling, it was his mother who convinced him to attend. He became an excellent student who graduated at the top of his class from Shibpur Engineering College, Calcutta, India, in 1950. For the next two years he taught at the Ahsanullah Engineering College, which later became the Bangladesh University of Engineering and Technology. In 1952 Fazlur was awarded both Fulbright and Ford Foundation scholarships for graduate studies at the University of Illinois, Urbana, in the United States. There he earned two M.S. degrees and a Ph.D. in structural engineering by 1955.

Khan's professional career in the United States began in 1955 with the well-known architectural firm Skidmore, Owings, and Merrill headquartered in Chicago. After working as a structural engineer for two years, Khan returned to his home country, East Pakistan, which in 1971 became the independent nation of Bangladesh. He took a position as technical advisor to the Chief Engineer's Office of the Karachi Development Authority. In 1960, while still in Karachi, he married Lislette Anne Olga Turba of Vienna, Austria, an artist with a degree in biology. In the following year the Khans had a daughter, Yasmin, who later followed in the footsteps of her father and became a structural engineer.

The Khans returned to the United States in 1960, and Fazlur resumed work at Skidmore, Owings, and Merrill. Khan soon achieved distinction by setting a new trend in the design of tall structures. He was concerned with both the social and visual impact of buildings and was constantly searching for new structural systems to enhance a building's natural strength. David P. Billington, a professor of civil engineering at Princeton University, described Khan as a great structural artist whose understanding of buildings was unsurpassed. Billington pointed out that Khan's remarkable understanding of building materials allowed him to combine steel and concrete in innovative ways.

Besides his two most famous structural creations, Chicago's John Hancock Center and the Sears Tower, Khan's designs include the tent-like Jeddah Airport, Hajj Terminal, in Saudi Arabia. Other U.S. buildings such as One Shell Plaza in Houston, Texas; the De-Witt Chestnut Building, Onterie Center, and the Brunswick Building in Chicago, to name a few, have all demonstrated Khan's ability to create forms that are structurally sound, aesthetically attractive, and environmentally safe. Khan's view was that modern cities, especially inner cities, could be made more habitable and inviting by having structures that were visually appealing, spacious, and safe.

An advocate of collaboration, Khan insisted on working closely with architects in designing and building complex tall structures. He not only reinforced the natural bond between engineering and architecture but brought practitioners from both fields closer together as builders. The fact that he truly believed in such cooperation and coordination of engineers and architectural activities was clearly demonstrated by a letter he wrote to *Newsweek* after the magazine published a story about him with his picture against the background of the Sears Tower captioned "Man at the Top," recognizing him as the designer of the tallest building in the world. In his letter Khan reiterated the role of collaboration in designing and building tall structures. In particular he emphasized the part played by his architect partner, Bruce Graham. Subsequently he was given a gold medal by the Association of Architects for his unique contributions to architectural engineering.

Khan received many national and international awards for his works, including the Agha Khan Medal for Architecture for the Hajj Terminal at Jeddah Airport, an honorary doctorate from Lehigh University, Pennsylvania, and the creation of a Chair in his name at both Lehigh and the Bangladesh University of Engineering and Technology. Additionally, Fazlur R. Khan Institutes devoted to research and design of high-rise buildings were established at each of the universities.

Khan remained involved and concerned with the social and political issues of his home country. During the conflict between East and West Pakistan of the 1970s, he organized an effective group of advocates to mobilize American public opinion concerning military actions taken against the people of East Pakistan. After a civil war between East and West Pakistan, the former became the independent nation of Bangladesh. Khan's advocacy group became known as the Bangladesh Foundation, an organization that continues to provide social services in Bangladesh today.

The Khan family made their home in Chicago. Fazlur R. Khan died on March 27, 1982.

Selected Bibliography

Bennett, David, et al. *Skyscrapers*. New York: Simon and Schuster, 1995.
Billington, David P. *The Tower and the Bridge*. New York: Basic Books, 1983.
Billington, David P., and Myron Goldsmith. *Technique and Aesthetics in the Design of Tall Buildings: Fazlur R. Khan Session on Structural Expression in Buildings*. Bethlehem, PA: Institute for Study of the High-Rise Habitat, Lehigh University, 1986.

McGraw-Hill's Construction Weekly, August 26, 1971.
Time, April 12, 1982, p. 45.

                                                    Zillur R. Khan

JAY KIM

(1939–   )

Congressman, Politician

Jay Kim was the first Korean congressman to be elected in the United States. In 1992 he was elected to represent the 41st District of California, which covers San Bernardino, Orange County, and Los Angeles. Following the election he was selected to be on the Public Works and Transportation Committee and the Small Business Committee.

Born in Seoul, South Korea, on March 27, 1939, Jay Kim came to California in 1961 at the age of twenty-two. He attended school in southern California, where he earned his Bachelor's and Master's degrees in civil engineering in 1967. He also earned a Master's in public administration from California State University at Los Angeles.

In 1976 Kim founded his own engineering design firm, which he later sold after being elected to Congress. It was one of the five minority-owned businesses to help rebuild Los Angeles after the devastating earthquake that crippled the city in 1992. During a decline in business, Jay Kim decided to run for Congress in 1992 after serving in the Diamond Bar City Council from 1990 to 1991 and, later, as the mayor of Diamond Bar, California, from 1991 to 1992.

Representing a predominantly white-collar and racially mixed district, he ran on a platform that supported abortion rights and favored fewer regulations on businesses. Kim went on to win the election to the 103rd Congress with 60 percent of the overall votes after a surprise victory in the Republican primary of the newly designated 41st District of California.

After winning his last three terms in office, on July 31, 1997, Jay Kim and his wife, June, were charged with concealing more than $230,000 in illegal campaign contributions. The Kims had been under investigation since 1993. On August 11, 1997, Congressman Kim and his wife pleaded guilty to misdemeanor violations of federal election law. In addition, his campaign committee was charged with violations of federal election law, although Kim is not being held personally responsible.

Facing a maximum of six months in prison and $635,000 in fines, Jay Kim was sentenced by Federal Judge Richard Paez on March 9, 1998, and placed on one-year probation, for two months of which he was required to wear an electronic monitoring device. He was also ordered to serve 200 hours of community service and pay a $5,000 fine. June Kim was sentenced to one-year probation with 250 hours of community service and a $5,000 fine. Kim's campaign committee was also convicted of criminal charges and was ordered to pay $170,000 and placed on five-year probation.

Due to his misdemeanor plea rather than a felony conviction, Kim is allowed to keep his seat in Congress. During his two-month home detention period Kim was able to fulfill his duties as a congressman and was allowed to travel between Washington, D.C., and California. Kim campaigned for reelection in California's June 1998 primary without success while under investigation for campaign violations and other misconduct allegations by a four-member panel of the House Ethics Committee.

Selected Bibliography

Burton, Jonathan. "A Dream Come True." *Far Eastern Economic Review*, vol. 155 (October 29, 1992): 55–56.

Lacayo, Richard. "The Outsiders." *Time*, vol. 140 (November 2, 1992): 44–46.

Pincus, Walter. "Rep. Kim Expects Confinement Won't Halt His Campaign." *Washington Post*, March 11, 1998.

Rosenzweig, David. "Rep. Kim, Wife Plead Guilty in Illegal Contributions Case." *Los Angeles Times*, August 12, 1997, p. B3.

———. "Rep. Kim, Wife to Plead Guilty to Misdemeanors." *Los Angeles Times*, August 1, 1997, pp. A1, A26.

Chae Reed

RICHARD KIM

(1932–)

Author, Educator

Richard Kim is one of the great inspirations for the Korean American Society. Through his works such as *Trans-Siberian Railway* and *Koreans in China and Russia*, people are educated about the lives and migration of the Korean people throughout Asia and Russia.

Born on March 13, 1932, at Hamheung, Hamkyeong namdo, Korea, to Chan Doh Kim and Okhyun Kim, Richard had dreams of receiving a good education and informing others about the Korean peoples. He attended Middlebury College from 1955 to 1959 and received his Master's degree in English Literature from John Hopkins University in 1960. Afterwards he attended the University of Iowa and received his M.F.A. degree in 1962. Then, while attending Harvard University, he earned another Master's degree in 1963.

He began his career at Long Beach State College as an instructor of English literature from 1963 to 1964, after which he moved to the University of Massachusetts as an associate professor from 1964 to 1969. In 1970 he taught briefly at Syracuse University and finally moved to San Diego State University in 1977, where he was a visiting professor until 1979.

Richard Kim received many awards in the field of arts, such as the National Endowment for the Arts fellowship in 1978; Fulbright fellowship, 1981–1983; Guggenheim Foundation fellowship, 1962–1963; a series of fellowships for the Ford Foundation, 1962–1963; University of Iowa writing fellowship, 1960–1962; and Johns Hopkins University Graduate Fellowship, 1959–1960.

However, he is best known for a series of documentaries, particularly the 1969 television documentary *Trans-Siberian Railway* that describes lives of Koreans who have struggled to put roots in Central Asia after they had been transported there from the Soviet Maritime Province by Stalin during the early 1930s. His other works include *Koreans in Russia* (1988), a photo essay entitled *Koreans in China and Russia* (1990), and novels *Lost Names* (1970), *The Innocent* (1968), and *The Martyred* (1964).

His first book, *The Martyred*, was hailed as a work in the psychological tradition of Job, Dostoevsky, and Camus by Chad Walsh of the *New York Times Book Review* in 1965. In this book, which is set against the background of the Korean War, Kim introduces fourteen Christian pastors who were taken prisoners by the North Korean Communists. Although they are portrayed initially as heroes who fought against Communism, a later investigation reveals that they died like dogs begging mercy from the Communist executors. Two of them survived, but one of them, Mr. Han, went insane because of torture. The other, Mr. Shin, had enough courage to spit in the face of his investigator, an army major who later described his encounter with these Christian ministers during his interrogation by a South Korean investigator. Mr. Shin, however, refused to talk about his heroism, thereby frustrating those who want to discover the truth.

The second book, *The Innocent*, is about a military coup d'état in Korea that involves two military officers set against each other because of a disagreement. One officer is viewed as righteous, whereas the other is considered ruthless. The reader must consider ruthlessness and righteousness in the context of a military revolution. Kim's third book, *Lost Names*, is set against the social and political background of Korea as a colony of Japan in which all Koreans were required to change their names into Japanese. Koreans were subject to this humiliating experience of loss of identity and alienation as they were forced to comply with the colonial policy of assimilation.

Kim married Penelope Groll Kim. They had two children, David and Melissa. He also served in the Republic of Korea's army as a first lieutenant in the infantry from 1951 to 1954.

Selected Bibliography

Benet's Reader's Encyclopedia of American Literature, 1st ed. New York: Harper Collins Publishers, 1991.

Cunningham, Eloise. "The Martyred." *High Fidelity*, vol. 32 (November 1982): MA33.

Kay, Ernest. *International Authors and Writers Who's Who*, 7th ed. Cambridge: International Biographical Center, 1976.

Hyung-chan Kim

DONG KINGMAN
(1911–   )
Artist, Educator

Dong Kingman, artist and educator, was born in Oakland, California, on March 31, 1911. He was the second of eight children of Dong Chuan-Fee and Lew Shee Kingman. His father immigrated to the United States from Hong Kong in 1900 and was a laundryman and dry goods merchant before returning with his family to Hong Kong. Kingman's mother painted in her spare time, and his father encouraged his love of theater by taking him to the Cantonese opera. Kingman attended school briefly in Oakland and completed his education at the Lingnam Grammar School in Hong Kong. After graduation in 1925, Kingman studied painting privately with headmaster Sze-to Wai.

In 1929, at age eighteen, Kingman returned to California and worked at a factory owned by his brother, a restaurant owner and a houseboy.

He attended art school in Oakland and held his first exhibition at the 1933 San Francisco Art Association Annual at the San Francisco Museum. In 1934 Kingman gave a one-man show at the Vallejo Library in San Francisco. From 1935 to 1940 Kingman was employed by the Works Progress Administration, painting and lecturing.

After the Metropolitan Museum of Art in New York City bought one of Kingman's paintings in 1940, he won a Guggenheim fellowship and traveled throughout the United States for two years. His first New York exhibition was at the Midtown Galleries in 1942. Kingman served in the United States Army from 1945 to 1946, preparing charts and graphs for the Office of Strategic Services. In 1948 he moved his studio to New York City. He went on a worldwide lecture tour at the invitation of the U.S. Department of State in 1954, visiting Japan, Korea, Taiwan, Hong Kong, Singapore, the Philippines, Malaya, Thailand, India, Turkey, Norway, Austria, England, and Iceland. Starting in 1957 Kingman has made summer painting tours of Mexico. In 1960 he was hired by *Life* magazine to make a painting of the filming of the movie *The World of Suzie Wong* in Hong Kong. He created a series of paintings for the film *Flower Drum Song* in 1961, which gave him widespread fame in the years thereafter.

Kingman began teaching art at the Academy of Advertising Art in San Francisco in 1938 and at the San Diego Art Gallery in 1941. He lectured at the University of Wyoming in 1944 and at Mills College in Oakland in 1945 and 1952. Kingman taught at Columbia University from 1946 to 1958 and at Hunter College, New York, from 1948 to 1953. Since 1953 Kingman has also taught art at the Famous Artists School in Westport, Connecticut.

Kingman's paintings are known for their inspired depiction of cities and urban scenes with splashes of color. His work is represented in the permanent collections of the Whitney Museum of American Art, the American Academy of Arts and Letters, Brooklyn Museum, Toledo Museum of Art, Joslyn Art Museum (Omaha), Boston Museum of Fine Arts, Metropolitan Museum of Art, Museum of Modern Art (New York City), San Francisco Museum, and Chicago Art Institute, among many others. He has created murals for the Bank of California (San Francisco), New York Hilton Hotel, R. H. Macy & Co., Franklin Square (New York), Boca Raton Hotel (Florida), Hyatt Regency Hotel (Hong Kong), Ambassador Hotel (Kowloon, Hong Kong), and Lincoln Savings Bank (New York City).

Kingman has received many awards for his painting. These include awards from the San Francisco Art Association (1936), Chicago International Watercolor Exhibition (1944), Audubon Artists Exhibition (1946, 1956), Philadelphia Watercolor Club, Pennsylvania Academy (1953), American Watercolor Society (1956, 1960, 1962–1965, 1967, 1972), National Academy for Design (1975), and the San Diego Watercolor Society (1984). He has also been named Man of the Year by the Chinatown Planning Council (1985), the Rotary Club (1991), and the Chinese for Affirmative Action (San Francisco, 1991).

Kingman is the illustrator of *The Bamboo Gate* by Vanya Oakes (1946), *China's Story* by Enid La Monte Meadowcroft (1946), *Nightingale* by Hans Christian Andersen (1948), *Johnny Hong in Chinatown* by Clyde Robert Bulla (1952), *Caen's and Kingman's San Francisco* by Herb Caen (1964), and *City on the Golden Hill* by Herb Caen (1967). He is the author, with Helena Kuo Kingman, of *Dong Kingman's Watercolors* (1980).

Over his long career, Dong Kingman has been known for his picturesque watercolors. Whether they be scenes from San Francisco, New York, or elsewhere, his works exude charm and a sense of playfulness. Literally everything seems suitable for his carefully crafted artistry. His many illustrations and paintings are distinguished by skill, integrity, and sensitivity to his subjects. His autobiography, *Paint the Yellow Tiger* (1991), was made into a documentary in 1997 with narration by actor Charlton Heston.

Kingman married Wong Shee in 1929, and the couple had two children, Eddie Kingman and Dong Kingman Junior. After his wife's death in 1954, Kingman married former Shanghai journalist and author Helena Kuo in 1956.

Selected Bibliography

Bulla, C. *Johnny Hong of Chinatown*. New York: Crowell, 1952. (Illustrated by D. Kingman).

Caen, H., and D. Kingman. *San Francisco, City on Golden Hills*. Garden City, NY: Doubleday, 1967.

Chinn, Thomas W. "Artist Shows First Exhibit in Bay Area in Over 10 Years." *AsianWeek*, September 16, 1982, pp. 12–13.

Gruskin, A. *The Watercolors of Dong Kingman, and How the Artist Works*. New York: Studio Publications, 1958.

Kingman, D. *Paint the Yellow Tiger*. New York: Sterling Publishing, 1991.

———. *Portraits of Cities*. New York: 22nd Century Film Corp., 1997.

———. *Watercolors Around the World*. Los Angeles: Hatfield, Dalzell Galleries, 1973.

Kingman, D., and H. Kingman. *Dong Kingman's Watercolors*. New York: Watson-Guptill Publications, 1980.

Franklin Ng

MAXINE HONG KINGSTON

(1940–   )

Writer

Author Maxine Hong Kingston was born in Stockton, California, on October 27, 1940. Her father, Tom Hong, a scholar and teacher in his native village of Sun Woi in the Guangdong province of China, came to New York City in 1924. Unable to find work in his field, Hong got a job in a laundry. Meanwhile, Kingston's mother, Ying Lan Chew Hong, trained as a midwife at the To Keung School in Canton and returned to Sun Woi to practice until she was able to join her husband in 1939. The family relocated to Stockton, California, where Tom Hong worked in a gambling house and later owned the New Port Laundry. There, Maxine was the first of six children born into the family. Two other children had died in China.

Kingston attended school in Stockton, struggling to learn English after speaking only Say Up, a dialect of Cantonese, at home. She received a number of scholarships that enabled her to attend the University of California at Berkeley, changing early from engineering to English literature. Kingston earned a Bachelor of Arts degree in 1962 and went back for a teaching certificate from 1964 to 1965.

Kingston taught high school English and mathematics at Sunset High School in Hayward, California, from 1966 to 1967. She then moved to Hawaii and taught at Kahuku High School (1967), Kahaluu Drop-In School (1968), Honolulu Business College (1969), Kailua High School (1969), and Mid-Pacific Institute, a private school (1970–1977). Kingston was a visiting professor at the University of Hawaii at Honolulu in 1977 and at Eastern Michigan University at Ypsilanti in 1986. She has been a chancellor's distinguished professor at the University of California at Berkeley since 1990.

In 1976 Kingston's first book, *Woman Warrior: Memoirs of a Girlhood among Ghosts*, was published. The autobiographical story of a Chinese American childhood, this book was an instant bestseller and won the National Book Critics Circle Award for the best nonfiction book of 1976. *China Men*, published in 1980, was written at the same time as Kingston's first book; it reveals the stories of the men in Kingston's family. It was a National Book Critics Circle Award nominee, and runner-up for a Pulitzer Prize. *Hawaii One Summer* (1987), *Through the Black Curtain* (1988), and *Tripmaster Monkey: His Fake Book* (1989), which won the PEN West Award in Fiction, followed Kingston's first two books. She has had short stories, articles, and poems published in magazines such as *Iowa Review, New Yorker, American Heritage, Redbook, Mother Jones, Caliban, Michigan Quarterly, Ms., Hungry Mind Review, New York Times,* and *Los Angeles Times.*

She has won the Anisfield Wolf Book Award (1978), Living Treasure of Hawaii (1980), Asian-Pacific Women's Network Woman of the Year Award (1981), California Arts Commission Award (1981), Hawaii Award for Literature (1982), Brandeis University National Women's Committee's Major Book Collection Award, (1990), and American Academy and Institute of Arts and Letters Award in Literature (1990). Kingston was inducted into the American Academy of Arts and Sciences in 1992.

Kingston married Earll Kingston in 1962. They have one child, Joseph Lawrence.

Selected Bibliography

Cheung, K. *Articulate Silences: Hisaye Yamamoto, Maxine Hong Kingston, Joy Kogawa.* Ithaca, NY: Cornell University Press, 1993.
Lim, G., ed. *Approaches to Teaching Kingston's* The Woman Warrior. New York: Modern Language Association of America, 1991.
Public Affairs Television, producer. *The Stories of Maxine Hong Kingston.* Alexandria, VA: PBS Video, 1990. [Videorecording]
Saffa, J., producer (for KQED, San Francisco). *Maxine Hong Kingston, Talking Story.* San Francisco: CrossCurrent Media, 1990. [Videorecording]

Franklin Ng

HARRY H. L. KITANO
(1926–   )
Author, Educator

Harry H. L. Kitano, educator and author, was born in San Francisco, California, on February 14, 1926, and grew up in San Francisco's Chinatown. Of Japanese descent, he went to school with mostly Chinese Americans and participated in varsity band and basketball in junior high school. During World War II, Kitano and his family were evacuated into the internment camps. Kitano became very active in the Topaz, Utah, camp high school as football team captain, class president, and gradua-

Harry H. L. Kitano

tion speaker. He addressed significant questions of identity as a Japanese American even while in the camps.

Kitano attended the University of Minnesota from 1945 to 1946 and the University of California at Berkeley, receiving a B.A. degree in 1948, an M.S.W. degree in 1951, and a Ph.D. in 1958. While in school, Kitano was active in the Stiles Hall YMCA and the University of California band. He was a trombone player during the Big Band era (1945–1960) and played professionally in the Midwest and in the San Francisco Bay Area.

Kitano held an endowed chair in Japanese American studies at the University of California. He was the director of the University of California Tokyo Study Center in 1970–1971 and was the first acting director of the Asian American Studies Center at UCLA.

His major areas of scholarly interest are the Japanese American community and race and ethnicity. Some of his major contributions focus on Japanese American culture, intermarriage, and alcohol use and abuse. In addition to publishing over sixty-five articles in professional journals, Kitano has written six books: *The Child Care Center: A Study of the Interaction among One-Parent Children, Parents and School* (1963); *Japanese Americans: The Evolution of a Subculture* (1969, 1976); *American Racism: Exploration of the Nature of Prejudice* (with Roger Daniels, 1970); *Race Relations* (1974, 1980, 1985, 1991); *Asian Americans: Emerging Minorities* (with

Roger Daniels, 1988, 1995); and *Generations and Identity: The Japanese American* (1993).

Kitano was honored by the Japanese American Citizens League with the Nisei of the Biennium Award in 1982.

Kitano is married and has four children from his first marriage and one child from his second.

Selected Bibliography

Niiya, Brian, ed. *Japanese American History: An A-to-Z Reference from 1868 to the Present*. New York: Facts on File, 1993, p. 204.

Steve Fugita

TOMMY TAMIO KONO

(1930–   )

Olympic Medalist (Weight Lifter)

Olympic athlete Tommy Tamio Kono—the only weightlifter to win three Olympic medals, including two golds, in three different Olympic games and three different weight categories—was born on June 27, 1930, in Sacramento, California. He suffered poor health due to asthma for much of his early life, so he missed approximately one-third of his schooling. When Kono was twelve years old he and his family were sent to Tule Lake Relocation Center in Tule Lake, California, during the period of Japanese internment. While there, Kono was encouraged by two friends to try weightlifting. He greatly enjoyed the sport and continued training when he returned with his family to Sacramento when he was nearly sixteen.

Kono studied mechanical engineering at Sacramento Junior College for two years and then left school to work fulltime. He was inducted into the United States Army in March 1951 and took his basic training at Fort Ord, California. He was scheduled to be shipped out to the Far East Command when the Army gave him the opportunity to be stationed at Fort Mason, California, so that he could try out for the U.S. Olympic Weightlifting Team.

Kono began establishing his long list of weightlifting records before entering the Army with a national record in the Press Lift in the middleweight division. He won the 1952 national title, setting the only na-

Tommy Tamio Kono

tional record made in the Championships, and also qualified for the U.S. Olympic Team in the lightweight division. At the 1952 Olympic Games in Helsinki, Finland, Kono won the lightweight weightlifting title. He also set Olympic and World records during the Olympic Games.

Kono went on to establish a number of weightlifting titles and world records:

Titles—Weightlifting (eight consecutive years):

1952	Olympic Lightweight Champion	Helsinki, Finland
1953	World Middleweight Champion	Stockholm, Sweden
1954	World Light-heavyweight Champion	Vienna, Austria
1955	World Light-heavyweight Champion	Munich, West Germany
1956	Olympic Light-heavyweight Champion	Melbourne, Australia
1957	World Middleweight Champion	Teheran, Iran
1958	World Middleweight Champion	Stockholm, Sweden

1959	World Middleweight Champion	Warsaw, Poland
1955	Pan American Games Light-heavyweight Champion	Mexico City, Mexico
1959	Pan American Games Middleweight Champion	Chicago, Illinois
1963	Pan American Games Light-heavyweight Champion	Sao Paulo, Brazil

Titles—Physique:

1954	Mr. World	Roubix, France
1955	Mr. Universe	Munich, West Germany
1957	Mr. Universe	Teheran, Iran
1961	Mr. Universe	Vienna, Austria

International Records Established:

26 World Records
7 Olympic Records
8 Pan American Games Records

Kono has held professional positions as a health food store owner, laboratory technician, and gym owner in Hawaii. From 1966 to 1968 he was National and Olympic Weightlifting Coach in Mexico, and from 1969 to 1972 he held the same position in West Germany. Kono also coached the U.S. Olympic team at Montreal in 1976. From 1973 to the present, Kono has served as a recreation specialist for the Department of Parks and Recreation, City and County of Honolulu, Hawaii.

Kono has received numerous awards during his career. In 1979 he received the SERTOMA Freedom Award (Service to Mankind Award for sports). He was selected for the Hawaii Sports Hall of Fame in 1980 and as Public Recreation Man of the Year from the Amateur Athletic Union of the United States. In 1990 Kono was inducted into the U.S. Olympic Hall of Fame as one of two Asians ever to be so honored. He was also the recipient of the Steve Reeves Award at the 10th Annual Fitness Award Banquet in New York City in 1990. In 1993 Kono was honored with the Mackey Yanagazawa Award at Aloha Stadium for his many years of contributions toward the promotion and support of sports. In 1994 he was inducted into the initial International Weightlifting Hall of Fame at the International Olympic Committee headquarters in Lausanne, Switzerland. In the same year Kono received the Excellence 2000 Award from the U.S. Pan Asian American Chamber of Commerce.

Kono and his wife, Florence, have three children: Jamieson, JoAnn, and Mark.

Selected Bibliography

Niiya, Brian, ed. *Japanese American History: An A-to-Z Reference from 1868 to the Present*. New York: Facts on File, 1993, pp. 208–209.
Zia, Helen, and Susan Gall, eds. *Notable Asian Americans*. Detroit: Gale Research, 1995, pp. 169–170.

Steve Fugita

FRED T. KOREMATSU

(1919–)

Community Leader

Fred Korematsu, who challenged the constitutionality of the Japanese American internment during World War II, was born in Oakland, California, in 1919. He was the third son of immigrant Japanese parents. The Korematsu family owned and operated a nursery on twenty-five acres in San Leandro. Fred spent most of his early years involved in sports—football, tennis, basketball—and other extracurricular activities.

Soon after Japan bombed Pearl Harbor on December 7, 1941, the U.S. government, concerned about spies and sabotage, began to harass Japanese Americans residing on the West Coast. Many were questioned by the FBI and suspected of being enemies of the state. In 1941, Korematsu attempted to enlist in the U.S. Navy but was rejected on the basis of his race. Soon thereafter he lost his job as a welder. Then, on February 19, 1942, President Franklin D. Roosevelt signed Executive Order 9066, which resulted in the wartime internment of more than 110,000 Japanese Americans from the West Coast

When the evacuation was ordered, Korematsu remained in San Leandro and tried to evade relocation and imprisonment because he wished to continue working and be with his fiancée. He even had plastic surgery in hopes of disguising his Asian features, but someone informed the police of his identity as a Nisei (second-generation) Japanese American, and he was arrested on March 30, 1942. Shortly after his arrest, the director of the American Civil Liberties Union in northern California proposed to test the legality of the Japanese American internment by using his case. Korematsu agreed to become the plaintiff in this case and challenge the constitutionality of the relocation program.

He was released on bail but was sent directly to Tanforan Assembly Center to join the rest of his family. There many of the Nisei saw him as a troublemaker. The family was later moved to Topaz internment camp, located in south-central Utah. Meanwhile, Korematsu was convicted of remaining in a military area in defiance of Executive Order 9066 and was sentenced to five years of probation. He appealed to the Ninth Circuit Court of Appeals and lost. In December 1944, shortly after the War Relocation Authority announced its decision to close the internment camps, the Supreme Court made its decision on *Korematsu v. United States*: "He [Korematsu] was excluded [from the Military Area] because we are at war with the Japanese Empire, because the properly constituted military authorities feared invasion of the West Coast . . . not because of hostility to him or his race." After release from camp Korematsu moved to Detroit, Michigan, where he married and worked as a draftsman until 1949.

In 1982 the Korematsu case, as well as *Hirabayashi v. United States* and *Yasui v. United States*, resurfaced as a team of ambitious Sansei (third-generation) Japanese American attorneys, including **Dale Minami**, decided to re-test the constitutionality of the wartime internment. On January 19, 1983, a writ was filed in the federal court of San Francisco in *Korematsu v. United States*. The attorneys were able to demonstrate to the court that the documents and testimony used to convict Korematsu in 1943 had been manipulated and that there actually had been no military necessity to evict Americans of Japanese ancestry from the West Coast. Thus, the government's rationale for relocation was shown to be invalid. In October 1983, Judge Marilyn Hall-Patel overturned Korematsu's original conviction.

President Bill Clinton awarded Korematsu the Presidential Medal of Freedom in 1998.

Selected Bibliography

Chan, Sucheng. *Asian Americans: An Interpretive History*. Boston: Twayne Publishers, 1991.

Chin, Steven A. *When Justice Failed: The Fred Korematsu Story*. Austin, TX: Raintree Steck-Vaughn Publishers, 1993.

Spickard, Paul. *Japanese Americans: The Formation and Transformation of an Ethnic Group*. New York: Twayne Publishers, 1996.

Zia, Helen, and Susan B. Gall, eds. *Notable Asian Americans*. Detroit: Gale Research, 1995.

Steve Fugita

MICHELLE KWAN

(1980–   )

Olympic Medalist (Figure Skater)

World champion skater Michelle Kwan was born on July 7, 1980, the second daughter of Danny and Estella Kwan, who had immigrated from Hong Kong to the United States. Danny had immigrated in 1971, married Estella in 1974, and settled in Torrance, California. The couple have three children—Ron, Karen, and Michelle.

After watching their older brother play ice hockey, the two sisters decided to take up figure skating. Acceding to their wishes, their father allowed them to take lessons. He drove them to lessons at Lake Arrowhead from Torrance and eventually moved there so that they could practice at the Ice Castle International Training Center. The two sisters competed in events sanctioned by the Ice Skating Institute of America and the United States Figure Skating Association.

By the age of twelve, Michelle was skating as a senior skater in the U.S. Senior Nationals at Phoenix, Arizona. Her coach was Frank Carroll. In the same year she took first place at the Gardena Spring Trophy in Italy and the U.S. Olympic Festival in San Antonio, Texas. In 1994 she won the silver medal at the U.S. National Championships in Detroit and took first place at the World Junior Championships, the Hershey's Kisses Pro-Am Championship, and the U.S. Outdoor Challenge.

Her successes continued to mount. In 1995 she took first place at Skate America, Skate Canada, the Nations Cup, and the U.S. Postal Service Challenge. In 1996 she came in first at the Champions Series Final, the Hershey's Kisses Challenge, the Continents Cup, the Trophy Lalique, the U.S. Postal Service Challenge, and others. Most important, she took first place at the World Championships and the U.S. Championships. In 1997 she took first place at the Skate America but finished second to Tara Lipinski at the U.S. Championships, the Champion Series Final, and the World Championships.

With Lipinski and Kwan as two of the top skaters in the United States, the media and the public were wondering who would win in the Olympics in 1998 at Nagano, Japan. Lipinski was younger at age fifteen and seemingly more athletic, whereas the seventeen-year-old Kwan was elegant and artistic. Kwan won first place in the U.S. Championships, which was closely watched as a possible clue to the Olympic contest.

However, at the Olympics, Lipinski won the gold medal while Kwan garnered the silver medal. Shortly thereafter, Lipinski declared that she would turn professional. In 1998 Kwan won her second world championship. Kwan has hinted that she may compete in the 2002 Olympics in Salt Lake City. For many, Kwan is the embodiment of a true champion with her skating performances displaying sophistication, beauty, and grace.

Selected Bibliography

"Americans Skate to the Top in Nagano." *Asian Week*, February 26–March 4, 1998, pp. 8–9.
Kwan, Michelle. *Heart of a Champion: My Story*. New York: Scholastic, 1997.
Longman, Jere. "A Turn on the Ice, A Turn in the Road." *New York Times*, April 6, 1998, p. C12.
————. "Chasing Gold at Varied Paces." *New York Times*, February 17, 1998, p. C11.
————. "Her Spirit in the Clouds, Kwan Finds Peace on the Ice." *New York Times*, February 1, 1998, p. L7.

Franklin Ng

HIM MARK LAI

(1925–   )

Author, Historian, Engineer

Him Mark Lai, researcher and writer, was born in San Francisco, California, on November 1, 1925. He attended Galileo Senior High School and graduated in 1943. Lai received an Associate of Arts degree from San Francisco Junior College in 1945 and a Bachelor of Science degree in mechanical engineering from the University of California at Berkeley in 1947. He did additional graduate work at Berkeley from 1951 to 1953.

From 1953 until his retirement in 1984, Lai was a mechanical engineer at Bechtel Power Corporation in San Francisco. Holding a deep interest in the experience of the Chinese in the United States, he has been active in historical research on Chinese American history since 1965. To promote research and understanding of the topic, Lai has written and edited, consulted, lectured, and been active in a number of projects and organizations.

From 1968 to the present, Lai has published articles on Chinese American history in journals such as *East/West: Chinese American Journal, San Francisco Journal, Bulletin of the Chinese Historical Society of America, Bridge Magazine, Amerasia Journal,* and *Journal of Overseas Chinese History.* He was assistant editor of *History of the Chinese in California: A Syllabus* (1969). Lai co-authored *Island: Poetry and History of Chinese Immigrants on Angel Island, 1910–1940* (1980). He also contributed a chapter to the *Harvard Encyclopedia of American Ethnic Groups* (1980) and *The Ethnic Press in the United States* (1987). In 1986, Lai compiled and edited *A History Reclaimed: An Annotated Bibliography and Guide of Chinese Language Materials on the Chinese of America.* Lai contributed the essay "The Kuomintang in Chinese American Communities before World War II" to *Entry Denied: Exclusion and the Chinese Community in America, 1882–1943,* edited by **Sucheng Chan** (1981).

Lai lectured at San Francisco State College in 1969 and at San Francisco State University from 1972 to 1975. He lectured at the University of California at Berkeley from 1978 to 1979 and in 1984. He has been an adjunct professor in the Asian American Studies Department at San Francisco State University from 1990 to the present. He consulted for a number of film projects, including *Carved in Silence* (1987) about the Chinese who passed through Angel Island, an immigration station in San Francisco Bay. He was consultant and curator for an exhibit called "Chinese of America, 1975–1980," which was shown in Shanghai (1985), Beijing (1986), and Hong Kong (1988).

To many researchers and scholars, Lai is considered the dean of Chinese American history. With his ability to research in both Chinese and English, he has been an inspiration and a source of encouragement to those who wish to learn more about the Chinese American experience. Generous with his time and guidance, he has helped to nurture many who are writing about the Chinese in the United States. Lai has been active in the Chinese Historical Society of America and has served as president (1971, 1976, 1977) and on its Board of Directors (1972–1981, 1984–1991). He has served on the Board of Directors of the Chinese Culture Foundation of San Francisco (1975–1985, 1987–present) and has served as president (1982) and Board co-chairperson (1983–1985, 1989). He serves on the Editorial Board of *Chinese America: History and Perspectives* (1986–present) and of *Amerasia Journal* (1979–present); he was also associate editor of *East/West: Chinese American Journal* (1985–1989). Lai has made numerous research trips to emigrant areas in China since 1976. He served on the planning committee of "The Repeal and Its Legacy: A Conference on the Fiftieth Anniversary of the Repeal of the Chinese Exclusion Acts" (Chinese Historical Society of America, 1992).

Selected Bibliography

Who's Who in America, 51st ed., 1997. New Providence, NJ: Marquis Who's Who, 1996.

Who's Who in Science and Engineering, 3rd ed., 1996–1997. New Providence, NJ: Marquis Who's Who, 1996.

Who's Who in the West, 25th ed., 1996–1997. New Providence, NJ: Marquis Who's Who, 1995.

Who's Who in the World, 13th ed., 1996–1997. New Providence, NJ: Marquis Who's Who, 1995.

Franklin Ng

RUTH ASAWA LANIER
(1926–   )
Artist

Artist Ruth Asawa Lanier was born on January 24, 1926, in Norwalk, California. She grew up on a truck farm, where her parents sometimes worked eighteen-hour days. From 1942 to 1943, along with thousands of other Japanese Americans who were removed from the Pacific Coast under the pretext that they were a threat to national security, she was interned in Santa Anita Assembly Center (formerly a racetrack) in Arcadia, California, and Rohwer, Arkansas. It was at Santa Anita that Lanier seriously began to develop her craft mentored by Nisei (second-generation Japanese American) Disney Studio veterans. Lanier graduated from high school at Rohwer and attended Milwaukee State Teachers College from 1943 to 1946, majoring in art. From 1946 to 1949 she attended Black Mountain College, an experimental college with an art-centered curriculum in North Carolina.

From 1946 to the present Lanier has lived and worked in San Francisco, California. Her work has centered on bas-relief sculptures and fountains, generally utilizing cast bronze or glass fiber–reinforced concrete. Some of her important commissioned pieces include "Andrea," a cast bronze fountain in Ghirardelli Square, San Francisco (1966); a cast bronze fountain at the Hyatt on Union Square, commissioned by the Hyatt Corporation of America (1970–1973); a glass fiber–reinforced concrete bas-relief wall at the San Francisco Parc Fifty Five Hotel (formerly

Ruth Asawa Lenier (photo by Laurence Cuneo)

the Ramada Renaissance; 1984); "Aurora," a stainless steel fountain at Bayside Plaza, San Francisco, commissioned by Hampshire Properties (1986); a glass fiber–reinforced concrete bas-relief fountain at Old Courthouse Square, Santa Rosa, California, commissioned by the Santa Rosa Redevelopment and Housing Agency (1987); a cast bronze fountain at Beringer Winery, St. Helena, California (1988); and the Japanese American Internment Memorial Sculpture, a cast bronze bas-relief sculpture commissioned by the City of San Jose, County of Santa Clara, and the local Japanese American community (1994).

Collections of Lanier's work are available for public view at the Whitney Museum of American Art (gift of Mr. and Mrs. Howard Lipman, 1958); Chase Manhattan Bank, New York (David Rockefeller, 1958); Oakland Museum of Art (Purchase Award, 1959; Women's Board Purchase Award, 1976); Williams College, Massachusetts (1965); City of San Francisco (San Francisco Art Festival Purchase Award, 1966); Addison Gallery, Andover, Massachusetts (1966); and the Solomon Guggenheim Museum, New York (Josef Albers Bequest, 1980).

Lanier's work has been featured in over thirty group and solo exhibitions since 1953. Museums that have showcased her work include the

San Francisco Museum of Art (1954, 1962, 1973); M. H. de Young Memorial Museum, San Francisco (1960); Pasadena Museum of Art (1965); Museum of Modern Art, San Francisco (1969); Fresno Arts Center and Museum (1978, 1988); the Los Angeles Museum of Contemporary Art (1989–1990); and the California Crafts Museum, San Francisco (1993).

Lanier has received numerous awards and fellowships throughout her career. In 1966 she was the first recipient of the Dymaxion Award for Artist/Scientist. Lanier received the Artist-in-Residence Award from the San Francisco Foundation in 1973, 1974, and 1977. In 1980–1981 she received the Artist-in-Residence Award, Chairman's Grant, National Endowment for the Arts. Lanier was awarded the Fine Arts Gold Medal by the American Institute of Architects in 1974. In the same year she received the Robert Kirkwood Award from the San Francisco Foundation. The date February 12, 1982, was designated Ruth Asawa Day by the City and County of San Francisco. The Asian Heritage Council awarded Lanier its Arts Award in 1983, and in 1990 the San Francisco Chamber of Commerce presented her its Cyril Magnin Award. In 1993 Lanier received the Women's Caucus for Art's Outstanding Achievement in the Visual Arts Award.

Lanier has contributed her time and expertise to the community through a number of organizations. In recent years she has been very active in the area of art education.

Lanier is married and has six children.

Selected Bibliography

Abrahamson, Joan, and Sally Woodbridge. *The Alvarado School Community Art Program*. San Francisco: Alvarado School Workshop, 1973.

Bancroft Library. *The Arts and the Community Oral History Project*. Berkeley: University of California, 1990.

Dobbs, Stephen. "Community and Commitment: An Interview with Ruth Asawa." *Art Education*, vol. 34, no. 5 (1981): 14–17.

"Guess Who Came to Dinner?" *San Francisco Examiner, Image Magazine*, May 29, 1988, pp. 8–11.

Harris, Mary Emma. *The Arts at Black Mountain College*. Cambridge, MA: MIT Press, 1987.

"History, Ruth Asawa Style." *San Francisco Sunday Examiner & Chronicle*, April 29, 1984, Scene/Arts, p.2.

Hopkins, Henry, and Mimi Jacobs. *50 West Coast Artists*. San Francisco: Chronicle Books, 1982.

Jepson, Andrea, and Sharon Litsky. *The Alvarado Experience*. San Francisco: Alvarado School Art Workshop, 1976.

Rubenstein, Charlotte Streifer. *American Women Artists*. New York: Avon, 1982.

———. *American Women Sculptors*. Boston: G. K. Hall, 1990.

San Francisco Museum of Art. *Ruth Asawa: A Retrospective View*. San Francisco: San Francisco Museum of Art, 1973.

Snyder, Robert, producer. *Ruth Asawa: On Forms and Growth*. Pacific Palisades, CA: Masters and Masterworks Production, 1978. [Film]
Woodbridge, Sally. *Ruth Asawa's San Francisco Fountain*. San Francisco: San Francisco Museum of Art, 1970.

Steve Fugita

BRUCE LEE
(1940–1973)
Martial Arts Expert, Actor

Bruce Lee, a martial arts expert and actor, helped make kung-fu movies popular and inspired a host of imitators. In many ways he was an innovator who nurtured the genre of martial arts movies in the United States.

Bruce Lee was born Lee Jun Fan to Grace Lee and Lee Hoo Chun on November 1, 1940, in San Francisco. His parents took him back to Hong Kong, where he spent his childhood. His father, a performer of Cantonese opera, had connections that opened the way for his son to star in movies at an early age. As a child actor with the stage name Siu Loong, or "Little Dragon," Bruce Lee had roles in some twenty films.

In 1958 his parents sent him back to the United States to finish his high school education. He then attended the University of Washington in Seattle, where he received a degree in philosophy. While there he met and married Linda Emery in 1964, with whom he had two children. Upon graduation, he taught martial arts and eventually opened a kung-fu academy in Los Angeles.

Interested in martial arts, Bruce Lee had studied a number of different styles. From this knowledge he developed a style known as *Jeet Kune Do*, or the Way of the Intercepting Fist. His students came to include noted actors such as Steve McQueen, James Coburn, and James Garner. As his reputation grew, it brought him to the attention of the television and film industry. From 1966 to 1967 he starred as Kato in the *Green Hornet* television series. He also acted in "Marlowe" with James Garner and "Longstreet" with James Franciscus. He appeared in episodes of series programs such as *Batman, Ironsides*, and *Blondie*, too.

In 1971 Bruce Lee moved to Hong Kong to make films with producer Raymond Chow for Golden Harvest (H. K.). His first film, *The Big Boss*, directed by Lo Wei, was distributed in the United States by National General Pictures and shown under the title *Fists of Fury*. His second film, *The Chinese Connection*, had been released in Hong Kong but was featured with the different title in the United States.

His films received an enthusiastic response from movie audiences, and in 1972 Warner Brothers worked with Bruce Lee to produce *Enter the Dragon*. Directed by Robert Clouse with Fred Weintraub and Paul Heller as producers, this was arguably the best of the Bruce Lee films. The cast included John Saxon and Jim Kelly from the United States, along with Shih Kien and Angela Mao-Ying from Hong Kong. The film included a famous scene with a hall of mirrors in which the villainous Han (Shih Kien) duels with Bruce Lee. *Enter the Dragon* was a tremendous box office success worldwide, and it transformed Lee into the prototypical kung-fu hero. Bruce Lee did not live to see the release of this film in 1973. He died on July 20, 1973, of cerebral edema in Hong Kong.

Another film distributed in the United States in 1973 after his death was *The Return of the Dragon*. Produced by Raymond Chow, this film starring Bruce Lee had actually been shown in 1972 in Hong Kong as *The Way of the Dragon*. Although it was made before *Enter the Dragon*, its title capitalized on the fantastic popularity of the Warner Brothers production with American audiences.

Other films tried to cash in on the kung-fu craze and the cult status of Bruce Lee. *Game of Death* was a film that Bruce Lee had started but was unable to complete. Featuring other actors such as Chuck Norris and Kareem Abdul-Jabbar, it relied on a Bruce Lee substitute to finish the film. Short episodes in the *Game of Death* presented Bruce Lee in action sequences, but overall it only tantalized and disappointed film-goers.

A number of different actors have tried to continue the legendary success of Bruce Lee in martial arts films. These have included Chuck Norris, Steve Segal, Jean Claude van Damme, and David Carradine. Among Chinese actors, probably the most noteworthy is Jackie Chan from Hong Kong. In 1993, Hawaiian-born actor Jason Scott Lee starred in *Dragon: The Bruce Lee Story*, a film that depicted Bruce Lee's life. In the same year Bruce Lee was posthumously awarded a Hollywood Boulevard Star of Fame along with veteran Asian American actors **Keye Luke**, George Takei, and Mako.

The legacy of Bruce Lee is a mixed one for Asian Americans. On the one hand, some do not like the fighting and feuding in his films, and they do not condone the violence associated with kung-fu movies. On the other hand, others see him as portraying a heroic and sympathetic screen image of Asians, in contrast to the usual medley of diabolical Fu Manchu, proverbial Charlie Chan, or comical Hop Sing stereotypes. For better or worse, Bruce Lee is the standard to be measured against in the genre of martial arts movies. His carefully choreographed action sequences, his flying kicks, his use of nunchaku sticks, his licking of his own blood on a bared chest, and his animal-like yelp before leaping into battle are all his signature trademarks that have contributed to a greater sophistication in the production of kung-fu films.

Selected Bibliography

Block, Alex Ben. *The Legend of Bruce Lee*. New York: Dell, 1974.
Clouse, Robert. *The Making of Enter the Dragon*. Burbank, CA: Unique Publications, 1987.
Gross, Edward. *Bruce Lee: Fists of Fury*. Las Vegas: Pioneer Books, 1990.
Lee, Linda. *Bruce Lee: The Man Only I Knew*. New York: Warner, 1975.
Magill, Frank N., ed. *Magill's Survey of Cinema: English Language Films*, vol. 2. Englewood Cliffs, NJ: Salem Press, 1981.
Mintz, Marilyn D. *The Martial Arts Films*. Rutland, VT: Charles E. Tuttle, 1983.

Franklin Ng

CHANG RAE LEE

(1965–)

Author, Educator

Chang Rae Lee, well known for his novel *Native Speaker*, was born in Seoul, Korea, on July 29, 1965. At age three he immigrated with his family to the United States and was raised in the Westchester suburbs of New York. Lee graduated from Phillips Exeter Academy in 1983 and received a Bachelor of Arts degree in English at Yale University. Then he attended the University of Oregon, where he completed his Master of Fine Arts degree.

In March 1995 Lee published his first novel, *Native Speaker*, which received great praise from literary critics. He has received more than eight honors and prizes for *Native Speaker*, including the American Book Award and the Barnes & Noble Discover Great New Writers Award. The book was named one of the Year's Best Books of 1995 by *Time* magazine. In the novel Lee explores the psycholinguistic problems associated with the identity and assimilation of people who are either first-generation immigrants or their descendants. Lee examines the power of language that shapes immigrants' life chances for success or failure in terms of their ability to manipulate and use English.

Currently Lee works and lives in Oregon with wife, Michelle, and serves as associate professor of creative writing at the University of Oregon.

Selected Bibliography

"Family: American Writers Remember Their Own." *Publishers Weekly*, September 2, 1996, p. 101.
Klinkenborg, Verlyn. "*Native Speaker.*" *New Yorker*, July 10, 1995, pp. 76–77. [book review]
Monaghan, Peter. "A Korean-American Novelist's Impressive Debut." *Chronicle of Higher Education*, April 7, 1995, p. A6.

Jennifer Kang

MING CHO LEE

(1930–   )

Set Designer, Educator

Ming Cho Lee, theatrical set designer, was born in Shanghai, China, on October 3, 1930. His father, Tsufa F. Lee, was a graduate of Yale University and worked for an international insurance company; his mother, Ing Tang Lee, divorced when Lee was six years old. On his weekend visits to his mother Lee was introduced to the world of film, theater, and opera, both Western and Chinese. He studied ink drawing and landscape painting with artist Chang Kwo-Nyen.

In 1949 the Lee family moved to Hong Kong, where Lee attended high school. He then went to Los Angeles to attend Occidental College. First majoring in art, Lee switched to speech and began designing sets for the college's theater productions. He received his Bachelor of Arts degree from Occidental in 1953 and then did graduate work in theater arts at the University of California at Los Angeles.

Lee began his professional work as an apprentice and assistant designer to Jo Mielziner, a well-known Broadway set designer, from 1954 to 1958. He worked on such productions as *Silk Stockings, Cat on a Hot Tin Roof, Guys and Dolls, The Infernal Machine, Madama Butterfly*, and *Crucible*.

Leaving Mielziner's studio in 1958, Lee became a freelance designer. He designed sets for the Peabody Institute of Music in Baltimore, Maryland; his work there included the operas *The Turk in Italy, The Old Maid and the Thief, Werther, Amahl and the Night Visitors,* and *The Pearl Fishers.* Lee also designed the set for the Baltimore Opera Company's production of *Katya Kabanova* and a touring production of *Madama Butterfly* for the Opera Company of Boston.

Lee designed sets for the San Francisco Opera in 1961 and then returned to New York City, where he designed sets for the New York Shakespeare Festival's Delacorte Theatre in Central Park. He designed sets for more than twenty Shakespearean plays during the next ten years, developing a minimalist style that was highly influential in the American theater. His design for the Festival's 1964 production of *Electra* won a Joseph Maharam Award for outstanding theatrical design, and he won the award again in 1968 for *Ergo.* Lee designed sets for the Festival's off-Broadway productions, such as *Hair, Invitation to a Beheading,* and *For Colored Girls Who Have Considered Suicide/When the Rainbow is Enuf.* He designed an Elizabethan-style, multilevel mobile stage for taking Festival productions to city parks and neighborhoods, and he redesigned the Delacorte Theatre.

Lee designed sets for the Juilliard Opera Theatre and the American Opera Center of the Juilliard School of Music, the Metropolitan Opera, and the New York City Opera. He has designed for a number of ballet and dance companies, including the Martha Graham Company, the Alvin Ailey Dance Theatre, the Joffrey Ballet, the National Ballet of Canada, Jose Limon, and Gerald Arpino. His Broadway productions include *The Shadow Box* (1977) and *K2* (1983), which won Lee a Tony Award, Outer Critics Circle Award, Drama Desk Award, and the Joseph Maharam Award for his stunning depiction of a massive ice-encrusted cliff. His sets for *Travelers in the Dark* (1985) won the Los Angeles Drama Critics Circle Award and the Hollywood Drama-Logue Critics Award. Lee has also worked with a number of nonprofit regional theaters and small, experimental theaters such as the Intar Hispanic American Theater (New York City), the Mark Taper Forum (Los Angeles), and the Long Wharf Theater (New Haven, Connecticut).

Lee has taught set design at the Yale University School of Drama since 1969, and he serves as co-chair of the Drama Department and as design advisor to the Yale Repertory Theatre. He received a Guggenheim fellowship in 1988 to explore the state of pre-professional training in the arts in the United States.

Lee received a special award from the National Opera Institute in 1980, the Mayor's Award of Honor for Arts and Culture (1984), and a Quinyun Award for Art and Culture from the China Institute of America (1984).

Lee was named Man of the Year by the Chinatown Planning Commission in 1986.

Lee married Elizabeth Rapport in 1958. They have three children.

Selected Bibliography

Huang, Yu-mei. "The Twists, Turns, Trials and Triumphs of a Theatrical Life." *Free China Review*, January 1984.

Lee, Ming Cho. "Designing Opera." In Elizabeth B. Burdick, Peggy Hansen, and Brenda Zanger, eds., *Contemporary Stage Design U.S.A.* Middletown, CT: Wesleyan University Press, 1975.

MacKay, Patricia. "Designers on Designing: Ming Cho Lee." *Theater Craft*, February 1984.

Franklin Ng

ROSE HUM LEE

(1904–1964)

Sociologist, Educator

One of the pioneers in the study of the Chinese in the United States is Rose Hum Lee. A second-generation Chinese American, she was born in Butte, Montana, on August 20, 1904, to Hum Wah-Lung and Hum Lin Fong. Hers was a large family, and she was the second of seven children. Her father died as she was growing up, and her mother assumed the direction of his business.

Rose Hum Lee graduated from Butte High School in 1921 and worked briefly as a secretary. She then married Ku Young Lee, a Chinese man who had been studying in Philadelphia. She returned with him to China in the late 1920s and worked in assorted jobs for both the government and private businesses. During the 1930s she served on committees to help in the relief of Sino-Japanese War victims and to evacuate civilians. Because of her facility in both English and Chinese, she also served as an interpreter. Active in Canton, she was president of its Women's International Club and a member of the American Association of University Women and the National Federation of Business and Professional Women's Clubs.

As the Sino-Japanese War intensified, Rose Hum Lee returned to the

United States with a war orphan whom she had adopted as her daughter. Wishing to continue her education, she supported her daughter herself by writing and lecturing. She enrolled at the Carnegie Institute of Technology in Pittsburgh and earned a B.S. degree in social work in 1942. She next went to the University of Chicago and received an M.A. degree in sociology in 1943 and a Ph.D. in sociology in 1947. Her Master's thesis focused on maternal and child health and welfare services in Canton, China. Her Ph.D. thesis was about the growth and decline of Chinese communities in the Rocky Mountain region of the United States, and she acknowledged the help and guidance of Professors E. W. Burgess and E. C. Hughes. Her receipt of a Ph.D. in 1947 marked her as the first woman of Chinese descent to earn a doctorate in that discipline in the United States.

Rose Hum Lee started teaching at Roosevelt University in Chicago in 1945. She served as chairman of its Department of Sociology from 1956 to 1961 and was promoted to the rank of professor in 1959. In the course of her career she published numerous articles and presented many papers. Her areas of interest included Chinese Americans, China, and urbanism.

Reflecting her training as a product of the University of Chicago School of Sociology identified with Sociologist Robert Park, she investigated the aspects of urban life. This commitment led her to conduct research and to coordinate interviews for the North Kenwood–Oakland survey in Chicago from 1955 to 1956. The Schwartzhaupt Foundation provided financial support to aid her research. In 1955 she also published *The City: Urbanism and Urbanization in World Regions*. Inspired by University of Chicago sociologist Louis Wirth in this book, she emphasized the need to study non-Western cities, too, and to examine nonindustrial factors that helped to promote urban growth. The work received favorable mention from scholars such as Don Martindale.

Rose Hum Lee's urban investigations led her to become immersed in civic activities. Her Master's thesis had reflected a fascination with social work, and she tried to further interracial harmony and unity. She was active in the Chicago Commission of Human Relations Education Committee and the National Conference of Christians and Jews. She served on the board of the Hyde Park–Kenwood Community Conference and was a contributing editor to the *Journal of Human Relations*. Her efforts received recognition, and in 1959 she was given the B'nai B'rith Women of Achievement Award for Greater Chicago.

Rose Hum Lee was also interested in China and international understanding. As a lecturer for the Speaker's Bureau of the Adult Education Council in Chicago, she frequently lectured on subjects relating to China and the Chinese. Popular topics included Chinese art and its symbolism, Chinese customs, and Christianity in China. Concerned about international affairs, she discussed issues such as peace in the Pacific, China as a battlefield for human rights, China's politics, and America's role in the Far East.

At one point in the 1940s, Rose Hum Lee wrote several plays for children. They included *Little Lee Bo-Bo* and *Shoes for Shoe Street*. The former was performed by the Goodman Theatre in Chicago and was published as a book.

However, Rose Hum Lee is most known today for her pioneering research on the Chinese in the United States. She wrote about the Chinese in the Rocky Mountain region, Chinatowns, and cultural conflict. In 1949 she received a grant from the Social Science Research Council to study new immigrant families in the San Francisco Bay Area. Her best-known work is *The Chinese in the United States* (1960).

During the Asian American movement for civil rights and ethnic identity of the late 1960s and early 1970s, Rose Hum Lee was criticized for being an assimilationist and a representative member of the University of Chicago School of Sociology. Her prediction that Chinatowns in the United States would disappear did not turn out to be valid because of the influx of Chinese immigrants and Southeast Asian refugees since 1965. Nevertheless, her research has proved invaluable to those who are interested in the Chinese American experience. Moreover, her desire for the Chinese to leave their Chinatowns and to become American Chinese was motivated by a desire to end the exploitation of its residents and a recognition of certain negative structural aspects of ethnic enclaves such as poverty, pidgin English, and increased school drop-out rates, as results of cultural isolation from mainstream society.

On leave from Roosevelt University in 1961, she taught for a while at Phoenix College in Arizona from 1962 to 1963. On March 25, 1964, Rose Hum Lee died at the Good Samaritan Hospital in Phoenix of a brain embolism. She was survived by her second husband, Glenn Ginn, a Chinese American lawyer whom she married in 1951, and a daughter, Elaine.

Selected Bibliography

Burr, William. "Lee, Rose Hum." In Barbara Sicherman and Carol Hurd Green, eds., *Notable American Women: The Modern Period. A Biographical Dictionary*, Cambridge, MA: Harvard University Press, 1980, pp. 414–415.

Lee, Rose Hum. "Chinese Immigration and Population Changes since 1940." *Sociology and Social Research*, vol. 41 (1957): 195–202.

———. *The Chinese in the United States of America*. New York: Oxford University Press, 1960.

———. *The City: Urbanism and Urbanization in Major Regions*. Philadelphia: J. B. Lippincott, 1955.

Lee, Rose Hum, and Charlotte B. Chorpenning. *Little Lee Bobo; or, The Chinatown*

Detective. A Mystery Play for Children in Three Acts. Anchorage, KY: Children's Theatre Press, 1948.

Lyman, Stanford. "In Memoriam: Rose Hum Lee (1904–1964)." In Stanford Lyman, ed., *The Asian in North America*, Santa Barbara, CA: ABC-Clio, 1977, pp. 259–260.

Phillips, Terri. "Rose Hum Lee (1904–1964)." In Mary Jo Deegan, ed., *Women in Sociology: A Bio-bibliographical Sourcebook.* Westport, CT: Greenwood Press, 1991, pp. 256–262.

Franklin Ng

SAMMY LEE

(1920–   )

Olympic Medalist (Diver), Swim Coach, Physician

Sammy Lee was the first male athlete to win two consecutive Olympic gold medals in platform diving. It was in London at the 1948 Olympic Games that Lee won his first gold medal as a member of the U.S. Diving Team. This was also the first time that an American of Korean descent won a gold medal. His second gold was won four years later at the 1952 Olympics in Helsinki, Finland.

Sammy Lee was born on August 1, 1920, to Korean immigrant parents in Fresno, California. He was told by his father that he was privileged to be an American and was raised on the ideal that in America, he could be anything he wanted, regardless of his race. His parents taught him to stand above racial prejudice and to use acts of discrimination to his advantage. They encouraged him to dream big dreams.

In 1932 Lee, in his youth, began to dream of becoming an Olympic champion. He was twelve years old when the Olympic Games were held in Los Angeles, where the Lee family had settled. There he discovered what the Olympic Games were about, and even though he did not yet know what sport he would compete in, Lee knew that someday he would be a part of the Olympics.

While he was a student at Occidental College, Lee won his first national championship as a diver in 1942. He was victorious in the 3-Meter Springboard and the 10-Meter Platform events. Lee stood at 5 feet and 1 inch but was able to use his height to his advantage by "tucking and turning faster than his opponents." He went on to the University of

Sammy Lee

Southern California Medical School and briefly retired from diving, but he returned to competition in 1946 and won the national championship in the platform event.

In 1947 Lee served his country as a member of the U.S. Army following his graduation from USC Medical School. He continued to dive, and at the 1948 Olympics in London, he won his first gold medal in the platform competition as well as a bronze medal in the springboard competition. In an interview with Terry Hong, Lee describes the two things he was proud of at that moment: "I was wearing the flag of my country on my chest and I was wearing the flag of my Asian ancestors on my face."

After the Olympics, Lee focused his attention on medicine and served as a doctor in the Korean War. While serving his residency as a lieutenant in the Army Medical Corps, Lee was approached by the U.S. Olympic coach to compete in the 1952 Olympics. Despite the fact that he rarely competed after winning his first gold medal, Lee qualified for the 1952 Olympic Games. In Helsinki, Lee won his second gold medal in platform diving and became the first male athlete to win two consecutive gold medals in that event. A year later Sammy Lee was awarded the James E. Sullivan Memorial Award for outstanding U.S. amateur athlete.

Lee retired from competitive diving as an athlete but remained active
as a coach for the 1960 U.S. Olympic Diving Team as well as the 1964
Japanese and Korean teams. He also trained gold medalists Bob Webster
and Greg Louganis. In 1968 Lee was inducted into the International
Swimming Hall of Fame, and in 1979 he became the first foreign coach
to enter China and evaluate its diving team.

Selected Bibliography

"Asian Americans: A 'Model Minority.' " *Newsweek*, December 6, 1982, pp. 39–
    42.
Bingham, Walter. "Swimming & Diving—Pathways to the Olympics." *Sports Il-
    lustrated*, August 1, 1988, pp. 43–47.
Wampler, Molly Frick. *Not without Honor: The Story of Sammy Lee*. Santa Barbara,
    CA: Fithian Press, 1987.

Jennifer Kang

TSUNG DAO LEE

(1926–)

Physicist

Tsung Dao Lee, Nobel Prize–winning physicist, was born on November
25, 1926, in Shanghai, China. He was the son of businessman Tsing-Kong
Lee and Ming-Chang Chang. He entered the National Chekiang University in Kweichow in 1943; when the University moved to K'un-ming in
1945 and became part of the National Southwest Associated University,
Lee followed. He received his Bachelor of Science degree in physics in
1946 and then attended the University of Chicago. While there, Lee studied with Physics professor Enrico Fermi. Lee received his Ph.D. in 1950.
    Lee was a research associate at the Yerkes Astronomical Observatory
in Lake Geneva, Wisconsin, and at the University of California at Berkeley in 1950 and 1951. In 1951 he joined the Institute for Advanced Study
in Princeton, New Jersey, and from 1960 to 1963 served as professor
there. Lee became assistant professor at Columbia University in 1953. In
1956, at age twenty-nine, Lee was the youngest person ever to become
full professor at Columbia. In 1963 he was named Enrico Fermi Professor
of Physics there.
    Lee and his colleague Chen Ning Yang had met as students at National
Southwest Associated University and began working together again at

the Institute for Advanced Study. They began to design experiments that challenged the law of the conservation of parity in the weak force (which acts in the emission of particles during radioactive decay). They found evidence for the law in strong and electromagnetic forces, but, surprisingly, found no evidence for the law in weak forces. When these experiments showed that the law did not apply in weak forces, Lee and Yang could better explain the problem of theta- and tau-mesons (which are weak forces), which had appeared to behave contrary to the law.

For their investigation of the law of the conservation of parity, Lee and Yang were awarded the Nobel Prize in Physics in 1957. In the same year Lee received the Albert Einstein Commemorative Award from Yeshiva University. In 1986 he was awarded the Order of Merit from the Republic of Italy.

Lee married Hui-Chung (Jeannette) Chin in 1950. They have two children.

Selected Bibliography

Crease, R., and C. Mann. *The Second Creation: Makers of the Revolution in Twentieth Century Physics*. New York: MacMillan, 1986.
Lee, T. D. *Particle Physics and Introduction to Field Theory*. New York: Harwood Academic Publishers, 1981.
Wasson, Tyler, ed. *Nobel Prize Winners*. Princeton, NJ: Visual Education Corporation, 1987.

Franklin Ng

YUAN-TSEH LEE
(1936–   )
Chemist, Educator

Yuan-Tseh Lee, Nobel Prize winner in Chemistry, was born on November 29, 1936, in the northern city of Hsinchu, Taiwan. His father was Tse Fan Lee and his mother was Pei Tsai Lee. Lee attended National Taiwan University and received his Bachelor's degree in 1959. In 1961 he received his Master's degree from National Tsing Hua University. In 1962 he began doctoral studies and research on the chemical ionization processes of electronically excited alkali atoms at the University of California at Berkeley. He earned his Ph.D. there in 1965.

Lee next worked with professor Dudley Herschbach at Harvard University; their research on the crossed molecular beams method was honored by the Nobel Prize in Chemistry in 1986. Lee became assistant professor and then professor of chemistry at the University of Chicago from 1968 to 1974. In 1974 he was offered a position at the University of California at Berkeley and continued his teaching and research there.

In addition to the Nobel Prize in Chemistry in 1986, Lee has received the Earnest Orlando Lawrence Award (1981), the Harrison E. Howe Award (1983), the Peter Debye Award (1986), and the National Medal of Science (1986). In 1993 he was named the University of California at Berkeley's faculty research lecturer, lecturing on "Steering Chemical Reactions by Laser Excitation."

In late 1993 Lee was appointed by Taiwan president Lee Teng-hui to succeed Wu Tayou as president of Academia Sinica, the Republic of China's highest academic institution. In this capacity Lee has plans to raise $37.7 million over three years to encourage overseas scholars to return to Taiwan. He hopes to promote Taiwan's technological and cultural development and provide better pay, housing allowances, and education subsidies for dependents for returning scholars.

Lee married Bernice Chinli Wu in 1963. They have three children.

Selected Bibliography

"Chemistry: Nobel Prize for 'Detailed Understanding of How Chemical Reactions Take Place.' " *Scientific American*, December 1986, p. 86.

Gwynne, Peter. "Nobel Prize Focus on Science of the Ultra Small." *Research and Development*, December 1986, p. 37.

Lee, Y. "Molecular Beam Studies of Elementary Chemical Processes." *Science*, vol. 236 (1987):793–798.

"Lee, Yuan T." *Current Biography*. New York: H. W. Wilson, 1987, p. 167.

Zoglin, Richard, Joe Levine, et al. "Nobel Prize Winners." *Time*, October 27, 1986.

Franklin Ng

VICTOR HAO LI

(1941–   )

Author, Educator

Victor Hao Li, law professor and author, was born in Hong Kong, China, on September 17, 1941. His mother was Wu Chu Fang, and his father, General Han Hun Li, was governor of China's Guangdong province from

1938 to 1945. Li came to the United States in 1947 and graduated from White Plains High School in White Plains, New York, in 1957. He received his Bachelor of Arts degree in mathematics from Columbia University in 1961. Li attended Columbia Law School and received a doctorate in jurisprudence in 1964. He also holds an LL.M. (1965) and an S.J.D. (1971) from Harvard Law School.

Li was visiting assistant professor of law at the University of Michigan Law School from 1967 to 1969 and assistant professor of law at Columbia Law School from 1969 to 1972. He was associate professor of law at Columbia from 1972 to 1974. From 1974 to 1981 he was Shelton professor of international legal studies at Stanford Law School, where he also served as acting professor of law. From 1981 to 1990 he was president of the East-West Center, an academic institution located at the University of Hawaii, Manoa campus. The Center promotes understanding between the United States and Asia-Pacific nations through cooperative study, training, and research.

Since 1990, Li has been co-chairman of the Asia Pacific Consulting Group.

Li's books include a series of studies on the normalization of U.S.-China relations. These are *Derecognizing Taiwan* (1977) and *The Future of Taiwan: A Difference of Opinion* (1980). Li's *Law in Radically Different Cultures (China)* (1983) was awarded the American Society of International Law's 1984 Certificate of Merit. Some of his other books are *Law and Politics in China's Foreign Trade* (ed., 1977), *Law without Lawyers: A Comparative View of Law in China and the United States* (1980), and *Transnational and Economic Law in the People's Republic of China* (1981). His current interests are Pacific trade and investment, U.S. relations with the Asia-Pacific region, China's legal system, and the cultural dimension in economic and political development.

Li is married to Arlene Lum, former publisher of the *Honolulu Star-Bulletin*. They have three children.

Selected Bibliography

Evans, Kani, and Peter F. Senecal, eds. *Leaders of Hawaii, 1983*. Louisville, KY: General and Associates, 1983.

Hartwell, Jay. "China Expert Picked to be Head of EWC." *Honolulu Advertiser*, December 25, 1980.

Lum, Arlene. *Sailing for the Sun: The Chinese in Hawaii, 1789–1989*. Honolulu: Center for Chinese Studies, University of Hawaii, 1988.

Watumull, David. *Prominent People of Hawaii*. Honolulu: Delta Publishing, 1988.

Franklin Ng

GENEVIEVE (GENNY) LIM

(1946–)

Author, Community Leader, Educator, Television Journalist

Genevieve (Genny) Lim, writer, performer, community activist, and educator, was born in San Francisco on December 15, 1946. She graduated from Galileo High School in San Francisco, California, in 1964. In 1974 she completed the Michele Clark Fellowship Program in Journalism at Columbia University. She received her Bachelor of Arts degree in English, with a creative writing emphasis and a minor in theater arts, from San Francisco State University in 1977. In 1988 she earned a Master of Arts degree in English, with a creative writing emphasis.

Lim began her multifaceted career as a broadcast associate for CBS News, National Assignment Desk. There, from 1972 to 1973, Lim did general reporting from network bureaus in Atlanta, Chicago, and New York and served as substitute host for CBS News' radio weekly, "Today's Woman," and as voice-over commentator for CBS National Syndication. Lim served as a freelance writer/reporter, television producer, and commentator from 1973 to 1981. During that time she co-produced the documentary *Bad Times on Gold Mountain* for WETA-TV (1974). Lim also coordinated, wrote, and co-produced local segments of WTTW-TV's special educational series on desegregation, *ASWESEEIT*. From 1976 to 1977, she was host on KGO-TV's weekly ninety-minute program, *Perspective*.

From 1979 through 1981 Lim was a performing member of Unbound Feet, a collective of six Chinese American women writers who staged their own work. Lim taught creative writing workshops to Asian community residents from 1981 to 1982 as a California Arts Council community artist-in-residence for the Kearny Street Workshop in San Francisco. In 1983 she served as visiting lecturer in creative writing at the University of California at Berkeley in the Department of Ethnic Studies. From 1981 through 1983 Lim was project investigator for the "Chinese Women of America, 1848–1982" project. This project was sponsored by the Chinese Culture Center in San Francisco under the Women's Educational Equity Act of the U.S. Department of Education. Lim was also artistic director of Paper Angels Productions from 1982 through 1987; from 1984 through 1985 she adapted her play, *Paper An-*

Genny Lim (photo © 1995 by Bob Hsiang)

gels, into an hour-long television drama for PBS's *American Playhouse* series.

Between 1986 and 1989 Lim shared her talents in several California elementary and middle schools as a writer-in-residence through the California Arts Council and through the California Poets in the Schools Program and the California Heritage Program. Lim was curator of Poets in the Galleries, a rotating exhibition of student poetry combined with art at the Fine Arts Museums of San Francisco from 1989 through 1993.

Since 1989 Lim has been a part of the Core Faculty in Humanities and coordinator of performance studies at New College of California. She is also co-chair of the undergraduate humanities program there.

Lim's theater productions include *Paper Angels*, which premiered at the Asian American Theater Company in San Francisco (1980). It won the James Wong Howe Award from the Asian American Pacific Actors' Association. *Pigeons*, a one-act play, premiered in 1983 at the San Francisco Chinese Culture Center. It was adapted by Christine Choy into a film entitled *Fei Tien*, which premiered in New York City in 1984. *The Only Language She Knows*, a portrait of Lim produced by **Steven Okazaki** and Amy Hill, aired on PBS's *Silk Screen* series in 1987. Lim's collaborations include *XX* (1987), which won the Zellerbach Family Fund

Community Arts Program grant, the Lee and Lawrence First Prize Playwriting Award from the San Francisco State University Creative Writing Department, and a California Arts Council Multicultural Program Fellowship. *The Pumpkin Girl* (1987), *Winter Place* (1988), *SenseUs: Rainbow Anthems* (1990), *La China Poblana* (1991), *Pins and Noodles* (1993), and *Bitter Cane* (1993) are some of Lim's collaborative works.

Lim's poetry and excerpts from her plays have been published in such magazines as *Y'Bird*, *Bridge*, *Bamboo Ridge*, *Contact/II*, and *Zyzzyva*. Her work has been included in a number of anthologies, such as *The Forbidden Stitch: An Asian American Women's Anthology* (1989), *Skin Deep: Women Writing on Race and Color in America* (1994), *Unbroken Thread: Anthology of Plays by Asian American Women* (1993), *Chinese American Poetry: An Anthology* (1991), and *This Bridge Called My Back* (1981).

Lim edited *The Chinese American Experience: Papers from the 1980 National Conference on Chinese American Studies* (1984). She co-authored, with **Him Mark Lai** and **Judy Yung**, *Island: Poetry and History of Chinese Immigrants on Angel Island, 1910–1940* (1980), which won the American Book Award from the Before Columbus Foundation in 1982. In 1989 a collection of Lim's poetry, *Winter Place*, was published. Lim also wrote *Wings for Lai Ho* (1982).

When asked about her perspective on Asian Americans, Lim says,

More and more we are edging towards the crossroads of self-extinction or self-evolution as Asian Americans. With each succeeding generation and with the increasing numbers of mixed marriages, the effects of racial and cultural assimilation will either erase us out of existence entirely or it will simply be a natural and progressive outgrowth of our successful survival in America. It all depends on how you look at culture and the importance of cultural preservation. For myself, I have a pragmatic view of culture as a dynamic human construct that has to be modified and changed from time to time, according to historical need. Certain elements of traditional culture can and should be discarded, such as feudal ideas of class and male worship; however, it is critical to preserve the philosophy, art, and mythology of a culture because they provide the ethos and marrow of cultural identity.

Lim says of Asian American studies,

Unless we can reframe the discourses of history, mythology, psychology, literature, religion, science, etc. in our own cultural terms, we will only fall further into the danger of self-institutionalization and neo-colonization. There must be more cross-pollination of disciplinary thinking and re-definitions of concepts, such as art, culture, knowledge, and self. We must continue to examine the cultural biases embedded in these Eurocentric concepts and teach them to our students so that they will not continue to accept cultural assumptions that marginalize us and waken us into stereotypes and alienated schizophrenics.

Lim adds that "History is very critical, especially for young people in understanding their cultural heritage and the impact of immigration and global policies on third world countries. The rules are constantly being made and maintained by those in power, while indigenous peoples throughout the world are exploited for American consumerism and corporate profits."

Lim is guided by her sense of social responsibility. She says,

We've all heard of the glass ceiling for Asian American professionals, but there is a substantial underclass of refugees and immigrants who struggle with health, housing, unemployment, youth gangs and drugs. While as a people we have accomplished a lot in terms of our historical contributions to the U.S., we must remember that we are only as advanced as the most deprived of us. The ideal of rugged individualism driving the competitive machinery of Western capitalism succeeds, ultimately, at the expense of communality and social responsibility.

Lim adds that the dichotomies of genres and disciplines

are the products of Eurowestern thinking, where bodies of knowledge are quantified, separated, and structured into categories, which satisfy its need to define all phenomena in absolute terms. These categories are then ratified and institutionalized by the state, which serves as the dominant culture, and we are thereafter their slaves. I have always mixed expressions—music with poetry, sculpture with song, without giving much thought to whether or not I was crossing over or breaking rules. These rules, confining genre to genre, paint to object, word to paper, are man-made and as such, they are artificial, not natural to my state of being or any other's.

Selected Bibliography

Houston, V., ed. *The Politics of Life: Four Plays by Asian American Women*. Philadelphia: Temple University Press, 1993.

Lai, H., G. Lim, and J. Yung. *Island: Poetry and History of Chinese Immigrants on Angel Island, 1910–1940*. Seattle: University of Washington Press, 1991.

Lim, G., ed. *The Chinese American Experience: Papers from the Second National Conference on Chinese American Studies*. San Francisco: Chinese Historical Society of America, Chinese Culture Foundation of San Francisco, 1983.

———. *Paper Angels and Bitter Cane: Two Plays*. Honolulu: Kalamaku Press, 1991.

———. *Winter Place: Poems*. San Francisco: Kearny Street Workshop Press, 1989.

Lim, S., M. Tsutakawa, and M. Donnelly, eds., *The Forbidden Stitch: An Asian American Women's Anthology*. Corvallis, OR: Calyx Books, 1989.

Moraga, C., and G. Anzaldua. *This Bridge Called My Back: Writings by Radical Women of Color*. Watertown, MA: Persephone Press, 1981.

Uno, R., ed. *Unbroken Thread: An Anthology of Plays by Asian American Women*. Amherst: University of Massachusetts Press, 1993.

Franklin Ng

JOHN KEUN LIM

(1935–)

Politician, Business Leader

John Lim, entrepreneur, state senator, and civil servant, was born on December 23, 1935, in Yeoju, Korea. Growing up with his parents, four brothers, and a sister, he learned early the value of cooperation and hard work. His father and uncle served as role models. They worked together as farmers and also operated the only sawmill in the small town near Seoul.

At age eight Lim became the first in his family to adopt Christianity. The decision—remarkable for so young a boy—shows how early his sense of self emerged.

In 1950 John's father, the local volunteer fire marshall, became one of the early casualties of the Korean War. Dealing with the hardships of war, the Lim family worked as hard as any to keep food on the table. Though for much of the war it was too dangerous to attend school, Lim made good use of the time by memorizing the 7,500 words in his English-Korean dictionary.

John also spent many years helping out at the orphanage behind his home. Before finishing high school he earned money as a houseboy for U.S. servicemen stationed in Korea. Later he supported himself with a variety of occupations, including house painter, custodian, messenger, gardener, and pot and pan salesman. These experiences, which others might have considered menial, were revelations for John. They planted in him the seed of service that years later bore fruit in the United States.

During the summers, while attending Seoul Theological College, John Lim earned money as an assistant pastor in many churches. He received his Bachelor of Arts degree in religion in February 1964. Two years later, in June 1966, Lim immigrated to the United States. In Portland, Oregon, he attended Western Evangelical Seminary and earned a Master of Divinity degree in May 1970. In 1996 the seminary presented Lim with an Honorary Doctor of Humane Letters.

For years John Lim and his wife, Grace, have worked diligently at building and maintaining a variety of small businesses including an international health and beauty products firm, a small grocery, and a com-

John Lim (photo © 1996 by Ron Karten Photography)

mercial and real estate firm. As a result of their successes, each year Lim
is honored with leadership positions in Oregon, the United States, and
abroad. His work has been cited in publications around the world. Most
recently he was honored by the Oregon Tourism Commission as Legislator of the Year. Also he was recently appointed to the executive committee of the Pacific Northwest Economic Region, or PNWER.

In 1990 Lim ran a notable campaign for the Republican nomination in
Oregon's gubernatorial race. Though he entered as an unknown, he won
more than 11 percent of the vote. With his hard-earned name recognition,
Lim returned to the campaign trail in 1992. He, his wife, children, and
campaign staff visited more than 30,000 homes in East Multnomah
County during that campaign. He wore out four pairs of shoes learning
what was on the minds of District 11 citizens. This time his efforts paid
off. In an election year of razor-thin margins of victory, Lim won the
state Senate seat with nearly 60 percent of the vote. As testimony to his
effective leadership, he ran for reelection in 1996 and won the nomination of the Republican party. Today Lim is chair of the state's powerful
Trade and Economic Development Committee and a member of the
Ways and Means Committee.

John Lim believes in giving back to the community. In 1990 he endowed the John Lim Scholarship to make higher education accessible to more Oregon state residents.

An outdoorsman when he has the time, Lim enjoys fishing, skiing, and playing golf. He likes to read about politics, economics, and religion. These wide-ranging interests give him a great respect for the diversity of American culture.

Married for more than thirty years, John and his wife, Grace, are the parents of three children: Peter, Bill, and Gloria. They also have one grandchild.

Selected Bibliography

Who's Who among Asian Americans, 1994–1995 ed. Detroit: Gale Research, 1994, p. 360.

Who's Who in American Politics, 16th edition, 1997–1998. New Providence, NJ: Marquis Who's Who, 1997, p. 1737.

Who's Who in American Politics, 14th ed., 1993–1994. New Providence, NJ: R. R. Bowker, 1993, p. 1444.

Jennifer Kang

MAYA LIN

(1959–)

Architect, Sculptor

Maya Lin, architect and sculptor, is probably best known as the designer of the Vietnam Veterans Memorial in Washington, D.C., and the Civil Rights Memorial in Montgomery, Alabama. She was born in Athens, Ohio, on October 5, 1959. She is the daughter of literature professor Julia Chang Lin, and Henry Huan Lin, a ceramist and dean of fine arts at Ohio State University. Her parents both immigrated from China to the United States in the 1940s.

Lin attended Yale University, majoring in architecture. During her senior year she submitted an entry in the competition to select a design for the Vietnam Veterans Memorial. Her design features two long, low black granite walls that meet to form a shallow "V." The names of almost 58,000 dead or missing veterans of the Vietnam War are inscribed on the monument's surface. Lin's design was chosen by a panel from 1,420 entries on May 6, 1981. Though some veterans protested the design, the memorial was dedicated on November 13, 1982, after a 48-hour vigil at the Washington Cathedral.

Lin briefly attended Harvard University's graduate architecture program, but in the fall of 1983 she returned to Yale University. She received her Master's degree from Yale in 1985 and her Ph.D. in 1987. Lin continued her design work on diverse projects, including a stage set in Philadelphia, a park outside the Charlotte Coliseum in North Carolina, and a new glass ceiling for the Long Island Railroad terminal in Pennsylvania Station in New York City. She has exhibited her sculpture at the Sidney Janis Gallery, the Tibor' de Nagy Gallery, and the Rosa Esman Gallery.

Lin was asked by the Southern Poverty Law Center in Montgomery, Alabama, to design a memorial for those who had given their lives in the struggle for racial equality. The sculpture was dedicated in 1989. The Civil Rights Memorial is composed of two elements. The first is a black granite disk inscribed with twenty-one landmark events in the history of the civil rights movement and the names of forty people who lost their lives in the struggle. The second element is a nine-foot wall with an inscription of Martin Luther King Jr.'s words: "until justice rolls down like water and righteousness like a mighty stream." Water runs down this wall and flows gently from the middle of the disk.

Lin also designed a monument commemorating the 100th anniversary of the admittance of women into Yale University's graduate school. Titled "The Women's Table," the sculpture is an oval table of green granite with water flowing slowly over it. Inscribed on the table is a spiral of numbers reflecting the number of women enrolled at Yale since its founding in 1701. It was dedicated in 1992 and is located on Cross Campus, the main quadrangle at Yale.

Lin continues both sculpture and architectural work in her private practice in New York City.

Selected Bibliography

Ashabranner, B. *Always to Remember: The Story of the Vietnam Veterans' Memorial.* New York: Putnam, 1988.
Gandee, Charles. "Life after Vietnam." *Vogue*, February 1993.
Malone, Mary. *Maya Lin: Architect and Artist.* New York: Enslaw, 1995.
Scruggs, J. *To Heal a Nation: The Vietnam Veterans' Memorial.* New York: Harper & Row, 1985.
Stein, J. "Space and Place." *Art in America*, December 1994.

Franklin Ng

DANIEL S. C. LIU
(1908–1986)
Law Enforcement Officer

Many people have heard of the fictional character Charlie Chan, who was based on a Chinese detective in Honolulu named **Chang Apana**. But few people today know about Daniel Siu Chong Liu, who was a Hawaii-born Chinese head of police for the Honolulu Police Department.

In 1908 Daniel S. C. Liu was born in Honolulu to Ah Seong Liu and Yin Kyau Ching. His father had emigrated from Beijing to open a grocery store in Hawaii, and his mother's family had come from South China. Daniel Liu attended Kaahumanu Elementary School and graduated from St. Louis High School in 1926. He also attended California Baptist College in Riverside, California.

In 1932, C. I. Howell came from Berkeley, California, to help set up a new police department in Honolulu in the wake of the furor over the nationally publicized Massie case, in which Thalia Massie was allegedly raped by a gang of "five dark-skinned youths." Instead of having an elected sheriff's system, there would be a chief of police under a police commission selected by the territorial governor. Being out of a job during the Depression, Daniel Liu took and passed the first merit system examination administered by the department.

He became a radio patrolman with the detective division and was assigned to a two-man, radio-equipped squad car. He gained experience working in police records and detective cases. From then on, he rose rapidly through the ranks. He attained the rank of sergeant in 1935. Six years later he was promoted to lieutenant and was also appointed secretary to the Police Commission. By 1945 he was captain, by 1947 he was assistant chief, and three months later he became deputy chief. On August 1, 1948, he accepted the top post of chief of police when William Hoopai retired. He thus became the first Chinese American to head a police department in an American city.

During World War II, the territory of Hawaii had been placed under martial law. At the end of the war in 1945, the Police Department was rocked by disclosure of graft in its vice squad. The scandal led to the departure of Police Chief W. A. Gabrielson and made a strong impression on Daniel Liu. That memory and his strong religious values strengthened his conviction that vice of all types—gambling, prostitution, and narcotics—should be eliminated. He also tried to curtail the use of pinball machines, fireworks, and the sale of beer at the Honolulu Stadium. These efforts, along with his attempt to ban Henry Miller's book *Tropic of Cancer* (1961) from the Library of Hawaii due to its "obscene language" and sexual content, were less successful.

From time to time, gambling syndicates from the U.S. mainland sought entry to Hawaii, tantalized by the prospect of easy profits from servicemen and tourists. Daniel Liu spurned attempts at bribery, threats, and political pressure, organizing a special anti-gambling squad within the vice division for the purpose of controlling gambling.

While leading efforts to combat crime and vice, Daniel Liu sought to upgrade and improve the professional stature of the police force. This entailed raising the level of education requirements to graduation from high school and, later, to several years of college. He also successfully raised the salary of officers and tried to improve their working conditions. On the whole, he stayed away from politics and avoided public controversy. A notable exception was when he opposed a proposal by the state legislature to give four counties rather than the governor the power to select Police Commission members. He believed that this bill would have introduced politics and compromised police operations.

Throughout his career he enhanced the image of the Honolulu Police Department and gave it a reputation for integrity and efficiency. He is credited with securing a police science program at the University of Hawaii and instituting a cadet training program. He also developed a crime laboratory, installed a computer system, and formed a community relations division. He cultivated ties with youth and worked with the YMCA, the Boy Scouts, the Police Activities League, and other civic organizations. A devout Christian, he was a trustee of the Olivet Baptist Church.

Daniel Liu's outstanding record in all aspects of law enforcement drew national and international attention. He was president of the FBI National Academy class in 1959 and president of the International Association of Chiefs of Police in 1963–1964. In 1966 he received the J. Edgar Hoover Gold Medal for his accomplishments in law enforcement and dedication to his profession. The American public sometimes confused him with Charlie Chan as his fame grew. He played himself in an espionage film, *Big Jim McClain*, in 1952 with actor John Wayne, and cartoonist Chester Gold even featured detective Dick Tracy working with Chief Daniel Liu on a case in 1960.

In 1969 Daniel Liu retired as police chief to serve as special assistant for international affairs with U.S. postmaster general Winton M. Blount in Washington, D.C. He later served as Pacific affairs director for American Airlines and was president of the Christian Broadcasting Association.

Daniel Liu married Jewell Mars, a former schoolteacher from Birmingham, Alabama, on June 2, 1937, in Hilo, Hawaii. She died in 1983, and he died on July 18, 1986.

Selected Bibliography

"50 Million Meet Police Chief Liu," *Honolulu Advertiser*, February 10, 1960.
"Dan Liu, Ex-Chief of Police, Is Dead." *Honolulu Star-Bulletin*, July 21, 1986.
"Dan Liu, Honolulu's Legendary Police Chief, Dies." *Honolulu Advertiser*, July 22, 1986.
"Honolulu's Amazing Mr. Liu." *Honolulu Advertiser*, January 13, 1957.
Jones, Gardiner B. "Liu Tells of Early Days: No Rules, No Training." *Honolulu Star-Bulletin & Advertiser*, May 18, 1969.
Liu, Daniel S. C. "Report of the Law Enforcement Staff Planning Committee of the Hawaii Model Cities Project. Report from Dan Liu to Arthur A. Akina." Honolulu Police Department, 1968.
"Liu Gets Order of the Splintered Paddle at Banquet." *Honolulu Star-Bulletin,* June 11, 1969.
"Liu's Career Reviewed." *Honolulu Advertiser*, April 27, 1969.
McMurray, Terry. "Chief Liu to Quit for D.C. Post." *Honolulu Advertiser*, April 26, 1969.
Mayo, Don. "Dan Liu: A Number One Enemy of Crime." *Paradise of the Pacific*, vol. 69, no. 9 (1957):24–25.
Verploegen, Mary. "A Portrait of Mrs. Dan Liu." *Honolulu Star-Bulletin*, May 28, 1969.
Walden, May Day Lo. "Many Chinese Active in City-County Posts." In Robert M. Lee, ed., *The Chinese in Hawaii: A Historical Sketch*. Honolulu: Advertiser Publishing, 1961.
Youngblood, Ron. "Tributes, Food Abundant at Liu's Aloha Banquet." *Honolulu Advertiser*, May 29, 1969.

Franklin Ng

GARY LOCKE

(1950–)

Politician, Governor, Attorney

A second-generation Chinese American, Gary Locke is the first Asian American to be elected governor of a state on the U.S. mainland. Prior to his election as governor of the state of Washington in 1996, other Asian

American governors included **George Ariyoshi** and **Ben Cayetano** of Hawaii.

Locke's grandfather had originally emigrated to Olympia, Washington, from the Taishan (Cantonese: Toishan) part of Guangdong province in South China. His grandfather eventually returned to China, but his father and mother, James and Julie Locke, came to Seattle in the late 1930s. They operated a Chinese restaurant in the Pike Market Place and later opened a grocery store. Gary Locke was born as the second child of the family on January 21, 1950.

In his youth, Locke worked for his parents and attended school. He found time to become an Eagle Scout and graduated from Franklin High School in 1968. Going east for his college education, he attended Yale University on a scholarship and received a B.A. degree in political science in 1972. Three years later he obtained a law degree from Boston University.

Locke returned to Seattle and served as a deputy prosecutor in King County. In 1982 he won election to the House of Representatives for Washington state. While in the legislature, he served on the Judiciary Committee and for five years was chair of the Appropriations Committee. In 1993 he successfully ran for the post of chief executive of King County, the largest county in the state.

Three years later, in 1996, he decided to run for governor of the state to succeed Democrat Mike Lowry. After winning the Democratic primary against Seattle mayor Norm Rice, he faced Republican candidate Ellen Craswell. Despite encountering negative ads in the last weeks of the campaign, Locke was able to register a landslide victory with 59 percent of the vote against his conservative Christian opponent. The gubernatorial victory by an Asian American candidate on the U.S. mainland was hailed by many in the Asian American community.

In his State of the Union address in 1997, President Bill Clinton introduced Governor Gary Locke to a national audience. Because Washington is the home of Boeing, a major manufacturer of aircraft, as well as Microsoft computer software and Yakima Valley apples, Locke has also been prominent in representing his state's economic interests before the world community. His election immediately made headlines in Asia, especially in Taiwan, China, and Hong Kong. He received invitations to visit China and Taiwan, and he received widespread coverage for his meetings with Chinese leaders such as President Jiang Zemin.

Locke is married to Mona Lee, a former television news reporter in Seattle. They have one child, who was born in 1997.

Selected Bibliography

Egan, Timothy. "Battle in Washington Brings Soul-Searching." *New York Times,* October 22, 1996, p. A18.

———. "Chinese Roots of Winner Delights Pacific Rim." *New York Times,* November 7, 1996, pp. B8, 11.

Eljera, Bert. "Coming Up a Winner." *Asianweek,* September 20, 1996, p. 10.

———. "Win Some, Lose Some." *Asianweek,* November 15, 1996, pp. 12–13.

Murphy, Kim. "Washington State Battle Inspiring Asian Americans." *Los Angeles Times,* November 1, 1996, pp. A30–32.

Weinstein, Henry. "7 Democrats, 4 in GOP Win Governorships." *Los Angeles Times,* November 6, 1996, p. A16.

Wong, Bill. "Great Aspirations." *Asianweek,* October 25, 1996, pp. 12–13.

Franklin Ng

JOHN LONE

(1952–   )

Actor, Director, Choreographer

John Lone, actor, director, and choreographer, was born in 1952 in Hong Kong, China. He trained for the stage at the Chin Chiu Academy in Hong Kong and at the American Academy of Dramatic Arts in Pasadena, California. Lone made his stage debut at the New York Shakespeare Festival's Public Theatre in 1980, playing the part of Steve in *F.O.B. (Fresh Off the Boat).* He choreographed that same production and appeared in the East/West Players production in Los Angeles in 1980. Lone next appeared in *The Dance and the Railroad* at the New Federal Theatre in New York City (1981) and at the Cricket Theatre in Minneapolis (1982). He also composed the musical score for both those productions. Lone directed and acted in the New York Shakespeare Festival's *Sound and Beauty* in 1983. He received Obie awards for his work in *F.O.B. (Fresh Off the Boat)* and *The Dance and the Railroad.*

Lone appeared in the films *Iceman* (Universal, 1984), *Shadows of the Peacock* (Laughing Kookaburra Productions, 1987), and *The Moderns* (Alive Films, 1987). He played Pu Yi, who became China's emperor at the age of three, in Columbia's *The Last Emperor* in 1987, winning a Golden Globe nomination for Best Actor in a Motion Picture. He starred in the enigmatic role of Song Liling in **David Henry Hwang**'s *M. But-*

terfly in the 1993 film directed by David Cronenberg. In 1995 he appeared in two films, *The Hunted* and *The Shadow*.

Selected Bibliography

Hilton, Pat. "The Sudden Success of John Lone." *Drama-Logue*, October 10–16, 1985.
"John Lone." *New York Times*, July 31, 1981.
Shewey, Don. "His Art Blends the Best of Two Cultures on Stage." *New York Times*, October 30, 1983.
Watson, Steven. "The Primitive Innocence of a Lone Iceman." *Newsday*, April 22, 1984.

Franklin Ng

BETTE BAO LORD
(1938–   )
Author

Bette Bao Lord, author and lecturer, was born in Shanghai, China, on November 3, 1938, and came to the United States with her family at age of eight. She is the daughter of Sandys Bao and Dora Fang Bao. Lord attended public schools in Brooklyn, New York, and received her Bachelor of Arts degree from Tufts University in 1959. She received a Master of Arts degree from the Fletcher School of Law and Diplomacy in 1960. Lord has also been honored with doctorates from the University of Notre Dame, Tufts University, Skidmore College, Marymount College, Bryant College, and Dominican College.

Lord is the author of *Eighth Moon: The True Story of a Young Girl's Life in Communist China* (1964). A captivating story, it was well received and was eventually published in fifteen foreign editions. Her second novel, *Spring Moon* (1981), about the tumultuous life in China during its Cultural Revolution, was a critical success. It became a *New York Times* bestseller and was nominated for the American Book Award. It subsequently was reprinted in eighteen foreign editions. Three years later Lord wrote a children's book, *In the Year of the Boar and Jackie Robinson*. A fictional account of her years as a grade school student in New York, it enjoyed favorable reviews and received the American Library Association Award. Her next book, *Legacies, A Chinese Mosaic* (1990), was

Bette Bao Lord (photo by Berle Cherney)

chosen by *Time* magazine as one of the ten best nonfiction books of 1990. It was also a *New York Times* bestseller and has been published in at least ten foreign editions. Her most recent book, *The Middle Heart* (1995), was also a *New York Times* bestseller. In addition to her books, Lord is the author of numerous articles that have appeared in the *Los Angeles Times, Newsweek, New York Times, USA Today*, and other publications.

Lord, whose husband is Winston Lord, assistant secretary of state for East Asian and Pacific affairs and former U.S. ambassador to China (1985–1989), is an expert on life in modern China. As a consultant to CBS News Lord helped to interpret the democracy movement launched by Chinese university students in Tiananmen Square from April to June 1989. She has appeared on *CBS Evening News, Face the Nation, McNeil Lehrer News Hour*, CNN, *48 Hours, Good Morning America, Larry King Live*, and *20/20*.

Lord co-produced the People's Art Theatre's Beijing production of *The Caine Mutiny*, directed by Charlton Heston, in 1988. She has been a featured guest lecturer at the Asia Society, the Council on Foreign Affairs, Harvard University, NASA, the National Council of Women, and the New York Public Library.

Interested in promoting human rights and political democracy, Lord is chairwoman of the Board of Trustees of Freedom House, an organization established in 1941 by Wendell Willkie and Eleanor Roosevelt to monitor the violation of political and civil rights and promote the growth of democratic institutions around the world.

Bette Bao Lord is an example of a remarkable and talented individual, committed to public life as an activist and author. In recognition of her achievements, she has won many awards throughout her career. These include the Barnard College Medal of Distinction, the Women of Honor Award from the National Council of Women, the New York Public Library's Literary Lion Award, membership in the International Women's Hall of Fame, the United States Information Agency Award for Outstanding Contributions, the American Women for International Understanding Award, the China Institute's Qingyun Award, the Distinguished American Award, the Chinatown Planning Council's Woman of the Year Award, and the National Graphic Arts Prize for Photographic Essay.

Lord married Winston Lord in 1963. They have two children, Elizabeth Pillsbury and Winston Bao Lord.

Selected Bibliography

Fox, Mary Virginia. *Bette Bao Lord: Novelist and Chinese Voice for Change*. People of Distinction Series. Chicago: Children's Press, 1993.

Lord, B. *Eighth Moon: The True Story of a Young Girl's Life in Communist China*. New York: Harper & Row, 1964.

———. *In the Year of the Boar and Jackie Robinson*. New York: Harper & Row, 1984.

———. *Legacies: A Chinese Mosaic*. New York: Knopf, 1990.

———. *Spring Moon: A Novel of China*. New York: Harper & Row, 1981.

Zia, Helen, and Susan B. Gall, eds. *Notable Asian Americans*. Detroit: Gale Research, 1995.

Franklin Ng

KEYE LUKE

(1904–1991)

Actor

Keye Luke was one of Hollywood's best-known Chinese American actors. Starring in many films and television shows, he was best known to the public as Charlie Chan's Number One Son and Master Po in the series *Kung Fu*.

Born in Canton, China, in June 1904, Keye Luke immigrated to the United States when he was a young child. Growing up in Seattle, Washington, he graduated from Franklin High School. He started out working as a publicity art director for the Fox and then the RKO studios. His duties included billboard design, caricature, and art work for newspaper columns. He also drew portraits of actors and occasionally wrote Chinese characters. Some examples of his art work may be seen in the murals in two Josef von Sternberg films, *The Shanghai Gesture* and *Macao*.

Keye Luke's entry into acting occurred accidentally. An M-G-M director needed a Chinese actor to speak in *The Painted Veil*, a 1934 film starring Greta Garbo based on Somerset Maugham's novel of the same name. It received good reviews. Once he was encouraged to become an actor, Luke found that his acquaintances and former advertising bosses in the film industry opened doors for him. Newspaper columnists whom he knew, such as Hedda Hopper, Louella Parsons, and Jimmy Starr, all helped spread the word about him. This favorable publicity was advantageous in advancing his acting career.

Keye Luke's ties with Hollywood landed him a role in Twentieth-Century Fox's Charlie Chan films. Phil Friedman, a casting director he knew, steered him to Jim Ryan, another casting director. Ryan said that the Charlie Chan pictures were going to include a Number One Son and that Luke was well suited for the part. Another acquaintance, Philip MacDonald, who was writing the script, saw to it that Luke would have a big role in *Charlie Chan in Paris*.

The 1935 film *Charlie Chan in Paris* gave Keye Luke the opportunity to become a regular in several Charlie Chan films. Acting as Lee Chan, Charlie Chan's Number One Son, Luke was the ideal counterpart to Warner Oland's Charlie Chan. The friendship between the two, both on and off the screen, communicated a sense of intimacy in the Chan family to movie audiences. Luke's informal "Hello, Pop!" conveyed warmth and informality between father and son. Warner Oland's affectionate response with news about his wife in Honolulu reminded moviegoers about Charlie Chan's Hawaiian background, adding personality and richness to the characters.

After this film Keye Luke was signed on contract. He did not appear in the next picture, *Charlie Chan in Shanghai*, the explanation being that the Twentieth-Century Fox studio was still thinking about the pairing. But by the time *Charlie Chan at the Circus* was filmed, the decision had been made and Luke was featured as the Number One Son in the Charlie Chan films of the 1930s. When Warner Oland died in 1938 while working on *Charlie Chan at the Ringside*, the movie was changed into a Mr. Moto film as *Mr. Moto's Gamble*. Mr. Moto was a character developed in writer John P. Marquand's detective novels. Keye Luke was retained in the Mr. Moto film so that the existing footage did not have to be discarded. The adaptation was somewhat awkward, with Number One Son being abruptly paired with a Japanese colleague.

In recent years the character Charlie Chan created by Earl Derr Biggers has been criticized by Asian American activists who see the portrayal as stereotypical and misleading. Fueling their ire is the fact that the role of Charlie Chan was never given to a Chinese actor. But Keye Luke takes pride in the series and defends them as welcome in casting a positive image at that time upon a Chinese detective. In particular, he values his close association with Warner Oland, whom he felt was a talented and dedicated actor. Although there would be others who assumed the role of Charlie Chan, he felt Oland was irreplaceable. Luke moved on to other parts, although from 1972 to 1974 he was the voice for Charlie Chan in the CBS series *The Amazing Chan and the Chan Clan*.

As a contract actor in the big-studio era of moviemaking, Keye Luke appeared in many movies, often with minor parts. But he won recognition for his fine acting in a number of major films. They included *Oil for the Lamps of China* (1935), *The Good Earth* (1937), *Across the Pacific* (1942), *Dragon Seed* (1944), and *Love Is a Many-Splendored Thing* (1955). He also acted as Kato's right-hand man in *The Green Hornet* film serials and as an intern in the M-G-M "Dr. Kildaire" films. In 1958 he played the leader of a Chinese American family in Richard Rodgers and Oscar Hammerstein II's musical *Flower Drum Song*, which had a long run on Broadway.

As television became a popular medium, Keye Luke played numerous television roles. The shows ranged from "Kentucky Jones," "Anna and the King," "Star Trek," and "Andy Griffith" to "M*A*S*H" and "Falcon Crest." He made guest appearances on many police and detective programs such as "Perry Mason," "Hawaii Five-0," "Judge Dee in the Monastery Murders," "MacGyver," and "Magnum, P.I." He especially enjoyed playing the role of the blind monk, Master Po, on the long-playing television series *Kung Fu* (1972–1975).

In a film and television career of nearly sixty years, Keye Luke acted in more than a hundred films and demonstrated his extraordinary versatility. Due to cultural stereotyping his roles were limited to Asian characters, usually Chinese or Japanese. As the norms in the film industry and society changed, he was pleased that some stereotypes fell by the wayside. In 1986 the Association of Asian/Pacific American Artists bestowed on him its first Lifetime Achievement Award. In December 1990 he was honored with a star in the sidewalk at the Hollywood Hall of Fame.

Keye Luke's last film was Woody Allen's comedy *Alice* (1990). In that movie he received warm praise for his role as Dr. Yang, an irascible, intelligent, and humorous doctor. He died on June 12, 1991, in Whittier,

California. His wife died in 1978. They had one daughter, Ethel Longe-
necker of Whittier.

Selected Bibliography

Champlain, Charles. "Keye Luke Was No. 1 in Every Role." *Los Angeles Times*,
    January 16, 1991.
Flint, Peter B. "Keye Luke, Actor, Is Dead at 86." *New York Times*, January 16,
    1991.
Hanke, Ken. *Charlie Chan at the Movies: History, Filmography, and Criticism*. Jeffer-
    son, NC: McFarland & Co., 1989.
Weil, Martin. "Keye Luke, Actor in Charlie Chan Films, 'Alice,' Dies." *Washington
    Post*, January 15, 1991.

                                                              Franklin Ng

---

WING LUKE

(1925–1965)

Politician, Attorney

Elected to the Seattle City Council, Wing Luke was a promising Chinese
American politician who seemed destined to have a bright future. His
successful campaign was an inspiration to Chinese Americans and encouraged Asian Americans to participate in the political process.

Wing Chong Luke was born on February 25, 1925, in Guangdong,
China, the son of Mr. and Mrs. Lung Sing Luke. In the 1930s his father
emigrated to Seattle and opened a grocery store. One of five children,
Wing Luke went to John Marshall Junior High School and graduated
from Roosevelt High School in 1944.

During World War II, Luke joined the U.S. Army and earned a Bronze
Star for service in the Philippines. After his military service he resumed
his education and earned a B.A. degree in political science from the University of Washington. He pursued graduate studies at the American
University in Washington, D.C., and then returned to earn a law degree
from the University of Washington in 1954.

Throughout his youth Luke had shown a lively interest in extracurricular activities and politics. He had been the Boy's Club student body
president and had been chosen president of the Seattle I ter–High School
Council. In college he became sophomore class president and headed the

Young Democrats, the campus YMCA, and other organizations. He got along well with his peers and showed leadership qualities.

After being in private practice in the law for several years, Luke accepted an appointment with the Washington state attorney general's office in 1957. He was assigned the responsibility of representing the State Board Against Discrimination and, later, the Real Estate License Division. In the course of his duties as assistant attorney general, he helped write the state's 1957 statute against discrimination in public accommodations, housing, and employment.

Five years later, in 1962, at age thirty-six, Luke decided to run for the Seattle City Council. He won the primary and faced his principal opponent, Dr. J. G. Aiken, a surgeon. No only did Luke have to contend with lack of name recognition, but he also had to face a smear campaign. In both the primary and the general election for City Council, rumors were spread that he was a communist sympathizer. Waging an aggressive campaign, Luke held coffee hours, distributed cards in buses, placed signs in windows, and mailed out campaign literature. He organized volunteers to help him canvass for votes. The 4,000 Chinese in the Seattle area rallied behind him, many participating for the first time in the political process.

Seeking a broad base of support, Luke did not run as an ethnic candidate. He highlighted his personal qualifications and vowed to represent his district. He solicited support from both Democrats and Republicans, regents from the University of Washington, educators, and Catholic and Jewish leaders. He also received endorsements from ethnic groups, the King County AFL-CIO Labor Council, and other organizations. As a result he easily won the election. His victory attracted considerable attention because of his youth and ancestry—he was the first Chinese to win a high public office in the Pacific Northwest—and he was even interviewed by the Voice of America.

While serving on the Seattle City Council, Luke became president pro-tem and, when the mayor was absent, filled in as acting mayor. One of his most noteworthy achievements, however, involved his efforts on behalf of an open-housing ordinance through the creation of a Human Rights Commission. He supported innovative preservation programs to save the historic Pike Place Market and campaigned to have a "living" ship museum for Seattle. He also welcomed and encouraged cultural exhibits, such as the Chinese exhibits in the Burke Memorial Washington State Museum. He continued to serve on civic groups such as the Board of Directors for the Urban League, the Jackson Community Service Organization, and the Chinese Community Service Organization.

Talented and popular, Luke was expected to win higher office in the future. But in 1965, while on a fishing trip, he and two fishing companions were reported missing; it was later learned that their small plane had crashed. In his memory the Wing Luke Memorial Museum, later renamed the Wing Luke Asian Museum, was established in Seattle's International District in 1986. As a tribute to his legacy it features the art, culture, and history of Asian Americans and Pacific Islanders.

Selected Bibliography

"25 Planes Hunting for Luke, 2 Friends." *Seattle Times*, May 18, 1965.

Chin, Doug. "The Intellectual Politics of Wing Luke." *International Examiner* (Seattle), October 1976.

"Councilman-Elect's Boyhood, School Years Spent in University District." *University District Herald* (Seattle), March 21, 1962.

Evans, Walter. "Bicentennial Biographies: Wing Luke." *Seattle Post-Intelligencer*, September 12, 1975.

Gee, Harriet. "Chinese Immigrant Boy Now Holds High Position in Washington State." *Honolulu Star-Bulletin*, March 7, 1959.

Guzzo, Louis R. "Councilman Luke Proposes Private Development Group to Save Market." *Seattle Times*, July 21, 1964.

Johnsrud, Byron. "Chinese Community Hopes for Miracle for Wing Luke." *Seattle Times*, May 25, 1965.

" 'Living' Museum: Historic Schooner Sails into History as Exhibit Here." *Seattle Post-Intelligencer*, January 17, 1964.

"Seattle Chinese Mayor May Set U.S. Precedent." *Seattle Post-Intelligencer*, July 29, 1964.

"Surplus Wing Luke Funds Distributed." *Seattle Times*, April 12, 1967.

Tomita, Paul H. "City Councilman Luke." Unpublished manuscript. Pullman, WA: Washington State University, January 1963.

Watson, Emmet. "Wing Luke: Anomaly in Seattle Politics." *Argus* (Seattle), July 19, 1963.

Winther, Alice Myers. "Chinese Wins in Seattle." *Christian Science Monitor*, April 7, 1962.

Franklin Ng

KALFRED DIP LUM

(1899–1979)

Educator, Author, Activist

An educated Chinese, Kalfred Dip Lum taught at the University of Hawaii and at many other universities. Concerned about the fate of China, he worked on its behalf in government and politics. He devised the name *Kalfred* by Anglicizing two Chinese characters that read "Kan-Fei."

Kalfred Lum was born to Lum Koon Chun and Leong Shee in Honolulu on December 25, 1899. His father was from the Chungshan area of Guangdong. Kalfred Lum attended the Kalihiwaena, the Jackson Chinese Institute, and Iolani School. In 1922 he graduated from the University of Hawaii; thereafter he said that he was the first Chinese student to receive a baccalaureate from the university. As early as 1917 he was a schoolteacher, founder, and later principal of the Min Hon Chinese School in Kalihi. In 1922 he was commissioner of Chinese schools in the Territory of Hawaii.

Wishing to further his education, Kalfred Lum went to Columbia University and received an M.A. degree in political science in 1923. His thesis examined the political influence of Asians in Hawaii and the "Oriental Problem," which refers to white Americans feeling threatened by Asian workers who were willing to work for lower wages. He concluded that there was no "Oriental problem," for he felt that the Hawaiian-born Asians were becoming Americanized and in two generations would be "real Americans." He then enrolled at New York University in 1923 and was awarded a Ph.D. in government and international law in 1926. His doctoral thesis focused on the evolution of government in Hawaii.

Returning to Honolulu in 1926, Kalfred Lum joined the University of Hawaii as an instructor in political science and was promoted to a professorship in 1928. He said later that he was the first person of Chinese ancestry born in Hawaii to hold the post of professor at the university. Over the next few years he was active in civic affairs and municipal improvement, often writing articles for the *Honolulu Star-Bulletin* about ways to improve the efficiency of governmental administration for the city and county of Honolulu. As one example, he called for reorganization of the police department with civil service examinations and suggested that the sheriff be appointed by the mayor.

Kalfred Lum also wrote in the local papers about contemporary issues. Thus, in one article, he explained why the U.S. Supreme Court in 1927 had found the territorial foreign language school law unconstitutional. He said that the law violated the due process clause of the Fourteenth Amendment and that the tax levied from the foreign language schools was more of a prohibitive, rather than a regulatory, measure.

As a scholar Kalfred Lum published several books. With Professor K. C. Leebrick he amended Robert Littler's *The Government of the City and County of Honolulu* (1927). Then he wrote *Outlines of Law* (1932), which addressed the scope and nature of law and jurisprudence. Three years later he produced *Chinese Government* (1935), which was an introduction to the organization and operation of the "five yuan," or divisions of the Nationalist government of China. He also wrote *Outline of Public Administration* (1935), which was printed in Chinese.

Kalfred Lum was actively involved with the Kuomintang, the ruling Nationalist Party of China. In Hawaii he served as executive secretary and chairman of the local chapter. He also was president of the *United Chinese News*, a Chinese-language paper affiliated with the Kuomintang. In 1931 he was elected to serve as the Hawaiian delegate to the National People's Conference in Nanking to draft a provisional constitution for China. In the same year he was appointed a commissioner of overseas affairs by the Chinese government and taught as a visiting professor of political science at Hangchow Christian College in China. In November 1931 he also was elected to serve as Hawaii's delegate to the Fourth Kuomintang Congress in Nanking.

In 1933 the Chinese government designated Kalfred Lum to be a special envoy for Kuomintang and overseas Chinese affairs in Hawaii and the Americas. In 1935 he served as a special envoy in the same capacity for the Dutch East Indies, the British Strait Settlements, and Thailand. Later that year he represented Hawaii at the Fifth Kuomintang Congress in Nanking and was eventually elected a member of its Central Executive Committee. He also acted as an advisor on foreign affairs to the Chinese government.

During these years Kalfred Lum taught at a number of different universities. From 1933 to 1934 he was a visiting professor of government and international relations at New York University. He also lectured at nearby colleges and universities such as Princeton, Syracuse, and Union. In the fall of 1934 he was a professor and department head of public administration at Chiaotung University in Shanghai.

As the Sino-Japanese War intensified in 1937, Kalfred Lum was sent to San Francisco. His purpose as an envoy from the Central Executive Committee was to end strife within the different Kuomintang factions. He successfully achieved this goal by appointing prominent community leaders to posts in the local branch of the Kuomintang. This strategy, to be repeated elsewhere, gave the Nationalist Party direct ties to the leadership in Chinatown communities. He also worked with the China War Relief Association to raise money from Chinese American communities to aid China in its war effort against Japan.

After the war Kalfred Lum worked in various businesses, including serving as a manager of the San Francisco office of Q. C. Lum Enterprises in 1962. Q. C. Lum, a big building contractor and property owner in Hawaii and a cousin of Kalfred Lum, was expanding his firm's operations to the mainland. Although the Republic of China retreated to the island of Taiwan in 1949, Kalfred Lum maintained his ties with the Kuomintang. He continued to serve as commissioner of overseas affairs and in other official capacities. During the Vietnam War he argued that the United States could win the conflict in Southeast Asia by making a declaration of war, launching a massive bombardment of North Vietnam, and letting Taiwan attack and recover the mainland of China.

Kalfred Lum married Elsie Kam-Lin Yee of Honolulu in 1930. Their children included Sherman and Shirley Lum. Kalfred Lum died in San Francisco on July 3, 1979.

Selected Bibliography

"Dr. Kalfred Dip Lum." In Kam Pui Lai, ed., vol. 2. *The Chinese of Hawaii*, Honolulu: Overseas Penman Club, 1936, pp. 58–59.

Lum, Kalfred Dip. *Chinese Government*. Shanghai, China: Mercury Press, 1935.

———. "Many Precedents for Supreme Court Rule; Dr. Lum Explains Why Language School Law Was Declared Unconstitutional." *Honolulu Star-Bulletin*, March 2, 1927.

———. *Outlines of Law*. Shanghai, China: Mercury Press, 1932.

———. "Sheriff Should Be Appointed by Mayor, Declares Lum." *Honolulu Star-Bulletin*, March 3, 1927.

Nee, Victor G. and Brett de Bary Nee. *Longtime Californ': A Documentary Study of an American Chinatown*. New York: Pantheon Books, 1973.

"The Strange Name of Kalfred Lum." *Honolulu Star-Bulletin*, January 30, 1962.

Franklin Ng

CHIN LUNG

(1864–1942)

Entrepreneur, Business Leader

Chin Lung was a Chinese entrepreneur who achieved success through acumen and hard work. Known as the Chinese Potato King, he was a contemporary of **George Shima**, who was known as the Japanese Potato King. Though better known because of his farming empire, he was like many other Chinese immigrants in the nineteenth and early twentieth centuries who helped to develop agriculture in the American West.

Chin Lung, also known as Chen Long or Chen Kangda, was born on December 12, 1864, in Namshan village in the Chungshan area of Guangdong. The fourth son in his family, he emigrated in the 1880s when he was eighteen or nineteen years old. He joined his older third brother in working for Sing Kee, a rice-importing firm in San Francisco. At night he went to the Chinese Baptist Church to study English.

In 1898 Chin Lung leased 200 acres for sharecropping from Ernest A. Denicke in Sacramento County, California. On this land he planted asparagus and vegetables. Two years later he leased 1,125 acres of delta land near Stockton in San Joaquin County from Ross C. Sargent and Elizabeth E. Barnhart. During the next few years he expanded his farming activities by also leasing land from Ellen Ryan, the Rindge Land and Navigation Company, Myra E. Wright, and others. In 1912 he purchased 1,100 acres northwest of Stockton under the name of Sing Kee in honor of his former employer.

To expand his farming operations, Chin Lung relied on a variety of methods. Besides sharecropping, he mortgaged some of his crops to his landlords until the rent was paid. He also secured loans from different creditors by pledging his crops as collateral. By the second decade of the twentieth century he was farming land that he leased and owned in San Joaquin County, Sacramento County, and Contra Costa County. He planted sweet and Irish potatoes, asparagus, beans, onions, and other vegetables. But he achieved fame principally through his production of potatoes in the Sacramento–San Joaquin delta and won widespread recognition as the Chinese Potato King.

To administer his vast agricultural holdings, Chin Lung traveled by boat or on horseback. He employed 500 Chinese workers and moved them from camp to camp in horse-carts. Besides owning over seventy horses and pieces of farming equipment, he had two barges to transport provisions as needed and to market crops for sale.

A shrewd businessman, Chin Lung knew how to negotiate with his workers, landlords, and creditors. He had to coordinate farming operations at varied sites and carefully monitor fluctuating prices and changing economic conditions. Moreover, he had to contend with the California alien land laws of 1913 and 1920 that imposed restrictions on his ability to lease for more than three years or to own land.

Fortunately, he knew how to diversify his business activities. He also bought land and property in Oregon and China. He operated as a labor contractor, hiring out his farm employees to salmon canneries during the off season. He also invested in several other ventures. For example, he opened a branch of the Sing Kee store in Sacramento. He started a combination import-export and baggage-manufacturing firm known as the Shanghai Trunk Company in San Francisco. And he owned stock in the Wing On Department Store in Shanghai.

Besides watching over his business operations and investments, Chin Lung brought relatives and people from his native district of Chungshan to work and to farm in the delta. From 1919 to 1932, members of the Chin clan established a Chinese American Farms corporation to oversee a wide range of enterprises. He also maintained an interest in the fate of his homeland and came to favor reform and change in China.

About three or four years after he first arrived from China in the 1880s, Chin Lung married Leung Kum Kew. She did not like living in the United States, and in 1904 she returned and settled in Macau with the children. The couple had five sons and two daughters; the sons later returned to help their father in various farm and business operations. In 1933 Chin Lung sold his lands and turned his businesses over to his sons. He then retired and returned to China. He died in Macau on February 25, 1942.

Selected Bibliography

Chan, Sucheng. "Chinese American Entrepreneur: The California Career of Chin Lung." *Chinese America: History and Perspective 1987* (1987).
———. "The Chinese in California Agriculture, 1860–1900." In Genny Lim, ed., *The Chinese American Experience: Papers from the Second National Conference on Chinese American Studies.*
———. *This Bittersweet Soil: The Chinese in California Agriculture, 1860–1910* (1986).
McCunn, Ruthanne Lum. *Chinese American Portraits: Personal Histories, 1828–1988* (1988).

Franklin Ng

YO-YO MA
(1955–   )
Cellist, Musician

Yo-Yo Ma, internationally renowned cellist, was born in Paris, France, on October 7, 1955. His father, musicologist, violinist, and composer Hiao-Tsiun Ma, came to Paris from a small village near Shanghai, China, in the 1930s. His mother, Marina, was a mezzo-soprano from Hong Kong. Ma's first teacher was his father, and after playing the violin briefly Ma decided to switch to the cello at age four. He began using an improvised cello, a viola with an endpin attached. His father, who specialized in the musical education of gifted children, had Ma memorize two measures of a Bach suite for unaccompanied cello each day. He had learned three Bach cello suites by the time he was five, and at age six he played one of them in his first recital at the Institute of Art and Archeology at the University of Paris.

Ma moved to New York City with his family in the following year, and his father began teaching at a school for musically gifted children. Violinist Isaac Stern, whose children attended the school, heard Ma playing the cello one day. Impressed by Ma's talent, Stern recommended him to Juilliard instructor Leonard Rose. Pablo Casals, who also heard Ma play, was instrumental in convincing conductor Leonard Bernstein to include Ma in the "American Pageant of the Arts," which was nationally televised in 1963. Ma made his New York City debut at age nine at Carnegie Hall in 1964.

Ma studied with Leonard Rose and Janos Scholz at Juilliard from the ages of nine to sixteen. He attended the Professional Children's School in New York City, graduating when he was fifteen years old. Ma attended Columbia briefly and then transferred to Harvard University. There he studied music history, theory, and appreciation, developing a more mature integration between his intuitive ability and his intellectual and analytic understanding of music. While at Harvard, Ma continued to perform, both on-campus and off. He received his Bachelor of Arts degree in humanities. In 1991 Harvard awarded Ma an honorary doctorate in music.

In 1978 Ma was selected as the sole recipient of the prestigious Avery Fisher Prize. The prize gave him the opportunity to perform with the New York Philharmonic, the Chamber Music Society of Lincoln Center, and other major orchestras around the country. Ma has performed with the Chicago Symphony, the Pittsburgh Symphony, the Los Angeles Philharmonic, the Boston Symphony Orchestra, the Philadelphia Symphony Orchestra, the Royal Philharmonic, the English Chamber Orchestra, the Berlin Philharmonic, the Orchestre Nationale de France, the Vienna Philharmonic, and the Israel Philharmonic, among others. He has also toured nationally and internationally to perform solo recitals and chamber music concerts with such artists as Itzhak Perlman, James Levine, Emanuel Ax, Young-Uk Kim, Isaac Stern, Jaime Laredo, Jeffrey Kahane, Peter Serkin, and Kathryn Stott.

Ma has won ten Grammy Awards, including two in 1993 for his recordings of the Brahms Cello Sonatas with Emanuel Ax and of Prokofiev's Sinfonia Concertante and Tchaikovsky's Rococo Variations with the Pittsburgh Symphony under Lorin Maazel. He continues a strenuous schedule of recording and performing of both classical and contemporary works. Ma also devotes time to working with young musicians, through master classes and informal interaction with student audiences, as well as through teaching and performing at the Tanglewood Music Center in Lenox, Massachusetts.

Ma married Jill Hornor in 1978. They have two children.

Discography

The Unaccompanied Cello Suites (J. S. Bach). Holland: CBS Inc., 1983.
Sonatas for Viola da Gamba and Harpsichord (J. S. Bach). New York: CBS Records, 1983.

Cello Concerto No. 1, C Major, and Cello Concerto No. 2, D Major (Haydn).
(With the English Chambers Orchestra, Jose Luis Garcia, Conductor). New
York: CBS Masterworks, 1987.
Ma, Yo Yo and Bobby McFerrin. Hush. New York: Sony, 1992.
Sinfonia Concertante for Cello and Orchestra (Prokofiev). (With the Pittsburgh
Symphony Orchestra, Lorin Mazel, Conductor). New York: Sony Classical,
1992.
Made in America. New York: Sony Classical, 1993.

Selected Bibliography

Blum, David. "Profiles: A Process Larger than Oneself." New Yorker, May 1, 1989.
"The Courage to Go Forth: Yo-Yo Ma in Conversation." Economist, February 15,
1992.
Eisler, Edith. "Yo-Yo Ma: Music from the Soul." Strings, May/June 1992.
Kuperberg, Herbert. "Yo-Yo Ma." Stereo Review, vol. 55, no. 4 (April 1990).
Oestreich, J. R. "1 Part Earnestness, 1 Blast of Laughter." New York Times Bio-
graphical Service, 1994.
Thorne, Richard. "The Magic of Yo-Yo Ma." Saturday Review, July 1981.

Franklin Ng

FREDERICK KINZABURO MAKINO

(1877–1953)

Newspaper Publisher, Union Organizer

Frederick Kinzaburo Makino, labor organizer and newspaper publisher,
was born in the Japanese seaport city of Yokohama to Joseph Higgen-
botham and Kin Makino in 1877. His father, an English silk merchant,
died when Makino was five years old. With his father's death, Frederick
took on his mother's name. He was raised in a Japanese family and
attended Japanese primary school. Makino learned English at an English-
Japanese school. As a young man he worked as a clerk in a Yokohama
business house, spending much of his leisure time and money at tea
house parties. After a confrontation with dancer Zenko Sakuragawa at
a tea house party that was written up in a newspaper, Makino's family
decided to send him away in an attempt to reform him.

Accordingly, Makino arrived at Naalehu on the Big Island, Hawaii, in
1899. There he joined his oldest brother, Jo, in the retail business. He

subsequently worked as a clerk at Kona Sugar Refinery and at Honokaa Plantation. Makino eventually opened his own drugstore in 1901 in Honolulu, the Makino Drugstore located at the corner of Nuuanu Avenue and Hotel Street. The store became very popular because of Makino's knowledge of the law and understanding of English, which were helpful to other immigrants.

Because of his familiarity with the law, Makino chaired a meeting at the Japanese Young Men's Christian Association (YMCA) in Honolulu at which higher wages for Japanese laborers were discussed. An outcome of the meeting was the formation of Zokyu Kisei Kai (Higher Wages Association). Makino became chair of the association.

Makino played an important role in the 1909 Sugar Plantation Strike, which was Hawaii's first major labor dispute in the sugar industry. The strike was initiated by the Higher Wages Association and lasted for four months. The Higher Wages Association demanded a raise for its members from $18 per month to $22.50 per month. The latter amount was what Portuguese and Puerto Rican laborers were making doing the same work as the Japanese. On May 9, 1909, workers began walking out. By June, 7,000 workers were on strike. Japanese consul general Senichi Uyeno urged the strikers to return to work. Ignoring his request, the strikers and their families were evicted from the plantations and forced to go to Honolulu. They received aid from the Higher Wages Association, the Japanese community, and others (e.g., Chinese merchants supplied rice). Finally the plantation owners offered $1.50 a month more. The offer was rejected.

On June 10, 1909, Makino and two other strike leaders from the Higher Wages Association were arrested by Sheriff William Henry and charged with conspiracy. Henry banned all mass meetings and public speeches during the strike. On August 22 the strike leaders were convicted of third-degree conspiracy, sentenced to ten months in prison, and fined $300. The strike leaders called off the strike on August 5. Three months after the conviction and sentencing of the strike leaders, wages were raised to $22 per month.

On July 4, 1910, Makino and the other imprisoned strike leaders were pardoned and released. Crowds of cheering people greeted them as they paraded through Aala Park to the Yamashiro Hotel. Because of their "radical activities," the strike leaders and the Higher Wages Association were condemned by conservative elements of the Japanese American press.

When Makino heard that the *Nippu Jiji*, a newspaper run by several of the strike leaders, was being given subsidies by the Hawaii Sugar Planters Association, he started his own paper, the *Hawaii Hochi*. The first issue was published on December 7, 1912. To distance it from the *Nippu Jiji*, which was tainted by the subsidy rumors, the *Hochi* claimed that the planters did not subsidize it. Additionally, the paper claimed that it was not an instrument of any Japanese society or institution and therefore was free to give an unbiased opinion on the issues.

In 1917 Makino hired attorney Joseph Lightfoot to petition the court on behalf of five language schoolteachers from Japan who had been denied entry into Hawaii. After the U.S. District Court in Honolulu ruled against the teachers, the case went to the Ninth Circuit Court in San Francisco, which held that the language schoolteachers should receive the same immigration rights as businessmen.

On January 1, 1923, Governor Farrington passed Act 30, which restricted foreign language schools. However, on December 28, 1922, the Palama Japanese Language School had filed a petition in the territorial circuit court challenging the Act. Fully 87 of the 143 Japanese-language schools ultimately became co-litigants. Circuit Judge James J. Banks held, on February 6, 1923, that the section of Act 30 that dealt with textbooks was valid, but that the portion that related to qualifications for attendance was invalid. Both parties appealed the case. On appeal, the case went to the U.S. District Court, to the Ninth Court of Appeals in San Francisco, and finally to the U.S. Supreme Court. On February 21, 1927, the Supreme Court unanimously ruled in favor of the petitioners. Thus, the language schools won a decisive victory. Makino had used the *Hochi* to spearhead the drive to test these restrictions in court.

Owing to its legal success in the language school case, the *Hochi* regained its financial viability. Two years later the *Hochi* became involved in another legal effort, this time defending Myles Fukunaga. On November 19, 1929, Myles Yutaka Fukunaga was hanged in Hawaii for the murder of George Gill Jamieson. Fukunaga had kidnapped the ten-year-old student and killed him by strangulation and blows with a steel chisel. (Here is the case background. Fukunaga was from a low socioeconomic class, working eighty hours a week to help support his parents and siblings. After a bout of appendicitis Fukunaga missed a week of work, and as a result his parents were evicted from their home. To raise money, Fukunaga kidnapped the boy for ransom.) Fukunaga was mentally unstable, depressed, and had previously attempted suicide. He eventually turned himself in and pled guilty. Many papers opposed the racially biased court trial and Fukunaga's hanging in spite of his obvious insanity. The *Hochi* was among the leading newspapers that objected to the court proceedings.

In a subsequent case, twenty-year-old Thalia Massie, a white woman, accused five men (two Japanese Americans, two Hawaiian Americans, and one Hawaiian Chinese American) of rape. Because the evidence was, at best, weak, the jury declared a mistrial. As a result outraged white residents took matters into their own hands, killing two of the five men. They were sentenced to ten years of hard labor, but Governor Lawrence

Judd commuted their sentences to one hour to be served in his office, where they were served cocktails. The *Hawaii Hochi* called for a fair sentence in this obvious case of miscarriage of justice.

The *Hochi* also attacked the oligarchy in Hawaii, urged Nisei (second-generation Japanese Americans) to break ties with Japan, attacked the Hawaiian caste system, and argued for full citizenship rights for all Japanese in the United States. The *Hochi* changed its name to the *Hawaii Herald* in 1942 but in 1952 switched back to the *Hawaii Hochi*. In 1962 the newspaper was sold to Japanese newspaperman Konosuke Oishi.

Frederick Kinzaburo Makino died on February 17, 1953, at age seventy five.

Selected Bibliography

Kotani, Roland. *The Japanese in Hawaii: A Century of Struggle*. Official Program Booklet of the Oahu Kanyaku Imin Centennial Committee. Honolulu: Hawaii Hochi, 1985.

Niiya, Brian, ed. *Japanese American History: An A-to-Z Reference from 1868 to the Present*. New York: Facts on File, 1993.

Okihiro, Gary. *Cane Fires: The Anti-Japanese Movement in Hawaii, 1865–1945*. Philadelphia: Temple University, 1991.

Steve Fugita

MIKE MASAOKA

(1915–1991)

Community Leader

Mike Masaru Masaoka, Japanese American Citizens League (JACL) leader, was born on October 15, 1915, in Fresno, California. He was the fourth child of Eijiro and Haruye Masaoka. His father was born in Aki-gun, Hiroshima prefecture, on January 10, 1878. He left for the United States in 1903 at the age of twenty-five. His mother, Haruye Goto, was born on February 11, 1898, in Kumamoto prefecture. She came to the United States on November 3, 1905. Masaoka's parents were married on July 3, 1908, in Riverside, California. The family moved to Salt Lake City, Utah, when Masaoka was one and a half years old. His parents had eight children: (oldest to youngest) Joe Grant, Ben Frank, sister Shinko, Mike, Ike Akira, sister Kiyoko (Okoe), Iwao Henry, and Tadashi (Tad). When

Masaoka was nine years old, on October 13, 1924, his father died in a hit-and-run car accident. Masaoka's mother became a widow with eight children.

Masaoka attended Japanese school daily for an hour after public school. He was a student at West High School in Salt Lake City, graduating in June 1932. He worked for a year and then attended the University of Utah, having turned down a four-year scholarship to Harvard. He graduated with honors from the University of Utah in 1937. At the university he was very active on the debate team. Masaoka was a Mormon.

After graduation he accepted a position to teach speech at the University of Utah. He was invited to his first JACL meeting on Labor Day weekend 1938, in Los Angeles. At this meeting he proposed nationalizing the JACL and making it a political organization.

In the fall of 1938 Masaoka enrolled in pre-law courses at the University of Utah. He was also an assistant high school debate coach and was on Utah senator Thomas's reelection staff. In September 1941 Masaoka left his position at the university to become the first paid executive secretary of the JACL. He helped the JACL gain national visibility. Known for his hyper-patriotic spirit, Masaoka was the author of the JACL creed, which was read into the *Congressional Record* by Senator Thomas of Utah on May 9, 1941.

During his time with the JACL, Masaoka encountered many anti-Japanese incidents. On one occasion he arrived in North Platte, Nebraska, with the intention of increasing JACL membership in that region. On Sunday, December 7, 1941, he was arrested by the local police, who were reacting to the Japanese attack on Pearl Harbor and who knew he was a Japanese American leader. Senator Thomas was able to obtain his release from jail.

Masaoka's brothers, sisters, and mother were all interned during World War II at the Manzanar War Relocation Camp in California. During the War, the continental United States were divided into defense zones. Masaoka escaped incarceration because he was outside of the Western Defense Zone.

Masaoka was the first Japanese American witness to testify at the Tolan Committee hearings. He urged policy changes to allow young Nisei (second-generation Japanese American) men in the War Relocation Authority camps (after their status had been changed to "4-C"—aliens not subject to military service—and "4-F"—persons unfit for military service) to help fight the war instead of being imprisoned. As soon as Secretary of War Stimson approved of the all–Japanese American 442nd Regimental Combat Team, Masaoka was sent to the Pentagon to be given advance word about the Team. He became the first Nisei to sign up for the 442nd. Before this, on February 14, he married Etsu Mineta. Masaoka was officially inducted on June 22, 1943, to the public relations staff, where he saw little combat. During the war he served as a war correspondent. Masaoka was awarded the Combat Infantryman Badge. He also received the Purple Heart, the Bronze Star, the Italian Cross for Military Valor, and the Legion of Merit awards, along with the Distinguished Service Cross.

After the war Masaoka traveled frequently to Washington to lobby in Congress for civil rights for Japanese Americans. He represented the JACL's Anti-Discrimination Committee. Etsu, his wife, was hired as secretary for the JACL branch in Washington, D.C., and Gladys Shimasaki was their typist.

As a lobbyist, Masaoka worked to get Issei (first-generation Japanese immigrants) naturalized and to block the deportation of many Japanese aliens. He worked for the Walter-McCarran Act (also known as the 1952 Immigration Act), which offered the Japanese a small immigration quota and allowed Issei to become naturalized. It narrowly passed with a five-vote margin that overrode the president's veto. Previously, in 1946, Masaoka had helped to defeat California's Proposition 15, which validated the Alien Land Law Act of 1920, prohibiting persons then ineligible for U.S. citizenship from purchasing land.

Masaoka helped defeat Title II of the Internal Security Act of 1950, which gave the government the power to evacuate and detain individuals thought to be a security threat, without trial, in times of war, insurrection, or invasion. President Nixon signed the bill to remove Title II from the statutes on September 25, 1971.

Masaoka has often been criticized for carrying his "Americanism" to an extreme. For example, he proposed the formation of a "suicide battalion" of Nisei whose actions would be guaranteed by Issei being held as hostages by the U.S. government. He also advocated turning over disloyal Japanese Americans to the FBI. Mike Masaoka, **James Sakamoto**, and other JACL members testified at the Tolan Committee hearings on the Nisei's Americanism and opposed the mass internment of the Japanese Americans but nonetheless pledged to cooperate with the government, if it should see fit to take such actions. Additionally, Masaoka opposed any legal challenge to Executive Order 9066, which authorized military commanders to remove, relocate, and intern all persons of Japanese descent, such as the *Yasui v. United States* case.

Masaoka's family also set legal precedent in a lawsuit involving Mrs. Haruye Masaoka and her five sons (Ike, Henry, Tad, Mike, and Joe Grant), who had transferred a land title in Pasadena to their mother. Under existing law, such a transfer was illegal even though three of the sons had served in the 442nd Regimental Combat Team and a fourth had died in combat. Judge Thurmond Clark declared that the Alien Law Act violated the equal protection clause and cited the *Fuji* land case, until the Commission on Wartime Relocation and Internment of Civilians hearing (CWRIC) caused him to change his mind.

Masaoka stepped down from the JACL and opened his own consulting office in Washington, D.C. His clientele were mainly Japanese Americans. During this period he and Etsu went to Japan for the first time. He visited his ancestral burial grounds in Hiroshima, while Etsu visited hers in Shizuoka. Masaoka received the Order of the Rising Sun and the Order of the Sacred Treasure from the Japanese government.

Masaoka and his wife adopted Midori Marie in 1955 and then Michael Edward in 1957. Midori passed away in 1986 and Michael seven months later. Masaoka had a minor heart attack in 1980 and another in Japan in the same year. He endured his third heart attack on Christmas Eve of the same year and then underwent double-bypass surgery. Mike Masaoka died on June 26, 1991. He published an autobiography entitled *They Call Me Moses Masaoka* with **William Hosokawa** in 1987.

Selected Bibliography

Daniels, Roger, Sandra C. Taylor, and Harry H. L. Kitano, eds. *Japanese Americans: From Relocation to Redress*. Seattle and London: University of Washington, 1991.

Hohri, William Minoru. *Repairing America: An Account of the Movement for Japanese-American Redress*. Pullman, WA: Washington State University, 1988.

Hosokawa, Bill. *Thirty-Five Years in the Frying Pan*. San Francisco: McGraw-Hill, 1978.

Masaoka, Mike, and Bill Hosokawa. *They Call Me Moses Masaoka*. New York: William Morrow, 1987.

Niiya, Brian, ed. *Japanese American History: An A-to-Z Reference from 1868 to the Present*. New York: Facts on File, 1993.

Wilson, Robert A., and Bill Hosokawa. *East to America: A History of the Japanese in the United States*. New York: William Morrow, 1980.

Steve Fugita

ROBERT T. MATSUI

(1941–)

Congressman, Politician

U.S. Representative Robert T. Matsui was born in Sacramento, California, in 1941 to second-generation Japanese American parents. He is a graduate of the University of California at Berkeley and the Hastings College

Robert Matsui

of Law. After founding his own law practice in Sacramento in 1967, he was elected to the Sacramento City Council in 1971. He won reelection in 1975 and became vice mayor in 1977. In 1978 he was elected to Congress and has been reelected ever since by wide margins. He has gained a national reputation for bringing into focus complex public policy issues such as trade, tax policy, Social Security, health care, and welfare reform.

Matsui has been a member of the U.S. House of Representatives Ways and Means Committee for thirteen years and is the ranking member of its subcommittee on human resources, a position that has allowed him to play a pivotal role on issues ranging from welfare reform and foster care to employment and disability. In 1993 he worked with children's advocates to ensure that for the first time in twelve years, new money would be included in the federal budget for family preservation programs. Matsui secured $1 billion over five years for programs designed to prevent child abuse and neglect and to keep families together.

Matsui is the ranking Democrat on the Ways and Means Committee's subcommittee on trade. During one of the most heated congressional battles of 1993, the fight to pass the North American Free Trade Agreement, he worked with a team that included Republicans and Democrats, cabinet secretaries from current and former administrations, academics, business leaders, and environmentalists to gain congressional approval of the agreement that reduces trade barriers between the United States, Canada, and Mexico.

Matsui's advocacy of aggressive legislative agendas has placed him at the forefront of economic, social, and environmental public policy debates. In 1992 he championed economic growth initiatives such as the Enterprise Capital Formation Act. He drafted legislation that became the backbone for child welfare reform, and his program to promote children's health insurance as a top national priority was regarded as a model during the Ways and Means Committee's health care reform deliberations. Matsui successfully changed the law to promote mass transit use through favorable tax treatment of employer-provided transit subsidiaries, and he instituted a tax credit for the production of renewable energy sources.

Matsui's substantive and thoughtful approach to public policy has gained him the respect of his colleagues and the national news media. His legislative endeavors and opinions on major issues have appeared in the *Wall Street Journal*, the *Washington Post*, the *Los Angeles Times*, and many other national publications. He has been a guest on news programs such as "Meet the Press," the "CBS Evening News," "MacNeil/Lehrer News Hour," C-SPAN, and CNN programs including "Crossfire," "The Morning Business Report," and "Both Sides with Jesse Jackson."

Matsui has served on the Democratic National Committee since 1991. In addition to his duties as a fundraiser for the Democratic Party, Matsui serves as a spokesman for the party and its candidates in forums across the country.

His legislative accomplishments have been recognized by both local and national organizations. In September 1989 he received the Chubb Fellowship, the highest honor Yale University confers on visiting lecturers. Matsui was also named one of California's outstanding legislators by Claremont College in 1990 and 1992. In 1992 he received the Excellence in Public Service Award from the American Academy of Pediatrics for his work on behalf of children's health issues. In the same year he was cited by the American Wind Energy Association for his work in promoting mass transit. The Children's Defense Fund honored him for his work on behalf of children in 1993. Matsui has been honored with the Lifetime Achievement Award from the Anti-Defamation League and was named Congressional Advocate of the Year by the Child Welfare League of America for his commitment to improving the nation's foster care system.

Matsui is married to the former Doris Okada, who is deputy assistant to the president and deputy director of public liaison for President Clinton. Congressman and Mrs. Matsui have one son.

Selected Bibliography

"Matsui, Robert." *Who's Who in American Politics*. New York: R. R. Bowker, 1993.
Zia, Helen, and Susan Gall, eds. *Notable Asian Americans*. Detroit: Gale Research,
    1995, pp. 238–240.

Steve Fugita

MASAYUKI "SPARK" MATSUNAGA

(1916–1990)

Senator, Politician

Masayuki "Spark" Matsunaga, United States senator from Hawaii, was born in 1916 on a sugar plantation on Kauai to poor Japanese immigrants. His father, Kingoro Matsunaga, ran away from a Japanese monastery at age nineteen and settled on Kauai Island. He married a Japanese immigrant widow with four children. While working on a sugar plantation, Kingoro was killed when 100-pound bags of sugar fell on him.

Spark Matsunaga worked his way through high school doing odd jobs as a stevedore, warehouseman, and store clerk. In 1937 he won $1,000 in a newspaper contest. He gave his parents $600 and used the rest to attend the University of Hawaii, from which he graduated with honors in 1948. At the University of Hawaii, Matsunaga was elected to Phi Beta Phi and Phi Gamma Mu and was active in forensics and theater arts. He majored in education.

At the University of Hawaii, Matsunaga participated in the Reserve Officer Training Corps (ROTC) program. After graduation he volunteered for active military duty in the Army and was assigned to Homestead Field on Molokai Island. He was commissioned as a second lieutenant in the United States Army Reserve after the attack on Pearl Harbor. Matsunaga was assigned to Camp McCoy in Wisconsin. He helped to draft a plea to President Roosevelt suggesting the formation of the 100th Infantry Battalion.

Matsunaga was a highly decorated member of the 100th Infantry Battalion of the 442nd and was wounded twice during combat in Italy. He was promoted to captain and earned the Bronze Star, the Purple Heart, the Legion of Merit, and the Army Commendation Medal. In 1945 Matsunaga was assigned to the Military Intelligence Language School (MILS) at Fort Snelling, Minnesota. His duties included giving tours for the War

Relocation Authorities, who were in the process of relocating Japanese Americans.

After he was discharged in 1945, Matsunaga became a veterans' counselor for the U.S. Department of the Interior in Honolulu. During this period he married Helene Tokunaga. He then attended Harvard Law School and graduated in 1951. At Harvard, Matsunaga lobbied to obtain statehood for Hawaii.

After graduation Matsunaga returned to Hawaii and served as a public prosecutor for the city of Honolulu. He was elected to Hawaii's Territorial House, serving from 1954 to 1959. In this capacity he pushed for vocational counseling programs in high schools, free adult classes in citizenship and English, and modification of the Workmen's Compensation Law, the Unemployment Compensation Law, and the Wages and Hours Law. In 1959 he unsuccessfully ran for the seat of lieutenant governor. Subsequently he successfully ran for the U.S. House of Representatives in 1962. He served seven consecutive terms. Matsunaga was a member of the Rules Committee, and in 1971 he helped sponsor legislation to repeal Title II of the Emergency Detention Act/Internal Security Act. This legislation allowed imprisonment without trial of people considered a "security risk" during times of war, insurrection, or invasion. President Nixon signed the repeal in 1971. Later, in 1971, Matsunaga joined the summit party as a Japanese interpreter at the request of President Jimmy Carter during the president's tour of Japan and Korea.

After U.S. senator **Hiram Fong**'s seat was vacated, Matsunaga ran against his friend and colleague **Patsy Mink**, defeating her in 1976. He served three terms as a U.S. senator from Hawaii. Matsunaga was on the Senate Finance Committee and chaired the international trade and aging subcommittees, along with the sugar and tourism subcommittees. He was president of the 88th Congress Club and secretary of the House Democratic Steering Committee. He also served as the Senate Democratic chief deputy whip, stepping down in 1988. Matsunaga also worked on the veterans' affairs and labor and human resources subcommittees. In 1964 he successfully completed a campaign to establish a national poet laureate. (One of his hobbies was writing poetry.) He also lobbied for twenty-two years for a U.S. Peace Institute, which was established by Congress in 1984.

As a senator, Matsunaga supported the joint U.S.–U.S.S.R. exploration of Mars. He also wrote a book entitled *The Mars Project*, which analyzes the history and politics of space exploration. In 1970 he co-sponsored the Newspaper Preservation Act. Additionally, he advocated for environmental awareness by sponsoring many measures to protect the environment, including the development of hydrogen planes and wind-powered commercial ships as an alternative to those using fossil fuels. During his term he also supported free trade.

Most important, Matsunaga was the main Senate sponsor of the Civil

Liberties Act of 1988. He introduced SB-2116 on November 17, 1983. The bill accepts the Committee on Wartime Relocation and Internment of Civilians (CWRIC) Act findings and provides for $12,000 redress payment for the Aleuts from the Aleutian Islands and $20,000 for Japanese Americans who were incarcerated during World War II. However, Matsunaga initially felt that monetary compensation inadequately addressed the issue and believed that a monument would be more appropriate. He also sponsored the bill to educate the public about the World War II incarceration of Japanese Americans and examine its long-term consequences.

In 1990 Matsunaga went to Toronto for treatment for prostate cancer, which had spread to his bones. His wife, Helene, and two of his five children were with him in Toronto when he died on April 15, 1990, in Toronto General Hospital at the age of seventy-three.

Selected Bibliography

Daniels, Roger, Sandra C. Taylor, and Harry H. L. Kitano, eds. *Japanese Americans: From Relocation to Redress*. Seattle: University of Washington, 1991.

Hall, Carla. "The Senator and His Space Refrain." *Washington Post*, August 13, 1986, p. C13.

Herman, Masako, ed. *The Japanese in America, 1843–1973*. New York: Oceana Publications, 1974.

Hohri, William Minoru. *Repairing America*. Pullman: Washington State University.

Hosokawa, Bill. *Nisei: The Quiet Americans*. New York: William Morrow, 1969.

Niiya, Brian, ed. *Japanese American History: An A-to-Z Reference from 1868 to the Present*. New York: Facts on File, 1993.

Wilson, Robert A., and Bill Hosokawa. *East to America: A History of the Japanese in the United States*. New York: William Morrow, 1980.

Steve Fugita

NOBU MCCARTHY

(1934–   )

Actress

Actress Nobu McCarthy was born on November 13, 1934, in Ottawa, Canada. She lived in Tokyo during World War II until the family home was destroyed. For the next two years McCarthy lived in the north of

Japan with students from an elementary school, separated from her parents. She survived the starvation and destruction of Japan following the war, and between the ages of eleven and eighteen she became a ballerina and Japan's top fashion model.

In 1956 McCarthy married and moved to the United States. She was discovered by the Hollywood film industry in 1957, landing her first leading role in *Geisha Boy* with Jerry Lewis. Numerous film appearances followed. Her films include *Five Gates to Hell, Wake Me When It's Over, Two Loves, Walk Like a Dragon, Lost Flight, Farewell to Manzanar, Karate Kid II, Pacific Heights* (the film version of **Philip Kan Gotanda**'s *The Wash*), and *Painted Desert*.

McCarthy has also appeared in television, guest-starring in episodes of *Playhouse 90, The Man from U.N.C.L.E., Batman, Quincy, Kung-Fu, T. J. Hooker, Hawaii Five-O, Magnum P.I., Island Sun*, and *China Beach*. She has been featured on talk shows such as "The Johnny Carson Show" and "The Mike Douglas Show."

In addition to her work in film and television, McCarthy starred in a number of stage plays beginning in 1970. These include *When We Were Young, Pineapple White, The Gold Watch, The Teahouse of the August Moon, The Year of the Dragon, Come Back Little Sheba*, and *Not a Through Street*. She played the leading role in **David Henry Hwang**'s play *As the Crow Flies*. McCarthy also played Masi in Philip Kan Gotanda's play *The Wash*, and it was in this production that she made her New York debut at the Manhattan Theatre Club. She played the role again in the Mark Taper Forum production in Los Angeles, winning the Los Angeles Drama-Logue Award for her performance. Her other drama awards include the Los Angeles Drama-Logue Award for her performance in *As the Crow Flies* and the Bernie Award from the *San Francisco Chronicle*.

McCarthy is also an accomplished stage director. She has directed *Webster Street Blues, The Gambling Den*, and the world premiere of Wakako Yamauchi's play *The Chairman's Wife* for East West Players. She has also directed Yamauchi's play *And the Soul Shall Dance* for California State University at Los Angeles.

From 1989 to 1994 McCarthy was artistic director of East West Players in Los Angeles. Founded in 1965, it is the oldest professional Asian American theater company operating in the United States. She also served as director of the theater's Professional Actors' Training Program and co-director of its Summer Workshop. She has taught at California State University at Los Angeles, was director of its Asian American Theater Project, and was a member of the California State Distinguished Artists' Forum.

In recognition of McCarthy's contributions to the southern California community, she has received awards and commendations from the State of California, the County of Los Angeles, the City of Los Angeles Board of Supervisors, and the United States Congress. She has received the Elaine Kashiki Arts Award from the Inner City Cultural Center of Los Angeles and has been recognized for her work by the Pacific Asian Family Center, the City of Hope, and the California State University, Los Angeles, Asian American Support Group. In 1990, in recognition of her contributions to the arts, McCarthy was presented with the Woman Warrior Award from the Asian Pacific Women's Network of Los Angeles. In 1991 she was an honored recipient of the On Screen Women in Film Career Achievement Award.

McCarthy is married to attorney William Cuthbert. They have two children, a son and a daughter.

Selected Bibliography

Niiya, Brian, ed. *Japanese American History: An A-to-Z Reference from 1868 to the Present.* New York: Facts on File, 1993, p. 220.
Zia, Helen, and Susan Gall, eds. *Notable Asian Americans.* Detroit: Gale Research, 1995, pp. 242–244.

Steve Fugita

ZUBIN MEHTA

(1936–   )

Conductor

Since 1958 Zubin Mehta has been conducting symphonies and through the universal language of music has attempted to override the barriers of countries and cultures. Born on April 29, 1936, in Bombay, India, he grew up in a musical environment. His father, Mehli Mehta, currently music director of the American Youth Symphony in Los Angeles, co-founded the Bombay Symphony. Zubin started studying the violin and piano in 1943.

Zubin Mehta enrolled as a pre-med student at St. Xaviers College, Bombay, during 1953 to 1954. However, at age eighteen he abandoned his medical studies to pursue a career in music. The Academy of Music in Vienna beckoned Mehta, and he spent the next four years there studying conducting, piano, composition, and string bass. In 1958 he won

Zubin Mehta (photo by Christian Steiner)

first prize at the Liverpool Conducting Competition and became associate conductor of the Royal Liverpool Symphony Orchestra.

Mehta made his U.S. debut when he conducted the Philadelphia Symphony Orchestra in 1960. At age twenty-five he conducted both the Vienna and Berlin Philharmonics; he has been conducting each of these orchestras every season since. In 1961, for the first time Mehta conducted the Israel Philharmonic, substituting for Eugene Ormandy. From 1961 to 1967 he acted as music director of the Montreal Symphony. The Los Angeles Philharmonic appointed him its music director in 1962, a post he held until 1978 when he accepted the appointment of music director with the New York Philharmonic.

In 1969 the Israel Philharmonic Orchestra appointed Mehta its music advisor, in 1977 its music director, and in 1981 its music director for life. Numerous concerts, recordings, and tours of all five continents have resulted in over 1,500 concerts with the Israel Philharmonic Orchestra. In 1981 Mehta co-founded the American Friends of the Israel Philharmonic Orchestra (AFIPO) with Frederic R. Mann. He served as co-chairman of AFIPO with Itzhak Perlman. Since 1986 he has acted as music advisor and chief conductor of the Maggio Musicale Fiorentino, the summer festival in Florence, Italy, where he recently completed a cycle of Mozart operas produced under the direction of Jonathan Miller.

As music director of the New York Philharmonic during 1978–1991, Mehta conducted over 1,000 concerts. He held the post longer than any other music director in the orchestra's modern history. He conducted the New York Philharmonic on a number of major tours during his thirteen-year tenure with the orchestra, among them a few concerts in India. In June 1988 he led the orchestra on a ten-day tour of the Soviet Union that culminated in a historic joint concert with the State Symphony Orchestra of the Soviet Union Ministry of Culture in Moscow's Gorky Park.

In May 1991, Mehta concluded his tenure with the New York Philharmonic with three performances celebrating the 100th anniversary of Carnegie Hall. This was followed by a series of performances of Schoenberg's *Gurrelieder*. Mehta returned to conduct the New York Philharmonic twice in 1992. One was the world premier of Oliver Messiaen's last symphony, "Éclairs sur l'Au Delà" and the other was in December 1992 to join in "A Philharmonic Celebration: 150th Anniversary Concert."

Fulfilling Mehta's plan to conduct more opera, a collaborative achievement in Rome in 1990 produced the recorded performance of "Carreras, Domingo, and Pavarotti in Concert." This recording of the three renowned tenors singing a medley of show tunes and opera classics became an unprecedented success in the field of classical music. Mehta conducted two productions of *Tosca* in 1992. The first was a live performance with Placido Domingo in early July, which was viewed in 107 countries. Each performance was performed at the exact locations and times of day as specified by Puccini in his original score. Simultaneously connected via television monitors and loudspeakers from a recording studio on the other side of Rome, the conductor led the Rome Symphony Orchestra and Chorus of Italian Radio. A second production of *Tosca*, with Luciano Pavarotti, opened the Covent Garden season in London two months later.

In the latter part of July 1992, Mehta joined the Israel Philharmonic Orchestra to back a concert version of *Aida*. For his 1993 debut with the Lyric Opera of Chicago, he began Wagner's Ring cycle, which continued through 1996, along with his other commitments.

The largest and most publicized of Mehta's concerts was "Encore! The Three Tenors," a reprise performance to the 1990 concert in Rome. Telecast live in 1994 to over 100 countries, the concert featured Jose Carreras, Placido Domingo, and Luciano Pavarotti, conducted by Zubin Mehta. They dazzled an audience of 56,000 people at Dodger Stadium in Los Angeles, California. Some 56,000 people paid up to $1,000 per ticket to sit in Dodger Stadium, and a radio and TV audience of one billion watched and listened. The audio and video recordings of the concerts sold thousands of copies. The production required the services of nearly 1,000 people. Flanked by trees, waterfalls, and columns on a specially built stage, the tenors were aiming for an even greater extravaganza than that of Rome in 1990. The tenors were accompanied by the Los Angeles Philharmonic and the Los Angeles Music Center Opera Chorus, with Mehta at the podium. There have been many concerts at Dodger Stadium, featuring the Beatles, U2, and even Eric Clapton, but never before had there been a classical music event.

Zubin Mehta's love for his native country drove him to bring home to India the Israel Philharmonic Orchestra. The orchestra's five concerts in 1994 in New Delhi and Bombay broke political barriers that had prevented them from performing for three decades. The invitation to perform came after India and Israel opened embassies in each other's capitals and embarked on an effort to increase both economic and cultural ties. The concert's high point was a performance of Tchaikovsky's Violin Concerto with Itzhak Perlman as soloist. Zubin Mehta, Itzhak Perlman, and the orchestra took no fee for the tour, which was financed primarily by commercial sponsors. To improve the acoustics at the Bombay Cricket Stadium where the concert was held, the specially constructed bandshell used in Los Angeles for the three tenors' concert at Dodgers Stadium was flown in.

Mehta had a fulfilled his dream. Hailed as the son of Bombay, he has earned a faithful Indian following. His concerts were attended by many of the country's top political leaders. One absentee, Prime Minister P.V. Narasimha Rao, wrote Mehta an apology explaining that electioneering in his home state of Andhra Pradesh kept him away.

Over the years Zubin Mehta has been awarded numerous honors. Among them are the Nikisch Ring, the Vienna Philharmonic Ring of Honor, Padma Bhushan—India's highest cultural award given to people of outstanding accomplishment in the arts and sciences, and the Defender of Jerusalem Award. An honorary citizen of Tel Aviv, Mehta was the only non-Israeli ever to receive a special award of appreciation.

In 1996 he celebrated his sixtieth birthday with both the Israeli Philharmonic and the Los Angeles Philharmonic at the Music Center in Los Angeles, California.

In 1998 Mehta took the position of General Music Director of the Bavarian State opera in Munich.

Selected Bibliography

"3×3 Tenors." *American Record Guide*, January–February 1995, p. 247.
"Berlioz: Symphonie Fantastique." *American Record Guide*, November–December 1994, p. 74.
Isenberg, Barbara. "3 Tenors Hit High Note with Arias in Arena." *Los Angeles Times*, July 17, 1994, pp. A1, 14.

"Music in the Ruins." *People Weekly*, July 4, 1994, p. 44.
Who's Who in America, New Providence, N.J.: Marquis Who's Who, 1998.

Visi R. Tilak

DAVID C. MENDOZA

(1944–   )

Activist, Artist, Judge

David C. Mendoza has become the leading national exponent of protecting and extending the First Amendment right to freedom of artistic expression. Since 1991 he has been executive director of the National Campaign for Freedom of Expression (NCFE), which was founded by a group of arts activists in 1990. As director of Artist Trust in Seattle, Washington, Mendoza conceived the original concept of this national network.

Mendoza was born in Auburn, Washington, in 1944, the eldest of three sons of a Filipino American immigrant and his Caucasian wife. His parents were farmers, and Mendoza recalls summers working with his father in the fields. When it was time to go to college he attended the University of Washington, where he received a Bachelor of Fine Arts degree in 1968. A person with extraordinary managerial skills and artistic knowledge, Mendoza became director of the Richard White Gallery (1969–1971) and the Foster/White Gallery (1972–1977), both in Seattle. As director he organized over 150 exhibitions of contemporary art, primarily by artists of the Pacific Northwest. He served as corporate art collections consultant for major Seattle corporations. For eight years Mendoza wrote arts criticism and did cultural reporting for various Pacific Northwest publications and national arts publications, as well as preparing feature articles on various subjects ranging from food and restaurants to fashion and style.

Mendoza moved to the East Coast in 1978 and for four years was executive assistant to Kitty Carlisle Hart, chair of the New York State Council on the Arts (NYSCA). In this capacity he served as liaison for the NYSCA chair with staff, elected officials, grantees, and the media. He sometimes mediated controversies. Mendoza conceived and produced a special statewide study report entitled "New York State Arts Geography," which was the first long-range planning document for the agency. In 1982 Mendoza became director of planning and development for NYSCA. He chaired the Individual Artist Task Force, a two-year NYSCA study of support for individual artists in the state. During his three-year tenure Mendoza developed a joint marketing campaign with the state Department of Commerce/I Love New York office entitled "I Love NY Celebrates the Arts." He developed a program that offered NYSCA funding to leverage new support from county governments at Brooklyn College in 1984.

Mendoza returned to the Pacific Northwest and became executive director for Artist Trust, a nonprofit organization founded in 1986 to provide programs—including grants and fellowships—and services for individual artists in all arts disciplines throughout Washington state. Artist Trust is a model program that is currently being replicated in New England and Portland, Oregon.

As director of Artist Trust, Mendoza became involved in the public controversy over free expression by artists, especially those seeking funding from the National Endowment for the Arts and public arts programs in Washington state. He served as public and media spokesperson on a variety of arts and political issues. He lobbied elected officials and testified before local, state, and federal legislative committees to affect public art policy. In 1990 Mendoza proposed, implemented, and now serves as chair of the Free Expression Network, a national network of forty-five organizations concerned with First Amendment issues—ranging from the American Library Association and Recording Industry Association of America, to the National Gay and Lesbian Task Force and the National Council of Churches.

For over twenty-five years Mendoza has demonstrated personal dedication and commitment to improve the support structure for diversity of artists and arts organizations and to elevate the role of artists and culture in public life.

Selected Bibliography

Seattle Post-Intelligencer, October 11, 1986, p. D1.
Seattle Weekly, June 19, 1991, pp. 6–9.
Seattle Weekly, November 8, 1995, p. 35.
The Weekly (Seattle), June 18–24, 1986, p. 39.

Dorothy Cordova

Benjamin Menor

(1922–1986)

Judge

Benjamin Menor was born in a split-bamboo house on stilts with a nipa (palm) roof—a humble beginning for a man destined to become one of the first Filipino lawyers in America, and a man who was eventually elected associate justice of the Hawaii State Supreme Court.

Benjamin Menor was born on September 22, 1922, in San Nicolas, Ilocos Norte, in the Philippines. The oldest of seven children, he came from a long line of farmers and sailors. In 1925, after hearing stories of prosperity in America, his father decided to migrate to Hawaii and become one of thousands of *sakadas*, or contract laborers, on the sugar plantations. The elder Mr. Menor was to go alone and send for his family as soon as possible. It was five years before they saw him again.

Although his father sent money from Hawaii it was barely enough, so his resourceful, Ilocano mother raised Menor and his sister by living off the land. She also took produce to market and was able to barter and trade for their other necessities. Despite their poverty, Menor recounts a closeness of family and relatives as they lived self-sufficiently to fulfill their basic needs.

In 1930 Menor, his mother, and his sister embarked on the long journey to join his father in Hawaii. Menor's mother had misgivings about leaving home but felt her family should be together. Upon arrival in Hawaii her doubts were magnified by the living conditions on the plantations. She did not mind the barracks-like living quarters as much as the sharing of a community tub for bathing. This, coupled with her homesickness, made life almost unbearable for her. If not for other families who helped the Menors, and the eventual births of five more children, Menor's mother may never have gotten over leaving the Philippines.

When Mrs. Menor saw how long and hard the laborers had to work, she realized that only an education could make a difference and vowed that none of her children would ever have to work in the cane fields if she could help it. She enrolled Menor and his sisters in the plantation school and instilled in them the desire for learning. Pahoa School consisted then of grades one to nine, and most of the 200 pupils were of Japanese descent. There were only half a dozen Filipino students, because most of the workers were single men or married men who had left their families in the Philippines.

At first it was difficult for Menor and his sisters to adjust in school. They were newcomers and unable to speak English. Of those students of Filipino ancestry who were in school when he started, Menor was the only one who went beyond the ninth grade. During those years the older Filipino children in Hawaii usually were required to leave school in order to work and help their families financially. Menor's mother was adamant about her son getting a high school education, and he also wanted one so he could get a white-collar job. His dream was elusive. As a resident alien and Philippine national, Menor was prevented by law from working for either the country or the territorial government.

In 1941 Menor graduated from Hilo High School as salutatorian in a graduating class of 517. He received a scholarship to the Honolulu business college and finally had an opportunity to go to school in Honolulu. He worked parttime as a live-in houseboy and yardboy for a Haole (Caucasian) couple. When World War II broke out, Menor went to work for defense contractors until he was drafted into the U.S. Army in 1944.

Menor was sent to San Luis Obispo, California, for training. After basic training he became an American citizen, along with thousands of other Filipino soldiers. Menor was sent to Leyte in the Philippines as part of the First Filipino Regiment. There he was able to visit Ilocos Norte and family members he had not seen since 1930.

Menor was discharged in 1946 and used the G.I. Bill to attend the University of Hawaii. He became a member of the varsity debate team, which enabled him to travel to different colleges on the mainland. Graduating in 1952, he decided to continue his education at the Boston University Law School. After graduating he moved back to Hawaii and set up a successful law practice.

In 1962 Menor was elected to the Hawaii State Senate as a Democrat. He was appointed circuit court judge in 1968 and associate justice of the Hawaii State Supreme Court in 1974. Menor was the first person of Filipino ancestry to hold those positions in the United States. In one of the ironies of life, Ben Menor—who once by law could not obtain a government job—was the circuit court judge who declared that very law unconstitutional on September 19, 1972, finding it to be in violation of the Equal Protection Clauses of both the federal and state constitutions. Shortly after this, the federal courts also declared such laws unconstitutional.

Menor never lost touch with the Filipino people and assisted them in many ways, but his greatest contribution was being a positive role model for young Filipino Americans. Judge Menor retired in 1983. He died in Hawaii on July 4, 1986.

Selected Bibliography

Filipino American Herald, March 15, 1982, p. 2.
Forgotten Asian American Oral History: Filipinos and Koreans. 1982.
Hawaii Filipino News, October 1–15, 1983, pp. 14, 15.
Philippine News, July 6–12, 1983, p. 15.

Dorothy Cordova

DALE MINAMI

(1946–   )

Attorney

Dale Minami, attorney, was born on October 13, 1946, in Los Angeles, California, to second-generation Japanese American parents. Educated in the Los Angeles public school system, he was active in sports and student governance at Peary Junior High School and at Gardena High School. Minami also worked parttime at his parents' sporting goods store and played in Pony League All Star baseball.

Minami studied political science and law at the University of Southern California, receiving his B.A. degree in 1968. He graduated magna cum laude and was a member of Phi Beta Kappa and Phi Kappa Phi. Minami received numerous sports awards in basketball and baseball during his college career. He received his Juris Doctor degree in 1971 from the University of California Law School and was active in the Nisei Trojan's Club and the Asian American Law Students' Association.

Minami's legal practice has specialized in personal injury, entertainment law, and civil litigation. He has been particularly committed to working toward empowerment of the Asian Pacific American community, through litigating cases on behalf of Asian Pacific American issues, supporting candidates and issues that advance the Asian Pacific American community, teaching Asian American studies, and founding and participating in organizations that serve the Asian Pacific American community. He has also actively supported the efforts of other minority groups, women, the disabled, and gay men and lesbians to gain legal rights.

From 1971 to 1972 Minami was an instructor in the Department of Ethnic Studies at Mills College in Oakland, California. He lectured at the

Dale Minami (photo © 1997 by Bob Hsiang)

University of California at Berkeley in Asian American studies from 1971 to 1983. Minami has lectured extensively on civil rights litigation and legal issues affecting Asian Pacific Americans at universities and conventions throughout the United States from 1976 through the present.

From 1972 to 1975 Minami was directing attorney of Asian Law Caucus, Inc., in Oakland, California. During this time he filed the *Chan v. City and County of San Francisco* lawsuit (1972), seeking injunctive relief for unconstitutional police sweeps of young Chinese Americans in Chinatown for mugshots and fingerprints without probable cause. These police sweeps ended after the lawsuit was filed. Minami also filed *United Filipinos for Affirmative Action v. California Blue Shield*, the first class-action lawsuit brought by Asian Pacific Americans on behalf of Asian Pacific Americans. Filed in 1974, this case was settled after certification as a first class action suit.

From 1975 to the present Minami has been a partner in private law practice (Minami, Tomine & Lew, 1975–1983; Minami & Lew, 1983–1987; Minami, Lew & Tamaki, 1987–1989; and Minami, Lew, Tamaki & Lee, 1989–present). During this time he has litigated a number of important cases. In *Wong. v. Younger* (1976) he filed an action to enjoin distribution of the attorney general's report on crime, which unfairly stereotyped

Chinese Americans as criminals. Minami was lead counsel in the 1978 class action lawsuit *Spokane JACL v. Washington State University* on behalf of Asian Americans to establish an Asian American studies program at Washington State University. This was settled successfully with the creation of such a program and counseling services. In 1982 Minami filed a *coram nobis* action (that a mistake was made in the original case due to prejudice) to erase a forty-year-old conviction for refusal to obey exclusion orders aimed at Japanese Americans during World War II, originally upheld by the U.S. Supreme Court in landmark decisions. In *Koromatsu v. United States* (1984) this conviction was vacated. Minami was the initial coordinating attorney for the companion actions of *Hirabayashi v. United States* and *Yasui v. United States*, which also resulted in vacated convictions. In 1989, in a case that generated widespread publicity over discrimination in academia, Minami acted as counsel for Professor Don Nakanishi. He filed and won two grievances that, along with political pressure, led to granting of tenure to Nakanishi (*Nakanishi v. UCLA*). Minami has litigated numerous employment discrimination cases over the years, challenging the "glass ceiling" (career limitations due to prejudice) and employment discrimination on the basis of physical disability, race, national origin, and sex.

He was founder of the Asian Law Caucus, Inc., in 1972; this was the first Asian Pacific American community legal service organization in the country. Minami also founded the Asian American Bar Association of the Greater Bay Area (1976), the first Asian American Bar association in the country. He founded the Asian Pacific Bar of California, a statewide consortium of local Asian Pacific Bar Associations, in 1988. Minami served on the Board of Directors of the ACLU of Northern California from 1973 to 1974 and on its litigation committee from 1990 to 1992.

Dale Minami has served the public in other roles as well. From 1981 to 1984 he served as a commissioner of the State of California Fair Employment and Housing Commission. He served in the State Bar of California's Commission on Judicial Nominee Evaluation from 1984 to 1987. Minami served as chair of the attorney general's Asian/Pacific Advisory Committee from 1988 to 1990 and as president of the Coalition of Asian Pacific Americans from 1988 to 1992, and as its secretary/treasurer from 1993 to the present. Minami was co-chair of Northern California Asian Pacific Americans for Clinton/Gore in 1992 and has been a member of Senator Barbara Boxer's Judicial Screening Committee from 1993 to the present.

A number of awards have been presented to Minami. In 1983 he received the Centro Legale De La Raza for delivery of legal services to the poor. In 1984 he received the State Bar of California's President's Pro Bono Service Award. He received the Coro Foundation Achievement Award in 1986 and the Harry Dow Memorial Fellowship "Justice in Action" Award in 1988. The Japanese Cultural and Community Center of Northern California presented Minami with its Community Award in 1988, and the Organization of Chinese Americans presented him with its Leadership Award in 1989.

Minami's publications include "Shikata ga nai: Legal Justice and Asian Americans" in *Church and Society* (1971); "Asian Law Caucus: Experiment Alternatives" in *Amerasia Journal* (1975); "Coram Nobis and Redress" in *Japanese Americans, from Relocation to Redress,* edited by Sandra C. Taylor and **Harry H. L. Kitano** (1986); "Guerrilla War at UCLA: Political and Legal Dimensions of the Tenure Battle" in *Amerasia Journal* (1990); and "Internment during World War II and Litigations" in *Asian Americans and the Supreme Court,* edited by Hyung-Chan Kim (1992).

Selected Bibliography

Personal interview, 1994.
Zia, Helen, and Susan B. Gall, eds. *Notable Asian Americans.* Detroit: Gale Research, 1995.

Steve Fugita

NORMAN Y. MINETA
(1931–   )
Congressman, Politician

Norman Y. Mineta, U.S. congressman from 1975 to 1995, was born in San Jose, California, on November 12, 1931. His father, an immigrant from Japan, had established the Mineta Insurance agency in 1920. As a child Mineta was one of 120,000 Americans of Japanese ancestry who were forcibly removed from the West Coast by the U.S. government during World War II and incarcerated. He later graduated from San Jose High School. Mineta earned a Bachelor of Science degree in business at the University of California at Berkeley in 1953.

After graduation Mineta entered active duty in the U.S. Army and served as a military intelligence officer during tours of duty in Japan and Korea. He left active service in 1956 but continued to serve in the reserves and attained the rank of major. Returning to San Jose, Mineta went to

Norman Y. Mineta

work for his father in the Mineta Insurance agency, a business that Mineta himself owned until 1990.

In 1962 Mineta became a member of San Jose's Human Relations Commission, his first public post. The City Council of San Jose then appointed him to a position on the city's Housing Authority. In 1967 he was appointed to fill a vacancy on the City Council, becoming the first ethnic minority member of the Council in San Jose's history. Mineta won election to a seat on the Council in 1969 and became vice mayor by appointment of the mayor and the Council.

In 1971 Mineta was elected mayor of San Jose, becoming the first Japanese American mayor of a major U.S. city. As mayor of San Jose, he quickly established himself as an aggressive and able spokesperson for urban America. He became a member of the Legislative Action Committee of the U.S. Conference of Mayors and a member of the Board of Directors of the National League of Cities. Mineta often appeared before legislative and administrative bodies on behalf of San Jose and the nation's other cities.

Mineta was elected to the U.S. House of Representatives in 1974, winning the seat vacated by a retiring Republican member of Congress. He immediately established himself as one of the leaders of the seventy-five new Democratic members in the 94th Congress when fellow new members elected him chair of the New Members Caucus.

Mineta's congressional service has been unusually varied and accomplished. He served on the House Budget Committee from 1977 to 1982, chairing its Task Force on the Budget Process from 1979 to 1980. Mineta was on the Democratic Policy and Steering Committee from 1981 to 1984 and has served as deputy whip for the House Democratic leadership from 1982 through the present. He was a member of the Post Office and Civil Service Committee from 1975 to 1976. He was also a member of the Science, Space, and Technology Committee from 1983 to 1992, becoming a senior member. As a representative of California's "Silicon Valley," Mineta continues to work on the technology and competitiveness issues that are key to the industrial base of the area. He served on the House Select Committee on Intelligence from 1977 to 1984.

Mineta was elected chair of the House Public Works and Transportation Committee for the 103rd Congress in 1993, becoming the first American of Asian ancestry to chair a major committee in the House. He served as chair of the surface transportation subcommittee (1989–1992), the aviation subcommittee (1981–1988), the investigations and oversight subcommittee (1979–1980), and the public buildings and grounds subcommittee (1977–1978). As chair of the Public Works and Transportation Committee, Mineta had leadership authority over much of the nation's public infrastructure investments—including roads, bridges, transit, safety, aviation, water resources, public buildings and grounds, and economic development assistance programs.

During the 100th Congress, Mineta was the driving force behind the passage of H.R. 442, the Civil Liberties Act of 1988, which redressed the injustices endured by Americans of Japanese ancestry during World War II. Overall, Mineta's broad legislative expertise includes transportation, high-technology industry, trade, NASA and the American space program, the federal budget, civil rights, and issues of specific importance to Americans of Asian and Pacific Island ancestry. After he left Congress in 1995 he joined Lockheed Martin as senior vice-president and managing director of transportation, system and services.

Mineta is married to Danealia Mineta. He has two sons, David and Stuart, from a previous marriage, and two stepsons, Bob and Mark Brantner.

Selected Bibliography

Niiya, Brian, ed. *Japanese American History: An A-to-Z Reference from 1868 to the Present*. New York: Facts on File, 1993, pp. 232–233.
Zia, Helen, and Susan Gall, eds. *Notable Asian Americans*. Detroit: Gale Research, 1995, pp. 259–260.

Steve Fugita

PATSY TAKEMOTO MINK

(1927–   )

Congresswoman, Attorney, Politician

Congresswoman Patsy Takemoto Mink was born on December 6, 1927, in Paia, Maui, Hawaii. Her father, Suematsu Takemoto, was a civil engineer, and her mother, Mitama Takemoto, was a boarding school–educated homemaker. Patsy began school at the age of four at Hamakuapoko Grammar School and decided early that she wanted to become a doctor. In fourth grade she and her brother Eugene transferred to the Kaunoa English Standard School. She graduated from Maui High School in 1944 as class valedictorian after being elected student body president during her senior year.

Patsy attended the University of Hawaii and in her sophomore year was elected president of the Pre-Medical Students Club and was chosen to be a member of the Varsity Debate Team. She attended Wilson College in Chambersburg, Pennsylvania, and then transferred to the University of Nebraska during her junior year. She returned to the University of Hawaii to graduate in 1948 with a Bachelor of Arts degree in zoology and chemistry. Disappointed by her rejection by medical schools, she decided to attend law school and was accepted by the University of Chicago Law School. She received a Doctor of Law degree in 1951.

She met and married John Francis Mink, a hydrologist and geologist, while attending the University of Chicago. After the birth of their daughter, Gwendolyn Rachel, in 1952, the family moved back to Hawaii. There John Mink was employed by the Hawaiian Sugar Planters Association. Patsy Mink was admitted to the Hawaii Bar in 1953 after challenging a state statute that considered her a resident of her husband's home state rather than of her own. Facing considerable gender bias as a woman attorney, Mink opened her own law practice and lectured at the University of Hawaii.

She then became active in party politics in Hawaii. She participated in Democratic Party platform reforms and reorganization and was instrumental in founding the Young Democrats organization, which became an important factor in Hawaiian politics in the following decades. During the 1955 territorial legislative session Mink served as a staff attorney, drafting legislation and learning more about the legislative process.

In 1956 she ran for a seat in the Territory of Hawaii House of Repre-

Patsy Takemoto Mink

sentatives. Along with a few supporters, Mink campaigned door-to-door in her large, rural district. She was elected by a wide margin and was the first Japanese American woman elected to the territorial legislature. On her first day in office Mink proposed a resolution protesting nuclear testing by the British in the South Pacific. The resolution passed, establishing her reputation as an outspoken advocate for controversial issues.

In 1958, after just one term in the territorial House of Representatives, Mink ran for a seat in the territorial Senate. Despite a lack of support by the Hawaii Democratic Party, Mink easily won the election. During her term in office she drafted the Senate's "equal pay for equal work" law and served as chair of the Senate Education Committee.

After Hawaii became a state in 1959, Mink ran for Hawaii's new House of Representatives seat but lost that election to **Daniel Ken Inouye**. In 1960 she served on the Drafting Committee of the Democratic National Convention's Platform Committee, and as vice-president of the National Young Democratic Clubs of America. In 1962 she ran for state Senate and won.

In 1964 Mink again ran for U.S. Representative and was elected, becoming the first Asian American woman to be elected to Congress. She served six consecutive terms, from 1965 to 1977. During her terms Mink served on the Education and Labor Committee introducing the first Early

Childhood Education Act, the Women's Educational Equality Act, and the Title IX amendments to the Education Act (1972). She also served on the Interior and Insular Affairs Committee (1965–1977) and was chair of the subcommittee on mines and mining (1973–1977). She also introduced the Regulation and Reclamation Act, which became law in 1977. Mink was a member of the House Budget Committee (1972–1976) and of the Select Committee on Outer Continental Shelf (1975–1976).

During this period Mink participated in a number of other congressional activities. She was vice-chair of the Democratic Study Group from 1966 to 1971 and from 1975 to 1976. She served as vice-chair of the Democratic Study Group's Task Force on Education in 1971 and as chair of its Congressional Reform Task Force in 1974. She also served as chair of the House-Senate Ad Hoc Committee on Poverty in 1968.

In 1971 Mink entered the Oregon presidential primary (there was no Hawaii primary) as an expression of her growing impatience with government inaction over the Vietnam War and with cutbacks in social programs. During this campaign, in April 1972, Mink flew to Paris with Representative Bella Abzug to meet with delegates from North and South Vietnam and the United States to urge resumption of the peace talks. Mink lost the presidential primary and was opposed in her next House of Representatives campaign by a group of Hawaii Democrats. She was reelected despite this opposition.

In 1976 Mink decided to seek election to the Senate seat being vacated by **Hiram Fong**. She lost the primary to Representative **Masayuki "Spark" Matsunaga**, who had the backing of the Democratic Party.

President Jimmy Carter nominated Mink in January 1977 for the post of assistant secretary of state for oceans and international, environmental, and scientific affairs. She served in that capacity from 1977 to 1979, working on issues such as the protection of whales, toxic waste disposal, and ocean mining.

Mink returned to Hawaii in 1980, and in 1982 she was elected to the Honolulu City Council, serving as chair and chief executive officer from 1983 to 1985. She remained on the City Council until 1987. In 1986 she ran for and lost a bid for governor of Hawaii, and in 1988 she lost the race for mayor of Honolulu. From 1979 to 1981 Mink was a visiting professor in women's studies and lecturer in political science and business law at the University of Hawaii.

In 1990 Mink ran successfully for U.S. Representative in special and regular elections to fill a seat vacated by Daniel Akaka. She was reelected in 1982 with a 77 percent majority. Her current committee assignments include Education and Labor (1990–present) and Government Reform. She is a member of the Congressional Travel and Tourism Caucus, the Environmental and Energy Study Conference, and the Congressional Caucus for Women's Issues.

Mink's major legislative accomplishments from 1990 to 1993 include sponsoring the Ovarian Cancer Research Act. She worked for amendments to the Higher Education Act, including making Pell Grants more accessible to nontraditional students, issuing loan forgiveness for nurses and medical technicians, and eliminating home equity from student aid formula calculations. She also continues to work legislatively on issues related to environmental preservation and national parks (such as Kaloko-Honokohau National Historical Park), elementary and secondary education, workplace fairness and equity, family and medical leave, universal health care, affordable housing, and agricultural industries.

In 1992 she received the American Bar Association's Margaret Brent Women Lawyers of Achievement Award, which honors women lawyers who have achieved professional excellence and have paved the way to success for others. Mink received a Distinguished Alumni Award from the University of Hawaii in 1987 and, in the same year, Distinguished Services Awards from both the Honolulu YMCA and the Hawaii Women Lawyers' Association. Some of Mink's other awards include the Distinguished Service Award from the National Association of Asian and Pacific American Education (1982), the Award for Creative Leadership in Women's Rights from the National Education Association (1977), the Human Rights Award from the American Federation of Teachers (1975), and the Nisei of the Biennium, Japanese American Citizens League (1972).

Mink has also made significant contributions through the legal process. In *Mink et al. v. EPA et al.* (1972) she sued for access to protected government documents, and the ruling provided the precedent used to obtain evidence in the Nixon Watergate scandal. In *Mink v. WHAR* (1976) a complaint filed with the Federal Communications Commission was approved, requiring radio stations to provide equal access for opposing views. In *Mink et al. v. University of Chicago* (1976) 1,000 women who were given the drug DES (diethyl stilbesterol) without their knowledge during the 1950s were awarded lifetime free medical care for reproductive malignancies. In *Mink v. Akahane, Matsumoto, and Pacarro* (1985) it was ruled that elected officials who have been recalled cannot run for election to succeed themselves.

Mink has published a number of articles in legal, education, and public policy journals during her career.

Selected Bibliography

Arinaga, E., and R. Ojiro. "Patsy Takemoto Mink." In M. Matsuda, ed., *Called from Within: Early Women Lawyers of Hawaii*. Honolulu: University of Hawaii Press, 1992.

Mink, P. "The Meaning of Politics." In *Five Asian and Pacific Perspectives on Educational Policy*. Berkeley: University of California Press, 1980.

———. "The Mink Case: Restoring the Freedom of Information Act." *Pepperdine Law Review*, vol. 2, no. 8 (1977).
Russell, A. *Patsy Takemoto Mink: Political Woman*. Ph.D. dissertation, University of Hawaii, 1977.

Steve Fugita

S. FRANK MIYAMOTO

(1912–   )

Educator, Sociologist

Shotaro Frank Miyamoto, sociologist, was born in Seattle, Washington, on July 29, 1912. He attended the University of Washington from 1930 to 1938, earning a B.A. degree in sociology in 1936 and an M.A. degree in sociology (with a minor in Far Eastern studies) in 1938. During these years Miyamoto was active in the Japanese Students Club, Alpha Kappa Delta, and the Pyramid Club. He was also awarded a graduate teaching fellowship from 1936 to 1939. From 1939 to 1941 Miyamoto attended the University of Chicago and was awarded a University fellowship. He earned a Ph.D. in sociology (with a minor in anthropology) in 1950 from the University of Chicago.

Miyamoto is best known for his study *Social Solidarity among the Japanese in Seattle*, which was written as a master's thesis at the University of Washington in 1938. He was greatly influenced by Professor Jesse F. Steiner, who arranged for its publication by the University of Washington Press. Miyamoto chose to study the local Japanese community because of its highly integrated social relations. His work was the only in-depth study of immigrant Japanese community life done before World War II.

Miyamoto's study caught the attention of Dorothy Swaine Thomas, who launched the Evacuation and Resettlement Study to examine the evacuation, detention, and relocation of Japanese Americans during World War II. She invited Miyamoto to join her project as a researcher at the Tule Lake Relocation Center. There, as a participant-observer, Miyamoto saw, and personally felt, the embitterment of people who were forcibly uprooted from their communities. Miyamoto's observations of life at Tule Lake were influenced by the social psychology of Professor

Herbert Blumer of the University of Chicago, and his work there became
the basis for his doctoral dissertation, *The Career of Intergroup Tension.*

Miyamoto taught in the Department of Sociology at the University of
Washington from 1945 to 1980. His teaching centered in the fields of
social psychology, collective behavior, and ethnic and race relations. He
became chairman of the department in 1965, the year when student protests and riots against the war in Vietnam began on the University of
Washington campus. In 1975 he was appointed associate dean in the
College of Arts and Sciences, with responsibilities for overseeing the social sciences and the emerging ethnic studies programs. In 1978 Miyamoto became acting dean of the college, a position he held until his
retirement in 1980.

Miyamoto's community service included serving on the Board of the
Civic Unity Committee from 1945 to 1950. This was a mayor's committee
to reduce problems of race and ethnic conflict in the Seattle community,
and especially to deal with problems of prejudice and discrimination that
faced the Issei (first-generation Japanese immigrants) and Nisei (children
of Issei) returning to Seattle after their incarceration.

Miyamoto is married to the former Michiko Morita, a piano prodigy.
He also has a son, John, who is a professor of psychology at the University of Washington, and a daughter, Jane Miyamoto Dell'Isola. His
current interests include supporting the career of his wife, who is a piano
teacher, woodworking, sports, gardening, computers, and writing.

Selected Bibliography

Ichioka, Yuji. *Views from Within: The Japanese American Evacuation and Resettlement
    Study.* Los Angeles: Asian American Studies Center, University of Cali-
    fornia, 1989.
Miyamoto, Shotaro Frank. "Problems of Interpersonal Style among the Nisei."
    Amerasia Journal, vol. 13, no. 2 (1986–87): 29–45.
———. *Social Solidarity among the Japanese in Seattle.* Seattle: University of Wash-
    ington Press, 1984.

Steve Fugita

HIROSHI H. MIYAMURA

(1925–   )

World War II Veteran, Congressional Medal of Honor Recipient

Hiroshi H. Miyamura, distinguished veteran of World War II and the Korean War, was born in Gallup, New Mexico, on October 6, 1925. His first tour of duty with the U.S. Army was from January 1944 to June 1946 with the 100th Battalion of the 442nd Regimental Combat Team in Europe during World War II. Miyamura's second tour was from September 1950 to October 1953 during the Korean conflict. He was assigned to the 7th Regiment, 3rd Division, where he achieved the rank of staff sergeant.

"Hershey" Miyamura received the Congressional Medal of Honor, the highest military honor that the Army can bestow, for heroism in Korea on April 24–25, 1951, near Taejon-ni. On the night of April 24, Corporal Miyamura, a machine gun squad leader, was occupying a defensive position when the enemy attacked. Miyamura engaged the enemy in close hand-to-hand combat, killing approximately ten of the enemy. He returned to his position to administer to the wounded and have them evacuated. When another assault came, after ordering his squad to withdraw he manned his machine gun until he ran out of ammunition. He then bayoneted through infiltrated enemy soldiers to a second gun emplacement. When it was necessary for his company to withdraw, he stayed behind to cover their movement. He killed more than fifty enemy soldiers before he ran out of ammunition and was severely wounded. Despite his painful wounds, he maintained his stand until his position was overrun.

In 1953 Miyamura received the Nisei of the Biennium Award from the Japanese American Citizens League. In the same year, Miyamura also received one of ten Outstanding Young Men awards from the National Junior Chamber of Commerce. He received the Department of Defense Award in 1981 during Asian Pacific Heritage Week. Miyamura has been honored with veterans' awards from cities throughout the United States from 1953 to the present.

Miyamura has made personal appearances throughout the United States on behalf of Nisei (second-generation Japanese American) veterans and Japanese Americans. He served as a member of his local draft board for ten years during the Vietnam War. He also served on the Board of Governors of the Japanese American Museum in Los Angeles.

Miyamura has owned and operated a service station in Gallup, New Mexico, for twenty-five years. He is married and has two sons and one daughter.

Selected Bibliography

Gall, Susan, ed. *The Asian American Almanac.* Detroit: Gale Research, 1995, p. 389.
Niiya, Brian, ed. *Japanese American History: An A-to-Z Reference from 1868 to the Present.* New York: Facts on File, 1993, p. 237.

Steve Fugita

TOYO MIYATAKE
(1895–1979)
Photographer, Artist

Toyo Miyatake, photographer and photographic artist, was born in Taka-shinomura in Nakatado County, Kagawa prefecture, Japan, and spent his childhood in Zentsuji. As a youth he enjoyed drawing, painting, and playing the saxophone in an orchestra called the Mikado Band.

During his fourth year of high school, Miyatake and his mother and brothers decided to sail to Seattle and reunite with Miyatake's father, who had previously immigrated to the United States in search of work. The family first resided behind his father's confectionery shop in what was then the Chinatown of Los Angeles. They later moved to a house on Jackson Street in Little Tokyo. Miyatake and his brother attended the Amelia Street Grammar School, where Miyatake shortened his name from Toyoo to Toyo at the principal's request.

While deciding on a career, Miyatake made money by picking grapes in Fresno. His love of drawing and painting initially influenced him to consider becoming an artist. However, he decided to pursue a career in photography, whereby he was able to become both an artist and a photographer.

At the age of twenty-one Miyatake began to study photography under Harry Shigeta, who developed methods of commercial photography known throughout the world. Miyatake bought the Toyo Photo Studio, which coincidentally bore his own name, in September 1923. He later opened a studio in Glendale and further developed his technique under the guidance of world-famous American photographer Edward Weston, who taught Miyatake about Japanese woodblock printing composition.

Miyatake won his first prize at a photographic art exhibition held by Japanese Americans. His reputation as a photographer grew when he received prizes at the 1926 London International Photography Exhibition and at various photographic art exhibitions in America. Miyatake's popularity increased as his friend, the famous dancer Michio Ito, introduced him to many Hollywood celebrities. Miyatake became the preferred photographer for Ito and Ito's pupils.

Throughout Miyatake's career, many Japanese who toured the United States visited Toyo Miyatake's studio and posed for his camera. Miyatake and his wife entertained many distinguished guests from Japan, and the portraits he did for these people were placed on display at the Mitsukoshi Department Store in Tokyo.

Miyatake's technique for taking portraits differed from the conventional Japanese pattern of having the client look directly into the camera. Miyatake would first make a quick study of the client's features and then take the photograph from the most suitable angle. Unlike most Japanese studios that used flat lighting, Miyatake's studio used three-dimensional lighting appropriate for the particular subject. Miyatake ensured that his clients were satisfied with the results and that the portraits could withstand objective scrutiny as portrait photographs.

In 1932 Miyatake photographed the Olympics in Los Angeles and donated his own money toward the direct transport of his news photos to Japan for the newspaper *Asahi Shimbun*. During the same year he returned to Japan owing to his father's illness and subsequent death. He remained in his homeland for about a year and then, after an unsuccessful attempt to establish a studio in Japan, returned to the United States. He next opened the prosperous Toyo Miyatake Studio in Little Tokyo in Los Angeles.

With the onset of World War II, Miyatake and his family were incarcerated in the internment camp at Manzanar, California. They departed on the morning of April 26, 1942, and arrived at Manzanar that evening. Initially, Miyatake spent most of his time reading the bestsellers sent to him by the Book of the Month Club. Camp authorities later made him an assistant in the art section of the museum at the camp. He received nineteen dollars a month, the highest salary paid in the internment camps.

In accordance with the Enemy Alien Control Law, Miyatake was not permitted to bring his cameras to camp and had them placed in storage.

With the help of a carpenter he built a camera body out of wood, which later came to be known as "Toyo Miyatake's hand-made camera," and attached a lens that he had concealed in his baggage. Miyatake was able to take pictures inconspicuously with his hand-made camera for approximately six months. Although photography was officially banned in the internment camps, Miyatake later received special approval by the camp administration to photograph Manzanar. With an ID card labeling him an official photographer, Miyatake sent for his camera and film in Los Angeles and freely photographed life in the camp. He received this privilege through the influence of Ansel Adams and other famous photographers who informed the head of the camp of his notable work as personal photographer of celebrities such as Thomas Mann and John Barrymore. Miyatake believed that his close friendship with Edward Weston also helped him obtain permission to take photographs, since Weston was an old friend of Ralph Merrit, the director of the camp. Most of Miyatake's photographs of Manzanar were taken as souvenirs. Over the years they have become valuable for their objectivity and documentary value.

In November 1945, following a three-year incarceration at Manzanar, Miyatake returned to Little Tokyo. He rented a vacant office on East First Street and opened the Toyo Miyatake Studio for the third time. The studio still exists under the ownership of his son Archie. In 1972 Miyatake was chosen as one of the pioneers of the year at the Nisei Week Festival. The Photographic Society of Japan presented him with a Distinguished Service Commendation in 1976. As a prominent figure in his community, he was named grand marshall of the Nisei Week festival in 1978. He received the Japanese Artist of the Year Award from the Little Tokyo Bijutsu no Tomo Association at a banquet in his honor.

Miyatake died in City View Hospital in February 1979. More than 2,000 people paid their last respects to him at memorial services held for him at Kohyasan Hall.

Toyo Miyatake and his wife, Hiroko, had two sons, Archie Atsufumi and Bob, and a daughter, Minnie Takahashi.

Selected Bibliography

Miyatake, Atsufumi, Taisuke Fujishima, and Eiko Hosoe, eds. *Toyo Miyatake behind the Camera, 1923–1979*. Tokyo: Bungeishunju Co., Ltd., 1984.

Niiya, Brian, ed. *Japanese American History: An A-to-Z Reference from 1868 to the Present*. New York: Facts on File, 1993.

Steve Fugita

RONALD TAI YOUNG MOON
(1940–   )
Judge

Chief Justice Ronald Moon, who currently serves on the Supreme Court of Hawaii, was born on September 4, 1940, in Honolulu, Hawaii, to Mary Lee and Duk Mann Moon. His grandparents were among the first wave of Koreans who immigrated to Hawaii between 1903 and 1905 to work as laborers on the sugar plantations. Born approximately one year before Japan's attack on Pearl Harbor, he grew up a third-generation Korean American in a small plantation town on the island of Oahu, near Honolulu. The Moons operated a "Mom and Pop" store, selling clothes and toys to the locals as well as to the soldiers and their families from the Schofield Barracks.

Although Moon grew up in an ethnically diverse community and the potential for losing one's ethnic/cultural identity was quite real, his parents and grandparents adamantly encouraged the younger generation to retain what they deemed Korean cultural values, that is, love of god, respect for elders, a strong work ethic, education, persistence, civility, and humility. In the Moon household, Korean customs and traditions, though diluted in form, were strongly emphasized.

Chief Justice Moon recalls a childhood incident after which he learned the definitive lesson that has guided his life. The eight-year-old Moon's fantasy of one day becoming a cowboy was rudely dismissed when he was told that there were no slant-eyed cowboys. That evening the young Moon had the first of many inspirational conversations with his parents. His father and mother reassured him that it is the character of one's person and not the characteristics of one's physical appearance that determines one's success in life. He recalls tears from his mother that evening as he lost his childhood innocence about race relations in the United States.

At age eighteen Moon moved to Iowa to attend the University of Dubuque and Coe College, pursuing an undergraduate degree in psychology and sociology. Then in 1965, after receiving his law degree from the University of Iowa, he returned to Hawaii and began work as a law clerk for one of Hawaii's most prominent and respected judges, Chief Justice Martin Pence, who has been a life-long mentor.

After one year of clerking, in 1968 he began his fifteen-year-long career

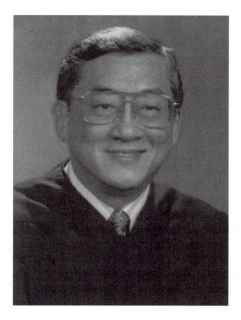

Ronald Tai Young Moon

as a trial lawyer in the firm of Libkuman, Ventura, Moon & Ayabe. In 1982 he was appointed by then-governor **George Ariyoshi** to the circuit court as a trial judge. From 1986 to 1988 Moon also served as adjunct professor at the University of Hawaii's Richardson School of Law. In 1990 and again in 1993, Moon was appointed by then-governor John Waihee to the Supreme Court of Hawaii as an associate justice. On March 31, 1993, Governor Waihee appointed Moon to be chief justice of the Supreme Court of Hawaii, where he remains today.

Chief Justice Moon and his wife, Stella, have six children.

Selected Bibliography

Who's Who among Asian Americans, 1994–1995 ed. Detroit: Gale Research, 1994.
Who's Who in American Law, 7th ed., 1992–1993. Wilmette, IL: Marquis Who's Who, 1991.

Jennifer Kang

TOSHIO MORI

(1910–1980)

Author

Author Toshio Mori was born in Oakland, California, the youngest of three boys. In 1915 Mori's family moved to San Leandro, where his father started a nursery and where Mori lived for the rest of his life. In addition to attending public school Mori, like most other American-born Japanese Nisei (second-generation Japanese Americans) attended Japanese language school. Every weekday afternoon he and fellow Nisei students went to the Buddhist church, which also served as the language school. Mori received Japanese schooling from the time he was eight years old until his third year in high school, and for a while he considered becoming a Buddhist missionary.

As a youth, Mori was interested in art and literature. He studied art at the Oakland schools and devoted much time to reading dime novels and short stories. He aspired to become either a writer or a major league baseball player. His high school coach even arranged a tryout for the Chicago Cubs. However, he was encouraged by his mother to favor the writing over baseball. His English teacher at Oakland High School, Mary B. Sheridan, also inspired Mori to pursue a writing career.

In 1932 Mori finalized his decision to become a writer and began to write each night from 10 P.M. to 2 A.M. He did this after working ten to twelve hours per day at the family nursery. Knowing that authors such as Sherwood Anderson and Ernest Hemingway had made their mark in their twenties, the 22-year-old Mori remained faithful to his rigorous schedule in order to improve his chances for publication. Unlike his colleagues, who often contributed to the Nisei vernacular press, Mori intended to publish his work in mainstream publications. His focus was on the Issei (first-generation Japanese immigrants) and Nisei in and around San Leandro and Oakland. He wanted to explain Japanese America to the American public.

Although he initially received numerous rejection slips, Mori succeeded in getting his first publication in the magazine *Coast* in 1938. Following his first publication he was "discovered" by William Saroyan, who encouraged him to get more of his work into print. Between 1940 and 1941, Mori published his work in such magazines as *Clipper, Iconograph, Writer's Forum, Common Ground*, and **James Omura**'s *Current Life*.

Caxton Printers of Idaho placed Mori's *Yokohama, California,* a collection of short stories based on Japanese American life in Oakland, on its Spring 1942 publications list; however, the publication was put off indefinitely with the onset of World War II.

Mori was sent to an assembly center hastily constructed at Tanforan Racetrack in San Bruno before being placed in the Central Utah Relocation Project in Topaz, Utah. In Tanforan, Mori wrote the "The Man with the Bulging Pockets," which commented on tragic-comic aspects of human nature. In Topaz, Mori was assigned to the documentation section and continued to write. He published his work in *Trek,* the literary journal at Topaz, along with several other Nisei artists including **Mine Okubo,** Jimmy Yamada, Taro Katayama, and Toyo Suyemoto. Beginning in 1942, the editors issued three magazines. Only Mori edited the fourth issue, entitled *All Abroad,* since the others had dispersed.

Mori and his family received permission to return to San Francisco after his brother, a member of the all-Nisei 442nd Regimental Combat Team, was injured and sent to the veterans' hospital in Auburn, California. Mori recalled some of this time in "Unfinished Message," which portrays a mother's concern. His earlier work, *Yokohama, California,* was published in 1949 and is reported to have been well received. He continued his writing and chronicled the lives of Japanese Americans in hundreds of short stories and six novels. One published novel by Mori, *Woman from Hiroshima,* illuminated the saga of Japanese American life from its origins in Japan to the period after World War II through the voice of an Issei woman speaking to her grandchildren. Five of Mori's novels remain unpublished, including *Send These the Homeless,* written in 1944 about the conflict between two Nisei brothers who are politically on opposite sides during World War II; and *Way of Life,* written in the 1960s about whites during the Great Depression. Many of Mori's works were published regularly in *Pacific Citizen* and *Hokubei Mainichi.*

Although Mori stopped writing in 1965, Sansei (third-generation Japanese American) students, writers, and critics rediscovered many of his works in the 1970s. In 1979 one of his novels and a second edition of his short stories were published. Mori participated as an honored panelist at many literary gatherings, including the Asian American Writers Conference sponsored at the Oakland Museum by the Combined Asian American Resources Project (March 1975); the Pacific Northwest Asian American Writers Conference at the University of Washington in Seattle (June 1976); and the Talk Story Ethnic Writers Conference at the Mid-Pacific Institute in Honolulu (June 1978).

In 1979 a second collection of Mori's short stories, *The Chauvinist and Other Short Stories* was published; however, the vast majority of his work remains unpublished. The settings of the stories in *The Chauvinist* include flower shops and nursery fields; Treasure Island with its Japanese pavilion and green tea ice cream; Chinatown; Oakland (sometimes called Ashland) and its Japanese getto; Tanforan Assembly Center; Topaz; and the veterans' hospital. Many of Mori's stories enable the reader to examine the home life of Japanese Americans, although some, such as "The Loser," contain no specific reference to ethnicity.

A common theme of Mori's work is the sense of order and purpose that prevails in the human spirit despite the hardships of depression, war, concentration camps, and prejudice. His writings are known for their portrayal of the daily struggles, aspirations, and joys of gardeners, housewives, artists, students, and shopkeepers who reflect the heritage of Asian Americans. Mori was the first Japanese American to have a book of short stories published in this country.

Selected Bibliography

Mori, Toshio. *The Chauvinist and Other Stories*. Los Angeles: UCLA Asian American Studies Center, 1979.

――――. *Yokohama, California*. Seattle: University of Washington Press, 1985.

Niiya, Brian, ed. *Japanese American History: An A-to-Z Reference from 1868 to the Present*. New York: Facts on File, 1993.

Steve Fugita

SADAO MUNEMORI

(1923–1945)

World War II Veteran, Congressional Medal of Honor Recipient

Sadao Munemori was a war hero and sole Nisei (second-generation Japanese American) recipient of the Congressional Medal of Honor for service during World War II. He was born in 1923 in Los Angeles, where he attended Lincoln High School.

Shortly after the bombing of Pearl Harbor, Munemori enlisted in the U.S. Army. He was immediately assigned to the Military Intelligence Service Language School at Camp Savage in Minnesota. After requesting a transfer, he joined the 442nd Regimental Combat Team at Camp Shelby, Mississippi. On May 8, 1944, he joined Company A of the 100th

Infantry Battalion at Anzio and earned his Combat Infantry Badge before
the end of the day.

Less than a year later Munemori received the Congressional Medal of
Honor, the highest military honor that the Army can bestow. He was
awarded the Medal after saving the lives of two American soldiers on
April 5, 1945, near Seravezza, Italy, as the 100th/442nd battled the Ger-
mans. During the battle Munemori took over the forward unit after its
squad leader was wounded. He then led the men through a minefield
within 30 yards of an enemy machine gun nest. Through heavy fire Munemori continued to advance and made a frontal, one-man attack and
knocked out two machine guns with a handful of grenades, about 15
yards away from the enemy. After wounding the two German gunners,
Munemori withdrew from the enemy's shower of grenades and headed
back toward a shell crater occupied by two of his comrades. As he approached the men, an unexploded grenade bounced off of his helmet
and rolled toward the two squad members. Munemori dove on the grenade to smother the explosion with his body and instantly died. His two
comrades, Akira Shishido and Jimi Oda, escaped alive. Shishido suffered
a concussion, and Oda received a fragment in the eye. Munemori's action
cleared the path for his company's victorious advance shortly after his
death.

The Congressional Medal of Honor commemorating Munemori's heroism was presented to his mother, Mrs. Nawa Munemori, on March 13,
1946. A military tanker was later renamed the USS *Private Sadao S. Munemori*, the first U.S. military ship to bear a Japanese name. In May 1993
a U.S. Army Reserve Center in West Los Angeles was named in Munemori's honor.

Selected Bibliography

"Building to Be Named for Munemori of 442nd." *Hokubei Mainichi*, May 8, 1993,
     p.1.
Hosokawa, B. *Nisei: The Quiet Americans.* New York: William Morrow, 1969.
Niiya, Brian, ed. *Japanese American History: An A-to-Z Reference from 1868 to the
     Present.* New York: Facts on File, 1993.
Tanaka, C. *Go for Broke: A Pictorial History of the 100/442nd Regimental Combat
     Team.* Richmond, CA: Go for Broke, 1982.

                                                      Steve Fugita

Josie Cruz Natori

(1947–   )

Fashion Designer

Josie Cruz Natori has changed world of fashion and in the process has changed the way women look at and use lingerie. She has parlayed a small business selling embroidered nightshirts operating from her living room into an international business retailing luxury lingerie featuring the intricate appliqué, embroidery, and detailing that has long been an art form in her native Philippines.

Before she became a New York fashion designer, "Josie" Cruz Natori was the first woman vice-president at the investment banking division of Merrill Lynch in the United States. Natori, born on May 9, 1947, is the oldest of six children of Felipe Cruz—a self-made man who ran an extremely successful construction business. Raised in a family that stressed independence for women, she recalled that the Philippines had a matriarchal culture that encouraged women to be entrepreneurial.

At age seventeen she left her home in Manila to attend Manhattanville College in New York City. A straight A student, she graduated with honors in 1968—receiving a Bachelor's degree in economics—and then took a relatively low-paying job at the corporate finance department at Prudential-Bache, Inc. Within months she was asked to help run the company's floundering Manila office and given the responsibility to hire and manage twenty people. She also became a registered stockbroker. After a disagreement between Bache and the Philippine government, the Manila office was closed and in 1970 she returned to Wall Street. This time she worked in Merrill Lynch's corporate finance department. Five years later, in 1975, she became Merrill Lynch's first woman vice-president in the company's investment banking division.

She met Ken Natori, a young Japanese American stockbroker, on a blind date. They married in 1971. The year after she became a Merrill Lynch vice-president, the couple's only child was born. After a short maternity leave she returned to work. Although she was earning a substantial salary and moving quickly up the corporate ladder, Natori felt dissatisfied, unchallenged, and not in control. She began to explore different business possibilities that she and her husband could pursue on their own. A brokerage was too expensive and a car wash was too mundane. She even considered a children's clothing shop. Natori wanted to start a business she could relate to and still have an advantage over her competitors.

Once she realized that being from the Philippines made her different, she went back there to consider her business options. She considered Filipino reproductions of Queen Anne furniture and Filipino baskets. Then a friend sent her several blouses intricately embroidered by "Manila artisans." When Natori began bringing her samples to department stores, a Bloomingdale buyer suggested she lengthen the blouses into nightshirts. Although she didn't know what a nightshirt looked like, she quickly learned and contracted small factories in the Philippines to produce and ship 1,000 units to the United States—each worth $12.50.

In 1983 the Philippines underwent political turmoil brought about by the assassination of presidential candidate Benigno Aquino. Natori moved some of her production to Antigua in the Carribean Islands to hedge against a possible closedown in the Philippines due to severe opposition to then–Philippine president Ferdinand Marcos. She planned to have the best Filipino seamstresses teach Caribbean labor how to embroider Philippine-style. It didn't work. She realized that "embroidery is an age-old Philippine skill . . . passed down from generation to generation." The Caribbean labor did not have time to master the skill. Shortly thereafter the Philippines underwent the "bloodless People's Revolution." Marcos fled the country, and Corazon Aquino assumed the presidency of the Philippines. Natori closed the Antigua operation and returned all production to her Philippine factory.

Natori is an astute, successful businesswoman who has revolutionized the world of lingerie fashion. She is the recipient of several awards, including the Galleon Award from Philippine president Corazon Aquino, the Ellis Island Medal of Honor, and the Department of Commerce "Salute to American Fashion Designers" Award. She served as a delegate to President Clinton's Economic Summit Conference in Little Rock and as a commissioner to the White House Conference on Small Business.

Josie Cruz Natori is also the mother of a college-age son, a wife who works successfully alongside her husband, and a granddaughter who followed the early advice of her Filipino grandmother—"that women should be independent and have their own careers—and never depend on a man for anything."

Selected Bibliography

AsiaWeek, April 14, 1996, p. 49.
Chicago Sun Times, December 20, 1995, p. 55.
Filipinas magazine, September 1992, pp. 6–9.
Impact 21, July 1996, p. 33.
Mirabella, March 1990, pp. 106–108.

Nation's Business, February 1995.
Savvy Woman, February 1991, pp. 42–45, 76–78.
Time, Fall 1990, p. 48.
Women's Wear Daily, July 22, 1996.
Working Women, November 1987, pp. 54–57.

Dorothy Cordova

HAING NGOR

(1947–1996)

Physician, Actor

Haing Ngor, know for his portrayal of **Dith Pran** in the film *The Killing Fields*, was born in a farming village south of Phnom Penh, the capital of Cambodia. His mother was Khmer and his father was an ethnic Chinese. He grew up in a war-torn country and had to work in the fields at an early age. However, overcoming poverty and adversity, his family was able to send him to school.

Haing Ngor studied in a local Chinese school and then went on to complete high school in a French *lycée* in Phnom Penh, where he lived in a Buddhist temple with the monks. He attended the national medical school in the capital, where he graduated with a specialization in obstetrics and gynecology. He became a successful young physician who operated his own clinic in the capital in addition to serving as a medical officer in the government army.

When Cambodian guerrilla fighters, the Khmer Rouge, overran Phnom Penh in 1975, Haing Ngor was among the intellectuals who had to hide for fear of being sent away to "re-education camps" or to a worse fate. He was forced to do manual work to survive while still trying to practice medicine in secret from the Khmer Rouge troops. In April 1975, along with thousands of his countrymen, Ngor joined the mass exodus from Phnom Penh. He was imprisoned, tortured, assigned forced labor; he also witnessed his mother being sent to a work camp in the jungle, and his father and brother taken to execution. In 1978 Ngor's wife died in childbirth owing to lack of medical care. Thereafter he witnessed Cambodian Communist leader Pol Pot's purge that became known to the world in *The Killing Fields*.

In 1979 Haing Ngor made it to freedom when he reached a refugee camp in Thailand. In August 1980 he flew to America and started his life as a refugee. He worked at odd jobs and went to school to learn English. Three months later, in November 1980, he was working as a caseworker with the Chinatown Service Center helping Vietnamese, Cambodian, and Laotian refugees to find work. In 1982 he was approached by a casting director from Warner Bros. Studio. In 1983 Ngor started filming *The Killing Fields*, a movie based on the story of Sydney Schanberg, the *New York Times Magazine*'s correspondent in Cambodia under Lon Nol, the Cambodian ruler installed by the United States prior to 1975, and Dith Pran, Schanberg's Cambodian assistant. The film relates horrors of the Pol Pot regime, the decade-long mass massacres and genocide efforts against the people of Cambodia. It also celebrates the bonds of friendship and the indomitable will to survive.

Without any previous acting experience, Ngor played the part of Dith Pran and won an Oscar for Best Supporting Actor in 1984. In his speech of acceptance Ngor said, "thank Warner Bros. for helping me tell my story to the world, let the world know what happened in my country." Since then Ngor acted in a number of television films and documentaries, but his main activities involved heading six humanitarian organizations devoted to caring for Southeast Asian refugees and assisting with their resettlement.

In his autobiography, *A Cambodian Odyssey*, written with Roger Warner and published in 1987, Ngor recounted the haunting ordeal of his people during the Khmer Rouge years. His tireless efforts to bring about changes in Cambodian took all his time. He actively sought assistance for Cambodian refugees and regularly returned to his homeland with medical and other vital supplies. He was also involved in the Cambodian community in Long Beach, California, and spent time and income supporting refugee groups. Ngor donated most of his royalties from the film *The Killing Fields* and his lecture circuit to the cause of Cambodians.

On Sunday, February 25, 1996, Haing Ngor was found shot to death in Los Angeles outside the two-bedroom apartment where he had lived alone before and after he became known as an Academy award–winning actor.

Selected Bibliography

Donahue, Deirdre. "Cambodian Doctor Haing Ngor Turns Actor in 'The Killing Fields,' and Relives His Grisly Past." *People*, February 4, 1985, pp. 43–44.
Michelmore, Peter. "Legacy of the Killing Fields." *Reader's Digest*, May 1997, pp. 60–66.
Noble, Kenneth R. "Haing Ngor, Cambodian Who Won Oscar for 'Killing Fields,' is Slain." *New York Times*, February 27, 1996, pp. A8, 16.

Le Hong Phan

ISAMU NOGUCHI

(1904–1988)

Sculptor, Artist

Isamu Noguchi, sculptor and artist, was born in Los Angeles in 1904. His mother, the Irish American writer Leonie Gilmour, and his Japanese father, Yonejiro Noguchi, met while on a trip to New York. They never married although their friendship continued. Noguchi's mother raised him. When he was two years of age they moved to Tokyo to join Isamu's father. Four years later Gilmour moved away with Isamu. She supported herself by teaching English. Occasionally Noguchi's father visited them, even though he married his Japanese house servant and they had several of their own children. He was a poet and a professor of English literature in Tokyo.

Due to his curly hair and grey eyes, Noguchi was a curiosity in Japan. When he was thirteen years old his mother sent him to a boarding school in Indiana. Here he also did not quite fit in, a recurring theme in his life. The school was closed for wartime use and Isamu moved into the home of a Swedenborgian minister in LaPorte, Indiana. After graduating from LaPorte High School, he entered Columbia University to begin premedical studies. Encouraged by his mother, Noguchi enrolled in an evening sculpture class. Soon thereafter he quit his medical studies to devote himself to sculpture. At this time he began using the name Noguchi instead of Gilmour.

In 1927 Noguchi was awarded a John Simon Guggenheim fellowship for travel to Paris and the East. In Paris he worked as an apprentice for innovative Romanian sculptor Constantin Brancusi. Noguchi returned to New York at the end of 1928. For the next decade he supported himself by producing portrait sculpture. In 1930 he traveled to Peking to study ink brush technique with Chi Pai-shih. He returned to Japan in 1931 for a difficult reunion with his father. In Kyoto, Noguchi saw his first Zen gardens and ancient Haniwa sculpture. He also studied pottery in Japan.

Noguchi had a long and successful relationship with modern dance choreographer Martha Graham, designing theater sets for her for over thirty years. Moreover, he designed sets for several other producers. In the commercial realm Noguchi designed an intercom for Zenith, a coffee table and dinette for Herman Miller, and rocking stools and a table for Knoll International.

Soon after the Japanese attacked Pearl Harbor, Noguchi organized the group Nisei Writers and Artists Mobilization for Democracy in order to work for the fair treatment of Japanese Americans. He traveled to Washington to try to reduce the hardships associated with their internment. He even protested the internment by voluntarily entering the Poston, Arizona, internment camp. Disillusioned, he left the camp and returned to New York six months later.

One of the exceedingly wide range of areas Noguchi worked in was the design of fountains. His first was for the Ford Motor Company for its building at the New York World's Fair. Others are found at the Hart Plaza in Detroit; in Palm Beach, Florida; in New Orleans at the John Hancock Insurance Company building; at the Art Institute in Chicago; and on the Missouri River between Nebraska and Iowa.

Many public projects were also undertaken by Noguchi. These include a stainless steel relief for the Associated Press building in Rockefeller Center; a waterfall wall and the "Red Cube," both in New York; "Portal" for the Cleveland Justice Center; "Sky Gate" in Honolulu; "Passage of Seasons" at the Cleveland Art Museum; "Unidentified Object" at the Metropolitan Museum of Art; "Constellation" for the Kimball Art Museum in Fort Worth; "California Scenario" in Costa Mesa, California; and "To the Issei" in the Japanese American Cultural and Community Center in Los Angeles.

Another area in which Noguchi made major contributions was the Akari lamp, a radically updated paper lantern. He also had a series of commissions in garden design through which his work blurred the line between sculpture and garden. Some of these are located at UNESCO in Paris; Chase Manhattan Plaza in New York; the Museum of Fine Art in Houston; the water garden at the Domon Ken Museum in Sakata, Japan; the IBM Headquarters in Armonk, New York; the Billy Rose Garden in Jerusalem; and the Beinecke Library at Yale University.

Later in life Noguchi began to explore hard stone. He moved to Japan and recruited a young stone cutter, Masatoshi Izumi. The resulting masterpieces integrate his many concerns.

On a trip to Japan in 1950 Noguchi met his future wife, actress Shirley Yamaguchi. They were officially married in 1952. They were divorced in 1957.

Noguchi was awarded many prizes and honors toward the end of his extraordinarily productive life. In 1986 he received the Kyoto Prize from the Inomori Foundation, in 1987 the National Medal of Arts, and in 1988 the Third Order of the Sacred Treasure from the Japanese government and the award for Distinction in Sculpture from the Sculpture Center. Noguchi died in December 1988.

In 1985, in the place where he accomplished many of his major achievements, the Isamu Noguchi Garden Museum was opened in Long Island City, New York.

Selected Bibliography

Altshuler, Bruce. *Isamu Noguchi*. New York: Abbeville Press, 1994.
Ashton, Dore. *Noguchi East and West*. New York: Alfred A. Knopf, 1992.
Grove, Nancy, and Diane Botnick. *The Sculpture of Isamu Noguchi, 1924–1979: A
    Catalogue*. New York: Garland Publishing, 1980.

Steve Fugita

ANGELA OH

(1955–)

Attorney, Political Activist

Angela Oh is currently working as a criminal defense lawyer in Los
Angeles for the firm of Beck, De Corso, Barrera & Oh. A practicing attorney and second-generation Korean American, she became known
around the nation as "the spokesperson for the Korean Americans" in
the aftermath of the 1992 Los Angeles riots. The riots resulted in the loss
and damage of over two thousand Korean-owned businesses in the Los
Angeles area. Oh has written numerous articles for national newspaper
publications and for *Ms.* magazine, becoming the voice for the victims
of the riots who lost not only their businesses but also a sense of trust
and belief in the system that failed to protect their life investments. She
has also participated in several academic conferences, both as a panelist
and a speaker. Her position has been to defend the Korean community,
which was often blamed for the racial tensions in Los Angeles, and to
promote racial harmony in the Los Angeles community.

Oh's work for the victims of the riot, which she did at no charge, was
recognized by the California Assembly. She was appointed special counsel to the Assembly Special Committee on the Los Angeles Crisis. As
special counsel she was to oversee the state's inquiry into the causes of
the riots and help in the preparation of a report concerning the rebuild-
ing of Los Angeles.

Angela Oh has worked as a community activist since her college years
at UCLA while studying for an undergraduate degree in psychology.
The list of civic and community affairs organizations with which she has
had extensive involvement include the ACLU, Korean Bar Association,
California Women's Law Center, and the Women's Organization Reach-

ing Koreans. Most recently Oh has been selected by President Clinton to be one of seven members on a race relations panel, the Presidential Advisory Board.

Oh's work as a spokesperson for the Korean Americans during the riots did not leave her simply with compliments and praise. In an article in the *New York Times*, Angela Oh states that the role as "spokesperson" was not one she sought out; she was just filling a void in the aftermath of the riots. As it turns out, she has had her share of criticisms. She explains that over 80 percent of the Korean community in Los Angeles are foreign-born, and they were very resentful that a second-generation person stepped out to speak on their behalf. Nevertheless she is still active in trying to convince people that the riots were not just about being victimized, but about other major failures in society.

April 1997 marked the fifth anniversary of the Los Angeles riots. When asked to assess the state of the city and of current race relations, Oh commented that she does not feel that things have gotten better and that there is still a long way to go. She feels strongly that the media plays a dangerous game of manipulation in covering "news" with incidents involving people of different races. According to Oh, the media injects racial overtones into every shooting incident involving convenience store owners and suggests that such incidents are about race, or a lack of respect for other cultures. This, Oh feels, is simply wrong.

Selected Bibliography

Chang, Edward Taehan, and Angela Eunjin Oh. "The Messengers Are Sending the Wrong Signals to L.A." *Los Angeles Times*, April 7, 1994, p. B7.

Hall, Carla. "A Dialogue, Five Years Later: Spokeswomen for the Korean American and African American Communities." *Los Angeles Times*, April 28, 1997, p. B1.

Ripston, Ramona. "Ramona Ripston in Conversation with Angela Oh." *Open Forum*, vol. 68, no. 4 (Winter 1993): 1–6.

Yoshihara, Nancy. "Angela Oh: Adding an Asian American Voice to the Race Debate." *Los Angeles Times*, July 13, 1997, p. M3.

Zia, Helen. "The King Verdict: Making Sense of It." *Ms.*, July–August 1992, p. 41.

Jennifer Kang

SOON TEK OH

(1933–   )

Actor, Educator

Soon Tek Oh, also a civic leader, is known to audiences around the world for his work in theater, film, and television. Born on June 29, 1933, in Korea, he was brought up in the difficult years of World War II and the Korean War. Despite hardships and exploits, after peace finally arrived Soon Tek Oh developed an undying love for acting while watching imported movies.

Soon Tek Oh first entered the United States after earning a scholarship to the University of Southern California (USC) cinema department in Los Angeles. He soon expanded his academic studies with a two-year program as a scholarship student at New York's much-respected Neighborhood Playhouse. After deciding to stay in the United States, he graduated from UCLA's motion picture department and the M.F.A. program in the theater arts department, where he taught as a graduate instructor. At the same time he became one of the founding members of Los Angeles' East-West Players, leading its workshops in performance and play development. From 1972 to 1973 he was guest professor in theater at Sogang University in Seoul and artist-in-residence/professor at the Seoul Institute of the Arts, formerly the Drama Center. In the intervening years Oh has organized theater teaching programs through the Korean-American Theater Ensemble and, since 1993, with his own company. His working approach to theater, as an educator and performer, has continued throughout his career.

Currently, Soon Tek Oh is artistic director for the Society of Heritage Performers, which he founded with the intention of developing the awareness of the American public to the contributions and potential of Korean American performers. To that end, he has directed two major productions combining the *mah-dang-nori* style of Korean drum-dance theater with the talents of American-trained actors, primarily young professionals of Korean American heritage. *Have You Heard '95* was the first production, a spectacle that earned them a City of Los Angeles Cultural Affairs grant to produce a second show in 1996, which was described by the *Los Angeles Times* as "the energetic heartbeat of L.A. theater." The Heritage Performers presented *Our Nori (Our Song): A Korean-American Celebration* to family audiences at the 1,200-seat open-air John Anson

Soon Tek Oh

Ford Amphitheater, sponsored by the County of Los Angeles. The Heritage Performers' production of an original drama, *Behind the Walls*, was described as "one of the most original productions of theater currently running in L.A. . . . This is a company with imagination. We look forward to more." For his socially conscious work in theater, Soon Tek Oh has been honored and recognized by government, church, and civic leaders throughout the United States.

Professionally, Soon Tek Oh has become internationally known as both "a protean actor" who can do anything (movie producer/director Hal Prince) and as a director noted for blending traditional with contemporary as well as for his nurturing abilities with new writers. His theater credits range far and wide: co-lead in Broadway's *Pacific Overtures* by Stephen Sondheim as staged by Hal Prince; the feature performer in the 1995 bi-coastal tour of *Woman Warrior* produced by the Berkeley Repertory Company; and stints at the Yale Repertory Company, the Mark Taper Forum/Center Theater Group in Los Angeles, the Drama Center in Seoul, and in over two dozen productions with the East-West Players. He has been active with the Los Angeles Theater Center, performing in plays aimed at addressing social issues: *Canned Goods* by African American playwright Silas Jones, and *Yellow Face* by Korean American playwright Philip Chung. Recently, heading his own troupe, the Society of Heritage Performers, he has performed in a number of staged readings as well as full-scale productions throughout southern California.

As a film and television actor, Oh is never far from the public eye. Art house audiences saw him in the independent feature *Yellow*—a complement to his British work in Mike Newell's *Sour Sweet*, an award winner at the Chicago Film Festival and the Moscow Film Festival. He is also featured in the Disney Studios and Animated Features production of *Mulan* (1998). In television, he had recurring roles in *M*A*S*H*, *Hawaii Five-O*, *Magnum P.I.*, and *Kung-Fu*. An Emmy Award nominee for *East of Eden* opposite Jane Seymour, Oh has also joined forces with James Bond in *The Man with the Golden Gun*, crossed fists as Chuck Norris's nemesis in *Missing in Action 2*, starred opposite Kathy Bates in *A Home of Our Own*, and played the co-starring role of the Master of Masters in the comedy *Beverly Hills Ninja*.

Recently, Soon Tek Oh has been involved in several new projects as a civic leader, an actor, and with the Heritage Performers. The Heritage Performers have been recipients of a Sony Pictures Entertainment grant to continue their cutting-edge theatrical work. Meanwhile, Oh has plans to work on a number of projects. As an actor, he provided a featured voice for the Disney animation feature *Mulan*. In television he had featured roles on "Touched by an Angel" and "Promised Land." As a director he will be working with producer Lauren Deutsch of KCRW-FM for the *Contemporary Korean Short Stories* series presented on National Public Radio. The socially conscious play *Model Minority*, directed and developed by Soon Tek Oh, has been invited to a convocation of church ministries in Korea. Finally, with the Society of Heritage Performers, Oh will be adapting the Korean novella *River of Tears* by Chung Channe for an English-language stage debut in the United States. They will also develop Korea's "Best Play of 1995," Man-Hee Lee's *A Small Darkness*, for an English-language feature film production.

Selected Bibliography

Joe, Jeanne. "Soon-Tek Oh and the Everlasting Struggle Against the 'Asians Can't Act' Syndrome," *Neworld*, 1977, No. 4, pp. 26–46.

Monji, Jana J. " 'Heard': High Energy Look at Korean American Experience," *Los Angeles Times*, Section E. Wednesday, September 25, 1996.

Ragan, David. *Who's Who in Hollywood: The Largest Cast of International Film Personalities Ever Assembled*. New York: Facts on File, 1992.

Chae Reed

VINCENT H. OKAMOTO

(1943–)

Attorney, Business Leader

Vincent H. Okamoto, attorney and businessman, was born in the Poston Relocation Camp in Poston, Arizona, on November 22, 1943, where his family had been interned along with many other Japanese Americans during World War II. He was the youngest of the ten children of Henry and Yone Okamoto. Following the family's release they moved to South Chicago, where his parents ran a small grocery store. The family later moved to Gardena, California, when Okamoto was twelve years old. He attended Gardena High School, where he served as senior class president, was a three-year letterman in track and football, and belonged to the Men's Honor Society.

Okamoto attended El Camino College from 1962 to 1965. From 1965 to 1967 he attended the University of Southern California, receiving a Bachelor of Arts degree in international relations in 1967. Okamoto became an Army 2nd lieutenant in 1967. He earned his commission from the University of California, Los Angeles, Reserve Officer Training Corps.

From 1967 to 1970 Okamoto served in the U.S. Army Infantry, attaining the rank of captain. He was stationed at Fort Bragg, North Carolina; in Vietnam; and in Berlin, Germany. He served as a rifle platoon leader, infantry company commander, airborne ranger, and intelligence officer attached to the Special Forces. During his military service Okamoto received the Distinguished Service Cross, the Silver Star, the Bronze Star, the Vietnamese Cross of Gallantry, and three Purple Hearts.

After his military service Okamoto attended the University of California Law School from 1970 to 1973 and received a J.D. in 1973. During law school he worked nights for the Los Angeles County district attorney as a law clerk. Okamoto served as deputy district attorney for Los Angeles County from 1974 to 1978. From 1978 to 1986 he was a partner in the law firm of Okamoto & Wasserman. In 1981 Okamoto became a founder of Pacific Heritage Bank. At this bank he has been chairman of the Board from 1981 to the present, chief executive officer from 1987 to the present, and president since 1994.

Okamoto served as Gardena City councilman from 1976 to 1980 and as mayor pro tem from 1977 to 1978.

Okamoto has spoken about the Vietnam War to a number of groups and is the author of an unpublished novel about the war.

Okamoto is married and has one son. He is an avid collector of Samurai swords and armor.

Selected Bibliography

Dobashi, Mas. "Born Captive, Okamoto Holds Pacific Heritage Reins." *Tozai Times*, vol. 5, no. 60 (September 1989): 1, 10.
Woo, Caroline. "California's Dynamic Twenty." *Transpacific* vol. 8, no. 43 (June 1993): 33.

Steve Fugita

STEVEN OKAZAKI

(1952–   )

Filmmaker

Steven Okazaki, filmmaker, was born on March 12, 1952, in Los Angeles, California. He attended San Francisco State University and received a B.A. degree in film in 1976. His films have garnered numerous honors, including an Academy Award for his documentary *Days of Waiting*. His varied filmography includes children's films, documentaries, and independent narrative works.

In 1982 Okazaki directed *Survivors*, the first English-language film in which survivors of Hiroshima recalled the day the bomb was dropped. Broadcast on PBS's "World," it was one of the highest-rated PBS documentaries of the season. *Unfinished Business*, nominated for an Academy Award in 1985, relates the story of three Japanese Americans who challenge the incarceration of their people. In 1987 Okazaki moved in a new direction with his first feature film, *Living on Tokyo Time*, a low-budget comedy about a Japanese dishwasher and her Japanese American husband. *Days of Waiting*, 1991 winner of the Academy Award for "Best Documentary Short Subject" and the prestigious Peabody Award, was broadcast on PBS, NHK, and the BBC. It tells the compelling story of artist Estelle Ishigo, one of the few Caucasians to be interned with the Japanese Americans during World War II.

In 1992 Okazaki produced the PBS documentary *Troubled Paradise*, a rich exploration of the culture, politics, and social ills of Native Hawaii. In 1993 he made *Hunting Tigers*, a film about art in Tokyo, and his second feature film, a low-budget romantic comedy entitled *The Lisa Theory*. Other projects include *American Sons*, a dramatic examination of racism against Asians in America, and a documentary special to commemorate the fiftieth anniversary of the Hiroshima atomic bombing. Okazaki has also directed several award-winning children's films and documentary shorts. His other work has included *The Only Language She Knows* (1983), *Judy and Paul* (1980), *A Little Joke* (1978), and *A-M-E-R-I-C-A-N-S* (1976).

Okazaki's awards include the Cinema du Reel, France (1993), CINE Golden Eagle (1977, 1985, 1990, and 1992), Academy Award for Best Documentary Short Subject (1991), George Foster Peabody Award (1991), Berkeley Arts Recognition Award (1989), Association of Asian Pacific American Artists Media Award (1986 and 1988), Steve Tatsukawa Memorial Award (1987), State of California Resolution of Commendation (1987), Focus Awards: Benihana Asian American Achievement Award (1986), San Francisco Foundation: James D. Phelan Art Award (1986), Media Alliance: Meritorious Achievement Award (1983), and *Instructor* Magazine: Best Educational Film Award (1978).

Okazaki's films have been selected and honored at a number of prestigious film festivals, including the Clermont-Ferrand Short Film Festival Grand Prize and Youth Prize (1991), San Francisco International Film Festival Special Jury Prize (1987 and 1990), National Educational Film Festival Bronze Apple (1990), Hawaii International Film Festival "Best Documentary" (1989), Chicago International Film Festival Silver Hugo (1989), American Film Festival Red Ribbon (1983 and 1985), American Film Institute Independent Filmmaker Grant (1985), and John Muir Film Festival Medical Sociology Award (1982).

Okazaki is an advisor to the National Asian American Telecommunications Association. He is a media consultant to the Japanese American Citizens League and the founder of Friends of Hibakusha, an atomic bomb survivors' support group.

Selected Bibliography

Matsumoto, Nancy. "Steve Okazaki." *AsiAm*, vol. 2, no. 8 (August 1987).
Notable Asian Americans. Detroit: Gale Research, 1995.
Okazaki, Steven. *American Sons*. Farallon Films, 1996.
"Steven Okazaki Wins 1991 Media Award from ACV." *New York Nichibei*, vol. 6, no. 1 (June 1991).

Steve Fugita

Mine Okubo

MINE OKUBO

(1912–)

Artist

Mine Okubo, artist, was born on June 27, 1912, in Riverside, California. Her mother was a calligrapher and painter who graduated from the Tokyo Art Institute. Okubo's mother married, came to the United States, and raised seven children, always encouraging her daughter's interest in art. Her father was an educated man who worked first in a confectionery store and later as a gardener.

Okubo studied first at Riverside Community College from 1930 to 1933 and continued her education at the University of California at Berkeley. She received a Bachelor of Arts degree in 1935 and a Master's degree in art in 1936. In 1938 she won the University's highest art honor, the Bertha Taussig Traveling Scholarship. This scholarship gave her the opportunity to travel to Europe, where she visited museums, hiked, bicycled, and produced a series of watercolor paintings. Okubo returned to California in 1939 at the outbreak of World War II. There she participated in the Federal Arts Program, creating mosaic and fresco murals for the U.S. Army at Fort Ord, Government Island, Oakland Hospitality House, and Treasure Island.

In 1942 Okubo, like all other West Coast Japanese Americans, was ordered into an internment camp. Okubo's family was split up; she and a younger brother were sent to Topaz, Utah. There Okubo began to document camp life in a series of 200 pen-and-ink drawings. These were published in 1946 in a book called *Citizen 13660*. She also created hundreds of paintings during this time, often working through the night. Okubo and a group of friends published several issues of a new publication, *Trek* magazine, while in the camp, and her illustrations were noticed by the editors of *Fortune* magazine in New York City. She was invited there to illustrate a feature story about Japan, and the magazine was able to secure her release from the internment camp in 1944.

Okubo pursued a successful career as a commercial artist in New York City, working for magazines such as *Fortune, Time, Life,* and *Saturday Review*; newspapers such as the *New York Times* and the *San Francisco Chronicle*; and leading book publishers. From 1950 to 1952 she lectured at the University of California at Berkeley and then returned to New York City to focus on pursuing her own inner vision of art. Okubo was awarded the National Women's Caucus of Art Award in 1991.

Selected Bibliography

Gesensway, D., and M. Roseman. *Beyond Words: Images from America's Concentration Camps*. Ithaca, NY: Cornell University Press, 1987.
La Duke, B. "On the Right Road: The Life of Mine Okubo." *Art Education*, May 1987.
———. *Women Artists: Multi-Cultural Visions*. Trenton, NJ: Red Sea, 1992.
Mori, T. *Yokohama California*. Seattle: University of Washington, 1985.
Okubo, Mine. *Citizen 13660*. New York: Columbia University Press, 1946.
Sun, S. *Mine Okubo, an American Experience*. Oakland, CA: Oakland Art Museum, 1979.

Steve Fugita

JAMES MATSUMOTO OMURA

(1912–1994)

Journalist

James Matsumoto Omura, journalist, was born in Winslow, Washington, on Bainbridge Island, on November 27, 1912. When he was a young boy his mother became ill and was taken to her sister's home in Nagasaki, Japan. The three youngest children were placed in the care of their grandmother, and the three oldest sons including James elected to remain in Winslow. In 1926 young Omura left home, working in the salmon canneries of Ketchikan, Alaska, and Anacortes, Washington, before settling in Pocatello, Idaho. There he began to attend school, and in 1928 he was named editor of the student newspaper and played baseball with an all-star American Legion team. In 1931 Omura returned to Bainbridge Island and was named a delegate in journalism to the State of Washington Student Leaders' Conference, the first Nisei (second-generation Japanese American) to be so honored in the state. Omura graduated from Broadway High School in Seattle in 1932. He was recruited for the University of Washington by Sid Spears, assistant dean of men, but the Great Depression intervened and he was never able to attend.

Omura's career in journalism was varied and controversial. He worked briefly as editor of *New Japanese American News* in Los Angeles from 1933 to 1934. From 1934 to 1936 he took over as editor of *New World Daily* in San Francisco. During this time Omura was criticized by the Japanese American Citizens League for an article on Nisei leadership. An effort to censure him at the group's Third Biennial Convention failed. Several other issues involving the Japanese American Citizens League also flared into the open, including whether the organization was nonpolitical, as it claimed to be, and whether it adequately supported the Oriental Veterans' Citizenship Campaign. Omura also promoted Japanese professional baseball and tennis in San Francisco and Sacramento. He resigned as editor of the *New World Sun* in January 1936 after the publication of a letter critical of him and the failure of the publisher to support him.

After working for several years in floriculture Omura returned to journalism, first writing a column called "The Passing Show" for the *Japanese American News* and then working with the new Nisei monthly, *Current Life*, which was inaugurated in October 1940. This publication sought upward mobility for the Nisei generation. On February 23, 1942, Omura was called to testify by the Tolan Committee the congressional committee to investigate the internment decision, and opposed the evacuation of Japanese Americans from the Pacific Coast and the cooperative policy of the Japanese American Citizens League. Expecting a multitude of Nisei to protest, he was surprised to find himself alone. He organized several meetings to oppose the Japanese American Citizens League's policy.

Eleven hours before the military deadline for evacuation, Omura drove to Denver, Colorado, where an office for *Current Life* had been set up. The magazine was seized by the Argonaut Press in San Francisco, and the Denver office became an Evacuee Placement Bureau, assisting Japanese Americans who fled to Denver. Omura filed three racial discrimination cases through the War Manpower Commission, and it is believed these cases led to the use of Nisei labor in war work and defense jobs. Omura also negotiated with the Washington, D.C., law firm of Callender, Callender & Wallace to sue for reparations on behalf of internees, but the attempt was halted when internees showed a lack of interest.

In January 1944 Omura became director of public relations for the Japanese Publishing Company and English editor of the *Rocky Shimpo*. He worked to defeat the proposed Anti-Alien Land Law. Omura's controversial editorial, "Let Us Not Be Rash," was published in the *Rocky Shimpo* in February 1944 and drew immediate scrutiny and debate. The editorial offered a practical basis for resistance to the draft by interned Japanese Americans, some of whom had already refused to appear for their physicals. In April of the same year, the Office of Alien Property Custodian informed the publisher of the *Rocky Shimpo* that it would close down the publication unless Omura was discharged. He offered to resign to prevent a shutdown.

Omura was then indicted by the grand jurors of Wyoming, along with seven visible leaders of the Fair Play Committee of Heart Mountain Relocation Center, on charges of conspiracy to aid and abet violation of the Selective Service Act of 1940. He was acquitted on the basis of his First Amendment right of freedom of the press. The other seven defendants, however, were convicted and served eighteen months at Leavenworth Federal Penitentiary before their conviction was overturned. Omura's acquittal did not mean vindication as far as the Japanese American community was concerned. He was ostracized by the community and was unable to find employment within it.

He then began a career in landscape contracting. He was twice president of the Colorado Landscape Association, a seven-year member of the Advisory Committee of the Colorado Department of Agriculture, and vice-president of the Associated Landscape Contractors of America, Inc.

Recognition for Omura's work has occurred only recently. In 1989 he received the Lifetime Achievement Award from the Asian American

Journalists Association. In 1994 he was honored by the National Coalition for Redress/Reparation with its Fighting Spirit Award. Omura's 1983 treatise on cultural heritage was featured in the Bainbridge Island Historical Exhibit that toured the state of Washington in 1988 and 1989 and the Boston, Massachusetts, schools in 1990. A number of historians (e.g. Nelson 1976) have noted the importance of his Tolan Committee testimony and his involvement in the Heart Mountain resistance.

Omura died on June 20, 1994. He was married and had two children.

Selected Bibliography

Chan, J. P., F. Chin, L. F. Inada, and S. Wong, eds. *The Big Aiiieeeee! An Anthology of Chinese American and Japanese American Literature.* New York: Meridian, 1991.

Daniels, R. *Concentration Camps U.S.A.: Japanese Americans and World War II.* New York: Holt, Rinehart, & Winston, 1972.

Drinnon, R. *Keeper of Concentration Camps: Dillon S. Myer and American Racism.* Berkeley: University of California, 1987.

Grodzins, M. *Americans Betrayed: Politics and the Japanese Evacuation.* Chicago: University of Chicago, 1949.

Hanson, A., ed. *Japanese American World War II Evacuation Oral History Project,* vol. 4. Westport, CT: Meckler, 1991.

Jacobs, P., and S. Landau. *To Serve the Devil,* vol. 2. New York: Random House, 1971.

Nelson, D. *Heart Mountain, the History of an American Concentration Camp.* Madison: State Historical Society of Wisconsin, 1976.

Niiya, Brian, ed. *Japanese American History: An A-to-Z Reference from 1868 to the Present.* New York: Facts on File, 1993.

Weglyn, M. *Years of Infamy: The Untold Story of America's Treatment of Minorities.* New York: Morrow, 1976.

Steve Fugita

YOSHINOBU OYAKAWA

(1933–   )

Educator, Swim Coach

Yoshinobu Oyakawa, teacher and swim coach, was born in Kona, Hawaii, on August 9, 1933. He was the youngest of three children, and when he was one year old the family moved to Papaikou. His Japanese

Yoshinobu Oyakawa

father was minister of the Papaikou Pilgrim Church. Oyakawa discovered his talent and interest in sports at a young age. When he was in ninth grade he participated in an American Red Cross swimming program at the Naval Air Station pool in Hilo. He was encouraged to join the Hilo Aquatic Team and began racing.

Oyakawa joined Hilo High School's first swimming team during his junior year, coached by Charles "Sparky" Kawamoto. His team placed second in the territorial swimming championships in 1950. In the same year Oyakawa swam in the Senior Nationals in Seattle, Washington. In 1951 he established a new Hawaiian record in the 100-yard backstroke, with the second-best time in the nation. That summer Oyakawa swam the fastest 100-meter backstroke worldwide; later he placed fourth in the Senior Nationals.

Oyakawa attended Ohio State University from 1951 to 1955, earning a Bachelor of Science degree in physical education with a minor in biological sciences. He participated in the university swimming team during this time, was selected co-captain during his senior year, and was named an All-American in swimming for all four years. Oyakawa was selected to the Ohio State University Hall of Fame in 1976.

He served in the U.S. Air Force from 1956 to 1958 as a first lieutenant stationed at Lockbourne Air Force Base in Ohio. From 1963 to 1965 he attended the University of Cincinnati and earned a Master of Education degree. He began his teaching career in physical education in Columbus, Ohio, and in 1960 moved to Oak Hills High School in suburban Cincinnati. He taught and coached swimming there for twenty-five years. Oyakawa had the largest swimming teams in the area during those years. His biggest honor as a coach was in 1972 when he was selected as Ohio's "Coach of the Year."

Oyakawa retired from education in 1985 and devotes much of his time to swimming in the Masters Swimming program. He is married to the former Mariko Yamane. They have five children and four grandchildren.

Selected Bibliography

Niiya, Brian, ed. *Japanese American History: An A-to-Z Reference from 1868 to the Present*. New York: Facts on File, 1993, p. 279.

Steve Fugita

YOUNG J. PAIK
(1930–   )
Business Leader, Inventor

Young J. Paik (Yeong J. Baek), born on March 19, 1930, in Seongch'on, P'yeong'an namdo, which is now located in North Korea, graduated from an agricultural high school in his native country. He attended Yonsei University in Seoul before he came to the United States in 1956 to study at the University of Oregon on a scholarship. He arrived in America with $50 in his pocket and has now created a large corporation that brings in total gross receipts of $150 million per annum.

Paik transferred from the University of Oregon to the Indiana Institute of Technology, where he studied engineering. In 1959 he graduated from the Institute. He then took employment as a county engineer with Van Wert County, Ohio. He moved to Los Angles and started an import-export business in the steel industry. Through hard work and creativity he invented the Paik Knee Joint, a column-and-rafter connection that facilitated the rapid construction of military facilities in Vietnam without the use of welding, heavy equipment, or experience on the part of the builder. During his years working for Soule Steel he engineered the con-

Young J. Paik

struction of prefabricated steel buildings for commercial warehouses such as the Los Angeles and Long Beach Port and Harbor structures. He continued his research and development by creating innovative products at Marcrest Steel. Through his research he was able to invent a lightweight I-beam (used to form the chassis of mobile homes and truck trailers, for instance) featuring a corrugated web.

His company, PACO Steel and Engineering Corporation, makes and sells the lightweight I-beam featuring a corrugated web that is approximately 25 percent lighter per foot with equal or better strength in comparison with the standard beam. His company is the exclusive supplier of domestic and imported corrugated beams along with welded beams. He worked diligently to make PACO Steel and Engineering Corporation successful as the largest distributor of lightweight beams in the world, with the main office located in Rancho Dominguez, California, and seven distribution bases nationwide.

Manufacturing will be the culmination of a long-term goal to complete the circle from product inception to engineering, testing, manufacturing, and distribution. In November 1995, PACO announced plans to build a $32 million, 50,000 sq. ft. lightweight beam production plant in Mississippi County, Arkansas, which is one of the largest steel-producing regions in the United States. The plant was completed in July 1997, as scheduled, and has now the capacity for producing 150,000 tons of steel per annum.

Paik, who now lives in Palos Verde, California, with Sue, his wife, was recognized as 1983 Businessman of the Year by the Asian Business Association, an organization supported by the Los Angeles Chamber of Commerce. They have one daughter and two sons.

Selected Bibliography

Iron Age, August 4, 1980.
Korea Times, December 28, 1996.

Hyung-chan Kim

CHAN HO PARK

(1973–)

Baseball Player

Chan Ho Park, starting pitcher/relief pitcher for the Los Angeles Dodgers, became the first Korean to play in major league baseball. He threw his first major league pitch in April 1994, and with his 95-mile-an-hour pitches Park struck out two hitters in his first appearance.

Born in Kongju City, South Korea, on June 6, 1973, Park was recruited by the Dodgers while still a student at Hanyang University in South Korea. He is the youngest member of the team, and although he spoke little English, the Dodgers thought his talents were good enough for them to take a gamble, signing him to a $1.2 million minor league contract. Soon thereafter he was moved from South Korea to southern California to start his professional baseball career.

Park has gotten reviews from both managers and players of different teams. Tommy Lasorda, Dodgers manager, said to a reporter that Park did well in his first appearance in the major leagues and believes that he has a great future. New York Mets manager, Dallas Green, was quoted by the March 8, 1994, issue of the *New York Times* as saying, "He's got outstanding stuff. He's got a good fast-ball . . . he's going to be a good one by the looks of it" (Frey 1994). The twenty-three-year-old Park went 5–5 in the 1997 season with 119 strikeouts and a 3.64 ERA (earned run average) over 48 appearances (10 starts), rather impressive statistics for any baseball player.

Chan Ho Park is only the fifth person of Asian descent to play in the major leagues. In the April 10, 1993, issue of the *New York Times*, reporter David Margolick stated that "he is the most heralded player of Asian decent." Many are looking to Park in hopes that he will help to shatter the stereotypes of Asians as bookish, clannish, unathletic, humorless, unfriendly, and even menacing. Those in the community believe that he will be a force for harmony among the different ethnic groups in the Los Angeles area.

Selected Bibliography

Frey, Jennifer. "No Ruling on Park's Delivery." *New York Times*, March 8, 1994, p. B10.
Margolick, David. "Bearing Kimchi, a Dodger Is a First." *New York Times*, April 10, 1993, pp. 10(N), 16(L).
Verducci, Tom. "Orient Express." *Sports Illustrated*, March 28, 1994, pp. 24–27.

Jennifer Kang

YONGMAN PARK
(1881–1928)
Social Reformer, Author, Political Activist

Yongman Park was a revolutionary who devoted most of his life to working for Korea's independence from Japanese control. His career as a revolutionary began early in his youth when he was imprisoned for involvement in political activities with the Korean Independence Association. He moved to the United States in 1905 soon after his release from prison.

Park entered the University of Nebraska, majoring in political science. During his years at the university he, along with the help of P. L. Johnson, established the Korean Youth Military Academy. Through his involvement with the academy he was able to author two books: *The National Military* (1911) and *Soldier's Requisite Knowledge* (1912). It was also during this time that he came to learn much about the military institutions of the United States. Upon completion of his studies at the University of Nebraska, Park was offered a position as editor of *New Korea*, a publication in Hawaii. He moved to Hawaii in 1912, and it was rumored that he invited **Syngman Rhee** to join him.

In Hawaii, Park began to launch his ambitious projects that would ultimately have an enormous impact on the Korean community there. His first project was to establish the All-Korean Association of Hawaii (AKAH). Through this organization Park attempted to put into effect his idea for government, much like that of the United States, with three main branches of power—the legislative, judiciary, and executive. He worked with the key members of AKAH and raised money for its headquarters, which was completed in 1914. His next project was the Military Corps, which was established on June 10, 1914, in order to train Korean youths in Hawaii for the regaining of Korea's independence from Japan. This was a result of Park's philosophy that Korea's independence could only be gained through military power. Park's third plan was to establish a middle school for the education of Korean youth, but owing to lack of financial resources from the Korean community in Hawaii this plan never materialized.

In 1918 the personal and political tension between Yongman Park and Syngman Rhee grew to the point that one would have to leave. The two had very different ideas on the methodology for gaining Korea's independence. Rhee dismissed Park's military strategies as "senseless adventurism" and insisted on more diplomatic solutions to Korea's colonial subjugation. The two finally had a falling out over the issue of who should take control of the Korean National Association of Hawaii. During that year Park bowed out of the association that he had helped to establish. Soon after the disagreement with Rhee, Park set out to seek other Koreans scattered around the globe in hopes of reorganizing for Korea's independence.

In 1919 he went to Vladivostok to unite the Koreans in the maritime region of the former Soviet Union. Initially he believed the Bolsheviks would be sympathetic to the cause of the Korean independence movement, but to his disappointment they were only interested in their own national ideology. Park continued his journey, which led him to Peking in 1921. It was there that he called for a meeting of the Military Unitary Preparation Conference, which was expected to gather representatives of various military organizations among overseas Koreans working toward Korea's independence. However, financial difficulties meant that the Military Unity Association, established by Park, could not be sustained. As a result Park became a businessman and took up banking. His bank, Business Promotion Commercial Bank, became the means by which he was able to raise money for purchasing farmland to be cultivated by his own army. It was his ultimate goal to strengthen his army for the purpose of challenging Japan's hold on Korea.

In July 1925 Park returned to Honolulu to attend the All-Pacific Youth Conference. Though the Department of Labor granted him a three-month stay in Hawaii, he remained for almost a year. He returned to Peking on June 1926, having been ordered to be deported. On October 17, 1928, Park was assassinated by a fellow Korean compatriot.

Selected Bibliography

Choy, Bong-youn. *Koreans in America.* Chicago: Nelson-Hall, 1979.

Hyon, John K. *A Condensed History of the Kungminhoe: The Korean National Association, 1903–1945.* Seoul, Korea: Korea University, 1986.

Kim, Warren. *Koreans in America.* Seoul, Korea: Po Chin Printing Co., 1971.

Lee, Chong-sik. *The Politics of Korean Nationalism.* Berkeley: University of California Press, 1963.

Pang, Chu-son. *Independence Movement among Koreans in America.* Korea: Hallim University Press, 1989.

Suh, Dae-sook, ed. *The Writings of Henry Gu Kim: Autobiography with Commentaries on Syngman Rhee, Pak Yong man and Chung Sun man.* Honolulu: Hawaii Center for Korean Studies, University of Hawaii, 1987.

Hyung-chan Kim

I. M. Pei
(1917–   )
Architect

Ieoh Ming (I. M.) Pei is one of the world's best-known architects, with projects ranging from the East Building of the National Gallery of Art in Washington, D.C., to the new entrance and renovations to the Grand Louvre in Paris, France. He was born in Canton, China, on April 26, 1917, the eldest son of banker Tsuyee Pei and Lien Kwun Chwong. His mother died when he was very young, and Pei grew up in Canton, Hong Kong, and Shanghai. He attended St. John's Middle School in Shanghai before coming to the United States to study architecture. He began these studies at the University of Pennsylvania but soon transferred to the Massachusetts Institute of Technology. Pei received his Bachelor of Architecture degree in 1940, and in that year he also received the Alpha Rho Chi Medal, the Traveling Fellowship, and the AIA Medal from the Institute.

In 1942 Pei enrolled in the Harvard Graduate School of Design, but his studies were interrupted for two years when he volunteered to work for the National Defense Research Committee in Princeton, New Jersey.

He returned to Harvard in 1948, completing his Master of Architecture degree in 1946 and serving as an assistant professor from 1945 to 1948. Harvard awarded him the Wheelwright Traveling Fellowship in 1951, enabling Pei to travel extensively in England, France, Italy, and Greece.

Pei joined the real estate development firm of Webb & Knapp in 1948 as its director of architecture. While there, he worked on a number of large-scale architectural and planning projects in Boston, Chicago, Denver, Montreal, Philadelphia, Pittsburg, and Washington. In 1955 he formed his own architectural partnership, I.M. Pei & Associates. The firm became I.M. Pei & Partners in 1966 and Pei, Cobb, Freed & Partners in 1989; it received the American Institute of Architects' Architectural Firm Award in 1968.

Pei has designed nearly fifty projects in the United States and abroad. More than half these projects have won major awards. One of the best known is his design for the National Center for Atmospheric Research in Boulder, Colorado (1961–1967). Comprised of reddish-brown geometric forms, the project reflects the blossoming of Pei's personal architectural style. Subsequent projects have included designs for the Everson Museum of Art in Syracuse, New York (1961–1964), the Herbert F. Johnson Museum of Art at Cornell University (1968–1973), and the Museum of Fine Arts/West Wing in Boston, Massachusetts (1977–1981).

Another of Pei's designs is the East Building annex to the National Gallery of Art in Washington, D.C. (1968–1978). Underwritten by the Mellon family, the design makes use of the same pink marble as the original building and features two triangular wings connected by an atrium lobby with an enormous skylight. The John Fitzgerald Kennedy Library in Boston, Massachusetts (1965–1979), is also one of Pei's most admired designs. The Morton H. Meyerson Symphony Center in Dallas, Texas (1982–1989), is a limestone rectangle surrounded by graceful curves of glass. He also designed the Rock and Roll Hall of Fame and Museum in Cleveland, Ohio (1996), an architectural landmark featuring a six-story central tower and pyramid-shaped glass facade.

Pei has designed a number of important buildings abroad. The Fragrant Hill Hotel in Beijing, China (1979–1982), is a synthesis of traditional Chinese and Western technologies and styles. The Bank of China Tower in Hong Kong (1982–1989), a seventy-story office building, houses the bank branch that Pei's father founded. The Grand Louvre project (1981–1989) consists of a large, glass pyramid that forms the new entrance to the museum. Pei considers it his greatest accomplishment. The Shinji Shumeikai Bell Tower in Shiga, Japan (1988–1991), and the Miho Museum of Art in Shiga, Japan (1991–   ), as well as a number of projects in the design stage, are among Pei's more recent foreign projects.

Pei has received a number of honors and awards throughout his career. He has received the American Academy of Arts and Letters' Gold

Medal for Architecture (1979), the American Institute of Architects' Gold Medal (1979), and the National Arts Club's Gold Medal of Honor (1981). L'Academie d'Architecture of France awarded Pei its La Grande Medaille d'Or in 1981. He was decorated by the French government as a *commandeur* in the Ordre des Arts et des Lettres in 1985, and in March 1989 French president François Mitterrand inducted him as a *chevalier* in the Legion d'Honneur. On July 4, 1986, at the rededication of the Statue of Liberty, Pei was one of twelve naturalized American citizens to receive the Medal of Liberty from President Ronald Reagan. He was awarded the Medal of Freedom by President George Bush in 1993. Japan awarded Pei the Praemium Imperiale for lifetime achievement in architecture in 1989.

Pei is married to the former Eileen Loo. They have four children.

Selected Bibliography

Diamonstein, B. *American Architecture Now*. New York: Rizzoli, 1980.

"I. M. Pei: A Feeling for Technology." *Technology Review*, April 1995.

Malesky, J. *Five Buildings in the Dallas Central Business District by I. M. Pei and Partner Henry N. Cobb: A Stamp on the City's Direction*. Thesis, North Texas State University, 1986.

"The Modern, Rooted in the Ancient." *New York Times*, April 19, 1998.

Pei, I., and E. Biasini. *Les Grands Desseins du Louvre*. Paris: Hermann, 1989.

Pei, I., and partners. *I. M. Pei & Partners Drawings for the East Building, National Gallery of Art. Its Evolution in Sketches, Renderings, and Models, 1968–1978: An Exhibition*. Washington, DC: Adams Davidson Galleries, 1978.

Suner, B. *Pei*. Paris: Hazan, 1988.

Wiseman, C. *The Architecture of I. M. Pei: With Illustrated Catalog of the Buildings and Projects*. London: Thames and Hudson, 1990.

———. *I. M. Pei: A Profile in American Architecture*. New York: H. N. Abrams, 1990.

Franklin Ng

ARATI PRABHAKAR

(1959–)

Engineer, Government Administrator, Physicist

"Create a dream together, turn everyone loose to make it happen, and measure the results." With this as her management credo, Arati Prabhakar has succeeded as a government administrator even though she

Arati Prabhakar (photo by Robert Rathe)

followed an unconventional career path. Prabhakar was the first woman
to earn a Ph.D. in applied physics from the California Institute of Technology (Caltech). She then moved to Washington, D.C., to become a congressional fellow at the Office of Technology Assessment (OTA). This
fellowship, which was denounced by some of Pabhakar's Caltech colleagues, provided a springboard to a career that has combined science,
technology, and policy.

As the tenth director in ninety-two years of the National Institute of
Standards and Technology (NIST) in the Department of Commerce,
Washington, D.C., she now leads the organization that was formerly the
unsung but vital National Bureau of Standards.

Born in New Delhi, India, she emigrated to America as a three-year-
old with her parents. Raised in Illinois and Texas, she says that the overwhelming influence in her life has been her mother, Raj Prabhakar, who
came to Illinois in 1961 to pursue a Master's degree in social services at
the University of Chicago. Her father, Jagdish Prabhakar, an electrical
engineer, is currently retired after having worked in the faculty at Texas
Tech and in California. Her parents were divorced while Arati Prabhakar
was in high school. Even though Arati followed her father's profession,
her mother was her main inspiration: for her desire to help others, her emphasis on education, and her view that nothing is impossible.

Arati attended graduate school at the California Institute of Technology with a full scholarship and stipend from the Bell Laboratories Graduate Research Program for Women. More important than the cash, she states, was the offer of two researchers to act as mentors: Robert E. Nahory, who later moved on to Bellcore, and Martin A. Pollack, who became her lifelong mentor and visited her once every year during her graduate studies and employed her during one summer.

At Caltech (which she chose over Stanford University because of its more intimate size) she switched her field to applied physics. Prabhakar admits she no longer breezed through classes there. She disliked isolated research for its own sake—the environment she found herself in at Caltech. However, with the motivation of her mother, she persisted with her coursework. More motivation came from mentors who talked about how a Ph.D. could help in areas other than research. All this helped her earn the first Ph.D. to be awarded at Caltech to a woman. Soon thereafter, Pollack pointed her to an ad in the IEEE newsletter for government policy work at the U.S. Congressional Office of Technology Assessment (OTA).

Prabhakar arrived at OTA, the technology policy think-tank of Congress, as a congressional fellow in 1984. At a time when Japanese strength in the global semiconductor market began to alarm the U.S. public about its own microelectronics industry, Prabhakar took the reins. She was the right person to examine the situation, with her Caltech degree, her Bell Labs experience, and her work during another summer at Lawrence Livermore National Laboratory. The result was a 35-page report, "Microelectronics Research and Development," which came out in March 1986. In it Prabhakar wrote how the once fiercely independent merchant semiconductor firms were starting to warm to the U.S. government. Her stalwart report lent credibility to the theory that the government should take more action. She concluded, backed by a blue-ribbon panel of reviewers, that the Japanese threat "will remain and quite possibly increase."

Her report led directly to a job offer from Richard A. Reynolds, then science director at the Department of Defense's Advanced Research Projects Agency (ARPA), who asked her to run a $6 million program funding research on gallium arsenide electronics. With that new job, Prabhakar seemed to be in a fairy tale situation: at OTA she had been able to assess a key problem; at ARPA she could address it.

Prabhakar attributes her big break to ARPA's willingness to take a risk when Reynolds hired her just a year out of graduate school. She noted the collaborative effort of her co-workers as the secret to the organization's success.

ARPA was arguably the most prestigious research and development agency in the federal government. It often hired the best and brightest and gave them responsibility, flexibility, and money to sponsor high-risk, high-payoff projects for its patron, the Department of Defense. Being at the right place at the right time is another secret of Prabhakar's. Within several years of her arrival Congress shifted money and power from the Pentagon to ARPA, raising its budget for microelectronics tenfold. Prabhakar rode the wave past many senior colleagues, and by 1991 she had commanded a budget of $300 million and all of ARPA's chip research.

During her several years at ARPA, Prabhakar estimates that she toured over 100 sites, from Bell Laboratories on the East Coast to Orbit Semiconductor on the West Coast. In that time she witnessed major changes. The assumption during the cold war that U.S. industry was fully capable of succeeding on its own gave way to a global economy in which virtually every U.S. industry has been challenged and some have been threatened.

Something about the way Prabhakar communicates appeals to people. She displays a sincerity and a casualness, a freshness and an astuteness, that are absent in many bureaucrats. Her exuberance can make topics such as the standard volt seem thrilling. She likes one-on-one conversations too. She stresses the importance of listening and communicating to keep up with the latest developments in science rather than always relying on journals. Her greatest joy comes from synthesizing what she has learned and passing information along to help in other areas. She is also intrigued by the fact that with the advancement of technology the rules of science are constantly being modified.

On May 23, 1993, Prabhakar was appointed the tenth NIST director by President Clinton. She is the first woman, the first foreign-born citizen, and the youngest person to direct the Institute. She oversees a staff of approximately 3,200 and a budget of nearly $1 billion. The first director of NIST who was trained as an engineer, rather than a scientist, she manages a portfolio of major programs that partner with industry in the pursuit of technology for economic growth: (1) a competitive Advanced Technology Program that provides cost-shared awards to industry for development of high-risk technologies with significant commercial potential; (2) a grassroots Manufacturing Extension Partnership designed to help small and medium-sized companies adopt new technologies; (3) laboratory research and services focused on "infrastructural technologies," such as measurements, standards, evaluated data, and test methods; and (4) the Malcom Baldrige National Quality Award and an associated quality outreach program.

Selected Bibliography

Adams, John A. "Arati Prabhakar." *IEEE Spectrum*, December 1993, p. 48.
Gibbons, Ann. "Traveling without Maps." *Science*, April 16, 1993.
Gibbs, W. Wayt. "Profile: Arati Prabhakar, Engineering the Future." *Scientific American*, April 1995, pp. 44, 48.

Holusha, John. "Profile: Arati Prabhakar, She's Not Just Setting Standards." *New York Times*, August 1, 1993.
Teresko, John. "NIST: More Than Weights and Measures." *Industry Week*, December 19, 1994, pp. 75, 78–80.

Visi R. Tilak

DITH PRAN

(1942–   )

Journalist, Author, Political Activist

Dith Pran, known for the bitter experiences he suffered under the government ruled by the Khmer Rouge in Cambodia, was born on September 27, 1942, in Siem Riep in the northwestern part of Cambodia located close to the Angkor Wat temples. He came from a middle-class family headed by his father, who worked as a senior government official in charge of supervising road-building in his hometown. Dith went to high school, where he learned French while learning English on his own. After graduating from high school in 1960, he went to work as an interpreter for an American military assistance group that was stationed in Cambodia.

When the Cambodian government severed its relations with the United States in 1969, charging that the U.S. government had attacked Cambodian villages and deployed its troops stationed in South Vietnam, American troops left Cambodia. Dith Pran found employment as a receptionist for a British film crew. He also worked as a tour guide. When a war broke out in 1970 between Cambodian guerrilla fighters known as the Khmer Rouge and the Cambodian government led by Lon Nol, who was supported by the U.S. government, Pran's hometown was not spared from military actions. The battle in the Siem Riep area brought Western journalists in contact with Dith Pran, who served them as an interpreter. Pran was deeply touched by the agony and suffering of his people, who fell victims to the senseless war, and he decided to tell their story by working as a journalist. He moved with his wife and children to Phnom Penh, where he could find work for a newspaper organization.

Although he was not trained to become a journalist, he assisted foreign television and newspaper reporters, among whom was Craig Whitney, the Saigon bureau chief of the *New York Times*. In 1972, when Sydney H. Schanberg, a recipient of the Pulitzer Prize in 1976 for his reporting on

Cambodia, came to Phnom Penh from Singapore to report on the war, Pran was assigned to work as his assistant. In the following year Pran was made a parttime correspondent for the *New York Times*.

In his book *The Death and Life of Dith Pran*, on which the film *The Killing Fields* is based, Schanberg describes the intense love and respect that developed between himself and Pran, who first came out to the Phnom Penh airport to meet him with a notebook full of suggestions for people to see and places to visit. Schanberg and Pran shared many of the same ideas and feelings concerning the war and its impact, which created an instant bond between the two.

As the Khmer Rouge army inched its way into Phnom Penh in April 1975, the U.S. government decided to pull out from the city, and Schanberg was able to arrange for Pran's family to leave the city with the Americans. But Schanberg and Pran decided to stay behind to report on the final hours of the war. After the fall of the city in the hands of Khmer Rouge army, Schanberg was forced to leave the city. Pran had to find his own way of escaping from his country. The excruciating experience Pran encountered while trying to survive every day as a laborer in a forced work camp, as a houseboy, or as a farmer with rice rationing of one spoonful per person per day, is vividly portrayed by **Haing Ngor** in *The Killing Fields*.

Dith Pran succeeded in escaping from Cambodia to Thailand, where he was sheltered in a refugee camp. When Schanberg was told that Pran had been found, he took the first flight to Thailand to see him and to bring him to the United States. This was in 1979, four years after the two were separated against their will. Pran was flown to San Francisco, where he was reunited with his family on October 19, 1979.

He has for many years worked for the *New York Times* as a photographer.

Selected Bibliography

Grogan, David W. "When Newsman Sydney Schanberg Was Expelled from Cambodia, His Best Friend Was Left behind in the Killing Fields." *People Weekly*, December 10, 1984, pp. 65–70.

Michelmore, Peter. "Legacy of the Killing Fields." *Reader's Digest*, vol. 150, no. 901 (May 1997): 61–66.

Schanberg, Sidney H. "The Death and Life of Dith Pran." *New York Times Magazine*, January 20, 1980, pp. 16–22.

Zia, Helen, and Susan B. Gall, eds. *Notable Asian Americans*. Detroit: Gale Research, 1995.

Hyung-chan Kim

SAFI U. QURESHY

(1951–   )

Entrepreneur, Engineer, Business Leader

From a garage-based start-up company in 1980, Safi Qureshy has built AST Computers into the world's fifth-largest personal computer company. It has about 6,800 employees worldwide and is ranked among the largest industrial corporations in America in the Fortune 500. Today AST Computers operates in more than 100 countries, with more than 10,000 dealers and retailers selling more than 1.4 million personal computers per year.

Safi U. Qureshy, a Pakistani native, came to the United States when he was nineteen years old to attend college. He is humble in a world of egomaniacal high-tech executives. Like many college students, he had parttime jobs, including working at a local 7-Eleven, while attending school. While driving through downtown Stockholm during a recent trip, he noticed a Burger King and a 7-Eleven and felt right at home.

AST was established in 1980 by Albert Wong, Safi Qureshy, and Tom Yuen to produce enhancement boards that expanded the functionality of the original IBM personal computers (PCs), making them faster and more flexible. The company was an early success based on its technological innovations, and by the time AST introduced its first personal computer in 1986 it already enjoyed a reputation for engineering design, quality, manufacturing expertise, and superior service.

Under the direction of Qureshy, AST Computers has earned a reputation for being an innovator in the PC industry to meet challenging market trends and customer requirements. His philosophy goes beyond "box-building" and brings forth a sense of responsibility to provide the best of technology.

In 1993 AST acquired Tandy Corporation's personal computer manufacturing operations. This allowed the company to increase manufacturing capability, add new technologies, broaden distribution, and increase purchasing leverage and market share. The integration of the acquired assets was completed in 1994, along with new manufacturing facilities that opened in Europe and China. This enabled AST to quickly deliver volume quantities of PCs to customers within each of its three operating regions.

AST's philosophy caught the attention of the White House in September 1993, when Vice-President Al Gore visited AST to learn how the company's methods could be applied to simplify the policies and procedures of the federal government. In early 1994 Qureshy also joined forces with the late commerce secretary Ron Brown's brigade of American business leaders on a trip to China.

AST's success rests on a global vision. Its aim is to look beyond selling only to Fortune 500 companies; instead it places its focus on worldwide markets. This global perspective has allowed AST to make a positive impact in emerging markets by providing access to information that will lead to economic growth, cultural autonomy, and individual expression in various parts of the world. For example, the company provided the PCs that were used to register voters in South Africa's elections in 1998.

In 1994 AST suffered a setback. While the rest of the industry was racking up double-digit sales, AST's revenues shrank by 5 percent. "We were trying to do too many things at the same time," admitted Qureshy; "we couldn't execute new products on time, we couldn't manufacture them on time, and we couldn't deliver them on time "(Armstrong and Nakarmi, 1995). However, AST did not take long to recover. It acquired a partner to see it through the troubled times.

AST entered into an agreement providing for an investment by Samsung Electronics Co., Ltd., of up to 40.25 percent in AST, as well as other strategic relationships, including component and joint procurement. Samsung's leading-edge screens and its memory chip technology were expected to give AST's PC lineup a badly needed boost. The AST link, on the other hand, was expected to give Samsung an entree into the worldwide PC business. Both companies are now in a position to play a role in the convergence of the computer and consumer electronics industries. The two companies have also discussed a home network of appliances controlled by PCs. Qureshy's challenge is to maintain AST as an independent company.

His commitment to change, growth, and entrepreneurship is evident in the activities he pursues outside of AST. He is chairman of the California Business–Higher Education Forum, a nonprofit organization that brings together representatives from higher education institutions, foundations, and California-based businesses to address key economic and educational challenges facing the state. He is also chairman of the Corporate Council on Africa, a nonprofit group organized to stimulate African economies through U.S. and African investments. He is a board member of the Washington, D.C., based American Business Conference and a board member of the Technology Leadership Council of California. He has earned acclaim from several national institutions, including 1994 International Entrepreneur of the Year from the University of Illinois at Carbondale in 1993 and Distinguished Alumnus for outstanding achievement from the University of Texas at Arlington.

Qureshy's goal is to become one of the top three personal computer makers in the world. "Our mission is to be recognized and respected worldwide as the easiest company to do business with in every way." Saying that this business is a people business, Qureshy adds, "To meet this goal, we are providing best-of-class PCs that are easy to use, easy to afford, and easy to obtain" (AST Research 1994).

Regarded as an industry visionary, Safi Qureshy sees the future of the computer industry in terms of its impact on the general population. The PC will play an increasingly important role in society, "empowering people as the 'great equalizer' by giving them access to the content, consumption and creation of information." He describes the convergence of new technologies such as the multimedia PC, wireless telephone, and interactive TV as providing "unlimited creativity, invention and opportunity for billions of users" (AST Research 1994).

Selected Bibliography

Armstrong, Larry, and Laxmi Nakarmi. "Can Samsung Usher AST to a Front-Row Seat?" *Business Week*, April 17, 1995, p. 92.
AST Research, Inc. "Biography, Safi U. Qureshy." August 1994, unpublished.
Rapaport, Richard. "Mission Imperative." *Forbes ASAP*, October 1994, pp. 76–82.

                                                              Visi R. Tilak

A. K. RAMANUJAN

(1929–1993)

Poet, Educator

After earning a Ph.D. in linguistics at the University of Indiana, A. K. Ramanujan joined the faculty at the University of Chicago to teach Tamil, a South Indian language, and to establish the first Tamil studies program in the United States. The author of seventeen books, Ramanujan was a noted poet, translator, and scholar. His *Speaking of Shiva* (1973), translations of medieval Kannada poetry, was nominated for a National Book Award. In 1976 the government of India honored him with a Padma Shri title for his contributions to Indian literature and linguistics. Ramanujan received a John D. and Catherine T. MacArthur Foundation five-year grant for distinguished scholars and creative artists in 1983.

A. K. Ramanujan, born on March 16, 1929, learned several languages as a child growing up in the Indian state of Karnataka. He spoke Tamil with his mother and conversed in English and Sanskrit with his father, a noted mathematician. Outside his home he spoke the local language, Kannada. Later in his writings and teaching he examined each of these languages and their literature. A colleague, David Shulman, noted that Ramanujan explored "the inner and outer spaces, mother-tongues and father-tongues, the folk-tales told by the former and the myths composed by the latter, with their different textures and structures of authority" (Shulman 1994).

At the University of Mysore, Ramanujan studied English language and literature. After completing B.A. and M.A. degrees he began his career by teaching English in colleges in the South Indian states of Tamil Nadu and Karnataka. His interest in theoretical linguistics led him to pursue graduate degrees in this field, first in India and then in the United States. Ramanujan started teaching at the University of Chicago in 1962. From the outset he helped shape the field of South Asian studies, which was beginning to develop in the United States. In the course of teaching he began translating ancient Tamil and Kannada poetry. Collections of these translations were published in volumes such as *The Interior Landscape* (1967), *Speaking of Shiva* (1973), and *Hymns for the Drowning* (1981). These books became widely used in South Asian and World Civilization classes across the United States. Ramanujan has been highly praised for his remarkable translation style. "So stunning and fresh. . . . He had the poet's perfect pitch, never using language carelessly or imprecisely" (Shulman 1994).

A prolific essayist and poet, Ramanujan contributed to countless academic and literary journals. He wrote poetry in Tamil, Kannada, and English, making a literary impact both in the United States and India. Among his four books of poetry written in English, *The Striders: Poems* (1966) received recognition from the Poetry Society of London. His colleagues described the close connection between his poetry and academic work: "as a poet, and as a translator between Tamil and English, he was perfectly brilliant. . . . His poetic sensibility, his way of thinking metaphorically, informed his scholarship which introduced new ideas about translation and the texture of the language" (*University of Chicago News* 1993).

Academic and literary commentators have described Ramanujan in terms of his brilliance, humanity, and modesty. In his writings and translations he aimed to make the cultures and literature of East and West mutually intelligible. He has been quoted as saying, "I am the hyphen in Indo-American" (*University of Chicago News* 1993). In his painstaking translations of Kannada and Tamil poetry, he illustrates the elegance and subtleties of the ancient literature, which in the case of Tamil dates back 2,000 years.

Among his students and colleagues, Ramanujan was appreciated for the passion that he brought to his work. Arshia Sattar describes a university seminar in which "the small man in the gray suit . . . took over the room—no one took their eyes off him, no one spoke, no one moved" (*Chicago South Asia Newsletter* 1993). He could weave together linguistic theory, folklore, literature, and anthropology in a manner that would engage both the academic and general audience. In the middle of an academic or theoretical discussion, he would use a folk tale or parable to make a particular point.

Ramanujan remained deeply interested in Indian folklore, from the stories his mother told him as a child to the folktales he collected from South Indian villages surrounding the regional centers of Mysore and Bangalore. He used a substantial portion of his MacArthur grant for a collection project to gather materials from these areas. In 1992 he published *Folktales from India*. His collection of Kannada stories, *A Flowering Tree and Other Oral Tales form India*, was published posthumously in 1997. The preface of the latter book includes a description of the volume in Ramanujan's words:

This is my oldest project. . . . In my twenties, I collected tales from anyone who would tell me one: my mother, servants, aunts, men and women in village families with whom I stayed when I was invited to lecture in local schools, schoolteachers and schoolchildren, carpenters, tailors. I wrote them down by hand and, years later, when I could afford a tape recorder, recorded them. I was just entranced by oral tales. . . . I had no idea I was doing what was called folklore (Blackburn and Dundes 1997).

Working in the field of folklore allowed Ramanujan to exercise his many scholarly capabilities, namely his fluency in languages, power of translation, theoretical analysis, and literary interpretation of the aesthetic form of folk tales. Although his focus remained literary, he took into account certain social aspects of folk expression including that of gender differences. Editors of *A Flowering Tree* point out that "one of the enduring contributions of his scholarship will be that, with others, he drew attention to the importance of women's tales in Indian folklore and culture generally" (Blackburn and Dundes 1997). Ramanujan described women's stories as sometimes being "counter-tales" that provided alternative interpretations of conventional cultural practices and norms.

In addition to teaching at Chicago, Ramanujan was visiting professor at Harvard University, the University of California at Berkeley, the University of Wisconsin at Madison, and the University of Michigan at Ann Arbor. He was elected to the American Academy of Arts and Sciences in 1990.

Ramanujan had a daughter, Krittika, and a son, Krishna. He died on July 13, 1993, in Chicago, Illinois. His former wife is Molly Daniels.

Selected Bibliography

"A. K. Ramanujan—Obituary." *University of Chicago News*, press release, July 14, 1993, pp. 1–2.

"In Memoriam: A. K. Ramanujan." *Chicago South Asia Newsletter*, Fall 1993, pp. 1, 5–6.

Ramanujan, A. K. *A Flowering Tree and Other Oral Tales from India*, eds. Stuart Blackburn and Alan Dundes. Berkeley: University of California Press, 1997.

———. *Folktales from India, Oral Tales from Twenty-Two Languages*. New York: Pantheon Books, 1991.

———. *Speaking of Shiva*. Harmondsworth United Kingdom: Penguin, 1973.

Shulman, David. "Attipat Krishnaswami Ramanujan." *Journal of Asian Studies*, August 1994, pp. 1048–1050.

Jane Singh

SYNGMAN RHEE

(1875–1965)

Politician, Social Reformer

Syngman Rhee (Seung-man, Yi), first president of the Republic of Korea when it was founded on August 15, 1948, and whose nom de plume was Unam, was born on April 26, 1875, in the village of P'yeongsan, Hwang-hae province, Korea. He was the last of the three sons of Yi Kyeong-seon, a distant descendent of a royal family. It was said that Rhee's father lived in abject poverty but was always proud of his royal lineage. Rhee also took pride in his lineage and always considered himself better than the average Korean.

Rhee came under the Western influence at the age of nine, when he was struck with a disease that resulted in his going blind. He was taken to an American missionary doctor, Horace Allen, who helped restore his sight. The power of Western medicine may have been a factor that made him turn toward the West for his search for national independence. At age nineteen Rhee entered Paejae Haktang, established by a Methodist missionary, Henry G. Appenzeller. Rhee learned of the Western world during his two-year stay at the school, where he was exposed to "full-fledged western education," to use his own words.

Rhee became a member of the Independence Club established by

Philip Jaisohn, who had returned from the United States with his American wife to Paejae Haktang in Seoul, where he began to teach. However, the Club was ordered disbanded by King Kojong, Korea's penultimate king, after it had sent a petition to him requesting that he change his government policy for leasing land to foreigners. The king ordered the members of the Club arrested. Rhee found refuge at the American Methodist Hospital before being arrested by court detectives. He was put in jail but later succeeded in escaping. His freedom did not last, however, and he was returned to serve a prison term of seven years. During this time he wrote a book, *Tongnip cheongsin* (The Spirit of Independence), which he smuggled out of his prison cell to be published in the United States. In this book Rhee pleaded with his countrymen to have love for their country and its independence. He told his countrymen that if their heart was not filled with love for their nation, then they should tear it out, for it is their own enemy.

In 1904 Rhee came to America to study at George Washington University, from which he graduated in 1907. After graduation he entered Harvard University to do postgraduate work in international relations and received his Master's degree in 1910. During the same year he received a Ph.D in international affairs from Princeton University. His doctoral dissertation was entitled "Neutrality as Influenced by the United States." Rhee thus became the first Korean to receive an American doctoral degree. He then returned to Korea to work for the YMCA in Seoul but left Korea in March 1912 as a delegate to attend the Quadrennial General Conference of the Methodist Episcopal Church in Minneapolis, Minnesota. He did not go back to his native country again until Korea was freed from Japanese colonialism in 1945.

He spent most of the period between 1913 and 1945 in Hawaii. During these years he established a number of Korean social, educational, religious, and political organizations. He founded *Korean Pacific Magazine* in 1913, which later became *Korean Pacific Weekly* in 1930. He became headmaster of the Korean Central Institute, which taught second-generation Korean youth not only the Bible but also English, Korean language, and Korean history. He was responsible for establishing the Korean Christian Church in 1918 in Honolulu. In order to support his political activities, which were aimed at restoring Korea's independence, he founded the Tongji-hoe, or Comrade Society, in November 1920. In 1919, while still in exile in Hawaii, Rhee was named premier of the Korean Provisional Government, which was established in Shanghai, China. In October 1934, at age fifty-nine, Rhee married an Austrian woman, Francesca Donner.

Rhee returned to Korea in October 1945 after Japan was defeated in World War II. Upon return to his native land he worked toward establishment of the Republic of Korea in the southern half of the Korean peninsula. He was elected to the National Assembly in 1948 and was chosen to be the assembly's speaker. He was elected first president of the Republic of Korea, which was founded on August 15, 1948. He was reelected in 1952 and 1956. During the 1960 presidential election, irregularities were discovered and students rose up against Rhee's regime. He was forced to resign from the office of presidency and went into exile in Hawaii, where he died on July 19, 1965.

Selected Bibliography

Allen, Richard C. *Korea's Syngman Rhee: An Unauthorized Portrait.* Rutland, VT: Charles E. Tuttle, 1960.

Lee, Han-wu. *Geodaehan Insaeng: Yi Seung-man gusimnyeon* (A Great Life: The Ninety Years of Syngman Rhee). Seoul: Choson Ilbo-sa, 1996.

Oliver, Robert T. *Syngman Rhee: The Man behind the Myth.* New York: Dodd Mead, 1954.

Yu Yeong-ik. *Yi Seung-man eui sam kwa ggum* (The Life and Dreams of Syngman Rhee). Seoul: Chungang Ilbo-sa, 1996.

Hyung-chan Kim

ROSHNI RUSTOMJI-KERNS

(1938–   )

Author, Educator

In her writing, editing, and teaching, Roshni Rustomji-Kerns examines the diversity and multicultural dimensions of American life and literature. She is particularly interested in exploring and giving voice to the experiences of ethnic Americans. Her groundbreaking anthology, *Living in America: Poetry and Fiction by South Asian American Writers* (1995), was the first such collection to be published on South Asian writing in the United States. In 1999 she edited *Encounters: People of Asian Descent in the Americas*, which focuses on Asian communities in the Americas. This anthology blends analytical, biographical, and personal narratives with fiction, photography, and artwork to examine the interaction of Asians with other ethnic groups in the Americas.

Rustomji-Kerns's family and national history reflect the many cultural strands that are found in her writings. She was born on October 25, 1938, in Bombay, India. Her parents were members of the Parsi, or Zoroastrian, community, a religious-ethnic group whose origins are in Iran. Her fa-

Roshni Rustomji-Kerns

ther was from Karachi, which later became part of Pakistan. Her mother was born in Japan, where the family was involved in commerce on the Japan-India-England trade route. Rustomji-Kerns's great-great-grandmother was a Chinese woman from Malaysia.

After the partition of India and Pakistan in 1947, the Rustomji family moved back to Karachi. Her parents, Behram and Goolnar Rustomji, were both educators, her father a high school principal and her mother a director of a Montessori school. They also worked in special education providing programs for adults, lower-income women and children, and the physically disabled. After school, Rustomji-Kerns assisted her parents with these programs.

In 1955 Rustomji-Kerns graduated from high school in Karachi and was selected to be one of the first Pakistani students to go the United States in the American Field Service Program. After one year in the United States she graduated with another diploma from Washington Park High School in Racine, Wisconsin. She then went to the American University of Beirut, Lebanon, to study English and American literature, graduating with honors in 1961. She returned to the United States to pursue a Master's of Arts degree in English, which she completed in 1963 at Duke University in North Carolina. She continued her advanced studies at the University of California at Berkeley, where she received a

Ph.D. in comparative literature (Sanskrit, Classical Greek, and English) in 1973.

Rustomji-Kerns spent the next two decades teaching and developing innovative programs at Sonoma State University in California. As the first coordinator of the India studies chair, she created a curriculum on South and Middle Eastern studies. She recruited visiting scholars for this program who came from disciplines such as political science, anthropology, art, music, history, psychology, and literature. She later coordinated the university's Interdisciplinary Studies Program incorporating Asian studies, Middle Eastern studies, and women's studies, among others. Rustomji-Kerns describes the link between her teaching style and her cultural background: "the way I teach and the way I learn is very deeply rooted in my Asian life and culture" ("Interview" 1995). She traces her personal style of teaching, her enthusiasm for learning, and her fascination with how people narrate their worlds through stories, myths, music, dance, and art to her early family life and education in India and Pakistan.

Since taking early retirement from Sonoma State University in 1992, Rustomji-Kerns has devoted most of her time to writing and editing. She was appointed professor emerita at retirement and continues to teach writing and literature when time permits. In Rustomji-Kerns's research and writings on the literature of migration, postcolonial experience, and the attempts to break free of colonized thinking, she points to the extensive works being written by those of Middle Eastern, South Asian, and Southeast Asian origins. She describes Asian American writings as not merely an extension or category of American literature but rather as a reworking of that which exists. She envisions the process as "a stretching, sometimes tearing apart of the existing literary structure . . . creating different patterns in American literature by interweaving new colors and textures" ("Interview 1995").

A central theme in Rustomji-Kerns's writing and research concerns women's issues. She attributes this interest to growing up in the company of strong women: her mother, grandmothers, aunts, and teachers. Aside from teaching courses in women's studies, she has co-edited a book, *Blood into Ink: South Asian and Middle Eastern Women Write War* (1994). This volume examines the ways in which women articulate violence and warfare and the ways in which they are victimized in times of war or political and social upheaval. It is the first anthology to focus on non-Western women's writings on the subject of war and conflict during the twentieth century.

Rustomji-Kerns considers herself to be primarily a fiction writer. Her short stories have appeared in journals and anthologies in the United States and Canada, and she has recently completed a novel called *The Braided Tongue*. In a 1996 interview she said, "My writing crosses continents, (featuring) places, houses, people. They are stories heard from my parents, grandparents, friends. I have always been surrounded by storytellers" (Gandhi 1996).

Rustomji-Kerns is currently a visiting scholar at Stanford University's Center for Latin American Studies. She and her husband, Charles Kerns, a multimedia specialist at Stanford University, live in Half Moon Bay, California.

Selected Bibliography

Cooke, Miriam, and Roshni Rustomji-Kerns, eds. *Blood into Ink: South Asian and Middle Eastern Women Write War*. Boulder, CO: Westview Press, 1994.

Gandhi, Parinaz. "Surrounded by Storytellers." *Parsiana* (Bombay, India), April 1996, pp. 17, 40.

"Interview with Rustomji-Kerns." Spring 1995, unpublished.

Rustomji-Kerns, R. *Encounters: People of Asian Descent in the Americas*. Boulder, CO: Rowman & Littlefield, forthcoming.

———, ed. *Living in America: Fiction and Poetry by South American Writers*. Boulder, CO: Westview Press, 1995.

Women of South Asian Descent Collective. *Our Feet Walk the Sky: Women of the South Asian Diaspora*. San Francisco: Aunt Lute Books, 1993.

Anu M. Mitra

JAMES YOSHINORI SAKAMOTO
(1903–1955)
Journalist

James Yoshinori Sakamoto, prizefighter and journalist, was born in Seattle, Washington, in 1903, the son of a Japanese businessman. In Seattle he attended Pacific Grammar School and Franklin High, where he was a star athlete in baseball, basketball, judo, and boxing and as a 128 lb. halfback in football. He tried to enlist in the U.S. Army shortly after the United States entered World War I but was rejected because he was too young. He moved to the East Coast before graduating from high school and attended school in Princeton, New Jersey.

For three years Sakamoto worked as an English editor of the *Japanese American News*, a Japanese immigrant newspaper published in New York City. He also pursued a boxing career and became the first Nisei (second-generation Japanese American, or son of Japanese immigrants) to fight in Madison Square Garden. In 1926 boxing injuries caused him to suffer detached retinas in both eyes, an irreversible condition at the time that later produced total blindness. Knowledge of his impending blindness motivated him to return to Seattle in November 1927.

When Sakamoto returned to Seattle, he found the second-generation Japanese American Nisei community split by a rivalry between two athletic clubs. As a respected member of the community, he became the mediator between the opposing forces. He viewed the nearly defunct Seattle Progressive Citizens League as a productive rallying point to push "Americanism" among the Nisei, who were now coming of age. Also, perceiving the need for a newspaper to give the Nisei a voice, Sakamoto accepted financial assistance from his father, Osamu, and founded the *Japanese American Courier* on January 1, 1928. As the first exclusively English newspaper for Nisei, the *Courier* featured national news, news from Japan, local community news, sports, and editorials urging full identification with America. Initially, Sakamoto and his wife single-handedly published the newspaper, but other Nisei journalists later assisted them.

Through his editorials in the *Courier*, Sakamoto espoused Americanism as the fundamental means of overcoming the economic, social, political, and racial barriers that challenged the Nisei. He believed that assimilation of the Nisei into the general American population would precede amalgamation of future Japanese American generations into American society. Sakamoto also believed that the Nisei, whom he referred to as "American-born Japanese" or "American citizens of Japanese ancestry," had a civic duty to educate fellow Americans about Japan in order to foster understanding between Japan and the United States. To popularize such views, Sakamoto published the supportive opinions of Japanese government officials, educators, and Nisei civic leaders such as Japanese ambassador Debuchi Katsumi and Japanese Seattle Progressive Citizens League president Clarence Arai, all of whom subscribed to the concept of the Nisei as a bridge of understanding between the United States and Japan.

From 1932 to 1934 Sakamoto promoted knowledge about Japanese culture among the Nisei by publishing a weekly column in the *Courier* on Japanese language, conversation, and civilization written by Henry S. Tatsumi. He endorsed *kengakudan*, or study tours of Japan, for Nisei students and cited the experiences of many students who had gained firsthand knowledge of Japan, emphasizing how their appreciation of Japanese culture helped them become good American citizens. In addition to addressing issues directly involving the Nisei, Sakamoto wrote about Far Eastern and European politics, business and labor problems, and tariff rates and banking policy. In 1934 he began a weekly 30-minute radio program on local station KXA that broadcast news from Japan as well as American news.

Sakamoto actively supported the Seattle Progressive Citizens League and managed its reorganization early in 1928. Sakamoto and other leaders of the League sought to establish an association of other Japanese American leagues along the West Coast. The Seattle organization's first major project was to hold a convention that attempted to form a federation called the National Council of Japanese-American Citizens Leagues. League members advocated the national council at a convention held on April 6, 1929, in San Francisco. The League's proposals, many of which were shaped in Sakamoto's office, called for Nisei civic clubs in Oregon and California to merge with the Seattle Progressive Citizens League to form the Japanese American Citizens League (JACL) in 1930. This merger was successful. The League's main objective was the education of young Nisei in American politics on a nonpartisan basis in order to prepare them for fulfilling civic duties when they reached voting age.

Between 1930 and 1940 Sakamoto and other founders of the JACL, including Dr. Thomas Yatabe and lawyers Saburo Kido and Clarence Arai, expanded the League to include 5,600 members organized into 50 chapters. The JACL met the economic and social needs of Nisei professionals and small businessmen by providing information about the educational and business achievements of the Japanese American community as well as by holding conferences, banquets, dances, and other social events. JACL leaders advocated the conservative strategies of enterprise, self-help, and patriotism in order to demonstrate their usefulness to American society.

In 1931 Sakamoto went to Japan to seek treatment for his blindness but immediately returned to the United States to work with the JACL. In 1934 he and JACL members adopted a resolution that endorsed the deportation of communists who were found to be "guilty of subversive acts." Sakamoto also wished to prohibit the Communist Party from participating in U.S. elections. He supported the establishment of the House of Representatives Special Committee on Un-American Activities in 1938. Under the chairmanship of Congressman Martin Dies of Texas, the Committee probed so-called subversives and investigated publicly supported conservative labor leaders, such as William Green of the American Federation of Labor, believing that conservative leadership would maintain the cooperation between labor and capital necessary for business recovery from the Great Depression.

From 1936 to 1938 Sakamoto served as national president of the JACL. Sakamoto and JACL members denounced dual citizenship at a convention in 1936 and called on the Nisei to demonstrate patriotism to the United States. In that year Sakamoto designed the JACL's "Second Generation Development Programs," which encouraged the Nisei to prove their American loyalty by contributing to the social life, economic well-being, and civil welfare of the country. He advocated that the Nisei live with other citizens in a common community of interests and activities promoting the national welfare. He urged them to assume roles in agriculture, industry, and commerce. He also emphasized the importance of becoming public-spirited citizens who voted intelligently.

In 1940 Sakamoto began to promote American patriotism, because the American public and government had both begun to question the loyalty of Japanese Americans. After Japan attacked Pearl Harbor, Sakamoto repudiated Japan's bombing in an editorial in the *Courier*. He appealed to the U.S. government to show tolerance toward Japanese Americans by publishing the transcript of a lecture by Louis Adamic that addressed the need for acceptance of racial diversity and education about immigrant groups. In 1940, at the JACL national convention in Portland, Sakamoto and other members publicly affirmed the undivided allegiance of the Nisei to the U.S. government and planned "Americanism Day" programs to promote patriotism. Sakamoto worked with government authorities to report "subversive" activities within the Japanese American community by organizing the JACL Emergency Defense Council. The Council worked with the FBI to report suspicious activities within the community. In February 1942 Sakamoto testified before the Tolan Commission to oppose the forced internment of Japanese Americans. However, similar to other JACL leaders, he consistently pledged to cooperate with the government's decisions. He urged Japanese Americans to obey the government's evacuation orders in an editorial that appeared in the final issue of the *Courier* on April 24, 1942.

During the war Sakamoto was appointed as the "chief supervisor" of the "Japanese staff" at Tanforan Assembly Center, an internment camp. He and his staff acted as liaisons between the inmate population and the Center's Caucasian staff. The power Sakamoto had gained through his supervisory position diminished when the Tanforan population was transferred to the War Relocation Authority Center in Minidoka, Idaho.

Sakamoto was married to Misao Nishitani. He was killed in an automobile accident in Seattle in 1955.

Selected Bibliography

Hosokawa, B. *JACL in Quest of Justice: The History of the Japanese American Citizen's League.* New York: William Morrow, 1982.

Ichioka, Y. "A Study in Dualism: James Yoshinori Sakamoto." *Amerasia Journal*, vol. 13, no. 2 (1986–1987): 49–82.

Kim, H., ed. *Dictionary of Asian American History.* Westport, CT: Greenwood, 1986.

Niiya, Brian, ed. *Japanese American History: An A-to-Z Reference from 1868 to the Present*. New York: Facts on File, 1993.

Steve Fugita

EDUARDO SAN JUAN
(1925–1988)
Engineer

Born in Manila in 1925, Eduardo San Juan was among the thousands of Filipino engineers who immigrated to the United States during the aerospace boom of the 1960s after being recruited by American aircraft companies. He was first hired by the Boeing Company in Seattle, and later he became part of the design team for the National Aeronautics and Space Administration (NASA).

At NASA, San Juan designed the lunar rover that was used by American astronauts to traverse and study the surface of the moon. The lunar rover, or LRV, had large balloon-like tires that resembled the dune buggies used to travel sandy beach areas. Thus, the lunar rover acquired the nickname "moon buggie." The lunar rover was first deployed on July 31, 1971, during the *Apollo 15* mission and was also used during the *Apollo 16* and *17* missions in the next two years.

San Juan was also a leader in the field of undersea research. He used his engineering skills to find ways to make transportation easier for all people on land, in air, or in water. After leaving Boeing he worked for the Lockheed Company in California. He also worked for the U.S. government on various projects at the American Research Center in Sunnyvale, California.

Eduardo "Ed" San Juan died on February 3, 1988, at the age of sixty-three.

Selected Bibliography

Philippine News, February 17–23, 1998, pp. 4, 15 and editorial.
Seattle Times, February 7, 1976, p. A4.
Your Public School, March 8, 1976, p. 4.

Dorothy Cordova

ROBERT SANTOS

(1934–   )

Community Leader

Robert Santos is a man of many accomplishments and interests—fearless community activist, director of several successful nonprofit poverty programs, visionary, entertaining raconteur, devoted father and grandfather, and most recently the representative in the Northwest for the secretary of the Department of Housing and Urban Development (HUD).

Santos—known as "Uncle Bob" to his thousands of admirers—was born in February 1934 in Seattle, Washington, to Virginia (Nicol) and Sammy Santos. His father was a well-known Filipino boxer who came to the United States during the 1920s. His mother, who was *mestiza* (having a Filipino father and French Canadian/Canadian Indian mother), died when he was very young. During the Great Depression, Santos went to live with his mother's older sister while his older brother, Sam, stayed with their great-grandmother. On weekends the boys visited their father, who lived in single room in Chinatown.

Santos graduated from high school during the Korean War and joined the Marines. He married shortly after his discharge, and the young couple eventually had six children. He worked in a variety of jobs and volunteered for a Knights of Columbus athletic program. When he was asked in the early 1960s to join the Archdiocese of Seattle's effort to bring about open housing, new vistas opened for him and he began the life that would bring him to the forefront of the civil rights movement.

In 1970 he became director of CARITAS, a tutoring program for inner-city youths. In 1972 he became director of Inter*Im (International District Improvement Association). In these roles Santos was to change the face and atmosphere of the once-decaying business/residential area of Seattle. Always a charismatic leader, he attracted idealistic young workers who wanted to effect social change. These were the final days of the civil rights movement, and young Asian Americans were beginning to make their voices heard. In addition to giving direct services to the elderly Filipinos and Chinese immigrants who constituted the majority of local residents, during his thirteen years at Inter*Im Santos established the district's first bilingual health clinic, community garden, public corporation, legal services, nutrition programs, and the Chinatown International District Preservation and Development Authority. His aggressive

Bob Santos

leadership coupled with political savvy made it possible to get the funds to rehabilitate deteriorating apartments and to build new housing complexes for the growing number of immigrants—old and recent, young and elderly—who were now seeking housing in the International District. Through Inter*Im, 700 new housing units were created.

For a time he was a legislative aide for Washington State congressman Mike Lowery. In 1989 he returned to the district to become executive director of the Seattle Chinatown-International District Preservation and Development Authority (SCIDPDA). Immediately he began to do what he did best—plan projects that would enhance the neighborhood of his youth. The ID Village Square began as a concept and Santos made it a reality. Because of the many years he had spent creating good relations with government agencies and the success of his earlier projects, Santos was able to secure needed land and funds.

His work in the International District caught the attention of Secretary of Housing and Urban Development Henry Cisneros, who was reorganizing HUD at the time. Santos's was one of eight resumés requested from the Northwest region. When Cisneros read his, the secretary realized Santos was already doing what the HUD reorganization called for—

"empowerment zones" and "enterprise communities." Santos flew to
Washington, D.C., for a short interview with Cisneros and received
White House approval less than a month later. As secretary's represen-
tative for the Northwest Region in the Department of Housing and Ur-
ban Development, Bob Santos is the highest-ranking Filipino in the
Clinton administration.

Selected Bibliography

Filipino-American Herald, May 15, 1994, p. 11.
International Examiner, January 1977.
International Examiner, May 2, 1984.
Modern Maturity, June–July 1992, p. 32.
Northwest Asian Weekly, April 2, 1994, p. 1.
Northwest Ethnic News, May 1985.
Seattle Times, July 5, 1970.
Seattle Times, September 9, 1997, Emmett Watson's column.

Dorothy Cordova

DALIP SINGH SAUND
(1899–1973)
Congressman, Farmer, Politician

Elected to the House of Representatives in 1956, Dalip Singh Saund was
the first Asian to serve in the U.S. Congress. Prior to his election Saund
was a farmer and businessman in California's Imperial Valley. Although
he was interested in local politics and civil issues, his political participation was limited because restrictive naturalization policies prevented
Asians from becoming citizens. To contest these policies, in 1942, he
helped form the India Association of America, which lobbied for non-
discriminatory immigration and naturalization laws. Once a bill was
passed that made Indians eligible for U.S. citizenship in 1946, he applied
for naturalization. Saund became a citizen in 1949 and immediately entered local politics by joining the central committee of the Democratic
Party in Imperial County and by running for a judicial post in the small
town of Westmorland. He held the position of judge in Westmorland
from 1953 to 1955. He then decided to run for a seat in the House of
Representatives.

Saund was born on September 29, 1899, in Chhajalwadi village in the northern Indian province of Punjab. Although the family had simple origins as village artisans, his father and uncles went on to become government contractors, building canals and railroads. They eventually became landowners. Saund's parents, Natha Singh and Jeoni Kaur, were Sikhs, members of a minority religion whose followers were concentrated in the Punjab. Saund attended schools in the nearby town of Amritsar and completed his B.A. degree with honors from the University of Punjab in 1919.

As a youth Saund was an ardent nationalist, participating in demonstrations to protest British colonial rule in India. Fearing that he might be arrested for his activities, Saund's elder brother encouraged him to leave the country to pursue graduate studies. Saund entered the University of California at Berkeley in 1920. He took classes in agriculture, food preservation, and mathematics, eventually majoring in math. He completed a Master's degree in 1922 and a Ph.D. in 1924 in mathematics at Berkeley.

Although Saund had planned to return to Punjab after his graduation, his family warned him that the anti-British speeches he had made while a student in California had been documented by the colonial government. Even though he decided to stay in the United States, Saund's life was unsettled as he drifted in a country where he could not become a citizen. Unable to decide on a career path, his first job after earning a Ph.D. was as foreman of the syrup department in a fruit cannery. He never used his math again.

Saund's next job was working as foreman of a cotton-picking crew near the town of Holtville in the Imperial Valley. While a student at Berkeley, he had attended religious services at the Sikh temple in nearby Stockton, California. There he met Punjabi immigrants who had become farmers in the Sacramento, San Joaquin, and Imperial Valleys. Saund was drawn to the Imperial Valley because of its abundant irrigation water from the Colorado River and year-round sunshine that allowed farmers to harvest two crops annually. With his earnings from the cotton-picking job, Saund began farming as a sharecropper.

Restricted from buying or leasing land because the California Alien Land Law prohibited noncitizens from buying land, Saund and other Asian immigrant farmers in the valley were quite susceptible to the ups and downs of the farming business—such as unavailability of land to rent, unpredictable harvests, and low market prices. Saund raised crops such as celery, melons, lettuce, and corn and was among the first in the valley to grow beets and Punjabi flax. Like other farmers, he had good and bad years and at one point found himself deeply in debt. Instead of filing for bankruptcy, he chose to pay off his debts over a period of several years.

In 1928 Saund met and married Marian Kosa, a second-generation Czech American who was then attending the University of California at Los Angeles. They made their home near the small Imperial Valley town of Westmorland, where Marian Saund joined her husband in farming activities. She said that her job one year was to "stand in the corner of a field and fire a .22 rifle under the clouds of blackbirds as they descended on the ripening corn. It worked too. The blackbirds did not get the corn" (MacKaye 1958).

The Saunds had three children, Dalip Jr. and daughters Julie and Eleanor. After some years in the valley, the severe heat had an ill effect on Marian Saund's health. The family was forced to relocate to Los Angeles, where she began teaching school. Saund then commuted between their home in Los Angeles and his work in Westmorland, driving approximately 1,000 miles per week.

Dalip Singh Saund had been farming in the Imperial Valley for twenty years when he decided to run for U.S. Congress. Yet when he was elected to the House of Representatives in 1956, even the most astute political observers were surprised. Although he had long been a farmer in the valley, had established a successful agricultural chemical business, and had served as a justice in the town of Westmorland, he was not well known throughout the 29th District, one of the largest in the county encompassing 11,460 miles. He was also the first Democrat to win election to Congress from that district. Moreover, his Republican opponent, Jacqueline Odlum, a famous aviator, businesswoman, and wife of a politically powerful millionaire, was reported to have spent three times as much as Saund on her campaign.

A newspaper reporter described the Saund family's role in the campaign. Marian Saund and daughter Eleanor concentrated on the voters in Riverside, where Saund was not well known, ringing doorbells and handing out literature. They registered voters and walked every precinct in the town. The married children, Dalip Jr. and Julie, took time out from school and work to campaign in the 29th District, which equaled the size of the states of Massachusetts, Delaware, and Rhode Island combined. Saund won the election by about 4,000 votes.

When the congressman reached Washington, he was immediately appointed to the House Foreign Affairs Committee and soon thereafter embarked on a diplomatic mission to Asia. This highly successful trip allowed him to fulfill one of his campaign declarations of promoting better understanding between the United States and Asian countries. He and his family were received by large enthusiastic crowds in Japan, Hong Kong, the Philippines, Burma, and India. During this trip Saund contributed to the cold war discourse of the period by extolling American democracy and downplaying racial prejudice in the United States.

Yet in his travels he did not deny that there had been discrimination against Asians and other people of color. He stated that prejudice thrives in all countries, but that in democracy people can change. He cited his own election as an example of that change.

As a legislator Saund supported bills on domestic issues such as an increase in Social Security benefits (July 1958), an increase in grants for federal action against water pollution (June 1959), and an extension of the tenure of the Civil Rights Commission (September 1959). Among the foreign affairs bills backed by Saund were the President's Mideast Doctrine (January 1957), increased U.S. subscriptions to the International Monetary Fund and the World Bank (March 1959), and U.S. participation in the Inter-American Development Bank (July 1959).

During Saund's first term in the House of Representatives there was much speculation in California's 29th District concerning his chances for reelection. Some observers attributed his successful bid for the House to the large number of Republican candidates in the 1956 primary that led to disunity in the party during the fall elections. In the 1958 election all major factions of the Republicans joined to support John Babbage, a forty-two-year-old lawyer who had received his degrees from the University of Southern California and Columbia University Law School. Settling in Riverside, he worked as a deputy district attorney before going into private practice. Babbage had also served two terms in the California state legislature after being nominated by both the Republican and Democratic Parties in the state primary.

In spite of a united Republican Party, a strong opposition candidate in the form of Babbage, and the lack of support of many of the large growers in the Imperial Valley, the voters of the 29th District returned Saund to the House of Representatives in the 1958 election.

Saund was serving his third term in Congress in 1962 when he suffered a serious stroke. Poor health forced him to give up his congressional seat. He died in California on April 23, 1973.

Selected Bibliography

Current Biography, 1960, pp. 359–360.
Diplomat, September 1958, pp. 1379–1381.
MacCann, Richard. "California Family Shares in Victory of Indian-Born Contestant for House." *Christian Science Monitor*, November 21, 1956, p. 6.
MacKaye, Milton. "U.S. Congressman from Asia." *Saturday Evening Post*, August 2, 1958, pp. 25, 53–56.
"A Sikh in Congress." *New York Times*, November 19, 1956, p. 13.

Jane Singh

GEORGE SHIMA

(1864–1926)

Farmer, Business Leader, Inventor

George Shima, farmer, was born in 1864 as Kinji Ushijima in Kurume City, Fukuoka, Japan. His family had farmed for generations. At a young age Shima developed an interest in Chinese literature, especially the works of Confucius, and in 1885 he went to Tokyo to become a scholar of Chinese culture. His limited knowledge of the English language prevented him from passing the entrance examination to Hitotsubashi University and motivated him to travel to the United States for further education. In 1889 he arrived in San Francisco, where he changed his name to George Shima and worked as a schoolboy.

He then began a challenging life as one of the *dekasegishosei*, a group of Japanese students who came to the United States with high ambitions about learning English or other skills required to make a living in the United States. Within a year he became a migrant farm laborer in the Sacramento Delta region. He worked for some time in New Hope, California, where he cared for the orchards of Arthur Thorton. He then became an agricultural labor contractor, supplying Japanese workers to white farmers. In the late 1890s he began to manage property, initially leasing fifteen acres of land. Shima expanded his holdings, leasing and purchasing underdeveloped swamplands in the San Joaquin Delta for a low price. He developed an elaborate system of dikes and drains to clear fertile land for more efficient farming. After experimenting with various crops, Shima found that the potato grew best in the delta's swampy soil. He was a pioneer in applying corporate managerial techniques to agriculture and in using the latest developments in agricultural science.

By 1912 he controlled 10,000 acres of potatoes valued at one-half million dollars. With 28,000 acres of land in production in 1913, he became known as the Potato King. His work force consisted of more than 500 agronomists, engineers, foremen, common laborers, and boat captains (the islands he owned were only accessible by water). Most of his employees were Japanese; however, they also included native and foreign-born South Asians and Caucasians. Shima became the delta's first large-scale potato grower. He was also the first shipper to adopt a trademark, specifically the "Shima Fancy" label attached to red potato sacks. By 1920, Shima controlled 85 percent of the potato crop, valued at more than $18 million. Emphasizing high product standards, he ensured that his potatoes were carefully washed and graded before packing. He held stock in a firm founded by local investors who developed a company called the California Delta Farms Company.

In 1909 anti-Japanese real estate agents and homeowners tried to prevent him from purchasing a home in Berkeley. This caused him to actively fight the anti-Japanese movement within California. As the first and life-long president of the Japanese Association of America, he tried unsuccessfully to prevent the passage of California's 1913 Alien Land Law, which prohibited aliens ineligible for citizenship, specifically Asians, from owning land.

In 1926 he was awarded the Fourth Rank Rising Sun Medal from the Emperor of Japan. On that same day, while on a business trip in Los Angeles, he suffered a stroke and died. Since his death Shima has been honored for his agricultural achievements through the establishment of the Shima Center at San Joaquin Delta College. His accomplishments as a philanthropist were recognized in 1975 at the dedication of the Shima Center, which recalled his efforts to help a number of youth attend Stanford University and the University of California. At Shima's funeral in 1926 the pallbearers included Davis Starr Jordan, the chancellor of Stanford University, and James Rolph Jr., the mayor of San Francisco.

George Shima married Shimeko Shima. The couple had a daughter, Taye, and two sons, Togo and Ringe.

Selected Bibliography

Daniels, R. *Asian American: Chinese and Japanese in the United States since 1850.* Seattle: University of Washington Press, 1988.

Japanese American Curriculum Project. *Japanese American Journey: The Story of a People.* Sacramento, CA: Japanese American Curriculum Project, 1985.

Niiya, Brian, ed. *Japanese American History: An A-to-Z Reference from 1868 to the Present.* New York: Facts on File, 1993.

Takaki, R. *Strangers from a Different Shore.* Boston: Little, Brown, 1989.

Steve Fugita

PAULL HOBOM SHIN

(1935–   )

Politician, Educator

The embodiment of the personal worth and success that come from hard work, discipline, and personal sacrifice, Paull Shin's life is the inspirational story of one man's determination to achieve the American Dream. Even though the United States is his adopted homeland, it is where Shin has built his life and found success.

Paull Shin was born in Seoul, Korea, in 1935. Abandoned as a four-year-old, he grew up as a street urchin, fending for himself on the streets of Seoul. When the Korean War erupted in 1950 he worked as a house-boy for U.S. military officers. An American dentist, Dr. Ray Paull, adopted Shin and brought him to the United States at the age of eighteen. In respect and deference to him, he assumed Dr. Paull's last name as his first. Shin had very little formal education when he arrived in America. Yet through his adoptive parents he was able to find a loving home, acceptance, and an education. Shin earned his high school diploma by studying for the GED (general equivalency diploma) test. The exercise in self-directed education prompted him to prepare himself for a test of even greater significance in his young life: the opportunity to become a citizen of the United States. Shortly after taking his oath of citizenship, Shin served for two years in the U.S. Army, stationed in Germany.

Upon his return Shin pursued higher education with renewed zeal, earning a Bachelor's degree from Brigham Young University, a Master's degree from the University of Pittsburgh, and a Ph.D. from the University of Washington. Convinced that education is the cornerstone of personal success and fulfillment, Shin embarked on a teaching career that led him from teaching at Brigham Young University to the University of Maryland, to a professorship at Shoreline Community College in Seattle, Washington. There he has cultivated the minds of students of all ages for over two decades.

Mindful that the best educators are those who balance the pursuits of academia with the challenges of the real world, Shin immersed himself in the affairs of business. He presently serves as chairman of the board for TTI, a long-distance telecommunications company. As his expertise in international business grew, Shin sought to apply his knowledge and skills to a matter close to his heart: providing economic opportunities for the residents of his home state of Washington. He found his niche in the political arena, where he served under numerous governors in the area of international trade. Shin's perseverance and vision have proven beneficial to the state of Washington's economy. Today, over 20 percent of its jobs depend on trade-related professions.

Successful at his first run for elected office, Shin served as a legislator in the Washington State House of Representatives from 1993 to 1994. As a state representative he honed his legislative skills while applying his professional expertise to the legislative process. During his tenure Shin served as vice-chair of the Committee on Trade, Economic Development and Housing and as an appointed member of the Committees on Transportation and Higher Education.

Shin ran an unsuccessful campaign in the Democratic primary for lieutenant governor in the fall of 1996 and has returned to his professorship at Shoreline Community College.

Selected Bibliography

Matthee, Imbert. "Shin Invited to Interview for Ambassador's Job to Seoul." *Seattle Post-Intelligencer*, January 4, 1997, p. A5.
Who's Who among Asian Americans 1994/95. Detroit: Gale Research, 1994.
Who's Who in America, 49th ed. (1995). New Providence, NJ: Marquis Who's Who, 1994.

Jennifer Kang

JOE SHOONG

(1879–1961)

Business Leader, Philanthropist

A successful businessman and philanthropist, Joe Shoong was a millionaire and the founder of the National Dollar Stores. His interests extended from retailing to real estate. His surname was Joe, but people often called him "Mr. Shoong."

Joe Shoong was born on August 30, 1879, in the Lungtowan area of Chungshan in the Guangdong province of China. His parents were Joe Gon Shoong and Wong Shee Shoong. Joe Shoong immigrated to the United States when he was young and worked as a garment worker.

Around 1901 he opened the Sang Lee dry goods store in Vallejo, California, with three partners. By 1903 he had bought out his partners and moved to San Francisco's Fillmore Street. Then, in 1905, he changed the location to Market Street in the downtown area and named it the China Toggery, J. Shoong Company. Its Chinese name was Chung Hing, which means "revival" or "rejuvenation."

Joe Shoong seized opportunities to open new branches of the store, which in 1928 had been named the National Dollar Stores. The first branch was built in Sacramento in 1916, and by 1920 there were eight branches and the store had been incorporated in California. Eight years later there were forty-three stores in Utah, Nevada, Washington, Oregon, California, and Hawaii with branches in cities such as Seattle, Tacoma, and Portland. Expansion continued until 1959, when there was a chain of fifty-four stores in seven western states worth $12 million and employing 700 workers. The stores sold moderately priced items such as apparel and dry goods. Each store was headed by a Chinese manager with clerks who were predominantly Caucasian.

Not content with only operating the National Dollar Stores, Joe Shoong diversified the company's interests. Around 1926 he bought 51 percent of the stock of the National Store Company. By this means he acquired controlling interest in a chain of thirty-two Reeves Shoe Stores on the West Coast by 1961. He also turned his attention to investment in real estate and the successful purchase of stocks. Consequently, at mid-century, Joe Shoong was widely known as one of the wealthiest Chinese Americans in the United States.

In 1938, Joe Shoong and his National Dollar Stores became involved in a complicated labor dispute with striking employees. To supply clothing for its chain of outlets, National Dollar Stores operated a sewing factory in San Francisco's Chinatown. The largest employer in Chinatown, it employed between 125 and 200 workers. When its factory workers organized a Chinese Ladies' Garment Workers Union, Local 341, for collective bargaining, the difficulties arose. After union representatives thought that they had secured a closed shop (a business place where union organization is forbidden) and increased wages, National Dollar Stores sold its factory to the Golden Gate Manufacturing Company. Lack of progress in the negotiations led the union to declare a strike on February 26, 1938. Although National Dollar Stores threatened to sue the union, the workers set up picket lines that were honored by the public. After thirteen weeks, National Dollar Stores and Golden Gate agreed to negotiate and to settle. But the victory was brief, for by the end of the year Golden Gate had closed down and the workers lost their jobs.

When Japan invaded China in 1937, Joe Shoong joined other Chinese in raising funds for the Chinese war effort. A China War Relief Association was created by San Francisco's Six Companies in 1937 to provide aid for China. Chinese organizations, churches, and concerned citizens raised large sums of money for the cause. Joe Shoong, like other businessmen, also gave large contributions. The China War Relief Association efforts included benefit dances, the sale of paper flowers, and other methods to raise money.

Joe Shoong was a noted philanthropist who gave to many charities and other worthwhile causes. In 1928 he built a Joe Shoong School in his home village of Lungtowan, Chungshan. For more than twenty years, from 1928 to 1949, he supplied over $200,000 for its operating expenses. At the same time he donated money each year to help run the Longdu Middle School near his village. In 1931 he paid off the construction debt for the Chinese Central High School in San Francisco. Six years later he gave $24,000 to the Chinese Hospital in San Francisco, and in 1938 he contributed $70,000 to the University of California to establish scholarships for needy students.

After World War II, Joe Shoong established the Joe Shoong Foundation with an endowment of $1,000,000. In the years to follow, scholarships for the University of California were increased. Sizable contributions were given to San Francisco's Chinese Hospital, Oakland's Chinese Community Center and Chinese School, Locke's Joe Shoong Chinese School, Sacramento's Chung Wah School, and the Chinese Historical Society of America. Several Christian churches in San Francisco, Oakland, and Berkeley were given funds, as were Bay Area charities and civic organizations. His son, Milton Shoong, has continued the philanthropic activities of the foundation.

In 1959 Joe Shoong retired from his business and his son, Milton, became the president. Joe died on April 13, 1961, in San Francisco. Married twice, his first wife was Rose Soo-Hoo. After she died in 1951, he was married again in 1952 to Ruth Chow. His survivors include his son, Milton, and two daughters, Mrs. Richard Tam and Mrs. Howard Byrd.

Selected Bibliography

Chinn, Thomas W. *Bridging the Pacific: San Francisco Chinatown and Its People*. San Francisco: Chinese Historical Society of America, 1989.

Fong, Patricia M. "The 1938 National Dollar Store Strike." *Asian American Review*, vol. 2 (1975):183–200.

"Joe Shoong, Chinese Merchant King, Dies." *San Francisco Chronicle*, April 15, 1965.

"Joe Shoong, 81, Bay Financier." *San Francisco Examiner*, April 15, 1961.

Lai, Him Mark. "Joe Shoong." Manuscript. Berkeley: University of California, Asian American Studies Library.

"Toggery Trouble." *Time*, March 28, 1938, pp. 55–56.

Franklin Ng

SICHAN SIV

(1948–   )

Educator, Government Administrator

One night while in the midst of a war-torn Cambodia, Chea Aun told her children that "hate does not end with more hate but with love. And from that we take hope." With this message, her son Sichan Siv escaped the war between the communist Khmer Rouge and the American-supported Lon Nol government to become the first Asian refugee to be appointed a ranking U.S. presidential aide.

Sichan Siv was born in Phnom Penh in 1948. After their father died when Sichan Siv was nine years old, Chea Aun was left to raise him, his brother, and two sisters. After graduating from college in Phnom Penh and working as an English teacher, Siv began working for CARE in 1974. As an employee of the U.S. relief agency, he was active in the effort to aid refugees fleeing from the wartorn countryside. It was Siv's dedication to the relief efforts that caused him to miss the last helicopter evacuating Americans and other relief workers five days before the Khmer Rouge entered Phnom Penh.

Knowing that the Khmer Rouge targeted for persecution, torture, or death all those who were educated or had associated with foreigners, Sichan knew he had to escape. After biking through over 200 miles of checkpoints, he was within 40 miles of Thailand when he was captured. After several months of manual labor, he escaped to Thailand in February 1976 by wandering for three days through a jungle. Soon thereafter he was arrested by Thai officials for illegal entry. Later, officials at CARE, contacted by the U.S. Embassy in Bangkok, petitioned the State Department to let him come to America. In honor of his mother, Siv was ordained as a Buddhist monk before he left Thailand. He later was told of his mother's death along with fifteen other relatives.

On June 4, 1976, Siv was granted refugee status and arrived in Wallingford, Connecticut, where he was sponsored by former Peace Corps officer Bob Charles and his wife, Nancy. After working as an apple picker and then a short-order cook at a local Friendly's restaurant, Siv moved to Manhattan, where he became a cab driver and eventually got a job counseling refugees for a Lutheran organization. While in New York City he sent letters to several universities describing his education, background, and career goals. In January 1980, Columbia University offered him a full scholarship to its School of International Relations and

Public Affairs. Siv earned his Master's degree in sixteen months and became a U.S. citizen in December 1982.

After a short stint at the United Nations, he joined the nonprofit Institute of International Education as director of Asia and Pacific programs in 1987. During this time Siv also volunteered to work on George Bush's presidential campaign. A Bush aide who was impressed with Siv's knowledge and honesty recommended him to presidential assistant David Demarest for the job of presidential aide. On February 13, 1989, Sichan Siv was sworn in as a deputy assistant to the president and became the first Asian refugee to become a ranking presidential aide. Siv was the president's primary connection to higher education associations and other special interest groups. He was also the leader of the White House Communications Task Force on National Security Issues, the cochairman of the U.S. delegation to the Geneva conference on refugees, the senior advisor the U.S. delegation to the Paris conference on Cambodia, and the deputy assistant secretary of state for South Asian affairs.

In 1993, after the end of the Bush administration, Siv became a senior vice-president of Commonwealth Associates, an investment bank and brokerage firm based in New York, where he heads the Asian and Pacific department. He resides in New York with his wife, Martha, whom he married on Christmas Eve, 1983.

Selected Bibliography

DeLoughry, Thomas J. "Former Prisoner of Khmer Rouge Now Provides Higher Education." *Chronicle of Higher Education*, September 6, 1989, pp. A21–22.
Friedman, Jack. "Escape from the Inferno." *People*, March 27, 1989, pp. 32–37.
Kelly, Sheldon. "The Rebirth of Sichan Siv." *Reader's Digest*, February 1991, pp. 138–142.
Zia, Helen, and Susan B. Gall, eds. *Notable Asian Americans*. Detroit: Gale Research, 1995, pp. 349–351.

Chae Reed

CHANG MOOK SOHN
(1944–   )
Economist

"When E. F. Hutton speaks, people listen," boasts a television advertisement. The same could be said of Dr. Chang Mook Sohn, executive director of the Office of the Forecast Council of the state of Washington.

Chang Mook Sohn

When Sohn speaks, Washington residents listen, because what he frequently speaks about in public is related to the economic health of their
state. His official responsibilities as chief state economist involve preparation and presentation of quarterly forecasts of economic activities in
Washington state and Washington's General Fund revenues, as well as
economic consultation to the Economic and Revenue Forecast Council,
the governor's Council of Economic Advisors, and the state legislative
committees. He also is responsible for development of staff capabilities,
management of the personal computer economic and revenue models,
press conferences, testimony before the Ways and Means Committee of
the state legislature, and presentations at various conferences and meetings.

Chang Mook Sohn was born on March 25, 1944, in Korea. He attended
public schools before he was admitted to Yonsei University, from which
he graduated in 1968 with a B.A. degree in economics. He came to the
United States on an academic fellowship to study at the State University
of New York at Albany in 1971, and in 1975 he received a Ph.D. in
economics. Upon graduation he moved to Oregon, where he worked as
state tax economist in the state's Department of Revenue between 1977

and 1980. Then in February 1980 he was promoted and moved to the Executive Department, State of Oregon, to assume full responsibility for quarterly state economic and revenue forecasting. He worked in that capacity until 1984, when he moved to Olympia, Washington, to work as executive director of the Office of the Forecast Council.

For his outstanding contributions, he was recognized with the Governor's Distinguished Management Leadership Award given by the governor of Washington in 1986. He was named the Asian American of the Year by the *China Post* in 1991. The Korean American Professionals Society in Seattle recognized him as the Korean American Professional of the Year in 1994, and in 1995 the Seattle *Times* named him one of the one hundred people of influence in the state of Washington.

He now lives with his wife, Sukjoo Sohn, in Olympia, Washington.

Hyung-chan Kim

YELLAPRAGADA SUBBA ROW
(1896–1948)
Physician, Scientist, Educator

Despite Subba Row's major contributions to modern medicine, he is neither widely known in the United States (where he conducted his research) nor in India (where he received his training as a doctor). Dr. Subba Row, whose scientific investigations resulted in the development of cures for many diseases found in both countries, decided to dedicate himself to medical research when he was a young man in India.

He enrolled at Madras University, where he told the registrar that he intended to conquer tropical diseases such as sprue. In 1921, after completing a Master of Science and medical degree, he became a teaching assistant at the medical school. He continued to be struck by the medical profession's inability to combat diseases such as sprue, cholera, pellagra, and leprosy, which were claiming many lives in India during this time. A year after his graduation, he decided to leave his family and Madras in order to continue his studies at the School of Tropical Medicine at London University in England.

While studying at London University, Subba Row worked with Dr. Richard Strong, a visiting professor of tropical medicine from Harvard University. Impressed by young Subba Row's determination to cure tropical diseases, Dr. Strong encouraged him to come to the United States for further study. Dedicated and curious, Subba Row was an enthusiastic young researcher.

He arrived in Boston in 1924 with less than $50 in his possession. He worked as a hospital orderly and a night librarian at the medical school and tended furnaces in order to cover his living expenses—a basement room, food, tuition, and books. He often went for days on very little food, eating only beans or shredded wheat and milk. During one particularly lean period he received an anonymous gift of cash, which was slipped under his door. He remembered the gesture throughout the years, and once he became well established he made a practice of helping struggling young students.

Subba Row completed his Ph.D. in biochemistry in 1930. He continued his studies of phosphorus compounds in muscle and liver, which eventually led to his isolating of chemical substances in liver extract that could be used in the treatment of pernicious anemia. He and his research team conducted ground-breaking investigations in vitamin chemistry that resulted in new insights about nutrition. In particular, his work contributed to the identification of nicotinic acid, a critical compound used to treat pellagra. Somewhat later, Subba Row won another victory in his fight against tropical diseases. With the synthesis of folic acid, he found a cure for tropical sprue.

In 1938 Dr. Subba Row accepted a faculty appointment at Harvard University. However, his preference for research over teaching led him to spend long hours in the laboratory. After 1933 he also collaborated with Dr. G. W. Clark at Lederle Laboratories in Pearl River, New York, where he often spent Fridays through Sundays using the well-equipped facilities to further his work on liver extract and nutrition. Subba Row's early work at Lederle resulted in the first isolation of vitamins from B-complex group. In 1940 he gave up his position as associate professor at Harvard University to become an associate director of research at the Lederle Laboratories Division of American Cyanamid. Within two years he became the director of research, leading a large research staff that synthesized new drugs such as folic acid, teropterin, sulfamethazine, and aureomycin.

Fellow researchers attributed Subba Row's achievements to his analytical capabilities and his flexibility: "Dr. Subba Row seemed instinctively to know when to let go of a particular approach and try another. When biotin seemed to him to show no particular results, he switched to folic acid. He was lukewarm to the synthesis of penicillin and streptomycin, but in aureomycin he saw a great antibiotic. Its effectiveness in conditions not responsive to penicillin or streptomycin, particularly certain viral and rickettsial diseases, shows that he was right" (*Lederle Laboratories Newsletter* n.d.). With reference to his capacity for analyzing data, his colleagues reported that "in learning a new subject he would read all related printed works, eliminate the hypothetical portions and realign the facts. Then he would meet personally every recognized authority in his new field. He firmly believed that there is no substitute for the personal contact. Finally, he would formulate his own manner of approach, usually taking the obscure or overlooked facts and replacing them in his new setting of a problem so that now they looked obvious and the only logical approach" (*Lederle Laboratories Newsletter* n.d.).

Subba Row served as director of research at Lederle Laboratories from 1942 until his death in 1948. He never failed to impress his associates with his perseverance and his abilities, which included an astonishing memory. "Once during a conference he was held up by the loss of a record sheet on some work done several months before. This sheet had contained two long rows of daily temperatures. Dr. Subba Row finally arose in disgust at wasting time and wrote the temperatures—from memory—on the blackboard. When the record sheet was found later that day, someone checked the figures—he had them almost perfect. At this time he was directing a great number of experiments, each with hundreds of daily temperature readings" (*Lederle Laboratories Newsletter* n.d.).

Known as a deeply spiritual man, Dr. Subba Row nevertheless discussed his belief system in scientific terms. In a letter written to the pastor of his church, he stated: "You see, to me, religion is a dynamic subject rather than a static code, or established principles. To me, it is an internal experience, a sort of unfolding self-revelation piece by piece" (*Lederle Laboratories Newsletter* n.d.).

Although Subba Row spent long hours in scientific research, he took up a number of hobbies in later life. He learned how to swim, ride horses, and fly planes. "[H]e developed an interest in orchids and was continually devising new methods to make them grow faster" (*Your Health* 1954).

A few years after Subba Row's death in 1948, Lederle Laboratories opened a plant in India at Bulsar near Bombay. The opening ceremonies included the unveiling of a plaque to honor the memory of Dr. Subba Row; it bears the inscription: "Science simply prolongs life—Religion deepens it." The Lederle plant in Bulsar symbolized Dr. Subba Row's scientific contributions made to the United States and India. Many of the pharmaceuticals produced under his direction have improved the quality of life for people in both countries and for millions of others around the world.

Selected Bibliography

"Yellapragada Subba Row, 1896–1948." *Lederle Laboratories Newsletter* (Pearl River, New York), n.d., pp. 6–9.

"Yellapragada Subba Row: Man with a Mission." *Your Health* (Calcutta, India), January 1954, pp. 22–24.

Jane Singh

STANLEY SUE

(1944–   )

Educator, Psychologist

Stanley Sue, professor of psychology, has done extensive research on the adjustment of, and the delivery of mental health services to, culturally diverse groups. A Chinese American, he is director of the National Research Center on Asian American Mental Health, a federally funded research center at the University of California at Los Angeles.

Sue was born on February 13, 1944, in Portland, Oregon. He attended high school in Portland, first at a technical school and later at a college preparatory school, where he developed an interest in psychology. Sue attended the University of Oregon and received a Bachelor of Science degree in 1966. He then studied at the University of California at Los Angeles and received his Master of Arts degree in 1967 and his Ph.D. in 1971.

Some of Sue's early research at UCLA found that Asian Americans tend to underutilize mental health services relative to their population, and that the few who do use mental health services are more severely disturbed. These findings aroused Sue's curiosity, and he was encouraged by colleagues to pursue his interests in ethnic research.

Sue was a predoctoral fellow at the UCLA Psychological Clinic and Student Health Psychiatric Services from 1969 to 1971. He was assistant and then associate professor of psychology at the University of Washington from 1971 to 1981. Sue has been professor of psychology at the University of California at Los Angeles since 1981. He served as associate dean of the UCLA Graduate Division from 1986 to 1988. Since 1988 he has been director of the National Research Center on Asian American Mental Health, which is engaged in research on assessing the prevalence of mental health problems in Asian Americans, determining the factors that predict positive treatment outcomes, and evaluating the effectiveness of mental health services.

Sue received the 1986 Award for Distinguished Contributions to Psychology in the Public Interest from the American Psychological Association. In 1989 he was honored by the Los Angeles County Society of Clinical Psychologists for Distinguished Contributions to Clinical Psychology. The Asian American Psychological Association honored Sue in 1990 with its Distinguished Contribution Award. He won an Outstand-

Stanley Sue

ing Mentorship Award from the Society for Community Research and Action in 1991, and the Janet E. Helms Award for Mentoring and Scholarship in Psychology from Columbia University Teacher's College in 1993.

Selected Bibliography

R. Endo, S. Sue, and N. N. Wagner, eds. *Asian-Americans: Social and Psychological Perspectives*. Palo Alto, CA: Science and Behavior Books, 1980.

Getz, W., A. Weisen, S. Sue, and A. Ayers. *Fundamentals of Crisis Counseling*. Lexington, MA: D. C. Heath, 1974.

Kitano, H. H., and S. Sue. "The Model Minorities." *Journal of Social Issues*, vol. 29, no. 2(1973):1–10.

Morishima, J., S. Sue, N. Teng, N. Zane, and J. Cram. *Handbook of Asian-American Mental Health Research*, (vol. I). Washington SC: DHEW Publication, U.S. Government Printing Office, 1979.

Sue, D., D. W. Sue, and S. Sue. *Understanding Abnormal Behavior*, 4th ed. Boston: Houghton Mifflin, 1994.

Sue, S. *Sociocultural Issues in the Assessment and Classroom Teaching of Language Minority Students*. Cross-Cultural Special Education Series, vol. 3. Sacramento: California Department of Education, 1988.

Sue, S., and T. Moore, eds. *The Pluralistic Society: A Community Mental Health Perspective*. New York: Human Sciences Press, 1984.

Sue, S., and J. K. Morishima. *The Mental Health of Asian Americans*. San Francisco: Jossey-Bass, 1982.

Sue, S., and N. N. Wagner, eds. *Asian-Americans: Psychological Perspectives*. Ben Lomond, CA: Science and Behavior Books, 1973.

Franklin Ng

HENRY YUZURU SUGIMOTO

(1900–1990)

Artist

Henry Yuzuru Sugimoto, artist, was born on March 12, 1900, in Wakayama, Japan. When he was a child, Sugimoto enjoyed copying scenes from Japanese scrolls in brush and ink, and he was encouraged by his grandfather to develop his artistic talent. In 1919 his family moved to California, where he attended Hanford High School and participated in swimming, fencing, baseball, and the school orchestra. Though he was a member of the school's swim team, Sugimoto could not practice with his team because he was Japanese (public accommodations were not open to people of color), and his teammates would often go with him to the municipal pool in the evenings, when it was open to him. Sugimoto graduated from Hanford High School in 1924.

In 1924 Sugimoto entered the California College of Arts and Crafts in Oakland, California; he earned a Bachelor of Fine Arts degree, with honors, in 1928. He pursued postgraduate study at the California School of Fine Arts from 1928 to 1929, and then at Academie Colarossi in Paris, France, from 1929 to 1931. In 1931 Sugimoto exhibited his work at the Salon d'Automne in Paris and in 1932 at the Musée de Crecy, which purchased his painting *Passage de Voulangis*.

After he returned to California, Sugimoto's work was featured in a one-man show at the California Palace of Legion of Honor Museum in San Francisco in 1933. In the same year his work was exhibited at the San Francisco Modern Art Museum and he was elected a member of the San Francisco Art Association. Other exhibits followed.

From 1942 to 1945 Sugimoto was interned with other Japanese Americans at Fresno Assembly Center, Jerome War Relocation Center, and Rohwer Relocation Center. While at Jerome and Rohwer camps, he taught high school art classes and painted camp life scenes. In 1944 he

Henry Yuzuru Sugimoto

was featured in a one-man show at Hendrix College Museum in Arkansas and in 1945 at the Baltimore Municipal Museum. He moved to New York City and continued to be featured in exhibitions in the United States throughout the 1950s. In 1962 he returned to Europe to study. His work was seen at the Salon des Artistes Français in Paris in 1963.

From 1963 to 1964, and again in 1969, 1972, and 1980, Sugimoto went to Japan, where his work was featured in Tokyo, Wakayama, Nagoya, and Osaka. In 1982 he was awarded the 6th Class, Order of the Rising Sun from the emperor of Japan; Konju hosho and Silver Medal from the Japanese government; and Bunka sho and Gold Medal from the City of Wakayama. In the same year his work was added to the permanent collection of the Tokyo National Museum of Modern Art.

The majority of Sugimoto's paintings were oils and watercolors. He also worked in woodcuts, linoleum, and lithography. His style was broadly French and realistic. His topics included landscapes and still life. Many of his works featured scenes of village life in France and New York City and daily existence in the Japanese American internment camps of World War II. Some of the latter are done on raw canvas acquired from other internees who used them to bring their meager belongings into the camp.

Sugimoto's work has been acquired by a number of museums, public collections, and private collections around the world. These include Musée de Crecy, France; California Palace of Legion of Honor Museum, San Francisco; California College of Arts and Crafts, Oakland; Hendrix College Museum, Arkansas; University of Arkansas; Residence of the Japanese Consul General, New York; Wakayama City Hall, Japan; Wakayama Modern Art Museum, Japan; Hiroshima Peace Memorial Hall, Japan; and Smithsonian Institution, Museum of American History, Washington, D.C.

Sugimoto supported Japanese American organizations such as the Japanese American Citizens League and the Japanese American Association, but for the most part political activities did not appeal to him. He did, however, have a passion for informing and educating people about the internment experience, and he testified before the Commission on Wartime Relocation and Incarceration of Civilians hearings held in New York City.

Sugimoto was married and had two children. He enjoyed raising African violets and Christmas cactus, was an avid New York Mets fan, and was actively involved in the Japanese American United Church. He died on May 8, 1990.

Selected Bibliography

Falk, Peter Hastings, ed. *Who Was Who in American Art*. Madison, CT: Sound View Press, 1985.
Hughes, Edan Milton. *Artists in California: 1786–1946*. San Francisco: Hughes Publishing, 1986.

Steve Fugita

BETTY LEE SUNG

(1924–)

Educator, Author

Betty Lee Sung, educator and author, was born in the United States on October 3, 1924, but moved to China with her family when she was nine years old. While in China, her mother died and her father returned to the United States to work. In 1935 Sung and her older brother and sister fled the invading Japanese army and joined their father in Washington, D.C. Sung attended the University of Illinois, studying economics and

Betty Lee Sung

sociology, and was elected to Phi Beta Kappa, Phi Kappa Phi (all-university honorary), and Alpha Kappa Delta (sociology honorary). She received her Bachelor of Arts degree in 1948. Sung received a M.L.S. degree in library science from Queens College of the City University of New York in 1968, and a Ph.D. in sociology from the University's Graduate Center in 1983.

After earning her Bachelor's degree, she became a radio script writer for the federally funded radio show Voice of America; she researched and wrote weekly programs about the lives of Chinese people in America that were broadcast throughout Asia. She found many stereotypes and little accurate information on Chinese Americans in the libraries she consulted, and this provided motivation for her future research and writing.

From 1954 to 1960 Sung concentrated on her family, eventually raising eight children. She was associate editor of *Islands in the Sun Club* Magazine from 1960 to 1961 and worked as an editor at several publishing companies in the 1960s and as a librarian at the Queens Borough Public Library.

Sung joined the faculty of City College of New York in 1970, advancing from instructor to professor and chair of its Department of Asian Studies. She initiated the first Asian American studies courses on the East Coast there in 1970. Sung retired from the college in 1992.

Sung's first book, *Mountain of Gold* (1967), the story of the Chinese experience in America, is based on her Voice of America scripts. It won a Special Award for Cultural Achievement from the Federation of Overseas Chinese in 1971. *The Chinese in America* (1973) is a children's book, and *Album of Chinese Americans* (1977) is a pictorial study of Chinese Americans. In 1976 Sung published *Survey of Chinese American Manpower and Employment*, based on research funded by the Department of Labor using a special tabulation of the 1970 Census. It won the Outstanding Book of 1976 Award from *Choice* magazine. *Statistical Profiles of the Chinese in the United States, 1970* (1979) is based on the 1970 Census as well. Sung's next two books, *Transplanted Chinese Children* (1979) and *Adjustment Experience of Chinese Immigrant Children in New York City* (1987), focus on the immigration experience of children. Some of this research was funded by a grant from the Department of Health, Education, and Welfare. Sung's latest book is *Chinese American Intermarriage* (1990). Her current research is a history of New York's Chinatown. Sung was awarded grants from the Chiang Ching Kuo Foundation and the National Endowment for the Humanities to establish a database for retrieval of archival records of early Chinese immigrants in U.S. archives.

Sung was honored in 1986 with the Champion of Excellence Award of the Organization of Chinese Americans. She was Honoree of the Year of the Chinese Alumni Association of City College of New York in 1987. Sung was honored by the Asian American Studies' 6th Annual Conference in 1989 with its Outstanding Service Award. She received the Distinguished Service Award in 1990 from the Asian Pacific American Librarians Association.

Sung is married to Charles C. M. Chung. They have eight grown children.

Selected Bibliography

McAlee, John J. "Mountain of Gold." *Best Sellers,* December 1, 1967, p. 357.
Towle, Lisa H. "Setting the Record Straight." *Clarion* (City College of New York), December 1990, pp. 7, 9.
Zia, Helen, and Susan B. Gall, eds. *Notable Asian Americans.* Detroit: Gale Research, 1995.

Franklin Ng

Amy Tan

(1952–)

Author

Novelist Amy Tan was born in Oakland, California, on February 19, 1952. Her father, John Tan, an electrical engineer and a Baptist minister, immigrated to the United States in the late 1940s from Beijing, China. Tan's mother, Daisy, was raised near Shanghai. At the onset of World War II she was able to escape to the United States in 1949, having to leave her two daughters behind. Tan had an older and a younger brother; her older brother and father both died of brain tumors within eight months of each other in 1968. After these deaths, Tan's family lived and traveled in Europe for a year.

Returning to the United States, Tan spent two semesters at Linfield College in McMinnville, Oregon. She then transferred to San Jose City College and later to San Jose State University and changed her major from pre-med to English and linguistics. She received a Bachelor of Arts degree from San Jose State University in 1973 and a Master of Arts degree from the same school in 1974. Tan pursued postgraduate study at the University of California at Berkeley from 1974 to 1976.

Tan became a language development consultant for the Alameda County Association for Retarded Citizens, and later director of a training project for developmentally disabled children. In the early 1980s she began freelance writing for corporate clients, writing speeches for executives and salesmen. Within a few years she was so successful that she was working ninety hours per week.

Tan began writing fiction at this point in an attempt to find her own unique voice. Her first short story, "Endgame," provided her entry into the Squaw Valley Community of Writers, a fiction writer's workshop. Her revised story was published in *FM* and *Seventeen* magazines. She was introduced to literary agent Sandra Dijkstra, who was impressed with Tan's first several stories and marketed them as the beginning of a collection of stories. After a trip to China with her mother to visit her half-sisters, Tan learned that G. P. Putnam and Sons Publishers had offered her a substantial advance for her book. She spent the next four months finishing what was to become her first novel, *The Joy Luck Club*.

The Joy Luck Club, published in March 1989, deals with the conflicted relations between Chinese American mothers and their daughters. An engaging but moving novel, the next month it appeared on the *New York Times* bestseller list. The book was a finalist for the National Book Award for fiction and was also nominated for the National Book Critics Circle Award for Fiction and the *Los Angeles Times* Book Award. It won the Commonwealth Club Gold Award (1989), the Bay Area Book Reviewers Award for Best Fiction (1989), and the American Library Association's Best Book for Young Adults Award (1989).

Tan's second novel, *The Kitchen God's Wife* (1991), is the story of her mother's tragic life in China. It was a 1991 *Booklist* Editor's Choice and was nominated for the Bay Area Book Reviewers' Award. *The Moon Lady* (1992) is a children's book and was illustrated by Gretchen Schields. In 1995 Tan wrote her third novel, *The Hundred Secret Senses*. Departing from her two previous novels, which had explored the ties between mothers and daughters, this book delved into the relations between two half-sisters. The story blends fact and fancy, with references to history and ghosts. Tan's essays and stories have been published in *Atlantic Monthly, McCall's, Threepenny Review,* and *Seventeen*.

Tan married Lou DeMattei, a tax attorney, in 1974. She enjoys playing billiards, skiing, drawing, and piano playing.

Selected Bibliography

Huntley, E. D. *Amy Tan: A Critical Companion*. Westport, CT: Greenwood Press, 1998.

Iyer, Pico. "The Second Triumph of Amy Tan." *Times*, June 3, 1991, p. 67.

Lehmann-haupt, Christopher. "Mother and Daughter, Each with Her Secret." *New York Times*, June 20, 1991, p. B2.

Melwani, Lavina. "Thirty Minutes with Amy Tan: Chinese American Writer Is Her Mother's Daughter." *Asian Week*, February 25, 1994, p. 80.

Tan, A. *The Hundred Secret Senses*. New York: Putnam, 1995.

———. *The Joy Luck Club*. New York: Putnam, 1989.

———. *The Kitchen God's Wife*. New York: Putnam, 1991.

———. *The Moon Lady*. New York: Macmillan, 1992.

Franklin Ng

TOGO WILLIAM TANAKA

(1916–   )

Business Leader

Businessman Togo William Tanaka was born in Portland, Oregon, on January 7, 1916. His family spoke Japanese at home, and he learned to speak, read, and write English when he began school in Hollywood, California. He entered Hollywood High School at age thirteen and graduated at sixteen. He was editor of the *Hollywood High School News*, was awarded an Ephebian Society ring, and earned membership in the California Scholarship Federation. Tanaka then entered the University of California at Los Angeles. He was a reporter for the *Daily Bruin* and a member of the John Dewey Club, Phi Beta Kappa, Pi Sigma Alpha, and Pi Gamma Mu. Tanaka earned a Bachelor of Arts degree, cum laude, in political science in 1936. While at UCLA he worked for the *Kashu Mainichi* (California Daily News), a bilingual daily published in Los Angeles's Little Tokyo district; in his senior year he was hired by the *Rafu Shimpo* (Los Angeles Japanese Daily News). He was English editor there until the newspaper was closed by Executive Order 9066 to evacuate in the spring of 1942.

After being arrested and imprisoned by the FBI for eleven days just after the bombing of Pearl Harbor, Tanaka was incarcerated at the Manzanar War Relocation Center with his wife and first-born daughter. There, he was given the job of "documentary historian." He was later moved to a camp in Death Valley. In 1943 Tanaka applied for a War Information position in Washington, D.C. Enroute he was a guest at a Quaker hostel in Chicago with his family; he volunteered there for work with the American Friends Service Committee. For three years he worked to find jobs and housing and to increase community acceptance for refugees from Auschwitz, Bergen Belsen, and other Nazi death camps of Europe, as well as for Japanese Americans who had been released from the war relocation centers.

In 1945 Tanaka got a job with the American Technical Society, textbook publishers in Chicago; in two years he became head of the Editorial Department. He remained with American Technical Society until 1955, having pursued studies at the University of Chicago in 1944 and the American School in Chicago in 1946–1947. Tanaka also co-founded Chicago Publishing Corporation, which published *Scene* magazine in three

Togo William Tanaka

languages; *Asia Scene*, of Tokyo, grew from that effort. In 1955 Tanaka and his family returned to Los Angeles, and he founded School-Industrial Press. In 1963 he acquired a real estate investment corporation, Gramercy Enterprises. From 1979 through 1988, he served as a director of the Federal Reserve Bank of San Francisco.

Tanaka has co-authored *English Composition and Rhetoric* (with Frank K. Levin, 1948), *How to Talk More Effectively* (with Dr. Jean Bordeaux, 1948), and *Easy Pathways in English* (with Alma Meland, 1949).

He has served the community in a wide range of organizations, including Goodwill Industries of Southern California, Methodist Hospital of Southern California, the American Heart Association, Boy Scouts of America, the Commission of Innovation for California Community Colleges, and Whittier College. He is a past president of Los Angeles Rotary Number 5.

Tanaka is married and has three children and five grandchildren.

Steve Fugita

CHANG LIN TIEN

(1935–   )

Educator

Chang Lin Tien, educator and university administrator, was born in Wu-han, China, on July 24, 1935. He received a Bachelor of Science degree from National Taiwan University in 1955 and a Master of Mechanical Engineering degree from the University of Louisville in 1957. Tien next studied at Princeton University, receiving a Master of Arts and a Ph.D. in mechanical engineering in 1959. His research interests include heat transfer, radiative heat transfer, thermal insulation and enclosure convection, and reactor safety heat transfer.

Tien began teaching at the University of California at Berkeley in 1959, becoming chairman of the Thermal Systems Division in 1969 and vice chancellor for research in 1983. He was named chancellor in 1990. Tien has served as a consultant to numerous organizations, including Lockheed Missile & Space Company (1963–1980) and General Electric (1972–1980). He has been associate editor of the *Journal of Quantum Spectros and Radiative Transfer* since 1971, and editor of the *International Journal of Heat and Mass Transfer* since 1981.

From 1988 to 1990 Tien was executive vice-chancellor at the University of California at Irvine. An able administrator who worked well with faculty and students, he also showed himself to be interested in providing a supportive environment for students of color. He frequently encouraged student attendance at conferences and made available a wide variety of multicultural activities for members of the student body.

In 1990 Tien was appointed chancellor of the University of California at Berkeley. The selection marked only the second time that an Asian American has headed a major research university, the first being Dr. Fujio Matusda of the University of Hawaii. Tien has continued his style of maintaining good relations with faculty and students, frequently walking across campus to be available to hear their concerns. His leadership and vision have been severely tested at a time when California has had to face a weak economic climate exacerbated by earthquakes, fires, natural disasters, and military base closures. He has witnessed the early retirement of many prominent senior faculty, some of them Nobel Prize winners, who are being replaced in an effort for the university

Chang Lin Tien

to retain its preeminent status among other institutions of higher learning by hiring younger scholars instead.

Nevertheless Tien has shown himself to be an adept leader. He has forcefully asked legislators to maintain the highest levels of state support for quality education and research at the University of California. He has also affirmed the importance of the university being responsive to the cultural diversity of the state's population and has been a strong advocate for affirmative action at the University of California. Throughout the United States, and especially in the San Francisco Bay Area, Tien has been a featured speaker and participant in many Asian American activities.

Tien married Di Hwa Liu in 1959. They have three children.

Selected Bibliography

Morain, Dan. "Chancellor Says Funding Research Is Best Economic Cure." *Los Angeles Times*, February 25, 1992.

Schoch, Russell. "A Conversation with Chang-Lin Tien." *California Monthly*, September 1990.

Shao, Mario. "He's Seen Our Future." *World Monitor*, July 1992.

Tien, C., ed. *Thermal Control and Radiation*. Cambridge, MA: MIT Press, 1973.

Tien, C., and J. Lienhard. *Statistical Thermodynamics*. New York: Holt, Rinehart, and Winston, 1971.

Tien, Chang-Lin. "Affirming Affirmative Action." *A. Magazine*, June/July 1995, pp. 87–88.

———. "Tool for a Colorblind America." *Honolulu Advertiser*, July 20, 1995.

Franklin Ng

SAMUEL CHAO CHUNG TING

(1936–)

Nuclear Physicist

Samuel Chao Chung Ting, Nobel Prize–winning nuclear physicist, was born on January 27, 1936, in Ann Arbor, Michigan. His parents, K. H. Ting (an engineering professor) and Jeanne M. Wong Ting (a psychology professor), were students at the University of Michigan, and the family returned to China a few months after Ting's birth. Ting was educated in China, excelling in mathematics, science, and history, and returned to the United States in 1956 to attend the University of Michigan. He began there as an engineering student but soon changed to physics. Ting received his B.S.E. degree in both physics and mathematics in 1959, his M.S. degree in physics in 1960, and his Ph.D. in physics from the same university in 1962.

In 1963 Ting was awarded a Ford Foundation fellowship to pursue research at the European Organization for Nuclear Research in Geneva, Switzerland. While there, he worked with Italian physicist Guiseppe Cocconi on the proton synchrotron, a kind of particle accelerator. A year later Ting became an instructor at Columbia University in New York. In 1966 he took a leave of absence from Columbia to become leader of a research group at the Deutsches Elektronen Synchroton in Hamburg, Germany. This group built a double-arm spectrometer and conducted experiments to study pairs of particles. In 1969 Ting was appointed professor of physics at the Massachusetts Institute of Technology, and in 1977 he was selected to be the Institute's first Thomas Dudley Cabot Institute Professor.

Ting won the Nobel Prize for Physics (with Stanford University physicist Burton Richter) in 1976 for "pioneering work in the discovery of a heavy elementary particle of a new kind." Ting called the new kind of particle the J particle. It provided experimental evidence for the existence of a fourth type of quark, called charm. Ting also received the Ernest Orlando Lawrence Award from the U.S. government in 1976 and the Eringen Medal from the Society of Engineering Science in 1977. The Government of Italy presented Ting with the DeGasperi Award in Science in 1988.

Ting's research in physics has centered on experimental particle physics, quantum electrodynamics, and the interaction of photons with matter. Some of his most important contributions to the field include the discovery of the anti-deuteron, the J particle, and gluon jets; a twenty-year series of experiments testing the validity of quantum electrodynamics and showing that electrons, muons, and tau mesons are pointlike particles; precision studies of leptonic decays of vector mesons, measuring the branching ratio and the production phase of these photon-like particles and providing an important check of the validity of the quark model; a study of photoproduction of vector mesons demonstrating the similarity between photons and vector mesons; a systematic study of muon pair production to investigate the scaling behavior and production mechanisms of heavy photons, and a precision measurement of muon charge asymmetry, demonstrating for the first time the validity of the Standard Electroweak Model.

Ting is a member of the American Academy of Arts and Sciences (1975), Academia Sinica (Republic of China, 1975), and the U.S. National Academy of Sciences (1977). He has been awarded foreign memberships in the Pakistani Academy of Sciences (1984), the Soviet Academy of Sciences (1989), the Hungarian Academy of Sciences (1993), and the Chinese Academy of Sciences (1994). He has received numerous honorary doctorates.

Ting is married and has three children.

Selected Bibliography

Bellini, G., and S. Ting, eds. *The Search for Charm, Beauty, and Truth at High Energies.* New York: Plenum Press, 1984.
Wasson, Tyler, ed. "Ting, Samuel C. C." In *Nobel Prize Winners: An H. W. Wilson Biographical Dictionary.* New York: H. W. Wilson, 1987.

Franklin Ng

EDISON UNO

(1929–1976)

Educator, Author, Activist

Edison Uno, teacher, writer, and activist, was born in Los Angeles, California, on October 19, 1929, the ninth of ten children born to George and Riki Uno. Immediately after the attack on Pearl Harbor in 1941, FBI agents took his father, George Uno, to several internment camps and prevented him from contacting his family for an entire year. While he was in camp, the rest of the Uno family was forced to vacate their home in Los Angeles and move to the assembly center at Santa Anita Race Track. They were then moved to the Amache War Relocation Center in Granada, Colorado, before being reunited with George Uno at the internment camp in Crystal City, Texas. When all the family members, except for George Uno, were released, Edison remained in the camp with his father for a year until he was persuaded to return to Los Angeles to complete his education. He spent more than four years in government camps by the time he finally left to begin high school in October 1946.

Uno was elected senior class president at Marshal High School in addition to being president of the Hi-Y, a YMCA youth group. At age eighteen he became the youngest president of the East Los Angeles Chapter of the Japanese American Citizens League (JACL). He attended Los Angeles State College and then enrolled in Hastings College of Law in San Francisco. Midway through his law school education, he had his first heart attack and was advised by physicians to give up his ambition of becoming a lawyer.

Uno went on to become a manager at an import-export company, the operations manager at the student union at the University of California at San Francisco, and the institution's financial aid officer.

Uno then became an activist for Japanese American concerns. In 1969 he spoke out in favor of the San Francisco State University students who held strikes over the issues of freedom of speech and the rights of ethnic minority students. During the early 1970s, Uno and Raymond Okamura helped organize a campaign that influenced the U.S. government to remove Title II of the Internal Security Act of 1950, a law that gave the president the authority to order detention of persons without trial if they were suspected of being saboteurs or spies during national emergencies. For fifteen years he tried to persuade U.S. Supreme Court justice Earl

Distinguished Asian Americans

Warren to publicly apologize for supporting the removal of the Japanese from California. In a memoir, Justice Warren eventually admitted regretting his role in the incarceration.

Uno worked to have a presidential pardon granted to Iva Toguri, a Japanese American who was found guilty of treason on September 29, 1949. Toguri had been one of the thirteen women broadcasters collectively labeled "Tokyo Rose." The women were hired to host a radio program of music, humor, nostalgia, and news on Tokyo Radio's "Zero Hour" show during World War II. When the war ended, the U.S. government believed that Toguri had utilized her broadcasting position to promote Japanese propaganda during the war. Between 1945 and 1946 she was imprisoned for twelve months, uninformed of the charges against her. She was again arrested on August 26, 1948, in Tokyo and charged with treason. Throughout the 56-day trial she emphasized that her job as a broadcaster only entailed entertaining the U.S. troops and that she had had no intent to betray the United States. However, she was convicted for one "overt act" of treason. She was sentenced to ten years in prison and given a $10,000 fine in addition to losing her American citizenship. Believing in Toguri's innocence, Uno and other members of the JACL publicized the fact that Toguri was enduring unjust imprisonment and humiliation. Their efforts succeeded when in January 1977, President Ford signed a "full unconditional pardon" for Toguri, the first pardon granted in a case of treason.

In addition to political activities, Uno wrote a children's book entitled *Japanese Americans: The Untold Story* (1970). He also assisted in the production of numerous television shows, including "Guilty by Reason of Race," an NBC production. He also taught a course on the evacuation of Japanese Americans at San Francisco State University in the early 1970s. At the age of forty-seven he suffered another heart attack and died on December 24, 1976.

Uno was married to Rosalind Kido. They had two daughters, Elizabeth Ann and Rosann.

Selected Bibliography

Howe, Russell Warren. *The Hunt for "Tokyo Rose."* New York: Madison, 1990.

Japanese American Journey: The Story of a People. San Mateo, CA: Japanese American Curriculum Project, 1985.

National Committee for Iva Toguri, JACL. *Iva Toguri.* San Francisco: National Committee for Iva Toguri, 1976.

Niiya, Brian, ed. *Japanese American History: An A-to-Z Reference from 1868 to the Present.* New York: Facts on File, 1993.

Steve Fugita

CHARLES B. WANG

(1944–)

Entrepreneur, Business Leader

Charles B. Wang has made a reputation in America as a shrewd businessman. In a computer industry known for creativity and individualism, he has found a way to bring together different businesses to form one of this nation's most formidable software giants.

Charles B. Wang was born in Shanghai, China, on August 19, 1944. His father had been a supreme court justice in China, but he brought his family to the United States in 1952 and became a law professor at St. John's University. Charles Wang was raised in New York with his two brothers. Working his way through college, he graduated from Queens College with a Bachelor's degree in mathematics in 1967. Noticing in a newspaper that advertisements for computer programmers were the most numerous, he decided to enter that field.

The Columbia University Electronics Lab hired Wang as a trainee in programming. Four years later he joined the Standard Data Corporation and worked in a department that provided software support for IBM mainframes for company clients. In 1976 he bought out Standard Data Corporation's software division and formed Computer Associates International, Inc. (CA). Knowing about a Swiss software company's desire to market its application program in the United States, Wang entered an arrangement that was satisfactory to both. He would have rights to the program in the United States, and in exchange the Swiss company would have an interest in Computer Associates. The arrangement worked out well, and several years later, in 1981, the firm went public.

Wang continued to employ the strategy of exchanging stock to purchase software companies. In selecting software companies, he always focused on the practical fit of their applications to business and to his production line. He aggressively implemented this strategy and rapidly acquired other firms. All the while, he kept his eye on serving corporate clients who had purchased various hardware systems at different times and later faced the problem of integrating into labor technologies through relevant software. Competitors often found that he was quick to exploit their weaknesses and seize the opportunity to buy them out if they could strengthen his line offerings or business position. He prefers to acquire a company for its products rather than for the opportunity to develop them. A good example is Legent Corporation. Legent specialized in managing networks of mainframes and smaller computers. In 1995 Wang acquired this rival company for $1.8 billion. By 1996 he had acquired over sixty other companies and products.

Far from presiding over a bloated conglomerate, Wang has gained a reputation for efficiency and cost-cutting. Critics charge that he is heartless and relentless in reducing the number of employees in the companies that he buys. Other observers comment that he was avoided redundancy in removing unnecessary executives, managers, and staff. He is particularly intent on avoiding duplication in the legal, marketing, and accounting divisions. Many employees who survive the initial cuts say that he offers generous compensation to his workers. He also provides good benefits such as free breakfasts, child care, and fitness centers. Those who remain with Computer Associates appear to be strongly loyal to Wang.

Charles Wang has compiled a remarkable record as chairman and chief executive officer of Computer Associates. In this role he planned the acquisition of more than 650 software companies. His company offers more than 500 products for large and medium-sized companies and helped to provide support for their computer networks and mainframes. Computer Associates employs more than 9,000 people in 36 countries and had a revenue in 1996 of $3.1 billion. From its humble origins of having four employees in 1976, it is now the second-largest independent software company in the world, behind Bill Gates's Microsoft. *Fortune* magazine has cited CA as being among the top 100 most valued businesses in the United States. The company is showcasing its Unicenter product, that helps manage computer networks that may be widely dispersed. It helps facilitate the flow of information and integrate seemingly incompatible technologies.

Witnesses Bill Gates of Microsoft and John Sculley, the former head of Apple, have been spokespersons and philosophers for the computer industry as a highway to the future, Charles Wang has generally shunned any such visible roles. He does not care to be a high-tech superstar. Instead, he prefers to maintain a low profile and considers himself more of a manager to broker technology that can serve business. In 1994 he authored a book, *Techno Vision*, that was a guide for business leaders and managers who were not familiar with information technology.

Nevertheless, the public spotlight continues to shine on Wang. In 1996 he returned to the China that he had left forty-five years ago. With his wife, Nancy Li, they toured sites such as the Great Wall, Beijing, and Shanghai and spoke before different audiences such as government leaders, reporters, and students. He is optimistic about helping to provide a powerful computer network for China. In 1996 he also gave $25 million to the State University of New York at Stony Brook to build an Asian American cultural center. The center will be endowed with state-of-the-art technology and wired to handle long-distance learning. It will include an auditorium, meeting rooms, a food court, and an art gallery. Although Wang himself was not an alumnus of the university, he sees it as a way to repay the community that is close to the headquarters of Computer Associates International, Inc. He hopes the Asian American cultural center will promote exchange between East and West in ideas, culture, and cooperation.

Selected Bibliography

Barry, Dan. "Anatomy of a $25 Million Contribution." *New York Times*, December 12, 1996, p. B11.

Cohen, Daniel. "Selling Software the Hard Way." *New York Times Magazine*, September 23, 1990, pp. 50–51, 73–76.

Cortese, Amy. "Sexy? No. Profitable? You Bet." *Business Week*, November 11, 1996, pp. 18, 93, 96, 98.

Karlgaard, Rich. "Charles Wang." *Forbes*, April 11, 1994, pp. S57–58.

Meyer, Michael. "No Sex, Just Scales." *Newsweek*, July 17, 1995, pp. 39–40.

Rapaport, Richard. "Can You Go Home Again? Charles Wang's Return to China." *Forbes*, February 26, 1996, pp. S86–91.

"The Software Scavenger." *Economist*, June 15, 1996, p. 62.

Tyler, Michael. "CA Goes Shopping Again." *Datamation*, August 1, 1994, pp. 50, 54.

Yip, Alethea. "Software Tycoon." *Asianweek*, December 14, 1996, p. 9.

Franklin Ng

WAYNE WANG

(1949–   )

Filmmaker, Director

Wayne Wang, film director, was born on January 12, 1949. His father, Wang Shen Lin, was an engineer and businessman from Shanghai who fled across the border into Hong Kong with his wife and first son just a few days before Wang's birth. The family settled in Hong Kong, where Wang attended an English-language Jesuit school. In 1967, at age seventeen, Wang sailed to California to attend Foothill College in Los Altos.

Originally planning to become a medical doctor or a dentist, Wang was intrigued by an art class and transferred to the California College of Arts and Crafts. There he studied painting, photography, and film. He received his Bachelor's and Master's degrees in film before moving back to Hong Kong in the early 1970s.

In Hong Kong, Wang worked on a television comedy series for several years and was assistant director for the Chinese sequences of *Golden Needles* (1974). He returned to the United States and filmed *Chan Is Missing* (1982) with grants from the American Film Institute and the National Endowment for the Arts. Wang produced, directed, wrote, and edited the film for a total cost of only $22,000. The film explored aspects of Chinatown and Chinese American culture, gently puncturing stereotypes that had been developed about Chinese Americans. In a comic way, it pointed out that Chinese Americans were diverse and did not conform to any uniform pattern. The film won critical acclaim despite the limitations of its small budget, and it continues to be a minor Asian American classic.

His next film, *Dim Sum: A Little Bit of Heart*, followed in 1984. It was a comedy focusing on the relationship between a Chinese mother and her American-born daughter who had not married. The film did not receive much attention among mainstream audiences, but it won praise from those who were familiar with the Chinese American community. Five years later Wang produced *Eat a Bowl of Tea* (1989). Based on **Louis Chu**'s novel by the same name (1961), the story revolves around New York's bachelor society in Chinatown. Because of exclusion and discrimination, the Chinese community in America had a heavily skewed ratio of men to women, with the former being dominant. Although the film received favorable reviews, it did not enjoy widespread box office success.

All that changed with *The Joy Luck Club* (1993), a film adaptation of the novel by **Amy Tan**. The story is an intricate one involving four pairs of mothers and daughters and the generational misunderstandings and reconciliation that take place. When news leaked out that Tan's bestseller would appear as a film, many wondered how the plot would be presented in a film. Would audiences be confused or alienated by the big cast of leading characters, the eight women in the roles of mothers and daughters? Wayne Wang worked closely with Amy Tan and Ronald Bass, who wrote the screenplay. Produced by Hollywood Pictures, a division of Walt Disney Studios, the film had a budget of $10.5 million.

Once the film appeared in theaters, it became a box office success. Film critics gave it good reviews. Stories soon circulated about how viewers went to the movies with handkerchiefs and tissues "for a good cry." It was a film that had universal appeal, and moviegoers found it sensitive and insightful in portraying the emotions of women. Wayne Wang's *The*

Joy Luck Club was an important milestone for Asian American filmmaking, for it demonstrated that even with a mostly Asian American cast, a film with certain requisite elements could have crossover success with a general audience. It also marked a growing trend of Asian American film directors enjoying critical acclaim. These include **Steven Okazaki** and Arthur Dong.

Wayne Wang has also produced the films *Dim Sum Take Out* (1987), *Slamdance* (1987), and *Life Is Cheap . . . But Toilet Paper Is Expensive* (1990). His film *Smoke* (1995), made with novelist Paul Auster, received favorable reviews as well. The film centered around a Brooklyn cigar-store manager who took photographs in front of his store each day at the same time for fourteen years. *Blue in the Face* (1995), another film collaboration with Auster, was a sequel to *Smoke*. His most recent film, *Chinese Box* (1998), starring Jeremy Irons and Chinese movie star Gong Li, is about the takeover of Hong Kong by China in 1997.

Wayne Wang is married to the Hong Kong actress Cora Miao. He became a U.S. citizen in 1984.

Select Bibliography

Chiu, Tony. "Wayne Wang—He Made the Year's Unlikeliest Hit." *New York Times*, May 30, 1982, pp. 17, 35.

Hsiao, Andy. "The Man on a 'Joy Luck' Ride." *Washington Post*, September 27, 1993, pp. B1, B3.

Kasindorf, Martin. "Wayne Wang's Subtle Film Punch." *New York Newsday*, August 3, 1989, pp. 3, 13.

Weinraub, Bernard. "I Didn't Want to Do Another Chinese Movie." *New York Times*, September 5, 1993, pp. 7, 15.

Franklin Ng

YUNG WING

(1828–1912)

Activist

Yung Wing figures in almost every account of Chinese modernization in the nineteenth century. As the first Chinese to graduate from a university in the United States, he played an important role in trying to help others receive a Western education. His failure to achieve success demonstrated some of the difficulties faced by those who tried to reform China. His name, Yung Wing, is the Cantonese pronunciation of *Jung Hung*.

Yung Wing was born in the village of Nam Ping in the Hsiangsham district (now Chungshan) of Guangdong province near Macao on November 17, 1828. His parents were Yung Ming-kun and Lin Lien-tai. He was sent to Protestant missionary schools, first in Macao in 1835 and then in 1841 at the Morrison Educational Society school in Hong Kong. When his teacher in Hong Kong, Samuel Robbins Brown, returned to the United States in 1847, he offered to take Yung Wing and two other Chinese with him. They arrived in Massachusetts, and Yung Wing was enrolled in the Monson Academy. Thereafter he entered Yale University in 1850 and earned his degree in 1854, becoming the first Chinese to graduate from an American university. During his years at the university he largely supported himself by working at a boarding house and being a librarian at a literary society. He also became a naturalized citizen of the United States in 1852.

In 1855 Wing returned to China to work in a variety of jobs. He served as a secretary to Dr. Peter Parker, the U.S. commissioner at Canton. He also was employed as an interpreter for the Supreme Court of Hong Kong. In 1856 he moved north to work as a translator for the Imperial Customs in Shanghai. He next worked for a tea and silk merchant before entering the same business himself. In all these jobs, his Western education was of benefit to him.

In the 1860s Chinese officials such as Tseng Kuo-fan and Li Hung-chang were inaugurating a policy of national "self-strengthening." After China had experienced defeats by European powers in the Opium Wars, fought between the Ch'ing dynasty of China and Great Britain in 1842, these officials wished to strengthen the country by adopting Western technology and methods. In 1864 Tseng Kuo-fan commissioned Wing to go to the United States to purchase machinery for the Kiangnan Arsenal near Shanghai. Three years later Wing persuaded Tseng to set up a school to train mechanics. By now he had been made an official and also served as a translator for the Chinese government.

Having studied in the United States, Wing was convinced that Chinese youth should be sent to study in the West. It would be practical and efficient, and China would not have to rely on foreign advisors or constantly buy expensive machinery because the Chinese students could learn about modern technology and introduce it to China themselves. Tseng Kuo-fan and Li Hung-chang endorsed the idea, proposed it to the throne, and in 1872 won approval for an educational mission to be sent to the United States.

Yung Wing and other Chinese officials were to supervise the 120 Chinese boys who made up the Chinese Educational Mission. The headquarters was located at Hartford, Connecticut, but the students were boarded with different families in the Connecticut Valley. The suggestion for this policy appears to have been made by Yale College president Noah Porter. In 1875 Wing married Mary Louisa Kellogg, the daughter of a New England doctor, with whom he had two children—Morrison Brown Yung and Bartlett G. Yung.

Meanwhile, the Chinese students acculturated quickly to American speech, dress, and deportment. Given their youth, this was to be expected. But the other more conservative Chinese officials were alarmed by the changes and the youths' neglect of Chinese studies. Ch'en Lanpin, a co-commissioner of the Chinese Educational Mission, and other officials complained to Li Hung-chang and others in Peking. In 1881 the Chinese government recalled the mission and the Western schooling came to an end. Former president Ulysses S. Grant and writer Mark Twain tried to intercede on behalf of Wing, but their effort was ultimately unsuccessful. The fact that the mission expenses were high, and the disclosure that the Chinese students could not be admitted to the U.S. Military Academy at West Point and the U.S. Naval Academy at Annapolis may have been considerations in the mission being recalled.

Despite the failure of the mission, many of the Chinese Educational Mission students were destined to be important leaders in China. T'ang Shao-i became the first premier of the Republic of China, and Liang Tunyen later served as the foreign minister for China. Admiral Ts'ai T'ingkan was a noted officer, and Jung K'uei served as part of the Chinese Legation in Washington for more than forty years. Though their education in the United States had been cut short, their knowledge of the West was helpful in their future careers.

Wing returned to China in 1882 but rejoined his wife in Hartford in 1883. He continued to be concerned about China's fate and remained deeply involved in relevant negotiations, enterprises, and projects. He was associated with reformers Liang Ch'i-ch'ao and K'ang Yu-wei, acting as an interpreter when the latter visited President Roosevelt in the White House in 1905–1906. In 1908 he supported the revolutionary leader Sun Yat-sen and his cause. In the next year he published an autobiography, *My Life in China and America* (1909). Three years later Yung Wing died on April 21, 1912, in Hartford. His wife, Mary Louisa Kellogg, had died before him on June 28, 1886.

Selected Bibliography

Clausen, Edwin. "With Open Arms: Chinese Students and Life in Nineteenth-Century American Society." In Lee Cat To, ed., *Early Chinese Immigrant Societies: Case Studies from North America and British Southeast Asia.* pp. 41–63.

LaFargue, Thomas C. *China's First Hundred.* Pullman, WA: State College of Washington, 1942.

———. "Jung Hung." In Arthur W. Hummel, ed., *Eminent Chinese of the Ch'ing Period (1644–1912).* Washington, DC: Government Printing Office, 1943, pp. 402–405.

Latourette, Kenneth Scott. "Yung Wing." In Dumas Malone, ed., *Dictionary of American Biography.* New York: Charles Scribner's Sons, 1964, pp. 638–639.

Leung, Edwin Pak-wah. "Education of the Early Chinese Students in America." In Genny Lim, ed., *The Chinese American Experience.* San Francisco: Chinese Historical Society of America and Chinese Culture Foundation of San Francisco, 1984, pp. 203–210.

Wing, Yung. *My Life in China and America.* New York: H. Holt and Company, 1909.

Franklin Ng

ANNA MAY WONG

(1907–1961)

Actress

Anna May Wong was the first well-known Chinese American actress. She acted in over a hundred silent film and sound screen pictures in a career spanning forty years.

Anna May Wong was born on January 3, 1907, in Los Angeles, to Wong Sam Sing and Lee Gon Toy. The second of eight children, she was named Liu Tsong by her parents. While her parents operated a laundry business, she attended public schools and helped them in their work. For amusement she often went to the local nickelodeons and was fascinated by silent films. She frequented casting offices and lined up at studios, hoping for parts as an extra. In 1919 she received her first role as an extra in the *The Red Lantern* and then in *Dinty* in 1920. Other minor roles followed: *Bits of Life* (1921), *The First Born* (1921), *Shame* (1921), and *Thundering Dawn* (1922).

Anna May Wong played her first leading role in *The Toll of the Sea* (1922). In that film she portrayed a Chinese girl who married a white man in China, only to meet with tragedy in America. Several other movies followed, including *Peter Pan* (1924), in which she played the role of Tiger Lily. But her real rise to fame came in *The Thief of Baghad* (1924), which featured Douglas Fairbanks. As a scantily clad Mongol slave girl, she captured moviegoers' interest as a sexy symbol of the mysterious and exotic East. With her striking beauty and poise she was a favorite of photographers, who found her attractive and glamorous. Publicists delighted in writing about her as a Chinese flapper-turned-screen-siren.

Anna May Wong was never cast in movies that did justice to her intelligence, beauty, and talent. The motion picture industry of the 1920s and 1930s consistently cast her in films pertaining to China, Chinatown, or sinister neighborhoods. Despite her popularity she was relegated to "B" quality plots and scripts. They involved mysteries and melodramas calling for her to act as either a helpless victim or an evil villain. It was a time when Hollywood subscribed to a star system limited to whites and screen images reflected racial and sexual stereotyping. By 1928 she had appeared in many low-budget genre films that placed her in these typecast roles. These films included *Mr. Wu* (1927), *The Devil Dancer* (1928), and *Chinatown Charlie* (1928).

Disappointed by her lack of challenging roles, Anna May Wong chose to try her luck in Europe. While under contract to Richard Eichberg she was cast in a leading role in her first German film, *Song* (1928). She was delighted by the critical acclaim that she received from the critics in Berlin. She starred in other films for Eichberg, but her performance in the English film *Picadilly* (1929) deserves mention. She starred as Sho Sho in this film by Alfred Hitchcock, which was nominated as one of the ten best films in Europe. During her time in Europe she learned to speak German and French fluently and to master the English accent. She also performed on the stage in Europe, showing talent in singing and dancing. In London she worked with Laurence Olivier in *Circle of Chalk* (1929). In Vienna she wrote and acted in a musical play entitled *Tschun-Tshi*. Europe welcomed her warmly, conferring on her international status as a celebrated star of stage and screen.

Despite the fame that she achieved abroad, Anna May Wong yearned to return to the United States. Although the country was in the throes of the Great Depression, she appeared on Broadway for the first time in Edgar Wallace's successful play *On the Spot* (1930), portraying a spiteful half-caste Chinese. In the next year she went to Hollywood to star in the title role of Ling Moy in *Daughter of the Dragon* (1931). The movie with a "yellow peril" theme (also known as *Gelbe Gefahr* in German, this refers to Asians who were considered a menace to Western civilization in the nineteenth century) was based on Sax Rohmer's novel *Daughter of Fu Manchu*. From 1932 to 1935 she appeared in a series of mystery and suspense melodramas such as *A Study in Scarlet* (1933), *Limehouse Blues* (1934), *Chu Chin Chow* (1934), and *Java Head* (1935). Her most notable role was in Josef von Sternberg's *Shanghai Express* (1932). Acting as a cool and nonchalant heroine who smoked, she played opposite Marlene Dietrich. Wong's performance in this classic film marked the peak of her career.

In 1935 Metro-Goldwyn-Mayer Studio offered Anna May Wong a supporting role of a vindictive concubine in the film adaptation Pearl S. Buck's *The Good Earth*. Desiring the lead role, she turned it down. The lead was given to Luise Rainer, who later won an Oscar for her performance. In January 1936, Anna May Wong decided to make her first visit to China. While there, she was dismayed to find that officials were critical of her negative portrayals of Chinese in her films. She explained that she was restricted in the roles that were available to her. In 1937 she acted in *Daughter of Shanghai*, a film that depicted the Chinese favorably. Although she was cast in other films during the 1930s, they were of the "B" category variety.

When Japanese forces invaded China in 1937, Anna May Wong joined with other Chinese Americans to raise funds to help in relief efforts. She acted in several films about the war in Asia, such as *Bombs over Burma* (1942) and *The Lady from Chungking* (1942). She also entertained American soldiers. After the war she acted only intermittently in films. In 1949 she appeared in *Impact* and in 1953 in *Ali Baba Nights*. She had by many accounts become a recluse in her Santa Monica home, which she shared with her brother Richard. She occasionally played guest roles in television shows such as "Wyatt Earp" and "The Big Valley." She had a small part as Tani, Lana Turner's maid, in *Portrait in Black* (1960). *The Savage Innocents*, in which she played Hiko, was released in 1961 and was her last film. She died in Santa Monica on February 3, 1961.

For students of her career, such as Judy Chu, Emma Gee, and Garland Richard Kyle, Anna May Wong was a Chinese American film pioneer. Aspiring to be a successful actress, she faced almost insurmountable odds in trying to escape stereotyped roles. The Hollywood of her era reserved star status for actresses such as Dorothy Lamour, Luise Rainer, or Myrna Loy, not an Anna May Wong. Nevertheless, she tried to craft a professional career as well as she could within the limitations of her era.

Selected Bibliography

"Anna May Wong Is Dead at 54; Actress Won Movie Fame in '24." *New York Times*, February 4, 1961.

Chu, Judy. "Anna May Wong." In Emma Gee, ed., *Counterpoint: Perspectives on Asian America*. Los Angeles: Asian American Studies Center, University of California, 1976, pp. 284–288.

Gee, Emma. "Wong, Anna May." In Barbara Sicherman and Carol Hurd Green, eds., *Notable American Women: The Modern Period. A Biographical Dictionary*. Cambridge, MA: Harvard University Press, 1980, pp. 744–745.

Kyle, Garland Richard. "The Legend of Anna May Wong." *Gum Saan Journal*, vol. II, no. 2 (December 1988): 7–11.

Franklin Ng

JADE SNOW WONG

(1923–   )

Ceramicist, Author, Entrepreneur

Jade Snow Wong, ceramicist, writer, and businesswoman, was born in San Francisco in 1922. She was the fifth daughter in a family of seven children. Her award-winning autobiography, *Fifth Chinese Daughter* (1950), describes her childhood as a Chinese American girl. Despite her father's disapproval, Wong attended City College of San Francisco, earning an Associate of Arts degree in 1940. She earned a Bachelor of Arts degree in economics and sociology from Mills College in 1942 and was elected to Phi Beta Kappa. In 1976 she was awarded an honorary Doctor of Humane Letters degree from Mills College.

Wong went on to develop her career as a ceramicist, working in enamels and pottery. Her work has been displayed in one-woman shows at the Chicago Art Institute, the Detroit Institute of Arts, the Joslyn Memorial Museum (Omaha), and the Portland Art Museum, as well as in Singapore, Kuala Lumpur, Penang, Rangoon, Calcutta, Delhi, and Karachi. She has participated in group exhibitions at the National Ceramic Exhibitions (1947–1951), the Cincinnati Art Museum, the Denver Art Museum, the M. H. de Young Memorial Museum (San Francisco), the Museum of Modern Art (New York City), the Oakland Art Museum, the San Francisco Museum of Modern Art, the Smithsonian Institution's National Collection of Fine Arts, and the Chinese Culture Center (San Francisco). Wong's work is part of the permanent collections of the Detroit Institute of Arts, Florida State University, the International Ceramic Museum (Faenza, Italy), the Joslyn Memorial Museum (Omaha), the Metropolitan Museum of Art (New York City), and the Oakland Art Museum.

Wong's autobiographical work, *Fifth Chinese Daughter*, won the Commonwealth Club's Silver Medal for Non-Fiction in 1951, and it was a Book of the Month Club and Christian Herald Family Book Shelf Selection. The book itself is frequently cited by those who seek to analyze facets of Chinese American literature or life in San Francisco's Chinatown. Her autobiography makes it clear, however, that Wong possessed a strong personality and independence that allowed her as a woman to rebel against her family and achieve success despite prevailing attitudes and her father's opposition. Her next book, *No Chinese Stranger* (1975), continues her story as a wife, mother, and traveler to China.

Wong operates Jade Wong Studios, a retail ceramic outlet for her work, and also operates a travel agency that she and her husband established. They were among the first to lead tours to Japan, and Wong has traveled extensively throughout Asia.

Wong has been active in her community, serving organizations such as the Chinese Culture Foundation of San Francisco, the California Council for the Humanities, the Center for the Pacific Rim, the San Francisco Public Library, and the Friendship Library in Shanghai. She has won a number of honors, including the Pioneer Award from the Asian American Teachers Association (1992), the Distinguished Service/Cultural Award from the Chinese Cultural Center, the Woman Warrior Award for Outstanding Contribution in Literature and Service from the Pacific Asian Women Bay Area Coalition, and two Awards of Merit for Outstanding Public Service from the City and County of San Francisco. *Fifth Chinese Daughter* was made into a PBS special in 1976 and won an award at the 1977 American Film Festival in New York.

Wong married Woodrow Ong on August 29, 1950, and was widowed in 1986. She has four children.

Selected Bibliography

Wong, J. *Fifth Chinese Daughter*. Seattle: University of Washington Press, 1989.
    (Originally published by Harper, New York, in 1950.)
———. *No Chinese Stranger*. New York: Harper & Row, 1975.

                                                                Franklin Ng

CHIEN-SHIUNG WU

(1912–1997)

Physicist

Chien-Shiung Wu, experimental physicist, was born in Liuhe, a small town near Shanghai, China, on May 29, 1912. Her father, Wu Zhongyi, had participated in the Chinese Revolution of 1911 and returned to Liuhe after the fall of the Manchu dynasty. Intrigued by the ideas of democracy and women's emancipation, he founded and led the area's first school for girls. His support and influence had marked effects on Wu's education and career. Wu's mother, Fan Fuhua, visited local families, encouraging them to send their daughters to school and to stop the practice of foot-binding.

Wu graduated from her father's school when she was nine years old. She then attended the Soochow Girl's School in Suzhou, with the encouragement of her father and great-great-grandmother. She studied a Western curriculum there and graduated at the head of her class in 1930 at age seventeen. While in high school, Wu pursued the teacher's training program but studied the books of her peers in the academic school at night, gaining the background in sciences and foreign languages she desired.

Wu was accepted to the National Central University in Nanjing and studied mathematics, physics, and chemistry during the summer before she enrolled, again encouraged by her father to pursue her dream of majoring in physics at the university. Wu became a leader in a student underground movement, and despite the political turmoil in China at the time she received her Bachelor of Science degree in 1934. She spent the next two years teaching at a provincial university and doing research in X-ray crystallography at the National Academy of Sciences in Shanghai. Encouraged by her family and her teachers to pursue graduate education in the United States, she left China in 1936. Although she intended to return to China as soon as she earned her Ph.D., Wu never saw her family again.

Wu at first considered attending the University of Michigan, but when she arrived in San Francisco she decided to study at the University of California at Berkeley. There she met Yuan Chia-liu (Luke Yuan), another physics student from China, whom she married in 1942. At this time the physics department at Berkeley included Ernest Lawrence, Robert Oppenheimer, and other prominent physicists, giving Wu the challenging environment she desired. She was recommended by the physics department for fellowships, but because of university prejudice against Asians she did not receive them. When China was invaded by Japan in 1937 and Wu was cut off from her family's support, Berkeley's physics department offered her assistance. Wu received her Ph.D. in 1940 and spent the next two years at Berkeley as a research assistant. Becoming well known for her work in nuclear fission, she lectured throughout the United States in 1941.

Because of prejudice against her as a woman (none of the nation's top twenty research universities at the time had a woman physics professor) and as an Asian (for example, Japanese Americans were being placed in internment camps during World War II), Wu was not hired to teach at Berkeley. In 1942 she taught at Smith College in Northampton, Massachusetts, and in 1943 she accepted a position at Princeton University, where war research had created a shortage of physicists and the university was willing to hire women. In 1944 Wu joined the Division of War Research at Columbia University in New York City and remained at Columbia as a teacher and researcher until her retirement in 1981.

Wu's doctoral thesis contained two parts: a study of the electromagnetic energy given off when a particle going through matter slows down, and a study of the radioactive inert gases emitted when the uranium nucleus splits. Her work for the Division of War Research focused on developing sensitive radiation detectors. From 1946 to 1952 she studied beta decay (the emission of electrons by atoms), confirming a theory that had been developed by American physicist Enrico Fermi but contradicted in a number of experimental trials. In 1956 she turned her attention to the puzzle of the behavior of K-meson particles, which seemed to violate the law of parity (which refers to the concept that in nuclear reactions there are an equal number of particles given out in directions left and right). This problem, conceptualized by **Tsung Dao Lee** of Columbia University and **Chen Ning Yang** of the Institute for Advanced Study in Princeton, New Jersey, became the focus of study for Wu and the team she assembled. Working at the National Bureau of Standards in Washington, D.C., Wu cooled radioactive cobalt nuclei to nearly absolute zero. Then, using a strong magnetic force, the nuclei were aligned and the direction in which electrons were being emitted was detected. The results of the study showed that the law of parity did not always hold true. This was an important step toward a unified theory that could explain both electromagnetic forces and weak forces, which are responsible for several forms of radioactivity.

Lee and Yang won the 1957 Nobel Prize for their conceptualization of the problem; Wu and other physicists were disappointed that she was not included in the prize for her experimental testing of it. Wu did, however, win a number of other prizes and awards for her contribution, including the first Wolf Prize in Physics from the state of Israel (1978). She was the first woman to win a Comstock Award from the National Academy of Sciences (1964) and the first woman to become president of the American Physical Society (1975), winning the Society's Tom Bonner Prize in the same year. Wu was elected to the National Academy of Science and became Pupin Professor of Physics at Columbia (1972–1981). She was awarded the National Medal of Science in 1975. She was Nishina Memorial Lecturer at the Universities of Tokyo, Osaka, and Kyoto in 1983. In 1990 researchers at Nanjing's Mt. Zijin Observatory named a newly discovered asteroid "Wu Chien-shiung's Asteroid."

Wu was a fellow of Academia Sinica and helped establish the first synchrotron radiation center in China.

She married physicist Yuan Chia-liu (Luke Yuan) in 1942. They had one child, Vincent Yuan, who is also a physicist. Wu died in 1997.

Selected Bibliography

Crease, R., and C. Man. *The Second Creation, Makers of the Revolution in Twentieth-Century Physics*. New York: Macmillan, 1986.

Gilbert, L., and G. Moore. *Particular Passions, Talks with Women Who Have Shaped Our Times*. New York: Crown Publishers, 1981.

McGrayne, S. *Nobel Prize Women in Science*. Secaucus, NJ: Carol Publishing Group, 1993.

Segre, E. *From X Rays to Quarks: Modern Physicists and Their Discoveries*. San Francisco: W. H. Freeman, 1980.

Wu, C. S. "Recent Investigations of the Shapes of Beta-Ray Spectra." *Reviews of Modern Physics*, October 1950, p. 22.

————. "Subtleties and Surprises: The Contribution of Beta Decay to an Understanding of the Weak Interaction." *Annals of the New York Academy of Sciences*, November 8, 1977.

Franklin Ng

NGUYEN HUU XUONG

(1933–)

Educator, Activist, Engineer

Nguyen Huu Xuong, known for his scientific research in relation to the "Xuong's Machine," was born in 1933 in Vietnam. He attended high school and college in France, where he graduated with a B.S. degree in electrical engineering in 1955, a M.S. degree in electronic engineering in 1957, and a M.S. degree in math at the Sorbonne in Paris in 1958. Xuong then continued his studies in the United States and received a Master's degree and a Ph.D. in physics from the University of California at Berkeley in 1962. In the same year he joined the faculty at the University of California at San Diego (UCSD), where he is still teaching and has achieved the highly unusual distinction of being professor in three disciplines: biology, chemistry, and physics.

Dr. Xuong's most important achievement was the invention of the "Xuong's Machine," which allows high-speed data collection for protein crystallography and has been used by researchers around the world. His invention allowed researchers to see for the first time what certain proteins look like and to unravel their structure. Xuong has also been doing on-going research on cancer and AIDS. In 1985 the National Institutes of

Health declared the "Xuong's Machine" a national resource, and in 1990 it was used in AIDS study of cells. Dr. Xuong was one of the first scientists to use a computer to analyze photographic film.

Xuong is equally well respected in the community, where he has been actively involved in the refugee cause. He was president of the Vietnamese Alliance Association (1976–1992) and chaired the Boat People S.O.S. Committee (1980–1990), which he founded during the peak period of the boat people crisis when hundreds of thousands of Vietnamese left their homeland in search of freedom and many perished at sea. With the help of funds raised in the community and others donated by European humanitarian organizations, the Committee sent a rescue ship every spring to pick up refugees in the South China Sea. It also provided continuing assistance to the boat people in the Southeast Asian refugee camps. Despite Dr. Xuong's attempts to bring worldwide attention to the plight of the refugees, the Committee's efforts ended in 1991 when formerly receptive nations ceased accepting boat people as refugees.

On the UCSD campus, Dr. Xuong instituted in 1989 a highly successful program that teaches Vietnamese culture, mostly to the younger generation of Vietnamese American students. Over the years he has received a number of awards and honors, including the Guggenheim Fellowship (1965–1966), a NATO Fellowship in 1977, and the UCSD Chancellor Associate Award in 1992. He has been keynote speaker at numerous functions. As an educator he believes that he has a duty to serve society.

Dr. Nguyen Huu Xuong resides in San Diego with his wife and their daughter.

Selected Bibliography

Los Angeles Times, February 12, 1989.
READER, vol. 14, no. 42 (October 24, 1989).
San Diego Union, December 3, 1990.
Who's Who in Technology, 7th ed. Detroit: Gale Research, 1995.

Le Hong Phan

Kristi Yamaguchi

KRISTI YAMAGUCHI

(1971–)

Olympic Medalist (Figure Skater)

Kristi Yamaguchi, figure skater, was born on July 12, 1971, in Hayward, California. She began ice skating at the Southland Rink when she was six years old. Besides spending hours in practice, she skated in show productions and in precision teams. During junior high school Yamaguchi, a Japanese American, became a national competitor and began representing the United States in international competitions. In high school she spent hours practicing before and after school, and by the time she was a junior in high school she had become the first woman to win the Junior World Championships in both ladies' singles and in pairs skating with her partner, Rudy Galindo. During her senior year in high school she made the World Team in both ladies' and pair events. She earned three National Titles during her high school years. Her crowning achievement was winning the gold medal in women's figure skating at the 1992 Winter Olympics in Albertville, France.

Since 1992 Yamaguchi has headlined the skating show tour "Stars on Ice" with skaters Scott Hamilton and Paul Wylie. Each year the show is performed in more than fifty U.S. cities and ten Canadian cities. She has also won the world professional figure skating championship numerous times.

Yamaguchi has been the spokesperson for the Christmas Seals Program of the American Lung Association since 1995. She has also contributed time to the Make-a-Wish Foundation, Rubicon of Fremont, and Daffodil Days for the American Cancer Society. She represents the United States Figure Skating Association's Memorial Fund Campaign to solicit funds for promising young skaters.

Selected Bibliography

Harvey, Randy. "Yamaguchi Is Good Enough for the Gold." *Los Angeles Times*, February 22, 1992, pp. C1, C6.
Janofsky, Michael. "Yamaguchi Not Perfect, But Perfect Enough." *New York Times*, February 22, 1992, pp. 33, 35.

Steve Fugita

CHEN NING YANG

(1922–)

Physicist

Chen Ning Yang, Nobel Prize–winning physicist, was born in Hofei, Anhwei province, China, on September 22, 1922. His father, Ko-Chuan Yang, was a professor of mathematics. In 1929 the family moved to Beijing, where Ko-Chuan Yang joined the faculty of Tsinghua University. After the Japanese invasion of China in 1937 the family moved again, following the relocation of Tsinghua University to K'un-ming. The University became National Southwest Associated University, and Yang earned a Bachelor of Science degree in physics there in 1942. In 1944 he earned a Master of Science degree and in 1945 began doctoral studies at the University of Chicago. He received his Ph.D. in 1948 and taught at the University in the following year.

In 1949 Yang joined the Institute for Advanced Study in Princeton, New Jersey. He later served as senior physicist for a year at Brookhaven National Laboratory on Long Island, New York (1953–1954). In the following year he was named professor of physics at the Institute for Advanced Study. He became the Albert Einstein Professor of Physics at the State University of New York at Stony Brook in 1965.

Yang first met **Tsung Dao Lee** at National Southwest Associated University, and the two physicists' paths crossed again at the Institute for Advanced Study in the 1950s. They began to meet regularly to discuss issues in physics. They became interested in the puzzle of the law of conservation of parity. Yang and Lee examined research reports and discovered that none tested parity conservation in weak interactions. K-mesons, particles that were observed after high-energy bombardment of atomic nuclei, did not appear to conform to the law of conservation of parity. After proposing the problem theoretically, experimental physicists were able to conduct experiments to test parity conservation in weak interactions. **Chien-Shiung Wu**, of Columbia University, working with the National Bureau of Standards, was the first to conduct such an experiment; the results showed that parity is not conserved in weak interactions. Yang and Lee shared the Nobel Prize in Physics in 1957 for their "penetrating investigation of the so-called parity laws, which has led to important discoveries regarding the elementary particles."

Yang's research interests continued to include the theory of fields and particles, statistical mechanics, and symmetry principles. In 1954 Yang and Robert L. Mills of the Brookhaven National Laboratory proposed a principle of particle and field interactions that spurred new developments in gauge theory.

In addition to the 1957 Nobel Prize, Yang received Yeshiva University's Albert Einstein Commemorative Award (1957), the American Academy of Arts and Sciences Rumford Medal (1980), the National Medal of Science (1986), and the Liberty Award (1986).

Yang married Chi L Tu in 1950. They have three children.

Selected Bibliography

Crease, R., and C. Mann. *The Second Creation: Makers of the Revolution in Twentieth Century Physics.* New York: MacMillan, 1986.

Yang, C. *Elementary Particles: A Short History of Some Discoveries in Atomic Physics.* Princeton, NJ: Princeton University Press, 1961.

———. *Selected Papers (1945–1980), with Commentary.* San Francisco: W. H. Freeman, 1983.

Yang, C., M. Ge, and X. Zhou, eds. *Proceedings of the XXI International Conference*

on Differential Geometric Methods in Theoretical Physics. River Edge, NJ:
World Scientific, 1993.

Franklin Ng

MINORU YASUI

(1916–1986)

Attorney, Community Leader

Attorney Minoru Yasui was born in Hood River, Oregon, in 1916. At age
sixteen he graduated as valedictorian of his high school. In 1933 he enrolled at the University of Oregon to study law. He graduated at age
twenty with a 4-point average and Phi Beta Kappa honors. As a ROTC
cadet he served in the Reserve Corps of the United States Army when
he turned twenty-one. Yasui attended the University of Oregon Law
School and in 1939 graduated with honors as the first Japanese American
to complete the school of law in Oregon.

In 1940 he accepted an offer to work as a legal attaché for the Japanese
Consulate in Chicago. He worked for the Consulate until he resigned
and volunteered for the U.S. Army in December 1941. After arriving at
his post at Fort Vancouver, he was immediately rejected on racial
grounds. Yasui returned to Oregon, where the Japanese community had
been experiencing the turmoil of the anti-Japanese movement of World
War II. He spent the next year helping members of the Japanese community file legal papers protecting their property and proving their citizenship. The need for his legal assistance increased when on February
19, 1942, President Franklin Roosevelt signed Executive Order 9066,
which authorized the War department to designate military areas from
which any or all persons may be excluded. The order permitted General
DeWitt of the Western Defense Command to exclude and remove all
persons of Japanese ancestry, both alien and nonalien, from the West
Coast. Believing the order to be racially motivated and unconstitutional,
Yasui tried to persuade other Nisei (second-generation Japanese Americans) to join him in a legal test case. His political voice was officially
heard when he challenged the curfew order issued by General DeWitt
on March 24, 1942, which required persons of Japanese ancestry to be
indoors between 8 P.M. and 8 A.M. After purposefully violating the order,
Yasui was arrested by police of the Second Avenue Station in Portland,

Oregon. During the trial, held in the Federal District Court of Oregon on November 16, 1942, Judge James Fee ruled that the curfew order was unconstitutional as it applied to American citizens. However, Judge Fee also decided that Yasui was guilty of violating the law because his position at the Japanese Consulate supposedly constituted forfeiture of his American citizenship. Yasui then served nine months in prison while he awaited the outcome of an appeal made by his lawyer, Earl Bernard.

On February 19, 1943, Yasui and fellow resistors **Fred Korematsu** and **Gordon Hirabayashi** presented their cases to the court of appeals. The three cases were presented to the Supreme Court in March 1943. Through a procedure called certification, the Supreme Court answered constitutional questions raised by the appellate court, including the ruling on Yasui's citizenship. On June 21, 1943, the Supreme Court ruled that Yasui had not forfeited his American citizenship; it also ruled that the curfew order was constitutional during a national crisis.

Following his release from prison Yasui was placed in a relocation camp in the desert near Minidoka, Idaho. Later, in 1943, Yasui responded to the U.S. War department's recruitment of Nisei to form the 442nd Regiment, a segregated, all Japanese American, army combat team. He volunteered to serve and visited various internment camps to encourage young Nisei men to volunteer. After the military did not accept him owing to his criminal record, Yasui received permission to relocate from Minidoka camp to Chicago, where he temporarily worked at an ice plant. In the fall of that year he moved to Denver, Colorado, where his mother, two sisters, and a brother had relocated. In order to help the resettled Japanese Americans sort out their legal affairs, he planned to practice law in Colorado; however, his past criminal record prevented him from immediately receiving his license. Members of the American Civil Liberties Union assisted in his appeal to the Colorado Supreme Court, which granted a favorable verdict.

In 1948 Yasui traveled throughout the nation to advocate for the Evacuation Claims Act of Congress, which authorized the partial reimbursement of financial losses for Japanese Americans who were incarcerated during World War II. Yasui also actively supported passage of the Walter-McCarran Act of 1952, which enabled Asian aliens to become naturalized American citizens.

For the next twenty years Yasui practiced law in Denver and served the community as a scoutmaster for an ethnic Boy Scout troop, a writer for numerous journals, an editor and producer of a local newspaper, a leader of various public school programs, and an activist for the rights of the poor, disadvantaged, and minority groups. In 1959 he was appointed to the Mayor's Commission of Community Relations in Denver. After eight years as a Commission member, vice-chairman, and chairman, he was appointed to the position of executive director of the Commission. In 1981 he was appointed chair of the National Japanese American Citizens League Committee for Redress. Following his retirement from the Denver Commission of Community Relations in 1983, he began a nationwide campaign to convince the public and U.S. senators to support redress. During that year Yasui and his lawyer, Peter Irons, filed a petition for a writ of error in Portland in order to reverse his conviction of 1943. The District Court of Oregon heard the case and granted the government's motion to reverse Yasui's conviction.

Yasui's contributions to his community were officially recognized beginning in 1976, when the monthly "Min Yasui Community Volunteer" Award was established in Denver. In 1984 the Oregon Bar Association honored him as Lawyer of the Year. During that summer the American Civil Liberties Union honored him at its annual meeting, applauding his stand against the government in defense of Americans' civil liberties. The mayor of Denver, Frederico Pena, and the governor of Colorado, Richard D. Lamm, proclaimed March 3, 1984, as Minoru Yasui Day.

In September 1986 Yasui underwent surgery for lung cancer. However, the malignancy could not be removed. Following the surgery he made his last public appearance at the Minoru Yasui Community Volunteer Awards celebration in Denver and died a few weeks later.

Selected Bibliography

Kim, Hyung-chan, ed. *Dictionary of Asian American History*. New York: Greenwood Press, 1986.

Niiya, Brian, ed. *Japanese American History: An A-to-Z Reference from 1869 to the Present*. New York: Facts on File, 1993.

Takaki, Robert. *Strangers from a Different Shore*. Boston: Ronald Takaki, 1989.

Yasui, Robert S. *The Yasui Family of Hood River, Oregon*. Hood River, OR: Desktop Publishing, 1987.

Steve Fugita

DO NGOC YEN

(1941–)

Journalist, Newspaper Publisher

Do Ngoc Yen, known as the founder of *Nguoi Viet* (the Vietnamese People), a newspaper well received by people in the Vietnamese American communities across America, was born in 1941 in Vietnam, where his newspaper career dated back to his childhood years. As a twelve-year-old boy he worked for an underground high school newspaper. As a teenager he was a student protester leader and with his fellow classmates petitioned the government for more scholarships and better classrooms. He was arrested and consequently suspended from school. He was drafted but could not serve because of his near-sightedness. Yen then became a reporter and editor for newspapers in Saigon. He also worked as an interpreter for French and American journalists.

After the fall of Saigon in April 1975, along with hundreds of thousands of others Yen and his family came to Camp Pendleton, California, as refugees. After taking some odd jobs, he moved with his family to Texas. In 1978 he came back to California after reading about the arrival of some 100,000 boat people. These were Vietnamese refugees who had escaped from Vietnam by boat and were about to be resettled in Orange County, California. Yen saw in the event an opportunity to get back to journalism. He wanted to write the stories of the boat people.

Yen did it on a borrowed typewriter. On December 6, 1978, using the family savings of $4,000, he printed 2,000 copies of his articles. It was the first issue of *Nguoi Viet*. Yen subsequently moved to Santa Ana, Orange County, with his wife and four children. The family rented one bedroom in a two-bedroom apartment. They shared the unit with several others, all journalist friends from Vietnam. Together, many working for free and out of their love for the profession, they continued to publish *Nguoi Viet*. Yen had been the publication editor-in-chief since 1980, and in 1994 he became the newspaper's publisher. Now a corporation with about $1 million in assets and stock, *Nguoi Viet* has offices in Little Saigon in Westminster, California, which is considered the cultural and business center of the Vietnamese community nationwide.

Yen is credited with having started the very first Vietnamese-language, hard-news daily newspaper in the United States. It now has 15,000 subscribers in southern California alone, as well as outside the United States, mostly in France and Australia. As a journalist Yen has always been concerned with staying on neutral political grounds when reporting the news. His newspaper not only reports the news but also chronicles the history of the Vietnamese community and the effects of changes in Vietnam.

Do Ngoc Yen lives in Garden Grove, California. His wife works in the newspaper's circulation and distribution department. One of his proudest moments, he said, was when his daughter graduated from the University of Southern California with a degree in journalism.

Selected Bibliography

Interview with Do Ngoc Yen, August 17, 1997.
Los Angeles Times, April 13, 1997.

Le Hong Phan

Jacqueline E. H. Young

JACQUELINE EURN HAI YOUNG

(1934–   )

Politician, Educator

Jacqueline Eurn Hai Young, the first Korean woman to serve as a U.S. legislator, was born in Honolulu, Hawaii, on May 20, 1934. Her grandparents arrived in Hawaii in 1904 among the first immigrants from Korea to work on the sugar plantations. Her grandfather, Cho Pyung Yo, was dedicated to the Independence Movement in Korea during the Japanese occupation and was an active member of the Korean community in Hawaii. From 1935 to 1947 he served as president of the Korean National Association, Kungminhoe. Young recalls a childhood rich with passionate discussions and community participation, all in the pursuit of equality of life for Koreans and for Korea's independence.

   In 1969 she received a Bachelor of Science degree from the University of Hawaii at Manoa in speech pathology and audiology. She went on to complete a Master's degree at Old Dominion University in Virginia in the area of special education, then a Ph.D. in communication and women's studies from the Union Institute of Ohio in 1989.

Young was elected to the Hawaii State House of Representatives in 1990, the first Korean American to serve as a legislator since 1961 and the first Korean American woman ever to serve in that capacity. In 1992 she was reelected and became vice-speaker of the House, the first woman to hold that position. Since leaving public office in 1994 she has served the Office of the Governor in Hawaii as director of the Office of Affirmative Action and is currently working as a management consultant. She is also an adjunct faculty member at Hawaii Pacific University, teaching courses on culture and gender communication. In 1995 Young founded J Young Productions, which produces television shows about Hawaii.

Selected Bibliography

Who's Who among Asian Americans, 1994–1995 ed. Detroit: Gale Research, 1994.

Jennifer Kang

JUDY YUNG

(1946–   )

Author, Educator

Judy Yung, educator and author, was born on January 25, 1946, in San Francisco, California. Her parents both immigrated from Guangdong, China, her father in 1921 and her mother in 1941. Yung was the fifth daughter in a family of five girls and one boy. Yung's father worked as a gardener, cook, and janitor, and her mother was a garment worker. Yung lived a sheltered life in San Francisco's Chinatown, where she attended public schools. For ten years she also attended Chinese language school after "American" school.

After high school Yung attended San Francisco State College, planning at first to become a secondary education teacher and later a librarian. She received her Bachelor of Arts degree in English literature and Chinese language from San Francisco State College in 1967 (magna cum laude) and her Master of Arts degree in library science from the University of California at Berkeley in 1968. In 1970 she earned the State of

California's Standard Teaching Credential with a specialization in junior college teaching. She received her Ph.D in ethnic studies from the University of California at Berkeley in 1990.

After receiving her Master's degree, Yung went to work at the Main Library of the San Francisco Public Library. Two years later she was assigned to the Chinatown Branch Library. During her time there, Yung's goal was to make the library serve the needs of Chinatown. She developed a Chinese-language collection and an Asian American collection, organized cultural events in the library, and did community outreach to publicize the library's services.

In 1972 Yung left the library to become associate editor of *East West Chinese American Weekly*. There she acquired the skills of a journalist, came to a deeper understanding of Chinatown, and learned to be proud of her Chinese American identity. Representing the weekly, Yung visited the People's Republic of China for the first time in 1974.

Returning to librarianship in 1975, Yung was hired by the Oakland Public Library to start the first Asian Branch Library in the country. With a grant from the California State Library, Yung developed a library that featured a popular multimedia collection for children and adults in six Asian languages, as well as English-language materials on Asia and Asian Americans. The library grew so quickly that it had to move to bigger quarters three times during the six years that Yung was branch librarian.

During this time Yung began to work with **Him Mark Lai** and **Genny Lim** to document the history of Asian Americans by interviewing Japanese immigrants who had been held at Angel Island, a processing center in San Francisco. The group translated the poems that several detainees had copied down from the the barracks walls and published them with the oral histories in *Island: Poetry and History of Chinese Immigrants on Angel Island* (1980). The book won the Before Columbus Foundation American Book Award in 1982 and was republished by the University of Washington Press in 1991.

In 1981 Yung embarked on a two-year research project funded by the U.S. Department of Education, Women's Educational Equity Act Program. Working with Genny Lim again, Yung began a national search for photographs and written accounts by and about Chinese American women. They also conducted over 250 oral history interviews with women of different generational and class backgrounds. Yung developed a pictorial exhibit, which opened at the Chinese Culture Center in San Francisco and traveled on to Honolulu, Seattle, Los Angeles, Houston, Chicago, New York, Boston, Philadelphia, and Washington, D.C. Yung also wrote *Chinese Women of America: A Pictorial History* (1986).

She enrolled in the ethnic studies Ph.D. program at the University of California at Berkeley in 1984 and wrote her doctoral dissertation on

Chinese women in San Francisco. Titled *Unbinding the Feet, Unbinding Their Lives: Social Change for Chinese Women in San Francisco, 1902–1945*, it was published in 1995 as *Unbound Feet: A Social History of Chinese Women in San Francisco*. After receiving her Ph.D. in 1990, Yung became a professor in American studies at the University of California at Santa Cruz.

Yung has received a number of honors, awards, grants, and fellowships, including the Junior Faculty Development Award (University of California at Santa Cruz, 1992–93, 1994–95), Faculty Research Committee Grants (University of California at Santa Cruz, 1990–1991, 1992–1993, 1993–1994, 1994–1995), a Dissertation Fellowship (American Association of University Women, 1988–1989), a Graduate Dissertation Fellowship (University of California at Berkeley, 1988), the Outstanding Asian Women of the Year Award (Asian Women's Resource Center, 1987), and the U.S. Department of Education Women's Educational Equity Act Program Grant (1981–1983).

Selected Bibliography

Asian Women United of California, ed. *Making Waves: An Anthology of Writings By and About Asian American Women*. Boston: Beacon Press, 1989.

Lai, H., G. Lim, and J. Yung. *Island: Poetry and History of Chinese Immigrants on Angel Island, 1910–1940*. Seattle: University of Washington Press, 1991.

Yung, J. "A Bowlful of Tears: Chinese Women Immigrants on Angel Island." In J. Zandy, ed., *Calling Home: Working-Class Women's Writings*, 1990.

———. *Chinese Women of America: A Pictorial History*. Seattle: University of Washington Press, 1986.

———. "Unbinding the Feet, Unbinding Their Lives: Chinese Immigrant Women in San Francisco, 1902–1931." In S. Hune, ed., *Asian Americans: Comparative and Global Perspectives*. Pullman: Washington State University Press, 1991.

———. *Unbound Feet: A Social History of Chinese Women in San Francisco*. Berkeley: University of California Press, 1995.

Franklin Ng

Appendix A: Fields of Professional Activity

ACTIVIST

Chew, Ng Poon

Choy, Bong Youn

Lum, Kalfred Dip

Mendoza, David C.

Uno, Edison

Wing, Yung

Xuong, Nguyen Huu

ACTOR/ACTRESS

Ahn, Philip

Cho, Margaret

Hayakawa, Sessue

Lee, Bruce

Lone, John

Luke, Keye

McCarthy, Nobu

Ngor, Haing

Oh, Soon Tek
Wong, Anna May

AMBASSADOR

Eu, March Fong

ANTHROPOLOGIST

Hsu, Francis Lang Kwang

ARCHITECT

Lin, Maya
Pei, I. M.

ART CRITIC

Coomaraswamy, Ananda
Hartmann, Carl Sadakichi

ARTIST

Aruego, Jose
Johnson, Indira Freitas
Kingman, Dong
Lanier, Ruth Asawa
Mendoza, David C.
Miyatake, Toyo
Noguchi, Isamu
Okubo, Mine
Sugimoto, Henry Yuzuru

ASTROPHYSICIST

Chandrasekhar, Subrahmanyan

ATTORNEY

Ariyoshi, George Ryoichi
Fong, Hiram
Locke, Gary
Luke, Wing
Minami, Dale
Mink, Patsy Takemoto
Oh, Angela
Okamoto, Vincent H.
Yasui, Minoru

AUTHOR

Barry, Lynda
Bulosan, Carlos
Chan, Sucheng
Chennault, Anna Chen
Chin, Frank
Choy, Bong Youn
Chu, Louis
Coomaraswamy, Ananda
DeSoto, Hisaye Yamamoto
Dhillon, Kartar
Eaton, Edith Maud
Hartmann, Carl Sadakichi
Hayslip, Le Ly
Ho, Ping Ti
Houston, Jeanne Wakatsuki
Hsu, Francis Lang Kwang
Kang, K. Connie
Kim, Richard
Kingston, Maxine Hong
Kitano, Harry H. L.
Lai, Him Mark
Lee, Chang Rae
Li, Victor Hao
Lim, Genevieve (Genny)

Lord, Bette Bao

Lum, Kalfred Dip

Mori, Toshio

Park, Yongman

Pran, Dith

Rustomji-Kerns, Roshni

Sung, Betty Lee

Tan, Amy

Uno, Edison

Wong, Jade Snow

Yung, Judy

AVIATION EXECUTIVE

Chennault, Anna Chen

BASEBALL PLAYER

Balcena, Bobby

Park, Chan Ho

BROADCASTER

Chu, Louis

BUSINESS LEADER

Chao, Elaine L.

Char, Tin-Yuke

Ching, Hung Wai

Chinn, Thomas W.

Ch'oe, Martha C.

Ho, Chinn

Lim, John Keun

Lung, Chin

Okamoto, Vincent H.

Paik, Young J.

Qureshy, Safi U.

Shima, George

Shoong, Joe
Tanaka, Togo William
Wang, Charles B.

CARTOONIST

Aruego, Jose
Barry, Lynda

CELLIST

Ma, Yo-Yo

CERAMICIST

Wong, Jade Snow

CHEMIST

Lee, Yuan-Tseh

CHOREOGRAPHER

Lone, John

COMEDIENNE

Cho, Margaret

COMMUNITY LEADER

Abiko, Kyutaro
Cheema, Boona
Ching, Hung Wai
Ch'oe, Martha C.
Hayslip, Le Ly
Hirabayashi, Gordon Kiyoshi
Itliong, Larry
Korematsu, Fred T.
Lim, Genevieve (Genny)

Masaoka, Mike
Santos, Robert
Yasui, Minoru

CONDUCTOR

Mehta, Zubin

CONGRESSIONAL MEDAL OF HONOR RECIPIENT

Miyamura, Hiroshi H.
Munemori, Sadao

CONGRESSMAN/CONGRESSWOMAN

Kim, Jay
Matsui, Robert T.
Mineta, Norman Y.
Mink, Patsy Takemoto
Saund, Dalip Singh

CULTURAL WORKER

Johnson, Indira Freitas

DIRECTOR

Lone, John
Wang, Wayne

ECONOMIST

Sohn, Chang Mook

EDUCATOR

Bose, Amar Gopal
Chan, Sucheng
Choy, Bong Youn
Das, Taraknath

Espina, Marina Estrella

Hayakawa, S. I.

Hirabayashi, Gordon Kiyoshi

Ho, Ping Ti

Hsu, Francis Lang Kwang

Hyun, Bong Hak

Inada, Lawson Fusao

Khan, Fazlur Rahman

Kim, Richard

Kingman, Dong

Kitano, Harry H. L.

Lee, Chang Rae

Lee, Ming Cho

Lee, Rose Hum

Lee, Yuan-Tseh

Li, Victor Hao

Lim, Genevieve (Genny)

Lum, Kalfred Dip

Miyamoto, S. Frank

Oh, Soon Tek

Oyakawa, Yoshinobu

Ramanujan, A. K.

Rustomji-Kerns, Roshni

Shin, Paull Hobom

Siv, Sichan

Subba Row, Yellapragada

Sue, Stanley

Sung, Betty Lee

Tien, Chang Lin

Uno, Edison

Xuong, Nguyen Huu

Young, Jacqueline Eurn Hai

Yung, Judy

ENGINEER

Khan, Fazlur Rahman
Lai, Him Mark
Prabhakar, Arati
Qureshy, Safi U.
San Juan, Eduardo
Xuong, Nguyen Huu

ENTREPRENEUR

Afong, Chun
Bose, Amar Gopal
Ho, Chinn
Lung, Chin
Qureshy, Safi U.
Wang, Charles B.
Wong, Jade Snow

FARMER

Saund, Dalip Singh
Shima, George

FASHION DESIGNER

Natori, Josie Cruz

FIGURE SKATER

Babilonia, Tai
Kwan, Michelle
Yamaguchi, Kristi

FILMMAKER

Okazaki, Steven
Wang, Wayne

FOOTBALL PLAYER

Chung, Eugene Y.

GOVERNMENT ADMINISTRATOR

Ch'oe, Martha C.
Prabhakar, Arati
Siv, Sichan

GOVERNOR

Ariyoshi, George Ryoichi
Cayetano, Benjamin J.
Locke, Gary

HISTORIAN

Char, Tin-Yuke
Chinn, Thomas W.
Coomaraswamy, Ananda
Lai, Him Mark

INVENTOR

Bose, Amar Gopal
Paik, Young J.
Shima, George

JAZZ PIANIST

Enriquez, Bobby

JOURNALIST

Chennault, Anna Chen
Chew, Ng Poon
Chinn, Thomas W.
Hartmann, Carl Sadakichi
Hosokawa, William K.

Kang, K. Connie
Omura, James Matsumoto
Pran, Dith
Sakamoto, James Yoshinori
Yen, Do Ngoc

JUDGE

Aiso, John Fugue
Barrett, Thang Nguyen
Choy, Herbert C.
Ito, Lance A.
Mendoza, David C.
Menor, Benjamin
Moon, Ronald Tai Young

LAW ENFORCEMENT OFFICER

Apana, Chang
Liu, Daniel S. C.

MARTIAL ARTS EXPERT

Lee, Bruce

MUSICIAN

Academia, Eleanor
Enriquez, Bobby
Ma, Yo-Yo

NEWSPAPER PUBLISHER

Abiko, Kyutaro
Chew, Ng Poon
DeSoto, Hisaye Yamamoto
Makino, Frederick Kinzaburo
Yen, Do Ngoc

NOBEL PRIZE RECIPIENT

Chandrasekhar, Subrahmanyan
Lee, Tsung Dao

Lee, Yuan-Tseh
Ting, Samuel Chao Chung
Wu, Chien-Shiung
Yang, Chen Ning

NUCLEAR PHYSICIST

Ting, Samuel Chao Chung

OLYMPIC MEDALIST

Draves, Victoria Manalo
Kono, Tommy Tamio
Kwan, Michelle
Lee, Sammy
Yamaguchi, Kristi

PHILANTHROPIST

Hayslip, Le Ly
Shoong, Joe

PHOTOGRAPHER

Miyatake, Toyo

PHYSICIAN

Hyun, Bong Hak
Jaisohn, Philip
Lee, Sammy
Ngor, Haing
Subba Row, Yellapragada

PHYSICIST

Lee, Tsung Dao
Prabhakar, Arati
Wu, Chien-Shiung
Yang, Chen Ning

PLAYWRIGHT

Chin, Frank
Gotanda, Philip Kan
Hwang, David Henry

POET

Bulosan, Carlos
Inada, Lawson Fusao
Ramanujan, A. K.

POLITICAL ACTIVIST

Ahn, Ch'ang Ho
Das, Taraknath
Dhillon, Kartar
Hyun, Bong Hak
Hyun, Soon
Jaisohn, Philip
Oh, Angela
Park, Yongman
Pran, Dith

POLITICIAN

Afong, Chun
Ariyoshi, George Ryoichi
Cayetano, Benjamin J.
Eu, March Fong
Fong, Hiram
Hayakawa, S. I.
Inouye, Daniel Ken
Kealoha, James K.
Kim, Jay
Lim, John Keun
Locke, Gary
Luke, Wing
Matsui, Robert T.

Matsunaga, Masayuki "Spark"

Mineta, Norman Y.

Mink, Patsy Takemoto

Rhee, Syngman

Saund, Dalip Singh

Shin, Paull Hobom

Young, Jacqueline Eurn Hai

PSYCHOLOGIST

Sue, Stanley

SCREENWRITER

Hwang, David Henry

SCULPTOR

Lin, Maya

Noguchi, Isamu

SENATOR

Fong, Hiram

Hayakawa, S. I.

Inouye, Daniel Ken

Matsunaga, Masayuki "Spark"

SET DESIGNER

Lee, Ming Cho

SOCIAL REFORMER

Park, Yongman

Rhee, Syngman

SOCIOLOGIST

Lee, Rose Hum
Miyamoto, S. Frank

SPORTS FIGURE

Babilonia, Tai
Balcena, Bobby
Chang, Michael
Chung, Eugene Y.
Draves, Victoria Manalo
Kono, Tommy Tamio
Lee, Sammy
Oyakawa, Yoshinobu
Park, Chan Ho
Yamaguchi, Kristi

SWIM COACH

Lee, Sammy
Oyakawa, Yoshinobu

TELEVISION JOURNALIST

Chung, Connie
Lim, Genevieve (Genny)

UNION ORGANIZER

Itliong, Larry
Katayama, Sen
Makino, Frederick Kinzaburo

WEIGHT LIFTER

Kono, Tommy Tamio

WORLD WAR II VETERAN

Miyamura, Hiroshi H.
Munemori, Sadao

Appendix B: Ethnic Subgroups

CHINESE AMERICANS

Afong, Chun

Apana, Chang

Chan, Sucheng

Chang, Michael

Chao, Elaine L.

Char, Tin-Yuke

Chennault, Anna Chen

Chew, Ng Poon

Chin, Frank

Ching, Hung Wai

Chinn, Thomas W.

Chu, Louis

Chung, Connie

Eaton, Edith Maud

Eu, March Fong

Fong, Hiram

Ho, Chinn

Ho, Ping Ti

Hsu, Francis Lang Kwang

Hwang, David Henry

Kealoha, James K.

Kingman, Dong

Kingston, Maxine Hong

Kwan, Michelle

Lai, Him Mark

Lee, Bruce

Lee, Ming Cho

Lee, Rose Hum

Lee, Tsung Dao

Lee, Yuan-Tseh

Li, Victor Hao

Lim, Genevieve (Genny)

Lin, Maya

Liu, Daniel S. C.

Locke, Gary

Lone, John

Lord, Bette Bao

Luke, Keye

Luke, Wing

Lum, Kalfred Dip

Lung, Chin

Ma, Yo-Yo

Pei, I. M.

Shoong, Joe

Sue, Stanley

Sung, Betty Lee

Tan, Amy

Tien, Chang Lin

Ting, Samuel Chao Chung

Wang, Charles B.

Wang, Wayne

Wing, Yung

Wong, Anna May

Wong, Jade Snow

Wu, Chien-Shiung

Yang, Chen Ning
Yung, Judy

JAPANESE AMERICANS

Abiko, Kyutaro
Aiso, John Fugue
Ariyoshi, George Ryoichi
DeSoto, Hisaye Yamamoto
Gotanda, Philip Kan
Hartmann, Carl Sadakichi
Hayakawa, S. I.
Hayakawa, Sessue
Hirabayashi, Gordon Kiyoshi
Hosokawa, William K.
Houston, Jeanne Wakatsuki
Inada, Lawson Fusao
Inouye, Daniel Ken
Ito, Lance A.
Katayama, Sen
Kitano, Harry H. L.
Kono, Tommy Tamio
Korematsu, Fred T.
Lanier, Ruth Asawa
Makino, Frederick Kinzaburo
Masaoka, Mike
Matsui, Robert T.
Matsunaga, Masayuki "Spark"
McCarthy, Nobu
Minami, Dale
Mineta, Norman Y.
Mink, Patsy Takemoto
Miyamoto, S. Frank
Miyamura, Hiroshi H.
Miyatake, Toyo
Mori, Toshio
Munemori, Sadao
Noguchi, Isamu

Okamoto, Vincent H.
Okazaki, Steven
Okubo, Mine
Omura, James Matsumoto
Oyakawa, Yoshinobu
Sakamoto, James Yoshinori
Shima, George
Sugimoto, Henry Yuzuru
Tanaka, Togo William
Uno, Edison
Yamaguchi, Kristi
Yasui, Minoru

FILIPINO AMERICANS

Academia, Eleanor
Aruego, Jose
Babilonia, Tai
Balcena, Bobby
Barry, Lynda
Bulosan, Carlos
Cayetano, Benjamin J.
Draves, Victoria Manalo
Enriquez, Bobby
Espina, Marina Estrella
Itliong, Larry
Mendoza, David C.
Menor, Benjamin
Natori, Josie Cruz
San Juan, Eduardo
Santos, Robert

KOREAN AMERICANS

Ahn, Ch'ang Ho
Ahn, Philip
Cho, Margaret
Ch'oe, Martha C.

Choy, Bong Youn
Choy, Herbert C.
Chung, Eugene Y.
Hyun, Bong Hak
Hyun, Soon
Jaisohn, Philip
Kang, Connie
Kim, Jay
Kim, Richard
Lee, Chang Rae
Lee, Sammy
Lim, John
Moon, Ronald Tai Young
Oh, Angela
Oh, Soon Tek
Paik, Young J.
Park, Chan Ho
Park, Yongman
Rhee, Syngman
Shin, Paull Hobom
Sohn, Chang Mook
Young, Jacqueline Eurn Hai

SOUTH ASIAN AMERICANS

Bose, Amar Gopal
Chandrasekhar, Subrahmanyan
Cheema, Boona
Coomaraswamy, Ananda
Das, Taraknath
Dhillon, Kartar
Johnson, Indira Freitas
Khan, Fazlur Rahman
Mehta, Zubin
Prabhakar, Arati
Qureshy, Safi U.
Ramanujan, A. K.
Rustomji-Kerns, Roshni

Saund, Dalip Singh
Subba Row, Yellapragada

SOUTHEAST ASIAN AMERICANS

Barrett, Thang Nguyen
Hayslip, Le Ly
Ngor, Haing
Pran, Dith
Siv, Sichan
Xuong, Nguyen Huu
Yen, Do Ngoc

Index

Editors and Contributors

EDITORS

HYUNG-CHAN KIM is Professor of Educational Administration and Foundations at Western Washington University. He is author of many books on Asian Americans, including *Asian Americans and Congress* (Greenwood, 1996), *Asian Americans and the Supreme Court* (Greenwood, 1992), and *Dictionary of Asian American History* (Greenwood, 1986).

DOROTHY CORDOVA is Executive Director of the Filipino American National Historical Society and Affiliate Professor in the American Ethnic Studies Department at the University of Washington.

STEPHEN S. FUGITA is Professor of Psychology and Ethnic Studies and Chair of the Department of Psychology at Santa Clara University. He is the author of *Japanese American Ethnicity: The Persistence of Community* and *The Japanese American Experience*.

FRANKLIN NG is Professor of Anthropology at California State University, Fresno. He is the author of *The Taiwanese Americans* (Greenwood, 1998), and is the former editor of the *Journal of American–East Asian Relations*. He is on the editorial boards of the *Amerasia Journal* and the *Journal of American Ethnic History*.

JANE SINGH is Visiting Lecturer in the Department of Comparative Ethnic Studies, with an Asian American Specialty at the University of California, Berkeley.

CONTRIBUTORS

ZILLER R. KHAN, Rosebush Professor of Political Science, University of Wisconsin, Oshkosh, Wisconsin

ANU M. MITRA, Visiting Professor of Humanities, Sichuan University, Chengdu, People's Republic of China

TAPAN MUKHERJEE, Program Director, National Science Foundation, Arlington, Virginia

LE HONG PHAN, Lecturer, Department of Ethnic Studies, University of California—Riverside

DILDAR GILL PISANI, Manager of Labor Relations, Kaiser Permanente Medical Care Program, Oakland, California

JENNIFER KANG

CHAE REED

VISI R. TILAK